OTTO SKORZENY
MY COMMANDO OPERATIONS

OTTO SKORZENY

MY COMMANDO OPERATIONS

The Memoirs of Hitler's Most Daring Commando

Translated from the German by David Johnston

SCHIFFER MILITARY HISTORY
Atglen, PA

I DEDICATE THIS BOOK
TO THE TRUE HEROES
OF THE SECOND WORLD WAR
THE COMMON
RUSSIAN AND GERMAN SOLDIER

Translated from the German by David Johnston.

This book published under the title,
Meine Kommando Unternehmen,
© 1993 by Universitas Verlag in F.A. Herbig Verlagsbuchhandlung GmbH, Munich.

This book was originally published
in 1975 by Edition Albin Michel.

Printed in the United States of America.
ISBN: 0-88740-718-8

We are interested in hearing from authors with book ideas on related topics.

Published by Schiffer Publishing Ltd.
77 Lower Valley Road
Atglen, PA 19310
Please write for a free catalog.
This book may be purchased from the publisher.
Please include $2.95 postage.
Try your bookstore first.

CONTENTS

PART I

PART II

PART III

PART I

1

ON THE RIGHT
OF SELF-DETERMINATION
OF PEOPLES

An invented triumvirate: Borghese-de Marchi-Skorzeny – My youth in Vienna – The tragedy of a German people in an East European state – The student: the time of the duels – Ban on fraternities by Baldur von Schirach – The engineer: work, sport and political commitment in favor of union with Germany – Goebbels in Vienna – Dolfuss declares Marxists and National Socialists illegal – Unexplained aspects of a failed putsch – Honeymoon trip to Italy – The oppression.

For almost thirty years certain correspondents, journalists and radio and television reporters have described me as "the most dangerous man in Europe." For example, at the end of November 1973 I was working in my office in Madrid, when I learned while skimming through Italian and Spanish newspapers that I was planning a coup d'état in Rome. I wasn't surprised; for in the fantasies of many journalists I had already organized countless coup d'états, plots and kidnappings, not only in Europe – noblesse oblige finally – but in Africa and both Americas. This time the Rome conspiracy had been directed by a triumvirate, consisting of Prince Valerio Borghese, the attorney de Marchi, leader of the M.S.I., and me. On completion of their preparations I was supposed to supply the Italian rebels with four Fokker aircraft. Where was I supposed to get them?

I gave the following statement during an interview with Manuel Alcala of the Madrid daily newspaper *Informaciones* on November 23, 1973:

"It's laughable: whenever the Italian government finds itself facing serious difficulties, it uncovers a plot which threatens it. It is no less strange that this is the second time within a short period that they have discovered a plot in which I was allegedly involved. More than a year ago they found letters I had written to Prince Borghese, which contained nothing astonishing. We became wartime friends in 1943. The exchange of letters in question had nothing to do with a plot or a conspiracy against the Italian government. For more than six months I haven't had the slightest contact with Valerio Borghese, and as far as Mr. de Marchi is concerned, I have never laid eyes on him in my life and didn't even know that he existed. I would like to once again state clearly that since the war I have never become involved in any political or military affairs of any country, and that I would reject any suggestion made to me in that direction."

This time I could deny the charges against me, and this denial was published. But I have thousands of articles from newspapers and magazines – most were sent by friends – which attribute to me the most fantastic, vile and perplexing actions and plans. Thousands of other publications all around the entire world spread rumors and defamations, sometimes in support of a political system.

Yet, I am not the only one affected. I think of the comrades at whose side I fought, of the brave soldiers I commanded and who died in the maelstrom of war: many fallen on the field of honor or lost forever in the steppes, forests or prison camps of Soviet Russia. I believe that people must know that these men never personally fought unfairly, even though they were involved in a dirty war. Even the enemy has acknowledged that.

In spite of all the ridicule, I firmly believe that there is military honor and that it will continue to exist as long as there are soldiers or until one half of our planet has destroyed the other half. But it is always possible to learn from the past.

This book is not intended as an "official denial." It is a book by a witness to recent history, one who had the time to reflect on events and people, on conditions and plans; a witness whose chief misfortune was to be a patriotic German who was born in Vienna, the capital city of Austro-Hungary in 1908.

When I spoke above of the alleged Borghese-de Marchi-Skorzeny triumvirate, I recalled, not without a certain nostalgia, two other triumvirates that I had to study in my class in Roman history in secondary school in Vienna in 1919. The first consisted of Caesar, Crassus and Pompeius, the second Octavius, Antonius and Lepidus: *Triumviri rei publicae constituendae* . . .

I was ten years old at the time. The Hapsburg Empire had just collapsed. Austria was now a country of six-million inhabitants (of which nearly 2 million lived in Vienna), 83,000 square kilometers in area. They had taken away the industries of Bohemia and the agricultural land of Hungary and had left it no access to the sea. It was therefore forced to live in misery or unite with Germany.

In March 1938 there was much talk of "rape by Hitler." But like Hitler, who was himself born in Austria, *we were Germans*! And we had the same right as the Saxons, the Bavarians, the Swabians, the Württembergers and all the other members of the German union, from which Austria had been expelled after the Battle of Königgratz in 1866.

For nine and a half centuries Austria, which in German means eastern empire, was part of the German Empire. This explains why an overwhelming number of Austrians voted for union. From 1918 to 1922, in the state of emergency of the defeated, we turned to the "Reich" out of an instinct for self-preservation. All parties supported reunification with Germany so strongly, that two laws were passed by the Austrian National Assembly, on November 12, 1918 and on March 12, 1919. They declared: "Austria is a fundamental part of the German Reich." This sentence was added to the nation's constitution. Furthermore, the new state was officially called *German-Austria*.

In spite of the "right of self-determination of peoples," the allies refused to take into consideration the will of the Austrian people at Versailles or St. Germain. We were not incorporated into the Reich. Ultimately, in September and October 1919, the allies demanded that the German and Austrian republics remove from their constitutions those articles relating to the union of the two countries. The Austrian government tried to "rouse democratic opinion" and organized regional referendums in Tyrol and Salzburg; that was in April and May 1921. The results: 145,302 Tyroleans voted for union, 1,805 against. However it was all in vain. These referendums were not "controlled by the nazis." There were none yet.

In 1931 former Foreign Minister Schober successfully concluded a customs and trade agreement with the Weimar Republic. The League of Nations and the International Court of Justice declared that this type of economic agreement was "incompatible with Article 85 of the Treaty of St. Germain." However the agreement of 1931 got Aristide Briand's plan for a European confederation under way. All these inconsistencies and willful decisions made no allowances for the economic, social, racial and historical realities; they must result in chaos and lead to a bloody revolution. The history of Austria from 1918 to 1938 is a tragedy which the people of my generation had to suffer.

My father, an engineer-architect and a reserve artillery officer in the Austro-Hungarian Army[1], was lucky to return from the war. Although medicine attracted me, I decided to become an engineer, following the example of my older brother. In 1926 I enrolled in the Vienna Technical College, where I found myself in the company of war veterans, who were much older than I and who wished to complete their studies, interrupted by the war and the subsequent terrible crises. These men, who had seen battle and who possessed experience we did not, exerted a strong influence on us.

My father, a liberal man, believed that a democratic regime would represent an advance over a double monarchy, which no longer corresponded to the times. In his opinion, politics should be run by selected, highly-capable specialists of unimpeachable character, relieving the citizens of the need to participate in the business of government. But neither the Social democrats, nor the Christian Socialists who succeeded them, provided such an ideal government. I must admit that politics were only of moderate interest to my generation.

What enthused me initially was the activity of the student fraternity to which I belonged, "the Markomannia *Duelling Society*." These fraternities, like the *Saxo-Borussia*, the *Burgundia* and the *Teutonia*, were famous in Germany and Austria since the time of the revolutionary movements of 1848, in which they played a mist active and vital role. A tradition of these old student fraternities was student duels on the "duelling floor" with long, double-edged swords.

In my opinion it was a place to teach courage, coolness and will. I myself fought fourteen times, which is where I got my duelling scars. They are tradition-rich, yes I would even dare to say, honorable wounds, on whose account the journalists dubbed me "the one with the duelling scars" or "scar-face." These traditional fraternities were banned in Germany from 1935 at the instigation of Baldur von Schirach, the later Gauleiter of Austria. He was leader of the Hitler Youth at the time.

The members of the student military societies and student corps were neither snobs nor drunkards, they worked for the fatherland. I was disappointed by Schirach's national-socialist reforms, and after 1938 I took the opportunity to tell him so. Later I said the same thing to the Reich Student Leader, Gustav Scheel. He agreed with me completely that the old student fraternities must be revived, for Baldur von Schirach's reforms had brought nothing positive in respect to the education of our youth.

The matter was close to my heart. During a conversation with Hitler at the end of 1943, I explained that student fraternities had sprung up all over the Reich in 1848, at the moment therefore when German youth manifested its will for change, and that this tradition had been kept alive in a good sense in Austria. While on their holidays the students forged links with the workers and farmers, forming a voluntary labor force which demonstrated a real socialist and national spirit. The vast majority had fought against the Red Front in the streets, and they had never understood that they were treated like snobs.

It seemed impossible to present to Hitler ideas which differed from his own. However this time he listened to me attentively. When I had finished he said, "Your arguments are fair and reasonable, Skorzeny. Thank you for stating them so candidly. But at the moment the duel is not so important. First we must win the war. Afterward we will talk about your questions again."

● ● ●

In the Markomannia we wore white caps, black bands and our breasts were trimmed with white and gold. Every year on the first Sunday in September the student groups joined with the masses of people at Heroes Square to officially demonstrate for union with Germany under the black-white-red flag. This was the sole political demonstration in which I regularly participated from 1920 to 1934.

On the other hand I played a great deal of sports: soccer, track and field, skiing, kayaking on our beautiful Danube and sailing on the lakes of our Alpine region.

In 1931 I passed my final exams for a diploma in engineering. However the future was very dark for young Austrians, no matter what class they belonged to. Like many other middle-class Austrian families, we had come to know want, sometimes even distress, during and immediately after the war and during the period of inflation, when food, coal and raw materials were in short supply. For too long unemployment had become a career for half a million Austrians.

After a visible improvement during the years 1926 to 1930 there came a worldwide depression. An economic catastrophe befell Austria just as I was about to begin working. Before I took any concrete steps in this direction I chanced to find work, although the pay was low, and later I was a participant in a significant scaffolding building operation.

As was usual in the building trade, some of my employees and workers were socialist-marxists, some communist, which did not prevent us from working closely together.

In the meantime the economic situation grew increasingly worse. Living on loans, the nation was dependent on greedy, foreign creditors who were ever more demanding and from whom the Christian-Democratic government couldn't or wasn't willing to free itself. It is impossible to understand the tremendous tragedy of the Second World War without considering my homeland. The division of Austria at Versailles created a dangerous vacuum in central Europe. The communist threat was not imagination. I was nineteen years old when the *Arbeiterzeitung*, the organ of the socialist-marxists, published its order for general mobilization in Vienna. That was in July 1927, and I can still see the demonstrations deteriorating into a bloody mutiny over two days. I still see how the communists charged police headquarters and set ablaze the Palace of Justice, which was soon one huge pillar of fire. All the land registry entries, which were kept there, were burned. That was without a doubt one of the objectives of the marxist mobilization. These violent street battles appeared to me to be extremely stupid. One thing was for certain: the citizens had been terrified.

The Marxists were the first to organize an armed militia, which was called the *Republikanischen Schutzbund*. Opposing them was the *Heimwehr*, led by the fanatical Prince Starhemberg, and Major Fey's *Heimatschutz*. Both formations, which were supposed to have been all-party, were in fact themselves political, revolutionary groups. In reality Starhemberg and Fey were more than a little ambitious. They only supported Dollfuss' government in order to replace him at some date. Thanks to Mussolini's support, Starhemberg dreamed of becoming regent of Austria, just as Admiral Horthy was regent of Hungary. However his hopes were soon dashed. Finally he consoled himself with actress Nora Gregor, with whom he was very much in love. Chancellor Schuschnigg, who in the Duce's view had the appearance of a "melancholy surveyor," exploited him and in May 1936 eliminated him from the picture politically.

● ● ●

After the unrest of 1927 the Marxists tried to take over the university. But we wanted to work in peace, and so the Academic Legion was formed. I was the legion's standard bearer at the usual demonstration at Heroes Square in September 1927. But the legion was soon infiltrated politically, was swallowed up by Starhemberg's *Heimwehr*, and finally became the *Heimatblock*. Then I left the movement.

The National-Socialist German Workers Party (NSDAP) made clear progress in Austria toward the end of 1929. A great many young supporters of reunification with Germany regarded this movement with sympathy. It has been written that I was "a founding nazi." That is not true. Speaking frankly, I doubted that my countrymen desired such a fundamental revolution as that advocated by the speakers.

The decisive event was in September 1932, when Dr. Goebbels came to Vienna to deliver a speech. The party was not yet banned, and the assembled crowd in the Engelmann Skating Palace was tremendously responsive. While the Austrian police kept order outside, it was the uniformed SA who maintained order inside. The swastika flags, the singing and the ceremony gave the meeting an impressive air.

Goebbels spoke for two hours, as he did when he was in his prime. His analysis of the international situation, the lamentable state of Europe since Versailles, the fruitless struggles of the parties, and Austria's position relative to Germany were all sound, completely reasonable and based on facts and the will toward constructive work in a finally-united people. The speaker was a tremendous success.

I admit that several weeks later, followed by many of my countrymen, I declared that I was joining. The National Socialist Party made a great leap forward in Austria. The next year, on June 19,

1933, Chancellor Dollfuss found only one means to prevent its growth: he banned it. And that was his first mistake.

In fact our unfortunate chancellor set up a proper dictatorship with his *Vaterländische Front,* which had the support of Starhemberg's and Fey's *Heimwehr.* He dissolved parliament, quarrelled with the organizations of the left and mixed up the struggle against Marxism with harassment of the workers. Blood flowed in Linz, Graz and Vienna in those frightful February days in 1934.

The victims? More than 400 killed and 2,000 injured, of which about 280 dead and 1,300 seriously injured were on the side of the workers. In this way the *Vaterländische Front* made sworn enemies of the workers. Social Democrats and National Socialists, both banned, came to each other's aid. Adolf Hitler had been Reich Chancellor in Germany since the beginning of the previous year, and several of my comrades believed that "the time had now come": the national-socialist revolution in Austria was now only a question of weeks. That was not my opinion. Strictly speaking, my activity within the National Socialist Party from September 1932 to June 1933 was not especially noticeable.

After the disbanding of the national-socialist movement in Austria, I limited myself to helping those comrades who had been jailed, were being sought or were living in the underground. My help also extended to numerous members of the *Schutzbund,* who were threatened with imprisonment. It wasn't a case of helping to defend a Marxist ideology, but of helping people, who had been drawn into a disastrous adventure, out of a predicament. One of my foremen, a man named Oehler, a true-blue communist, who had fought at the barricades, later did his duty so bravely in Russia that he was decorated with the Iron Cross, First Class as a common soldier. From 1934 to 1938 there was a real union of the outcasts from the Marxist and national-socialist camps under the sign of the underground movement.

But very few of the supporters of reunification with Germany could foresee the unbelievable events that were at hand at the beginning of the month of June 1934: it was the national-socialist putsch, in the course of which Federal Chancellor Dollfuss was to be killed.

Today we know that on April 9, 1934 Hitler sent a secret report to the envoys of the Reich abroad (see: Documents on *German Foreign Policy*, Vol. II, Series C-459), in which stated:

"At the moment the Austrian problem can obviously not be settled by means of union. We must let the Austrian thing run its course; for any attempt of this sort would make the European powers of the Little Entente enemies of the plan. Under these circumstances it appears more advisable to us to wait."

The leaders of the National Socialist Austrian Party in the underground could not pretend to be ignorant of these directives. Nevertheless, a plot was hatched which was supposed to force Dollfuss to resign. In his place a man they trusted, namely Anton Rintelen, Austrian ambassador in Rome, was to be named chancellor. There were indiscretions and Major Fey was informed. According to official sources, Dollfuss was fatally wounded in a dark hallway of the *Bundeshaus* by one of our comrades, Otto Planetta. The dictator was there with Major Fey, Generalmajor Wrabel, the new State Secretary for Security Karwinsky and the doorman Hedvicek. That was on July 25, 1934. Later I found that the role of Minister Fey and the autopsy on the chancellor's body, which was carried out with undue haste and under strange circumstances, allowed this "confused affair" to be seen from another point of view.

Those who wanted to "present the Reich with a fait accompli" contrary to the directives from Berlin were surely acting in good faith. What they didn't know was that many senior functionaries were playing a double game. The young conspirators, whose intention was not to murder the chancellor, were unaware that all their movements were watched by Fey's agents since the morning of July 25. It would therefore have been easy to stop them before they were able to storm the chancellor's office and the Radio House. However they let them have their way.

They had orders to use their weapons only in extreme emergency and then to aim at the feet. It was 1 P.M. when Planetta fired at a shadow in the passage that led to the palace archives. However he could have been arrested at least three hours earlier.

Older than I, the putschists were already experienced activists before the disbanding of the party. I didn't know them personally. What I was able to find out was that Planetta repeatedly claimed that he had only *fired once*. But the chancellor was hit by two bullets, one of which, having become lodged in his spine, was obviously fatal. When Planetta turned himself in to prevent his comrades from being executed, he was under no illusions; he knew that his days were numbered. Even if one of his comrades at his side had fired, he would definitely have said that he fired twice in order to save him. There are several very mysterious aspects of this case which were never explained. Certain historians have said that I participated neither in the organization of the conspiracy nor in the putsch. In reality, in May I had just married a young girl named Gretl, whom I had known for four years and who was then nineteen years old. We had set out for Italy in a motorcycle and sidecar. In the course of this very sporty honeymoon trip we visited Bologna, Venice, Ravenna, Pisa, Florence, Rome and drove through the region of Abruzzi.

At the Piazza Venezia in Rome I heard Benito Mussolini for the first time. He was speaking to a crowd from the balcony of the old Austrian embassy. The Duce made a good impression on me, and I suddenly found that, here among the Italians, my prejudices against Italy disappeared. In general I made similar discoveries on my trips through the various nations of Europe and I realized: we are one big family and we could easily get along with everyone, as long as we respect each other and each of us guards that which makes him special. Europe is like a rainbow of nations, whose colors must remain clear and separate. But scarcely had I returned from my trip to Italy, when I found myself in the middle of a political uproar. It had seized Styria, Kärnten and Tyrol after the radio said that the putsch was successful and the Dr. von Rintelen had been asked to form a new government. In truth Rintelen, who had walked into the trap, chose to commit suicide.

As for the putschists, after being assured twice that they would be taken safe and sound to the Bavarian border, they surrendered their weapons and – were then immediately arrested! The official published casualty figures were: 78 dead and 165 injured on the government side and more than 400 dead and 800 injured among our friends. Many of the politically-active National Socialists were able to escape to Germany. Those less lucky, thousands of our other comrades and marxists, found themselves in the concentration camps that had been set up by Dollfuss on September 23, 1233 and which they hypocritically called "administrative internment camps." Those of Woellersdorf and Messendorf near Graz remain a sad memory. More than two-hundred conspirators were brought before a court-martial and sentenced immediately. Sixty of those sentenced to death had their sentences reduced to life at hard labor by the President of the Republic, Miklas; but seven national-socialist leaders, among them Franz Holzweber, who was assigned to take the chancellor's office, Otto Planetta, Hans Domes, Franz Leeb and Ludwig Maitzen, were hanged, as were two young members of the *Schutzbund*, Rudolf Ansböck and Joseph Gerl, in whose possession explosives were found.

The scale of the oppression by the "authoritarian and christian" dictator was revealed by the amnesty decree issued in July 1936 by Federal Chancellor Schuschnigg, Dollfuss' successor: it resulted in the release of 15,583 political prisoners.

Two years earlier those condemned to be executed went bravely to their deaths. As they walked to the gallows they called out, "Long live Germany! Heil Hitler!"

On that 25th of July 1934 Hitler was taking in a performance of Wagner's *Das Rheingold* in Bayreuth. He received the news of the tragic events with anger and dismay. At the same time he learned that Mussolini had moved five divisions to the Brenner Pass and that Yugoslavian troops were massing along the border with Styria and Kärnten.

"Good God, protect us from our friends!" he said to Göring. "That would be a new Sarajevo . . ."

At the same time, with the agreement of the president's office of Field Marshall von Hindenburg, he sent the pope's secret treasurer, Franz von Papen, to Vienna. It is significant that relations between Berlin and Vienna were not broken off. They were in fact maintained, and the Austrian tragedy was unfortunately not over.

Notes

[1] The Austro-Hungarian Army lost about 1,200,000 men killed in the First World War.

2

THE ANSCHLUSS

Physical training in the German Gymnastics League – Schuschnigg proposes a peculiar plebiscite or "secret without voting booths" – The night of March 11, 1938 – Seyss-Inquart, chancellor – In the presidential palace: a drama between the SA and the guard battalion is avoided – We see Hitler from our scaffold – Recantations and the triumph of the plebiscite – The men from the other side of the Main.

On July 11, 1936 Kurt von Schuschnigg, Dollfuss' successor, officially admitted that "Austria was fundamentally a German state." Nevertheless he was against union with Germany and mobilized his police to ruthlessly suppress everyone who expressed views which were friendly toward Germany.

Although the Hitler-Schuschnigg meeting of February 12, 1938, which was held at Berchtesgaden, gave us hope for a normalization of relations between Austria and Germany, we had no reason to be optimistic that we would soon be incorporated into our German fatherland. The National Socialist Party was permitted again under certain conditions. But since 1935 I had been a member of the German Gymnastics League, a sports association which existed in Germany as well as Austria. By chance I met again there many former members and supporters of the disbanded party. It is probably unnecessary to mention that the 60,000 members of the gymnastics league all desired unification with Germany.

Within our gymnastics league we were organized in the form of military platoons. I was leader of one such formation. We were very aware that the communists and social democrats had become masters at camouflaging their troops. Above all we knew that Moscow had given the Austrian leaders specific instructions to prepare a people's front under communist direction and to take revenge for what had happened in Berlin in Vienna. Certainly Schuschnigg had shuffled his cabinet after his return from Berchtesgaden and named Seyss-Inquart to the post of Minister of the Interior. Seyss-Inquart was a brilliant lawyer and a catholic, who, like a majority of all Austrians, was in favor of union with Germany, without, however, belonging to the National Socialist Party at any time. But at the same time the chancellor made extraordinary efforts to reach an agreement with the leaders of the extreme left against us. Moscow's pressure soon became stronger and Schuschnigg decided to plunge himself into an adventure which was to be decisive for the fate of Austria.

On Wednesday, the 9th of March 1938, a thunderclap! In Innsbruck the chancellor announced a plebiscite (direct ballot) for Sunday, March 13, for or against a "free, German, independent, social, Christian and united Austria."

Berlin immediately accused him of "intentionally failing to comply with the Berchtesgaden agreements," "being in league with Moscow" and "wanting to proclaim a Soviet republic in Vienna." As French historian Jacques Benoist-Méchin (*Histoire de l'Armée allemande,* Vol. 4) stated, "they were in fact witnessing a strange spectacle, which Hitler's propaganda soon put to good use: apart from the *Vaterländische Front,* only the communists were openly in favor of the plebiscite."

Today we know that the chancellor was the victim of several deceptions, as well as promises that could not be kept. He had disposed of monarchist demands by rejecting a proposal for its restoration, which was made to him by Archduke Otto von Hapsburg. The latter signed his manifesto "Otto I.R.", for Imperator Rex, exactly like Carl the Fifth. Nine days later, on February 26, the French foreign minister, Yvon Delbos, announced his satisfaction to the Austrian chancellor in front of the French parliament with the following words:

"France cannot leave Austria to its fate: it confirms today that the independence of Austria represents an indispensable element in the European balance of power."

In his memoirs, Franz von Papen wrote that, "the French envoy in Vienna, Paux, a personal friend of Schuschnigg's, was the father of the idea of the plebiscite."

The chancellor reckoned on foreign support, in order to prevent or at least delay union by means of a successful plebiscite. This was not forthcoming, however. In London, Foreign Minister Anthony Eden had just resigned. Chamberlain, who replaced him with Lord Halifax, thought the project was a "hazardous business." Dr. Masty, the Czechoslovakian envoy in Berlin, assured Göring that President Benes had no intention of interfering in Austrian affairs.

Late on the morning of March 7, Colonel Liebitsky, the Austrian military attache in Rome, handed Mussolini a copy of the speech that Schuschnigg intended to give in Innsbruck. Genuinely startled, the Duce immediately tried to talk the chancellor out of the idea, which he said "could turn against him immediately." But Schuschnigg completely disregarded the advice. Was he perhaps expecting firm, official commitments from the French? That is questionable. A few weeks earlier the Chautemps government had won a vote of confidence in parliament, 439 votes to 2. One day after the Innsbruck speech, on the morning of March 10, Camille Chautemps spoke a few words to the house. He stepped down from the rostrum and left the room; his ministers followed him in silence. Chautemps and his cabinet had resigned while still holding a majority.

Our physical training in the gymnastics league did not prevent us from reading numerous foreign newspapers: the *Times*, the *Daily Telegraph*, the *Frankfurter Zeitung*, the *Temps* and the Swiss press. On the evening of March 10 we learned that Schuschnigg had lost his nerve, that he had isolated himself.

One should know that the plebiscite was supposed to be held as follows: as the last vote for the National Assembly had taken place in 1929, there were no voting lists on hand; they told us that none were necessary. The *Vaterländische Front*, which was the only organization to organize the plebiscite, would take care of everything. At first the officials were obligated to vote at their places of work; every citizen over 25 years of age in Vienna and over 24 in the provinces could vote, and needed only to show the family register, a rent, gas or light receipt, a bank book, an identity card issued by the *Vaterländische Front* or the *Landbund* and so on. Voters known to the election overseers didn't even need personal identification papers! It was said that the vote was public and that the polling stations only had YES ballots.

There were no voting booths. Those citizens who wished to vote in the negative had to bring with them a ballot marked NO and ask the election overseer for an official envelope in which to place it!

Under these circumstances it was easy for a band of fifty wags to give Schuschnigg several thousand votes if they began their route through the various polling stations, which were not closely watched by the election overseers, early in the morning. At the same time Austrian radio and the government press continued to remind the people that, "every citizen who votes NO is guilty of high treason." Therefore anyone so naive as to bring with him a NO ballot would have identified himself as a traitor.

Such behavior was of course not very honorable; nevertheless the organizers thought it was wonderful.

During the night of March 10 Schuschnigg issued a mobilization order for the class of 1935. Ready for action were the militias of the *Vaterländische Front.* But what caused more anxiety was the reappearance of the old *Schutzbund* troops, who were ultra-marxists. Some of them were in their camouflage – light grey uniforms – of the *Ostmärkische Sturmscharen,* the combat units of the *Vaterländische Front.* Whatever one might have said about these things, Schuschnigg had thrown all the logs in the fire, and on the trucks that drove around Vienna on the morning of this March 11, one could see the propagandists of the *Vaterländische Front,* their fists raised in the communist salute. We knew that Schmitz, the mayor of Vienna, had called together the factory militias, and we were convinced that weapons had been distributed. Furthermore columns of trucks came from the suburbs flying the red flag with the hammer and sickle. Workers raised their fists, sang the *Internationale* and shouted:

> "Vote YES for freedom!
> Down with Hitler! Long live Moscow!"

Meanwhile aircraft bearing the red and white cocarde dropped tons of leaflets with the instruction: "Vote YES."

What could such a bizarre vote, organized in seventy-two hours, mean to a government that lacked any popular basis? Since the evening before, discussions in the chancellor's office had taken on an increasingly bitter character. It was a theater coup: the Wiener *Neuesten Nachrichten* published a manifesto by Dr. Jury, adjutant to Seyss-Inquart in the Ministry of the Interior, in which he declared the vote "arbitrary and illegal" and called upon the population to boycott it. It was impossible to obtain a copy of the paper.

What was happening? After much speculation, at about 1 P.M. the chancellor, hoping to gain time, announced that the wording of the question was to be changed. But Göring telephoned and demanded that the government simply resign (4:30 P.M.). It was known that German troops were massed along the border. Schuschnigg asked Dr. Zehner, State Secretary of Defense, whether the army and the police were ready to defend Austria's borders. He soon realized that nothing could prevent the German troops from advancing to Vienna, "the population is enthusiastically in support of it."

● ● ●

When the mobilization of the workers militias was announced, the leaders of the German Gymnastics League called the defense platoons together. Under no circumstances did we want to relive the bloody days of 1927 and 1934.

Towards evening a huge crowd of people gathered in front of the chancellor's office. My comrades and I were also there, alternating between depression and hope as various rumors circulated through the crowd. Suddenly, at eight in the evening, Seyss-Inquart called upon everyone to be calm and asked "the police and the National Socialist security service to ensure that peace and order were maintained." To my great amazement I saw that a large number of people, including some of the police, had put on swastika arm bands. All had become good national socialists once they learned that the President of the Republic had accepted Schuschnigg's resignation.

At first President Miklas refused to name Seyss-Inquart as Schuschnigg's successor, although he was the only minister who had remained in his office, at the request of the president himself. The latter was an honorable man, who had principles and fourteen children. What he didn't know was that two of them belonged to the underground SA!

What they have called "the rape of Austria" began that night in the form of a tremendous torchlight parade through the streets of

Vienna and in front of the chancellor's office. At Heroes Square people cried, laughed and hugged each other. When the swastika flag appeared on the balcony of the chancellory at about eleven o'clock, there was no holding back, it was like in a delirium.

While his children were shouting "Heil Hitler!" in the square, President Miklas stubbornly continued to search for a successor to the resigned Schuschnigg. Seyss-Inquart didn't suit him. Göring, who was hosting two Austrian brothers-in-law, at first suggested, then demanded that he accept Seyss-Inquart. Miklas retired to the chancellery where he sounded out a dozen personalities, all of whom declined to accept the position. They included the State Secretary, Dr. Skubl; the former head of a Christian-Socialist government, Dr. Ender; and finally the Inspector General of the Army, Schilkawsky. The main concern of them all was to prevent a confrontation between brothers. Near midnight Miklas gave in and at last appointed Seyss-Inquart chancellor; the latter immediately gave him a list of new ministers.

My comrades and I were still in front of the chancellor's office when Seyss-Inquart appeared on the balcony: an enormous cry of jubilation greeted him, and we saw that he had become chancellor. He gave a brief speech to the crowd, but in the tumult we couldn't make out a single word. Suddenly everything grew quiet, and with bared heads we all joined in singing the German national anthem. I will never forget that moment, which made up for much suffering and sacrifice and many humiliations.

I have read that "democratic principles were violated" on this occasion. But not a shadow of democracy had existed in Austria. Chancellor Dollfuss had dissolved parliament in March 1933. After Dollfuss' tragic death, Miklas named Schuschnigg chancellor without consulting the Austrian people. Understanding our attitudes then and how we felt requires good faith and a knowledge, even if only a superficial one, of historical events.

● ● ●

I can still see myself on that memorable night, in the company of my comrades of the German Gymnastics League. We had been ready for action since ealy afternoon, all wearing mountaineering coats, which could be seen as uniforms; we also wore riding or ski pants. We had no arm bands.

We were so happy that we felt neither hunger nor cold. But there was nothing left for us to do at Heroes Square, so my comrades and I made our way to a side street behind the chancellor's office, for I had parked my car there. After the initial enthusiasm had faded, we almost thought we were dreaming. Was Seyss-Inquart really a true national socialist? We had formerly seen him as a middleman. How would the extreme left react? Were the rumors that Hitler had given the order for German troops to march into Austria true?

At that moment a black limousine pulled out of a driveway onto the street. As we stepped aside to let it pass, I heard someone calling to me. The man who had hailed me and several others had also come out of the palace. He approached quickly and I recognized him as Bruno Weiss, the president of our German Gymnastics League. He appeared nervous and asked if I had a car.

"Very good," he said. "It's lucky that I ran into you here. We need a man with a cool head and common sense. Did you see the big limousine that just pulled out? Good, it's carrying none other than President Miklas. He is driving to his palace on Reisner Strasse, which is occupied by a unit of the guard battalion. We have just learned that an SA battalion from Florisdorf has received orders to go to Reisner Strasse too, for the federal president is also supposed to receive the protection of the new government. A confrontation between the two formations must be avoided at all costs. Do you understand?"

"Completely, my dear Herr Weiss. But I have no authority..."

He interrupted me with a wave of his hand, "In the name of the new chancellor, I instruct you personally to go to Reissner Strasse and calmly, but energetically intervene to avoid any incident. Assemble some of your comrades, but don't waste time. I will inform the chancellor that I have given you this mission. I will try to reach an agreement by telephone, but it would be better if you could be there. Telephone the chancellery as soon as you arrive. Now get going, my dear fellow. The minutes are precious."

And they were that! Luckily I was able to recruit a dozen comrades on the spot, who were loaded into two or three cars or jumped onto their motorcycles. We roared into the night, straight through the crowd, which cleared a path for us. We arrived in front of the palace just as the president drove in. We stayed right behind him and I ordered that the large entrance gate be closed.

The president was just about to go up the stairs when we entered the hall. A young guards lieutenant appeared at the second floor balustrade and drew his pistol. The confusion reached its climax: the loud shouts of the guards soldiers and those of the president's entourage mingled, and finally Frau Miklas appeared, completely distraught.

I shouted louder than the others:

"Quiet!"

"Weapons ready to fire!" ordered the lieutenant.

This officer, who later became my friend, and whom I met three weeks later as a captain in the Wehrmacht, was just doing his duty. Fortunately we had neither weapons nor arm bands, but our unusual get-up scarcely spoke in our favor. The situation was as follows: about twenty guards soldiers, who were standing along the second floor gallery and down from the upper steps of the stairway, held us in check. The president was still standing in the middle of the stairs, looking at his wife without saying a word. From the street could be heard a growing tumult. The SA people, who had jumped down from their trucks, were demanding that they open the gate. I prayed that it would hold.

"Quiet gentlemen!" I shouted again. "Herr President, I ask that you listen to me."

He turned and looked at me in surprise:

"Who are you sir, and what do you want?"

"Allow me to introduce myself: engineer Skorzeny. May I call the chancellor on the telephone? He will confirm to you that I am here on his orders."

"Certainly, but tell me, what does all that noise outside mean?"

I knew what the noise meant, but I couldn't say it. One would have thought that the SA intended to take the presidential palace by storm, and that would probably have resulted in a firefight.

"Please excuse me a moment, Mr. President, I will go and see at once."

With the help of my friend Gerhard and our comrades from the gymnastics league, we were finally able to calm everyone. As President Miklas looked on, I called the chancellor's office; Dr. Seyss-Inquart came on the line straightaway: fortunately Bruno Weiss had taken the necessary steps and the new chancellor spoke with the president for a few minutes. Then Miklas handed me the receiver. Seyss-

Inquart congratulated me on my determined conduct and asked me to wait at the palace for further instructions and assume command of the guards battalion detachment. I was to see to it that the latter unit maintained order inside the palace, while the SA kept order outside.

For three days and nights I conscientiously carried out my mission, to the general satisfaction of those in charge and without incident. In the end Chancellor Seyss-Inquart thanked me with a heartfelt handshake. I was still young then and somewhat naive: I believed that I had entered active politics, not by chance, but through the big gate.

• • •

I witnessed Hitler's triumphant entry into Vienna from a very lofty vantage point, namely from one of the tall scaffoldings that had been erected for the overhauling of a museum located on the ring road. My workmen were even more enthusiastic than I was, and I understood how they felt. They were welcoming one of their own, one of our own. We looked down on this extraordinary man from our tall scaffolding. Whatever they might say about him today, he had endured hunger in Vienna. There, before our eyes, he took his place among the greatest Austrian rulers: it was the place of a Rudolf, Maximilian, Carl, Ferdinand or Josef, all of whom had been German emperors. It was impossible, yet it was true. Hundreds of thousands shouted out with us that it was true.

The spectacle on the ring itself was in keeping with the significance of the event: it was magnificent, wonderful, with a sea of flags and flowers, endless applause and martial music. The German troops received a welcome the like of which no other army had ever seen in Austria. Then, at a given moment, we sensed a general movement and curiosity in the crowd. It was the arrival of the SS-Leibstandarte Adolf Hitler.

I have never been able to explain to myself where my countrymen got hold of the tens of thousands of swastika flags. I expect that every family had prepared one or two such flags in anticipation of the "rape of Austria." Many other things surprised me too, things that are forgotten nowadays. For example, on March 10, Cardinal Innitzer, the Archbishop of Vienna, warmly endorsed Schuschnigg's plebiscite, declaring:

"As Austrian citizens we are fighting for a free, independent Austria!"

Eight days later, on March 18, Cardinal Innitzer, the Prince Bishop of Salzburg Hefter, the Bishop of Klagenfurt Pawlikowski, the Bishop of Graz Gföllner and the Bishop of Linz openly made a declaration to the contrary, namely: "That they considered it their duty as Germans to speak out in favor of the German Reich."

They said literally, "Out of the most inner conviction and with a free will, we, the undersigned bishops of the church province of Austria, declare on the occasion of the great historical events in German-Austria that: We joyfully acknowledge that the national-socialist movement has done and is doing outstanding work in the areas of national and economic development as well as social policy, for the German Reich and people, and especially for the poorest strata of society. We are convinced that the national-socialist movement will have the effect of keeping at bay the threat of all-destroying, godless bolshevism.

The best wishes of the bishops go with this work and they will exhort the faithful in this vein.

For us priests, on the day of the plebiscite it is our obvious duty as Germans to declare ourselves for the German Reich, and we expect that all Christian believers will realize what they owe their people."

What should one say about the attitude of the social-democratic leader Dr. Karl Renner, first chancellor of Austria in 1918-1919 and president of the National Council until 1933?

On April 3, 1938 he told the *Illustrierten Kronenzeitung* of Vienna:

"The twenty-year wandering of the Austrian people is now over, and it is returning united to the starting point, to its solemn declaration of will of November 12, 1918. The sad interlude of the half-century from 1866 to 1918 hereby goes down in our common thousand-year history.

"As a social democrat and therefore as the representative of the right of self-determination of the nation and as past president of its peace delegation to St. Germain, I will vote JA."

On that same April 3 Herr Dr. Renner confirmed to the *Neuen Wiener Tageblatt*:

"If I were not to welcome the great historical act of the reunification of the German nation with a joyful heart, I would have to disavow my entire past as a theoretical champion of the right of self-determination of nations and a German-Austrian statesman. As a social democrat and thus as a representative of the right of self-determination of nations, as first chancellor of the republic of German-Austria, and as past president of your peace delegation in St. Germain, I will vote JA."

Karl Seitz, a former leader of the social democrats and former mayor of Vienna, agreed with this declaration: After the _Anschluss_ Dr. Karl Renner lived in Goggnitz at the foot of the Semmering and thanks to the pension which was freely granted to him he survived the Second World War peacefully and unharmed. The invading Red Army found Dr. Renner and persuaded him to write a letter to Moscow. The following is an extract from that letter:

"Your excellency Marshall Stalin, Moscow

Honored comrade!
In the early days of the movement I made many personal friendships with Russian champions... The Red Army found me when it entered my home town, where I trustingly awaited the occupation with party comrades.. For this I thank the Red Army and you, its glorious supreme commander, personally and in the name of the working class of Austria, sincerely and humbly... The Austrian social democrats will come to terms fraternally with the communist party and will work on an equal footing with it in the refounding of the republic. That the future of the land belongs to socialism, is unquestionable and needs no emphasis."

The results of the plebiscite held on April 10, 1938, which in reality was a free and secret vote, were:

For the union of Austria with the Reich:	4,284,295 votes
Against:	9,852 votes
Spoiled ballots:	559

But why did we now have to be disappointed? Some of those whom we welcomed with such enthusiasm treated us with a lack of insight and a condescension which, under other circumstances, would have been comical.

Surrounded by the halo of the triumph he had achieved in the Saar Region three years earlier, Gauleiter Joseph Bürckel, a Rhinelander, brought with him to Austria neither a healthy common sense nor political understanding. But not all of those who came from the other side of the Main River were like him. First-class people should have been sent to Austria, but unfortunately this was not always the case, and the functionary type we received often resembled a Bavarian public school teacher from the year 1900 or a village policeman. But we also had our mistakes. We tried to smile and to understand those who did not understand us. The exaggerated strictness and sometimes also the tactlessness of the Prussians and Saxons were often hindrances to the truly fraternal union we longed for. These difficulties have been exaggerated or forgotten by historians to some extent, according to their personal attitude toward the subject.

3

WAFFEN-SS

Danzig and the German-Russian Pact – "If we should ever lose this war..." – Drafted into the Luftwaffe and admitted into the Waffen-SS – Errors and mixups – Origins of the SS and the Waffen-SS –The Death's Head Formations – General Paul Hausser – Esprit de corps and ideologies – European warriors, who received no orders from Himmler – Inquiry by the historical section of the Israeli Army: a study for the classification of the soldiers of both world wars – Prince Valerio Borghese.

On September 27, 1938 Sir Neville Chamberlain spoke the following words to the English people in a broadcast on the BBC:

"It would be frightful, fantastic and unbelievable if we were forced to dig slit trenches and put on gas masks on account of a dispute which has broken out in a distant land among people of whom we know nothing. And it seems even more incredible that this dispute, which in principle is already settled, might lead to a war!"

Frankly speaking, in the course of the following summer I still believed there would be no war. The Munich Agreement seemed to us to be the prelude to a general agreement by the European powers for a revision of the treaties of 1919/1920, which, as the brilliant French statesman Anatole de Monzie wrote: "Had created a half-dozen Alsace-Lorraine in the heart of Europe." It seemed impossible to me that the Europeans, who together shared such a high level of culture and civilization, should not reach an understanding: it was after all in the interest of everyone. The Czech problem was solved, Poland had recovered the Teschen region – a point that is always forgotten – and the 3,500,000 Sudeten Germans had again become citizens of the Reich. My father, whose family came from Eger in Bohemia,[1] was deeply moved by their return. We all thought that the Germans of Danzig would not be kept much longer from becoming our fellow citizens.

The whole world knew that Danzig, the home of Fahrenheit and Schopenhauer, had been the capital of West Prussia in 1918 and that it was taken from the Reich the following year. Its population was German, something which Article 448 of the Versailles Treaty could not change. It seemed to us that our scattered, torn-apart people, which had suffered frightfully from 1918 to 1925, could not be held responsible forever for the mistakes made by its government in the years from 1914 to 1918.

In August 1939 I was spending my vacation with the family of Professor Porsche, designer of the Volkswagen, on the Wörthersee in Austria, when we heard the news of the signing of the German-Russian pact. We were all deeply dismayed. There are few examples in history of such a sensational change of allegiances. I certainly wouldn't have believed it if someone had said a year earlier that Hitler would one day conclude a pact with Stalin. Both governments declared that their ideologies were not looked upon articles for export, but we very soon realized what this pact meant.

On August 31 Mussolini proposed in vain that an international conference be called for September 5 to review the clauses of the Versailles Treaty, which, as he said, were the cause of the present unrest. No one listened to him. At 5:45 A.M. on September 1 the Wehrmacht entered Poland. Great Britain declared war on Germany at 12:00 P.M. the next day, followed by France at 5:00 P.M., "in order to defend the independence of Poland."

No German was pleased and I believe that Göring expressed all our thoughts when, during the night of August 31, he said to von Ribbentrop: "God help us if we should ever lose this war!"

● ● ●

I had not yet done my military service. As I was about to take my final tests as a pilot, I was called up by the Luftwaffe. They were of the opinion, however, that at 31 I was too old to fly. But I had not the least intention of spending the war in some lowly position in an office. I applied for a transfer to the Waffen-SS. I was one of only ten out of a hundred applicants to be accepted, after a series of extremely demanding physical tests and medical examinations.

Countless books have been published about the SS and apparently will continue to be published. Many, however, fall far short of the mark in providing a clear picture of this organization. In recent years serious historians have admitted that the SS possessed an extremely complicated structure, and that its various branches were animated by quite differing spirits and played vastly different roles. Nevertheless the confusion continues and the Waffen-SS is still often equated with the Sicherheitsdienst (SD). In reality any confusion was out of the question, for one could identify a member of the SD simply by looking at his uniform: one could read large and clear on the left sleeve: SD (Security Service) and the two SS symbols were absent from the right collar insignia.

Further clarifications are necessary: writers always claim that Heinrich Himmler was the founder and commander of the SS. This is a double mistake. He was always only its first functionary.

Seen from the political and military standpoint, Hitler was obviously the commander of the *Schutz-Staffel* and we, the soldiers of the Waffen-SS, swore loyalty to him.

It was at the end of 1924, when Hitler left Landsberg Prison, that the problem of reorganizing the National-Socialist Party became acute. The *Sturm-Abteilungen* (SA) were banned in most provinces of the Reich. Hitler sent for his chauffeur Julius Schreck and tasked him, together with Rudolf Hess, with the formation of a small motorized formation made up of trustworthy people. It must be capable of protecting the leader and speaker of the party under any circumstances and of defending a hall where he was speaking. Such groups appeared in the larger cities and first in the interiors of the assembly halls, where they earned the name *Schutz-Staffel* (protection unit). In cities where the wearing of a uniform was not forbidden, they wore a white shirt with brassard, a tie, riding breeches, boots and a black cap. On this was a death's head, so that we were always aware of death.

The death's head has been characterized as a barbaric and frightful symbol. In reality there have been death's head hussars in the

German cavalry since 1741, these having served under the command of Frederick the Great. At Waterloo General Delort's much-feared cuirassiers were attacked bravely by von Lützow's Black Uhlans, who also wore the death's head as their insignia. In Great Britain the death's head was the insignia of the 17th Lancers, earned in the Battle of Balaklava in 1854. Many remember the silhouette of General von Mackensen in his great uniform of the Death's Head Hussars: the famous marshall's face was so alarming and gaunt that one thought he was seeing a second death's head beneath the one on his cap.

But the first SS men were not people from another world. They bravely did their duty, which at times was difficult, and many of them were killed in the fight against the Red Front. Toward the end of 1928 they numbered about 300, and it wasn't until the following year that Hitler tasked Himmler with organizing the SS; this was to be done under the completely new concept of military-political fighters who were to stand out above the mass of the SA men.

The SS played a very special role following the assumption of power and the very serious attempt to bring about a second revolution, which was undertaken by the SA's Chief-of-Staff Röhm and the SA leaders Heines (Silesia), Karl Ernst (Berlin-Brandenburg), Heydebeck (Pomerania), Hayn (Saxony), Schneidhuber (Bavaria) and others at the end of June 1934.

The first armed unit of the SS was the *Leibstandarte Adolf Hitler* under the command of a rough Bavarian, an old tank fighter of the Great War, Sepp Dietrich. This parade regiment with its white leather accoutrements, which we had seen march past flawlessly in Vienna, was Hitler's personal guard.

Soon afterward two further regiments were formed under the designation *SS-Verfügungstruppen;* these were active, military units of the SS. At the end of 1937 there were three SS infantry regiments, the *Deutschland* Regiment, the only one whose organization was complete, the *Germania* Regiment and the *Leibstandarte.* Administration and military training were entrusted to Paul Hausser, retired Reichswehr Generalleutnant and commander of the Braunschweig Junkersschule.

The military training of the Waffen-SS featured some interesting innovations. After an extremely strict physical selection process, the recruits, whether they were officers, NCOs or simple soldiers, had to play sports intensively. Discipline was even stricter than normal in the Wehrmacht. The officers took part in the lives of their men one hundred percent. Comradeship, trust and mutual respect were the rule. Relationships within the hierarchy of the Waffen-SS were simpler, more human than in the Wehrmacht, and we had none of the caricatured type of arrogant officer.

One will perhaps be surprised to hear that freedom of conscience was absolute in the Waffen-SS. One could find agnostics, practicing catholics and protestants there.[2] The chaplain of the French SS-Brigade *Charlemagne* was Monsignore Mayol de Lúpe, a personal friend of Pope Pius XII, and I had in my unit a Romanian catholic priest who served as a simple soldier.

While the majority of the SA men were members of the National-Socialist Party, not only was party membership not obligatory in the Waffen-SS, it wasn't even recommended. People don't want to understand this. We were without a doubt political soldiers, however we defended an ideology which superseded politics and parties.

The motto engraved on our belt buckles read: "My honor is loyalty." And so it remained.

We did not see ourselves as soldiers who were superior to the others; we did however strive with all our hearts to serve our fatherland as well as it was within our power to do.

It cannot be denied that the Waffen-SS possessed an esprit de corps, but that is nothing new, for every army in the world at that time had an esprit de corps. I believe it even existed in the Red Guard and in certain Siberian divisions, the elite troops of the Soviet Army.

One unique feature of the Waffen-SS was that it was a volunteer army, in which from 1942 European soldiers from many lands and peoples could be found: Albanians, Bosnians, Britons, Bulgarians, Cossacks, Croats, Danes, Dutch, Estonians, Finns, Flemings, French, Georgians, Greeks, Hungarians, Italians, Latvians, Lithuanians, Norwegians, Romanians, Russians, Serbs, Slovakians, Swedes, Swiss, Ukrainians, Walloons; as well Armenians, Byelorussians, Hindus, Kirghizes, Tartars, Turkmen and Uzbeks served under their own flags in the Waffen-SS. Almost all of these peoples were represented in my unit. The only ones missing were Albanians, Bosnians, Britons, Cossacks, Georgians, Greeks and Serbians.

It only remains to be said that as part of the army we neither had to receive nor did receive operational orders from Himmler during the war. Himmler was neither a serving soldier nor a military commander, even though he tried to appear to be one at the beginning of 1945.[3]

The real creator of the Waffen-SS was thus General Paul Hausser, whose nickname "Papa Hausser" was a symbol of the affection we felt for him. Together with Felix Steiner, an old warrior from the Baltic,[4] and Sepp Dietrich, he gave the Waffen-SS a style and an offensive spirit which could perhaps be compared with that of the Napoleonic Guard.

How can it escape a person's notice that this army, consisting of about a million young Europeans, all of whom displayed the same cold-bloodedness toward death, thoroughly and absolutely failed to confirm Reichsführer der SS Himmler's nebulous "Theory of the Nordic Man?" Hitler himself was not an adherent of this doctrine.

I must also admit that the doctrine of Reichsleiter Alfred Rosenberg always struck me as blurred. Rosenberg, whom I met later, was sincere, but he was given responsibilities which were beyond him. It was only with difficulty that I managed to read to the end his book *Myth of the Twentieth Century*. I've met few people who have read all 700 pages.

What sort of general opinion can one form concerning the conduct of the Waffen-SS in the course of the Second World War?

In 1957 the historical section of the general staff of the Israeli Army sent a questionnaire to more than a thousand military chiefs or experts around the world, as well as to historians and war correspondents. It requested that they answer the following questions in regard to both world wars: Which armies do you consider the best? Which were the bravest soldiers? The best trained? The most skillful? The most disciplined? Which had the most initiative and so on.

Among those who responded to the questionnaire were Generals Marshall (USA), Heusinger (NATO), G.F. Fuller (Great Britain), Koenig (France), as well as the famous military author Sir Basil Liddell Hart, authors Leon Uris, Hermann Wouk and others. The armies that participated in World War One were classified as follows:

1.   German Army
2.   French Army
3.   English Army
4.   Turkish Army

5.   American Army
6.   Russian Army
7.   Austro-Hungarian Army
8.   Italian Army

Where World War Two was concerned, the classification allowed for a maximum of 100 and a minimum of 10 points.

The results were as follows:

1. The German Armed Forces	93 points
2. Japanese Army	86 points
3. Soviet Army	83 points
4. Finnish Army	79 points
5. Polish Army	71 points
6. British Army	62 points
7. American Army	55 points
8. French Army	39 points
9. Italian Army	24 points

Where the air forces were concerned, the RAF followed the Luftwaffe, then came the American Air Force, the Japanese Air Force and that of the USSR. The British Navy placed ahead of the Japanese and American, while the German stood in first place.

Finally, among the elite units the Waffen-SS held first place, followed by the Marines (USA), the British commandos and the French Foreign Legion.

Naturally objections can be raised against any classification of this type. Opinions were very divided on placing the Polish Army in fifth place. In my opinion the Italian soldiers were not without merit, they were just often poorly armed, very badly supplied and commanded by officers who were not always equal to the task. In Africa the black shirt divisions were good. Italian submarine crews and fliers achieved some extraordinary personal achievements and successes. Italian units fought well on the Eastern Front and the *Savoia* Cavalry Regiment fought heroically in Stalingrad in November 1942. The manned torpedoes of the X-MAS Flotilla of Prince Junio-Valerio Borghese and Teseo Tesei distinguished themselves through sensational successes in the Mediterranean. These should have been taken into consideration.

I will come back to Prince Valerio Borghese, an aristocrat in the truest sense of the word. I met him in 1943 under circumstances I will describe later. He himself took part in two very dangerous, successful operations, one in Gibraltar Harbour and the other in Alexandria Harbour. In March 1945, when many of his countrymen were changing their colors, he said to me, "My dear Skorzeny, we're fighting for the same cause, for a free Europe. Rest assured that I will fight to the end, come what may." He kept his word.

Notes

1. Eger was an old fortress city of the Austro-Hungarian Empire. The Skorzeny family moved there from Posen, from the vicinity of Lake Skorzenczin, therefore its name. Posen, in western Poland, had been German until 1918. According to family documents written in German, the Skorzenys, at first landowners and farmers, were the ancestors of a family that could be traced back to the end of the Sixteenth Century.

2. SS leaders at least, were required to leave the church; however this regulation was not generally enforced (editor).

3. In *Erinnerungen eines Soldaten* Generaloberst Guderian said that Himmler's greatest ambition was to earn military laurels. In the view of the military experts this was a catastrophe. Guderian, then chief of the army general staff, feared the worst and sent General Wenck to assist. But Wenck fell victim to an auto accident en route (February 17, 1945). "Without Wenck," wrote Guderian, "Himmler demonstrated his total incompetence... The situation worsened from day to day." At Guderian's request, Hitler removed Himmler as commander-in-chief. His place at the head of Army Group Vistula was finally taken by General Henrici, who had formerly been commander-in-chief of the First Panzer Army (March 20, 1945).

4. A free corps formed after the collapse of the German front in the Baltic lands in 1918-19. It withstood the first bolshevik onslaught in Lithuania, Estonia, Latvia and even East Prussia.

4

WHY WE DIDN'T LAND IN ENGLAND & TAKE GIBRALTAR

The "Moonlight Company" – Campaign in France with the SS-Division Verfügungstruppe – Tiger hunt in a Bordeaux suburb – Operation Felix, the planned assault on Gibraltar – Canaris, Chief of the Abwehr, an "Admiral with seven souls" – His goal: "To prevent Germany from winning the war by any and all means" – General Franco's demands – Operation Otario – Misleading information from the Chief of the Abwehr – Frankness on the part of Winston Churchill.

It was February 1940 when I was assigned to the 2nd Company of the reserve battalion of the *SS-Leibstandarte Adolf Hitler* in Berlin-Lichterfelde. Although I was an engineer-officer candidate, I had to endure six weeks of intensive training with youngsters of sixteen to eighteen. The other recruits who were my age – doctors, chemists, lawyers and engineers – had to clench their teeth to avoid staying behind with this "moonlight company," which had thoroughly earned its name. The company commander had a decided preference for conducting exercises at night, and we had had enough of it.

My time in the "moonlight company" was followed by special training with the reserve battalion of the Waffen-SS Regiment *Germania* at Hamburg-Langenhorn. In May 1940 I passed all my military-technical tests in Berlin and was named an officer candidate.

The Polish Campaign had lasted only eighteen days. Russia, which occupied half of the country without fighting, also subsequently destroyed the small but heroic Finnish Army, while the Wehrmacht stole a march on the Anglo-French expeditionary Corps and occupied

Denmark and Norway on April 9, 1940. Sweden subsequently permitted free transit of German troops as well as the transport of ore from Norway.

My comrades joked: "We'd better hurry if we want to get in on the fighting, for the war will soon be over."

But not everyone was so optimistic. I hoped that it might be a short war, and that we would not have to directly attack either France or Britain, for the greatest threat was not from the west, but from the east.

Nevertheless, in May 1940 I, like everyone else, found myself in a field-grey uniform with the eagle emblem on the left sleeve, on the roads of Holland, Belgium and France. I was a member of the artillery regiment of the *SS-Division Verfügungstruppe*. This was the future *Das Reich* Division. Our commanding officer, "Papa" Hausser, already had three motorized infantry regiments – *Deutschland*, *Germania* and *Der Führer* – and the artillery regiment, which consisted of three battalions of light artillery and one of heavy artillery, to which I belonged, under his command.

Our division made a very rapid advance, in Brabant as well as in Flanders and in the Artois. We crossed the Somme on June 6 and 7 after very heavy fighting and the "Weygand Line" collapsed. At the height of the battle the month before, our division, which had suffered heavy casualties, received more than 2,000 replacements. One night my heavy artillery battalion was bombed by the enemy's air force and placed under very accurate fire by the French artillery. One of our munitions trucks exploded and a Hauptsturmführer was blown apart by a mine.

On June 12, my birthday, I was in Creusot, where the large Schneider Works were located. After guarding the left flank of the panzer division advancing on Dijon, we received orders to veer off in a southwesterly direction.

During all these battles and our advance through the lovely country of France, I was struck by the frightful consequences of war: ruins, abandoned farmhouses, vacant villages with plundered shops, unburied bodies and countless suffering people, refugees, elderly, children, women, some on the run all the way from Belgium. We overtook them and sometimes, when we made a halt, gave them food. This war between western countries was absurd, and the cease-fire concluded with the French government on 22 June at first seemed to me like the beginning of a lasting peace in Europe.

I cannot recall any expressions of absolute loathing or hate on the part of the civilian population.

An unusual adventure awaited me in a suburb of Bordeaux. As I was driving through the suburb at the wheel of my Kübelwagen I noticed that something out of the ordinary was going on. I slowed my vehicle. They called to me: "An animal...down there...a wild animal!" All the people then disappeared as if by magic, and I soon saw what was going on. There, scarcely one hundred meters in front of me, standing on the sidewalk at the top of a hill on a small road, stood a full-grown Tiger. It was just about to eat a hind quarter of an ox it had stolen from a nearby butcher's shop. I stopped my car, and in a quite natural reflex placed my hand on my pistol holster. But I immediately shrugged my shoulders, for what effect would a pistol bullet have on such a magnificent and powerful animal? So I took my chauffeur's rifle and killed the tiger, something I wasn't exactly proud of, but which very much relieved the inhabitants of Bordeaux. The butcher told me that the tiger had escaped from a circus and had caused a panic in this suburb. The butcher was also friendly enough to save me the pelt, which I picked up later.

We went into garrison in Dax, where I frequently used the French military aircraft at the field to fly over the countryside and the Basque region. We went swimming at Biarritz and often crossed the border into Spain, always in uniform. Our comrades of the Spanish Army always gave us a warm welcome.

Somewhat later I learned that our stationing on the border was no coincidence. Our division and various other elite units of the Wehrmacht were supposed to traverse Spain to take Gibraltar with the agreement of the Spanish government. This was to be Operation Felix. However the operation never took place, which calls for further explanation.

It was said that this operation was thwarted by the Chief of the Abwehr (the Wehrmacht's intelligence and counter-espionage service) Admiral Wilhelm Canaris. At this point we must take a closer look at Canaris, whom I got to know personally in 1943/44 and who played an extremely important role in the course of the Second World War.

On visiting his Berlin villa in Grunewald, the first thing one saw in the vestibule was a monumental portrait of a hero of the Greek war of independence (1823), Constantin Kanaris, a scimitar in his hand, cleaving Turkish heads.

The Abwehr chief claimed very seriously that this Constantin was his ancestor, although his family had emigrated from Italy to the Rhineland at the end of the eighteenth century. Canaris also told certain Spaniards that some of his distant Greek ancestors, who were courageous seamen, had reached the Canary Islands, which supposedly accounted for their name.

Born not far from Dortmund on January 1, 1887, Canaris became a cadet in the Imperial Navy in 1905 and served with the rank of Oberleutnant zur See on board the small cruiser *Dresden*, which was sunk by its crew in Chilean waters in March 1915 to prevent it from falling into the hands of the British cruiser *Glasgow*. Canaris reached Spain toward the end of 1915 and served as an officer of the German intelligence service in Madrid until 1916. He ended the war as a Kapitänleutnant in the German submarine service. One can say that he wasn't very highly thought of by his comrades. In answer to a question from attorney Otto Nelte, Grossadmiral Dönitz declared in front of the Nuremberg court on May 9, 1946:

"In the navy Admiral Canaris was an officer who inspired little trust. He was quite different from all the others. We said of him that he had seven souls."

Although Canaris called himself a monarchist, he served the Weimar Republic with great zeal. In 1924 he was promoted to Korvettenkapitän and in 1930 to Fregattenkapitän. Finally he was named Chief-of-Staff of the North Sea Station. In 1935 he became head of the Abwehr, succeeding Kapitän zur See Conrad Patzig.

At Nuremberg on June 3, 1946 Generaloberst Alfred Jodl, Chief of the Operations Staff of the OKW (Wehrmacht High Command) characterized the Abwehr under the direction of Canaris as a "nest of traitors." One of Canaris' most important department heads, Oberst Erwin Lahousen, declared before the same tribune on November 30, 1945:

"We were unable to prevent this war of aggression. The war meant the end of Germany and of us, and thus a disaster and a catastrophe of the greatest proportion. But a triumph by this system would have been a disaster even greater than this catastrophe, and using all the means at our disposal to prevent this had to be the ultimate essence and purpose of our struggle."

To return to Operation Felix, it didn't appear that it would take any great effort on the part of Admiral Canaris to convince General Franco to allow German troops to march through Spain to get at Gibraltar. The Chief of the Abwehr certainly knew the Cuadillo; it was even said that they used the familiar "du" form of address. Canaris made an inordinate number of trips to Spain, two alone in the summer of 1940, in July and August, and it was on the latter occasion that the admiral discussed the matter of Gibraltar with Franco.

I cannot reveal the military sources that informed me that Canaris convinced the Cuadillo to demand the following of Hitler in return, demands which definitely had to be rejected: wheat, fuel, weapons and ammunition in enormous quantities, and above all the annexation into the Spanish colonial region of all of French Morocco and the Departement of Oran in Algeria.

This was impossible. Why should Hitler give away something that he didn't possess and that he had never demanded from France? He was still of the opinion that a policy of honest cooperation and friendly relations with France was very desirable. This friendly policy was outlined in October 1940 in Montoire during talks with Marshall Pétain.

Following Canaris' visit to Spain, the Reich's ambassador in Madrid, Eberhardt von Stohrer, related the following in a report to the Wilhelmstrasse on August 8, 1940:

"(Even if the German government accedes to all of Franco's demands) the date for the beginning of preparations and the action (Gibraltar) itself must be adjusted to correspond to the expected developments in England (successful German landing in England), so that we avoid a premature entry into the war by Spain, which would mean an unbearable length of conflict for Spain and the possible creation of a source of danger for us."

Nowadays most of Canaris' subordinates and agents who actively worked on the fall of the government are known. One of the most determined was Oberst, later General, Hans Oster, head of the central department in the *Amt Ausland Abwehr*. It was he who sent the young Ewald von Kleist-Schmenzin to London in August 1938 to ask the British government for help and support against Hitler.

Kleist-Schmenzin established contact with Sir Robert Vansittart and Winston Churchill in the name of a group of German generals who were preparing a coup d'état – General Beck, his successor as Army Chief of Staff Halder, Generals Witzleben (later promoted to Generalfeldmarschall), Stülpnagel, Brockdorff-Ahlefeld, Hoepner and others. On August 29, 1938, after returning to Berlin, he received a very encouraging letter from Churchill which he passed on to Canaris, who then informed Halder and Witzleben. Halder himself subsequently sent two proxies to London, Oberstleutnant Hans Boehm-Tettelbach and Theodor Kordt. Indeed they expected that London would give them a free hand to bring down the government. The Munich Agreement confounded these people, who called themselves "German patriots."

On March 11, 1939 Oster informed the British and also the Czech secret service that the German Army would march into Bohemia and Moravia at 6 A.M. on March 16. This allowed the Czechs to fly their best intelligence specialists and most important archives to safety in England on March 14.

On March 16, 1948, Colonel J.G. Sas, who before the war had been the Dutch military attache in Berlin, made a statement before the Dutch Commission for Historical Documentation, in which he declared that Oberst Oster had given him a great quantity of the most vital, secret information over the course of several years. This included the exact date of the German attack against Norway, as well as much information concerning the offensive in the west (May 10, 1940).

At the same time as Oster was passing his information to the then Major Sas, on May 30, 1940 the Abwehr notified its "colleague" in Rome, Josef Müller, of the news. Müller had established contact with Belgian, Dutch and British representatives with the Holy See. This organization was called the "Black Orchestra," as opposed to the "Red Orchestra," which I will come back to. What is more, Canaris and Oster had an agent in Switzerland, Hans Bernd Gisevius, Vice Consul in Zurich, who later maintained an outstanding relationship with Allen Welsh Dulles, head of the American intelligence service in Europe. Dulles later became head of the CIA.

The Abwehr established itself in Zossen, which from 1943 was the seat of the Army General Staff. Oster kept extremely compromising documents in a safe there, which were found in September 1944 after the attempt on Hitler's life. Further documents were found in another safe at the beginning of 1945 in the form of twelve volumes of a private diary kept by Canaris. Convicted of conspiring against the security of the state, Canaris defended himself by maintaining that he had joined the conspirators in 1938 so as to be better able to expose them.

While on his way to the shower, Canaris was able to whisper to Theodor Strünck, one of Oster's liaison agents in Zurich who was likewise arrested and charged with treason, "Incriminate Oster and Dohnanyi." Dohnanyi was a direct subordinate of Oster's. Canaris played a double game to the end. He even denied for a moment that he and Oster had worked together!

With the chances of Operation Felix becoming a reality appearing more and more remote, our division was withdrawn from France and stationed in Holland to prepare for Operation Sea Lion (Otario), the landing in England. Toward the end of July, however, I received two weeks leave, which I spent with my family on the banks of the Wörthersee, where the beginning of World War Two had caught me by surprise. Afterwards I returned to Amersfoort near Utrecht, where my regiment was in garrison.

In January 1943 I had a conversation with Generaloberst Jodl about the Sea Lion plan. Jodl explained to me:

"Operation Otario was planned relatively late, namely on July 2, 1940. In order to be able to understand why it wasn't taken into consideration earlier, one must consider what happened on May 24, 1940, when the Führer ordered Reinhardt and Guderian's XLI and XIX Panzer Corps to halt their advance on Dunkirk and Calais. On the following day it became clear that we no longer had to fear being attacked or cut off on our left flank. Nevertheless the Führer kept his order in place until about noon on May 26. I believe he was then convinced that we could come to terms with Great Britain, and on these grounds wished to avoid embarrassing the nation by capturing Lord Gort's entire expeditionary corps."

Hitler wanted to come to an understanding with the European powers, and especially with Great Britain. Documents from the German archives, which were seized by the allies in 1945 and which are accessible today, prove that in 1936 the Duke of Coburg informed Hitler that King Edward VIII was very well disposed toward an alliance. Far from being aimed against France, this alliance was to include France. King Edward suggested installing a direct telephone line from Buckingham Palace to the Reich Chancellery.

I am convinced today, that from June 16, 1940 (we were crossing the Loire at that time) Hitler was hopeful of a successful outcome to the negotiations for a peace with Great Britain which were being conducted through Switzerland, Spain, Sweden and Italy with his knowledge, and that he erred in this matter. He also believed Reichsmarschall Göring, who declared that he could prevent the embarkation of the expeditionary corps with his Luftwaffe alone. As a result the English succeeded in evacuating 230,000 of their 250,000 men, albeit without weapons and equipment, back to England.

The evacuation by sea was carried out with civilian craft, some small yachts, and it is still my view that the Dunkirk evacuation was an unbelievably brave accomplishment by the British people.

Nevertheless, an enormous amount of materiel had been destroyed or abandoned. In his famous speech broadcast by the BBC on June 4, 1940, Churchill said:

"...we will fight on the beaches, at the landing sites, we will fight on the land and in the streets!"

The Deacon of Canterbury later stated that the speaker placed a hand over the microphone at that moment and added: "And we will throw beer glasses in their faces, for that is in fact all we have." Later the English Prime Minister officially admitted to the American Congress (December 26, 1941):

"We were lucky to have time. If Germany had landed in the British Isles after the collapse of France in June 1940, and if Japan had declared war on us then, disaster and suffering on an indescribable scale would have come over our land."

However Canaris was standing guard. On July 7, 1940 he gave Keitel confidential information which stated that the Germans would meet about twenty first-line divisions in an eventual landing in England, with another nineteen in reserve. However, in his memoirs Montgomery stated that at this time there was only one adequately armed and equipped division available, namely the 3rd under the command of Montgomery himself.

The false information from Canaris explains the demands made by Generalfeldmarschall von Brauchitsch, whom Hitler had entrusted with the overall command of the landing forces: he wanted to land on a wide front with 41 divisions, six of these panzer divisions and three motorized! Grossadmiral Raeder naturally answered with a *non possumus*; he didn't have enough ships to cover the landing at sea and furthermore demanded total air superiority on the part of the Luftwaffe.

The preparations for Otario were nevertheless actively pursued. One morning my commanding officer, Standartenführer Hansen, and Hauptsturmführer Emil Schäfer, who commanded the regiment, ordered me to build a loading ramp for th*e following day.* The ramp was to be able to bear mobile loads of 20 to 30 tons (tractors and heavy guns). It was obvious that they thought that they had given me an order which would take five or six days to carry out.

I immediately made a sketch of the design and was fortunate to find the necessary materials in Utrecht, which I had prepared in the workshops there. About 100 men worked through the night with light provided by the headlights of twenty trucks. Finally we succeeded in completing the loading ramp with the limited means available. At dawn I became the first to try out the ramp, driving a gun tractor over it with the regiment's heaviest howitzer in tow. Afterward they woke the Standartenführer and the Hauptsturmführer, neither of whom could believe the news.

"I would like to tell you, my dear Skorzeny," declared Hansen, "that you will pay dearly if this is a joke."

But it was no joke... We later carried out numerous loading tests and landing maneuvers on the Helder, using Rhine barges with their bows cut off. They nearly went under in heavy weather. In spite of our great enthusiasm we asked ourselves what would happen if the landing took place at the end of August or in September when the weather was generally very unfavorable in the English Channel.

Göring's air offensive, the "Battle of Britain," did not achieve the desired success. On September 16 and 17, 1940 we were bombed day and night by the RAF, and on 21 September a dozen transport ships and numerous Rhine barges were sunk or damaged. We suffered dead and wounded, which at the time led to rumors that we had tried a landing, which had been repulsed.

In June or at the beginning of July we could have landed about fifteen divisions in three or four attack waves. That would have been very possible. Since the British Expeditionary Corps was surrounded by our panzers in France, the Luftwaffe could have carried out a useful "demonstration" against the RAF and the Home Fleet.

On September 19 Hitler gave the final order to disperse the landing fleet and on October 12 Operation Otario was quietly put off until the next spring. It was also at this time that the OKW again considered Operation Felix against Gibraltar, however without taking any action.

It was clear that Hitler did not recognize the full strategic significance of the Mediterranean. The Italians should have occupied the "aircraft carrier," the island of Malta, but we could also have advanced to Gibraltar and occupied the rock in June 1940. As soon as we had taken possession of this and barred the entrance to the Mediterranean, the war would have taken an quite different course. The English would have had to sail around Africa and the Cape and through the Suez Canal in order to supply their forces in Egypt and North Africa. Admiral Dönitz's submarines would have wreaked havoc along the west coast of Africa, and I believe it is not an exaggeration to claim that Field Marshalls Alexander and Montgomery would only have received about thirty percent of the troops and materiel which in fact arrived directly via Gibraltar.

The Anglo-American landings in North Africa, Italy and France would have been impossible.

Those who maintain nowadays that Operation Otario would have ended in defeat in July-August 1940 should consider the following "confession" by Churchill, which he made to officers of the Home Guard on May 12, 1940:

"After the fall of France we were not only a people without an army, but also a people without weapons. If the enemy had fallen from the sky or landed in various parts of the country, he would have found only a handful of poorly-armed men guarding searchlight positions."

This, however, was not in tune with the assurances given by the German intelligence service under Admiral Canaris.

5

FROM THE ENGLISH CHANNEL TO THE BALKANS

Operation Otario postponed "sine die" – Explanations by Ambassador Hewel – In France: Arrest of President Laval and Operation Attila "A soldier of the SS may not fall under suspicion" – An entente with France, foundation of a new Europe – Ambassador Abetz, overtaken by events – In the Balkans – "Stoi!" – Thoughts on the capture of the island of Crete –Belgrade – Neither Gibraltar nor Suez nor Malta – Return to Austria

In Holland we had no idea that Operation Otario had been postponed "sine die," and we still believed that we would land in England in early 1941. Training continued at a rapid pace and discipline was strictly maintained.

Our aircraft had taken detailed photos of the English coast from low altitude. We therefore knew exactly where our battalion of heavy artillery was supposed to land and what natural obstacles we would have to overcome. We were told that we had to fear that the English would set their coast afire and cover the sea with a layer of burning liquid. This reminded me of the mysterious Greek Fire, which had first been used by the emperors of Constantinople, such as Justinian in the sixth century and finally also by the Empress Theodora against Russian ships.

This story of setting the coast afire seemed rather fantastic to me, for it wouldn't have been so simple to set, say twenty kilometers of coast, the area necessary to land two divisions, on fire. But we would get through in any case, with or without Greek Fire, we would get through bullets, bombs, machine-gun fire, the entire Home Fleet and any bad weather if it should be necessary, and we would advance to

London. We had not the least doubt that we would be successful. We also knew that our submarines had sunk 63 British ships totalling 352,407 tons during the month of October 1940 alone.

After our attack on ships of the allied fleet at Anzio with manned torpedoes in 1944, Grossadmiral Dönitz received me very cordially in his headquarters near the Wolfsschanze. On this occasion he told me that this success in 1940 had been achieved with only 8 U-boats and that he had pressed for 100 submarines at the time!

In October 1940 Dönitz commanded just the submarine arm. If his suggestions had been followed since 1938, England would have been driven out of the Mediterranean, the Battle of the Atlantic would have taken a different course and Operation Otario could have been carried out in September 1940.

The misadventure later suffered by the Royal Navy at Dakar showed even the allied storm troops that the English were far from unbeatable at sea. For three days, from the 22nd to the 25th of September 1940, a strong expeditionary sent by the English and de Gaulle tried to seize Dakar and a considerable quantity of gold which belonged to the national banks of France, Belgium and Poland. This fact is little known. In spite of all the rumors it is a fact: there wasn't even the shadow of a single German soldier in Dakar.

But the English fleet was met by cannon fire. Two cruisers were heavily damaged – the *Resolution* was hit by torpedoes and left listing and the *Barham* was set afire by a salvo from the modern cruiser *Richelieu*. The aircraft carrier *Ark Royal*, three other cruisers, the destroyers, torpedo boats, tankers and transport ships were forced to withdraw in order to prevent the entire affair from ending in catastrophe. Neville Chamberlain resigned on October 3 and Churchill, under pressure from the opposition, was forced to shake up his war cabinet. But there was no doubt that Hitler had already trained his gaze toward the east at the end of September.

During my stay at Führer Headquarters in the autumn of 1944 I gained a better insight into the grounds that had moved Hitler not to give the order for the attack on England. Certainly the false information from Canaris was decisive in the months of July and August, but envoy Hewel, who was the liaison man between the OKW and the Foreign Ministry, told me that at that time Hitler had not yet given up the idea of reaching a peaceful arrangement with Great Britain.

"The difficulties of a landing did not seem insurmountable to him in the summer of 1940," Hewel said to me. "What appeared to be significantly more difficult, was the necessity of feeding a nation of 47 million inhabitants which received about half its foodstuffs from abroad and then would receive no more. The Royal Family, Churchill and the government would go to Canada with the bulk of the Home Fleet. Should we proclaim a republic in Great Britain? 'Where,' he asked, 'are we to find a Cromwell?' Churchill wanted to see to it himself that the unity of the victorian empire was defended. We would find ourselves having to control an island amid an increasingly hostile population suffering from cold and hunger, while the worst was to be expected from Stalin." This was the reason why Operation Felix seemed more advisable than Operation Otario. He had already offered Great Britain what he could in his speeches to the Reichstag on October 6, 1939 and again on October 8, 1940: peace, guarantees for the British Empire and cooperation with all the nations of Europe. All the other, more or less secret attempts, had failed. But at the moment at which Otario was abandoned and Felix was impossible to carry out, it became clear that the solution would have to be sought in the east before it became too late. Stalin hoped that we would plunge into Operation Otario in early 1941. That would have been just right for him to attack Germany during the summer or at the beginning of autumn!

In mid-December we were again brought to a state of readiness. Christmas leave was cancelled and on December 18 we received the order to leave Holland, destination unspecified.

We returned to France via Düsseldorf, Wiesbaden, Mainz, Mannheim and Karlsruhe and drove through the Vosges to Vesoul. The journey was extremely demanding: It snowed continuously, and I had to retrieve more than 150 vehicles and trucks which had become stuck in the snow-covered Vosges.

There was no rest in Port-sur-Saóne either. I was informed that the SS-*Verfügungstruppe D*ivision was to be ready to leave for Marseille with munitions, fuel and food by December 21. During the night of December 20 I noticed that the largest of our fuel trucks had two badly damaged tires. I sought out an army dump in the vicinity of Langres, where, following lengthy negotiations with an insignificant Feldwebel, I had to resort to theoretical threats to get my two tires. I finally got them in exchange for a regulation voucher.

A few hours before our departure to cross the demarcation line and march to Marseille by the shortest route the order was changed: departure was planned for December 22, then for 4 A.M. on the 23rd, and finally the entire order was withdrawn.

Operation Attila, which was to see the occupation of the entire free zone of France, including the French *departements* in North Africa, was not carried out.

On December 13, 1940, Marshall Pétain in Vichy had separated himself from the president of the privy council, Pierre Laval, and even had him arrested. Poorly informed, ambassador Abetz, who saw Laval as the only guarantee of political cooperation with Germany, allowed himself to become confused and sent overly hasty reports to Berlin. Laval certainly accepted the policy of a joint conduct of the war at Germany's side as perhaps possible, especially with the goal of retaking the equatorial region of Africa, which had broken away.

At the same time Hitler had given back the ashes of Napoleon's son, the Duke of Reichstadt, which rested in the Capuchin Church in Vienna, so that the young eagle could find his place next to his famous father in the Hôtel of the Invalides. Marshall Pétain was represented by Admiral Darlan at the ceremony, because the French head of state had been informed that we would detain him if he should come to Paris! Hitler was furious when he learned of this. In reality what was going on in Vichy was a palace revolution and shabby intrigues. "Purely a matter of internal politics," Admiral Darlan explained to Hitler on December 25. At the time I had no way of knowing that I would later be given a delicate mission in Vichy, which thank God I did not have to carry out, namely to seize the person of the famous marshall.

After the departure order was ultimately withdrawn on December 23, 1940, I was again assigned leave. I was in Vienna with my family when I was recalled by telegraph. I was to report to the commander of my division immediately on my return: the people of the military general staff administrative section were demanding that I be severely punished. Generalleutnant Hausser informed me that I was charged with threatening a Feldwebel that I would level his tire dump if he didn't hand over the urgently needed tires.

"Gruppenführer," I explained, "the fuel truck's twelve tons of gasoline had to reach their destination! Every minute was important... The tires were lying there... Anyway I gave him a voucher."

"Skorzeny, you must understand that the stores administrators are very formal and bureaucratic people, who believe that the material they administer is their personal property. You were doubtless very courteous to them, but this Feldwebel must have been shocked by your persistence. These gentlemen of the administrative section are demanding that you be punished as an example to others. Therefore consider yourself punished in principle. Then we'll see. Meanwhile you can go back on leave. Go on then."

In Russia I had the opportunity to learn first-hand that certain gentlemen of the administrative section were in fact extremely bureaucratic.

We moved into our winter quarters on the Langres Plateau, and it deserves to be mentioned that our relations with the French population were outstanding. Any incorrectness on our part was punished firmly. I can offer two examples as typical:

On May 18, 1940 our regiment passed through a small village near Hirson (Aisne) whose name I cannot remember. Lying scattered on the sidewalk were bales of cloth from a shop which had been destroyed by a shell. The artillerists of our battery took one of the bales, it was a yellow material, and made themselves neckerchiefs from it. The next day the following division order, applicable to all units, was read out at roll call:

"Soldiers of the division have been seen wearing neckerchiefs which apparently have been made from French materials. The division is hereby reminded that the appropriation of any item from the street, be it cloth or other thing, is considered plundering. The division's officers are therefore advised to consider any soldier wearing such a neckerchief as a plunderer. The same are to be arrested immediately and brought before a court martial which will sentence them on account of this offense."

On the Langres Plateau and the Haute-Saóne some of us were put up in private quarters and therefore shared the family life of the resident hosts to a certain degree. This resulted in a number of situations.

In February 1941 numerous French prisoners of war were released to return home as a result of the cease-fire agreement. One of the French soldiers arrived home unexpectedly late one night and surprised one of our comrades with his wife. The woman claimed that she had been raped by him, hoping to escape the wrath of her husband. One can't blame her for that. However our countryman was arrested, brought before a court martial and sentenced to death. Several of us officers and NCOs vainly asked our general for mercy, for we were convinced that it was not a case of rape, rather that the affair had been going on for several weeks. After he had listened to us "Papa" Hausser said:

"Not a single member of the Waffen-SS, which is an elite force, may fall under suspicion of having committed an act which would shame a true soldier. The sentence will be carried out."

And it was carried out.

During the hard winter of 1940/41 we asked ourselves various questions on the Langres Plateau. What were we doing there? I saw no hatred of Germans in France, just as the Germans did not hate France. Both peoples had earned enough glory on the battlefield against each other to now build a united Europe, which was a possibility at that point in time, side by side.

Among those who believed it necessary to build a united Europe and join its peoples, peoples whose cultures made them so close and who also had common interests, as soon as possible, the meeting of French Marshall Pétain with Hitler in Montoire awakened great hopes. I confess that I was a convinced European all along and I haven't changed my opinion to the present day.

The meeting in Montoire, which could have turned out to be one of the high points of modern history, was unsuccessful.

Certainly there were people in Germany and France who lusted for revenge, but it seemed to me that this short-sighted and pitiful nationalism could be overcome. A great, positive revolution was waiting to be carried out on the old continent: we all had this feeling, and it was primarily a revolution in social justice. As in the present day, then too the lack of such social justice was the best weapon in the hands of the action groups of the Communist Internationale. The French, in particular, were in a position to carry out this revolution without having to emulate the fascists or the national socialists.

The suffering of an unfortunate people has never brought with it advantages for its neighbor. I later saw in Vichy how France, in order to survive, had to adopt a double-faceted policy in the face of a victor who did not allow the nation to plan and carry out policy on a large scale.

The French had a first-class agent in the person of Jacques Benoist-Méchin, a historian for the German Army, who achieved noteworthy advantages for his country. On June 25, 1940 several million French soldiers were sent to Germany by the Wehrmacht as prisoners.[1] One million of them were set free a month after the cease-fire; roughly 1,900,000 were brought to Germany, of which half were gradually sent back to France by January 1, 1944.

How unfortunate that my country had not immediately adopted a policy of cooperation without recrimination and concluded a peace treaty with the French government, which was conscious of the great threat facing Europe and the civilized world, instead of adopting a short-sighted diplomacy which showed very little generosity!

In the end it was the German, but also the European, soldiers who had to pay a high price for this haughty, clumsy and hesitant diplomacy.

Today West Germany and France work actively and closely together although no peace treaty and not even a cease-fire was ever signed by the two governments.

The lives of many millions of people, civilians and soldiers alike, had to be sacrificed to achieve this coming together. It would have been much more intelligent and humane to have achieved an understanding in 1939 or 1940! Everyone lost in this war, not only Germany, but France, England, Italy, Belgium and Holland as well. And unfortunately it produced no solution, neither in Europe nor in the rest of the world.

However, after the false readiness order of December 1940 we still clung to the illusion that not all the hopes for peace were lost. At the beginning of 1941 we assumed that our diplomacy would make the greatest efforts in this direction.

It soon turned out, however, that things were developing in a rather unfavorable way for the Axis, first of all in East Africa, where the Italians were defeated. Following a successful offensive by Marshall Graziani in North Africa, which led to the capture of Sollum and Sidi Barani in September 1940, in January and February 1941 the English launched a counteroffensive and occupied Tobruk and Benghazi. On February 26 the Africa Corps under the command of Rommel was forced to intervene.

In Europe itself the theater underwent an expansion that for us was completely unexpected. Without informing Hitler beforehand, the Duce invaded Greece with his badly-trained, poorly-provisioned and indifferently-led army. Our allies were soon thrown back and in the end overrun in Albania. On top of that a coup d'état took place in Yugoslavia: our ally, Prince Regent Paul, was overthrown on March 27, 1941.

Several days later the new head of government, General Simovich, signed a friendship pact with Stalin guaranteeing mutual support!

In the last days of March 1941 our division suddenly received orders to march to southern Romania. I was given leave to spend one night at home in Vienna and rejoined my unit the next day at the Hungarian border. We received a jubilant welcome when we marched through Budapest, as if we were victorious Hungarian soldiers. We reached the Romanian border near Gjola. The weather was poor and our equipment began to suffer to an unsettling degree. The roads were in the worst condition and they were no better through the entire Balkans Campaign.

We attacked at 5:59 A.M. on Sunday, April 6, after a five-minute artillery barrage. The Serbs defended themselves, setting one of our armored cars on fire. They fought at close quarters from behind a broad anti-tank ditch, but this couldn't prevent us from quickly overrunning them. I experienced this, my baptism of fire, with Hauptmann Neugebauer, a veteran of the First World War. After the first artillery salvoes my stomach felt the way it did before a practice duel. Neugebauer passed me a bottle of schnapps and said, "Have a drink, it's not very warm this morning!"

After the anti-tank ditch, where there were killed and wounded, we moved ahead to Pancevo, where we learned that our division's advance battalion commanded by Hauptsturmführer Klingenberg had become the first to cross the Danube, in a surprise attack, and had entered Belgrade.

I myself was sent ahead to scout east of our advance road as the leader of two small motorized patrols. We were 24 men all told, and I passed through Werschetz, which still had all the character of an old city of the Austro-Hungarian monarchy. We were advancing cautiously toward Karlsdorf when the entire population came out to meet us enthusiastically: it was an old German colony. We passed the village. Serbian troops were reported and we soon made contact in a difficult area of terrain covered with vegetation. When my right group was attacked it responded energetically. Suddenly about thirty Serbian soldiers appeared in front of me. I gave the order not to fire, while the Serbians came ever nearer. I shouted with all my might, "Stoi!" (Halt!)

Surprised, they listened, but then more Serbs came from all sides. What should I do? Shoot or not shoot? For me that was now the decisive question. Luckily at that moment my second group appeared behind them, which caused the Serbians to thrown down their weapons and raise their hands.

We returned to Karlsdorf with five officers and more than sixty captured soldiers. But we were ourselves held prisoner in Karlsdorf for three hours: the mayor gave a welcoming speech in front of the town hall and I had to shake his hand when he solemnly declared that the population had never forgotten its German fatherland. Afterward there was a festive meal in the school, and I believe that neither Brueghel or Teniers ever had the opportunity to paint such a festive occasion.

I naturally gave instructions that our prisoners should receive their share. As well as the five Serbian officers and the other prisoners, we brought our regiment not only the best food, but also a number of bottles of wine, which were welcomed enthusiastically. I gave my report to Standartenführer Hansen, who found the story extremely interesting.

We were quartered with German farmers of the agriculturally rich area of Banat. I found lodgings with a brave farmer's wife whose husband had been called up by the Romanian Army and who only got leave when he bribed his superiors! That gave me cause for reflection.

Soon afterward I was summoned to the officers' mess by Standartenführer Hansen.

"That patrol operation the other day," he said, "could get you the Iron Cross. Instead I chose to recommend you for promotion to Untersturmführer, and my recommendation has been accepted. My sincere congratulations on your promotion and I hope that you agree with my idea."

I joyfully gave my blessings. Several hours later I was called for again and learned that my promotion to Untersturmführer had also arrived via official channels and was retroactive to January 30, 1941.

Hansen said with a laugh, "Since you were already an Untersturmführer, your promotion of this morning was obviously to Obersturmführer!"

One can easily imagine my surprise and joy. All I had to do was fill up the glasses again.

The Yugoslav Army surrendered on April 17 and hostilities ceased the next day. Croatia had declared its independence on April 10. The new state, whose president was Doctor Ante Pavelich, was immediately recognized by Germany, Italy, Slovakia, Hungary, Bulgaria, Romania and Spain, while the Swiss signed a mutually beneficial trade agreement with Dr. Pavelich somewhat later (September 10, 1941).

On April 8, 1941 the German Twelfth Army (List), led by the Leibstandarte Adolf Hitler, broke through the Metaxas Line and occupied Saloniki, where a British army had landed. Most of the English troops were hastily evacuated across the sea to Crete, while on April 17 the German troops marched into Athens and the Greek Army surrendered.

The first large operation by parachute and airborne troops was carried out against Crete from May 20 to 31. The action was under the command of General Student. 22,000 men took part, our single parachute division, our only glider regiment and the 5th Mountain Infantry Division, which had not yet completed its training. The operation was a complete success. The Royal Navy was only able to save 16,500 of the 57,000 English, Australian, New Zealand and Greek troops that had sought refuge on the island, and at the cost of heavy losses.

Unfortunately our own losses, in large part due to the difficult terrain, were not insignificant: 4,000 dead and somewhat more than 2,000 wounded. In the years 1942-1943 I had occasion to thoroughly study the various episodes of the Battle of Crete, in order to find means of reducing to the maximum degree possible the risks involved in any future airborne operations that I might undertake. It seemed clear to me that such operations could not be carried out with inadequately-trained troops.

The losses suffered during the airborne assault of Crete made a strong impression on Hitler, who would not allow such operations to be repeated in Cyprus, Suez or Malta.

Napoleon, who had correctly recognized the strategic importance of the Mediterranean in general and of Egypt and Malta in particular, found himself facing the Third Coalition in 1805 when he tried to retake Malta, which he had conquered in 1793 and lost again two years later. He had also tried to capture Gibraltar.

It was a fortunate fact that the Balkan Campaign ended quickly and victoriously. In 1940 General Weygand, then the chief of the French forces in the Levant, proposed a plan from Beirut to Paris, which foresaw a landing in Saloniki, and even, "according on the reaction of the USSR," an eventual offensive in Asia Minor. The French also considered bombing the oil sources of Batum and Baku and made detailed plans. Undoubtedly General Weygand intended to play the same decisive role that Marshall Franchet d'Esperey had done toward the end of the First World War.

In pursuing a victorious war on the continent, the Mediterranean Sea was of even greater strategic importance in 1941 than in 1805 or 1914, and we had conquered neither Gibraltar nor Suez. Without doubt our Italian allies would have been able to take Malta in a surprise attack in July-August 1940, but the Luftwaffe, then in the midst of the Battle of Britain and Operation Otario, was in no position to help. Later Malta and Gibraltar, both held by the allies, were the main reason for our defeat in North Africa.

I soon had cause to visit Belgrade on official business, and it interested me to get to know this city, which had been conquered by the Turks repeatedly since 1521 and which they did not surrender for good until 1866.

I knew that the city had been bombarded, and it was there that I first got to know the worst side of the war. Our Stukas and level bombers had reduced entire quarters of the city to rubble. We were not yet used to such scenes of devastation and were therefore strongly impressed. Instead of the friendly, smiling faces of the people who had welcomed us so warmly in Werschetz, Karlsdorf and Pancevo, all we saw here were hostile, hate-filled expressions. To whose benefit was all this destruction and suffering? I felt for the unfortunates and in the bottom of my heart I expected nothing good for Europe from this war.

Soon afterward we received orders to pull back to Austria. I was happy to be able to spend a brief leave with my family. My father was more moved than he wished to admit at seeing me as an officer.

"You have been promoted quickly," he said to me, "I congratulate you. But don't start thinking you'll get the Knight's Cross some day. Keep a cool head."

"Certainly father."

"It's a great honor to be an officer. You must now lead your people with intelligence and courage, especially in difficult situations. My son, your duties to your fatherland must be sacred to you."

Today such words might sound banal or naive. But I have never forgotten them.

Notes

1. In Volume One of *Life in France during the Occupation*, Robert Moreau, the general commissar for repatriated prisoners of war, gives the figure of 3,000,000 French prisoners of war in German hands.

6

UNKNOWN FACTS ABOUT THE FLIGHT TO ENGLAND BY RUDOLF HESS (MAY 10, 1941)

The war could have ended in March 1940 – The personality of Rudolf Hess – Decisive supporter of an entente with Great Britain – Hitler's deputy and successor – Careful preparations for the flight – The unsuccessful efforts of Gauleiter Bohle. – Professor Haushofer – No war on two fronts – Meeting between Hitler and Darlan, May 11, 1941 – Findings by the American Mercury since 1943 – Hess believed he had a contact in the Duke of Hamilton – Hess' proposals in Hitler's name – Did Hitler see what was happening in the end, or did Hess take off with his full approval? – Churchill refuses to exchange Hess in 1943 The Nuremberg Tribunal

I t was after our campaign in the Balkans, and shortly before the beginning of our air landing on Crete, when our radio announced the sensational news. In this way I learned on the evening of May 11, 1941 that Rudolf Hess, the second most important personality in the state – Göring was at that time only third in significance – had flown to England the previous evening.

The official statement said that Hess' health had left something to be desired for some time, that he had "hallucinations," and that "this incident would in no way had any effect on the war, which was forced upon the German people by Great Britain."

After the initial shock had passed, it occurred to none of us that Hess might be a traitor. In early 1941 neither my comrades nor I felt that the war might be so long and pitiless and that the civilian population would have to suffer as much, or perhaps more, than we soldiers. I wasn't the only one who thought that Hess had flown to England, not as the result of a crazy brain wave, as was officially announced, rather more likely for the purpose of trying to contribute to an ending of a civil war among Europeans.

With the war already in progress, Sumner Welles, acting American Foreign Minister, was sent by Roosevelt on a special mission to Europe, where he created certain illusions. Welles held lengthy discussions with Chamberlain, Daladier, Mussolini, Ribbentrop, Schacht, Göring and with Hitler himself. Today we know that it would have been possible to end the war in March 1940. But the opportunity to convene a world peace conference, to be chaired by Roosevelt himself, was allowed to pass. Hitler gave his approval immediately. But after the return of Sumner Welles the project for a conference was torpedoed by Foreign Minister Cordell Hull.[1]

Of course in 1941 we knew nothing of these details. We did know that Hitler had proposed peace negotiations following the campaign in Poland. We also knew that his deputy was a man of unquestioned integrity and loyalty. Hess had a reserved, sometimes mystical character, without however ever giving any indication of mental imbalance. In the end we assumed that he had perhaps believed he was tasked with a great mission which he couldn't bring to a successful conclusion. In spite of our uncertainty we weren't far from the truth.[2]

Held prisoner for decades, condemned to life imprisonment as a "war criminal" at Nuremberg, Rudolf Hess is today more than eighty years old. Watched alternately by Soviet, American, English and French soldiers, Hess is now the last and only prisoner in Spandau Prison. Although the three western allies are in favor of his release, motions to this effect have been passed in the British parliament and countless petitions for mercy have been submitted by various personalities from all over the world, the Russians refuse to release this last prisoner. (Hess died in 1987)

● ● ●

Many facts concerning the odyssey of Rudolf Hess have been known for several years; however, others, extremely important, remain unknown to the general public.

First of all, who is the prisoner in Spandau? He came from a well to do family and his mother was of British descent. Born in Alexandria, where he spent part of his youth and was brought up "in the English style," he fought bravely with the German Air Force in World

War One. He later completed his studies at the University of Munich. It was there that he came into contact with the National-Socialist German Workers Party. After the putsch of November 9, 1934 he was imprisoned with Hitler at Landsberg. He became Hitler's truest friend, and the future Führer dictated part of his book *Mein Kampf* to Hess.

Reichsminister in 1933, in 1935 he was officially named deputy to the Führer, who in 1939 publicly named him his successor in the party.

Hess was a longtime advocate of an entente between Great Britain and Germany. This seems plausible to me, and a number of historians share my opinion that Hess flew to England as an extraordinary emissary to bring about a peace with England on the eve of the war against Stalin.

Many historians contend that Hitler was unaware of the planned flight. But it had been prepared down to the last detail far in advance. The minister carried out approximately twenty test flights, some even with directional guidance by radio, in an Me 110 specially equipped under the direction of Professor Messerschmitt. But all the world knew that Hess had been strictly forbidden to fly an aircraft himself since 1938, on orders of the Führer.

In contrast to statements by many alleged witnesses, Hitler did not appear especially surprised when he was informed that Hess had flown to the castle of the Duke of Hamilton in Scotland.

● ● ●

Hess had his adjutant deliver a letter to Hitler, in which he said: "...Should my mission fail, I am ready to be disowned... It will be easy for you to explain that I acted in a moment of mental confusion." I have not seen this letter, but extracts from same have been quoted, especially by the English historian James Leasor in his book about Hess. Moreover in 1945/46 I had the opportunity to speak with Hess' adjutant in the witness wing at Nuremberg, who told me the same thing. The letter in no way corresponded to Rudolf Hess' mental state at the beginning of his mission, which was neither that of a criminal, nor of a madman, but that of an emissary of peace.

It is known that numerous discussions concerning peace in the west took place in 1940/41. The negotiations were conducted by official persons or German and English special representatives, such as Richard Butler, adjutant to Lord Halifax in the Foreign Office, neutral diplomats, for example the Swedish emissary in London Bjoern Prytz, and others. Negotiations were also carried out in Switzerland, in Madrid, Lisbon and Ankara.

One of the most active adherents of a peace with London was Ernst Wilhelm Bohle, leader of the *Volksbundes für das Deutschtum in Ausland (DVA)*. Born in England and raised in South Africa, he studied at Cambridge and was an energetic propagandist for his pacifist world view, which was also often expressed by Hitler, publicly and privately, until 1941.[3] He declared: "Like the Roman church, the British Empire is one of the pillars of western civilization."

● ● ●

I met Bohle at Nuremberg. He had been charged in the so-called "Wilhelmstrasse Trial" of having promoted the "criminal ideas" of our foreign ministry. It is odd that he, who had previously been a complete agnostic, should find refuge in the catholic religion. A great piety had come over him: his cell was decorated with holy pictures, a privilege permitted him through the efforts of Sixtus O'Connor, a captain in the American Army and the resident catholic priest. O'Connor was a devoted Christian who was sympathetic to almost all the prisoners and to whom I shall return later.

But in the end the steps taken by Gauleiter Bohle failed to lead to success. Hess had met the Duke of Hamilton at the Olympic Games of 1936. At that time a large part of British public opinion was of the view that the Versailles Treaty had to undergo a revision if Europe was to be reorganized and the German people allowed a place on the continent. Edward VIII shared this view during his brief reign. After he became the Duke of Windsor he visited Chancellor Hitler with the duchess. Likewise the leader of the Labour Party, David Lloyd George, made his way to the Berghof, although he had had a hand in creating the Versailles Treaty. The proponents of an entente with Germany in London were more numerous than we are led to believe today. The loud manifestations of Sir Oswald Mosley's blackshirts undoubtedly had an absolutely negative effect in regard to an entente between the English and German peoples – which, by the way, Sir Oswald admitted in his book *My Life*, published in 1968. Men like

Lord Rothermere, Redesdale, Beaverbrook, Nuffield, Kemsley, Admiral Sir Barry Domvile and the Duke of Hamilton also believed that war with Germany was contrary to the interests of the British people.

After the war had broken out and our official diplomacy completely disappeared, it became increasingly difficult to end the bloody struggle and the mass death of peoples in the west. The *Daily Mail* stopped praising Hitler in the name of a "very honorable peer of the realm," Lord Rothermere. The British mentality changed. Hess probably knew this, but continued to believe that many people in London were still of the opinion that this war was absurd.

Hess' most important advisor in the politics of a peace with London was one of his old friends, Professor Haushofer, the inventor of geo-political science and the editor of the magazine *Geopolitik*, which Hitler read. Since September 1940 Hitler's personal deputy had been in possession of a long memorandum by Professor Haushofer on *the possibilities of concluding a peace with England*. Hitler probably read this memorandum and discussed it with Hess. In his compilation of the Hess-Haushofer conversations, which were written down by the latter, James Leasor noted that the professor explained to Hess that it was the view of influential Englishmen that Ribbentrop was playing "the same role as Duff Cooper or Churchill in the eyes of the Germans."

In the professor's opinion it might have been possible to establish a reasonable contact with the deputy minister O'Malley, who was the envoy in Budapest, with Sir Samuel Hoare, who was in Madrid, and with Lord Lothian, Great Britain's ambassador in Washington. Haushofer had known the latter for a long time.

Hitler would gladly have achieved in the west what he had accomplished in the east in August 1939. In order to avoid having to fight on two fronts, he wanted to replace the treaty he had signed with Stalin with a treaty or at least a *modus vivendi* in the west, and not just with Great Britain.

It is not without a certain significance that on May 11, 1941, the same day that Hess was in principle supposed to be discussing peace terms with Great Britain, Hitler received Admiral Darlan, head of Marshall Pétain's government, and the president's general secretary, Jacques Benoist-Méchin, at the Berghof. Certain concessions were made to the Frenchmen,[4] and they were given assurances that their country would play an important role in Western Europe. It was too early – especially on account of Italy – to conclude a peace treaty and thus give a guarantee for France's colonial empire. Hitler however expressed his good will and told the admiral that "his peace would not be a revenge peace."

From this one can infer that Hitler was not only fully informed about Hess' planned flight, but that he had also given his official representative full powers to speak in his name. And this at the beginning of the war. In reality the flight was preceded by lengthy negotiations, and Rudolf Hess was certain that he would be received by very senior persons on the other side of the English Channel, even if he hadn't been officially invited.

● ● ●

I believe that a correct explanation of Rudolf Hess' flight was given in a very well-documented article in the American magazine *The American Mercury* in May 1943. According to the author, who wrote anonymously, it was Hitler himself who from January 1941 concerned himself with the possibility of direct negotiations with Great Britain for the purpose of concluding a lasting peace. The following is an extract from *The American Mercury*:

"Hitler turned not to the English government, but to a group of influential Englishmen belonging to the already disbanded English-German Society – of which the Duke of Hamilton had been a member. A diplomat with an international reputation served as courier."

The American Mercury did not give the name of this diplomat, but it was without a doubt a German diplomat. From the anonymous account it is apparent that the British responded to the offer with an evasive, lukewarm reply. Negotiations went on in this way for four months, "with caution and restraint" on both sides, until the moment when Hitler suggested continuing the negotiations in a neutral country, which the English refused to accept. They even rejected Bohle as middleman, while the Turkish and South American press reported that Bohle had "received an important and confidential mission abroad."

This was the moment when Hess intervened. As deputy Führer he had full authority to make arrangements in Hitler's name. On May 10, 1941 he flew to Dungavel, the Duke of Hamilton's castle in Scotland, near which there was a small private airfield. They were expecting him there, but Hess, who parachuted from his aircraft and landed approximately 16 kilometers from the castle, injuring his ankle in the process, was in no doubt as to the identity of the people waiting for him.

In May 1943 *The American Mercury* reported, "The first contacts in 1941 were intercepted by the British secret service, which from that moment on took charge of the entire affair."

When RAF Fighter Command located the unidentified Messerschmitt aircraft, which failed to respond correctly to the radioed queries, the duty officer called the fighter commander, who was stationed in Scotland: "For God's sake tell them that they're not to shoot him down!" In this way Hess received an "honor guard" of two English fighters. He noticed the presence of one of the fighters. Had he not taken to his parachute and had instead landed at the Duke of Hamilton's private airfield, the secret would never have been known. But after Hess landed in a field belonging to a farmer named David MacLean, he was taken by the man to his house. He said his name was Alfred Horn and demanded that they notify the Duke of Hamilton.

With some imagination one could imagine that the brave Scottish farmer, who, pitchfork in hand, watched Hess fall from the sky, belonged to the same clan as Donald MacLean, who passed important atomic secrets to the Soviets and years later, in 1963, escaped to Russia after falling under suspicion. That would be an interesting theme for the lover of historical anecdotes. In this case, however, something quite different was involved.

Hamilton, a wing commander in the RAF, was at his post. When he was notified by telephone he declared that he did not know an Alfred Horn. The next day when he saw Rudolf Hess, whose visit he was not expecting, he was extremely surprised. The people waiting for Hess at the small airfield were senior officials of the intelligence service and secret service officers, who had set a trap for Hess.

They had to take Hess-Horn away from a half-dozen members of the home guard, which had been notified by MacLean. The secret service officers conducted the first interrogation of Hess in the barracks at Maryhill, Glasgow. Then he was taken to a military hospital.

The American Mercury wrote:

"Hess believed that he had to go a long way until he reached the top. But this happened much more quickly than he had imagined. Churchill sent Sir Ivone Kirkpatrick, master spy from the First World War and British diplomatic advisor between the wars, to him. He was supposed to listen to Rudolf Hess' proposals and lay them directly before the British government."

According to *The American Mercury*, Hitler offered the following: a cessation of hostilities in the west, a withdrawal from all occupied lands except Alsace-Lorraine and Luxembourg, withdrawal from Yugoslavia, Greece and the Mediterranean basin in general. In return he demanded Great Britain's benevolent neutrality with regard to Germany's policies in the east. No country, whether a combatant or neutral, was to demand reparations. According to *The American Mercury*, Hess insisted that it was necessary to eliminate the danger posed to the whole world by communism once and for all. Germany offered to carry out this mission alone, for which it needed the war production of France and Great Britain.

Hess also spoke with Lord Beaverbrook, Minister of State, whom he knew, with Lord John Simon "and other members of the war cabinet." He did not see Churchill, who notified Roosevelt directly. The answer to Rudolf Hess' proposals was of course negative.

When Hess realized that he had walked wretchedly into a trap, and from the very beginning, and that Great Britain was in reality already an ally of the Soviets, Hess was in fact the victim of a nervous breakdown, as *The American Mercury* tells us:

"The lie about his alleged derangement had almost become reality."

When he learned that the battleship *Bismarck*, which had sunk the British battleship *Hood*, had herself gone down (May 27, 1941), he wept the whole day.

The fantastic and noble character of his flight kept numerous commentators from realizing that their reports, seen from their point of view, sounded improbable.

The English preparations, cleverly camouflaged as ultimate cooperation toward peace, would not have found any good faith in Germany had it not been for the Halifax-Butler precedent, as well as the peace proposals which the Foreign Office made to the Swedish ambassador Prytz (June 17, 1940).

The honest character of Rudolf Hess has never been placed in question, neither by his friends nor by his family. He would never have spoken the name of Hamilton if he had not been convinced that the duke was acting in the name of very high English governing circles. Furthermore all the statements by witnesses agree that Hess asked directly that they should notify the one he saw as his middleman, namely Lord Hamilton, who was supposed to place him in contact with senior empowered members of the government.

It is an insult to the Duke of Hamilton to believe and to write that he was an accomplice of the British secret service. His astonishment when he saw Hess was real, for as *The American Mercury* tells us, "his handwriting had been imitated on falsified letters," so that it could be compared with that which possibly existed on pre-war correspondence in Berlin.

It would of course be interesting to see this correspondence. We hope, although not too confidently, that it same might someday be made public. I myself have little hope that it will.

If the Duke of Hamilton and other English personalities had secretly been in contact with Germans for four months, especially with Hess, how is it that they were not tried and convicted for dealing with the enemy after Hess' flight? Nothing of the sort happened.

I therefore believe the theory put forward by the *American Mercury*, which in 1974 recalled that the facts published in 1943 came from an "observer with a first-class reputation," who based his information on especially secure sources.[5]

Hess said to Ivone Kirkpatrick, "I come in the name of peace and humanity. The thought of a prolongation of the war and the needless sacrifice is terrible to me."

Hitler's reaction is also understandable. It is very likely that he became mistrustful after he read all the files pertaining to this peace feeler to the west. It is possible that he noted certain suspicious things. Hess, who was less intuitive and more trusting, must then have been disavowed by Hitler.

The historian Alain Decaux put forward another theory in his *Dossiers secrets de l'Histoire* (1966). He scrutinized the reactions of Hitler and Göring before, during and immediately after Hess' flight. He quoted facts and witnesses, especially those concerning the meteorologists and radio service of the Germans. He reasoned that Hess had flown to Scotland with Hitler's approval, and that a letter he left behind was supposed to allow Hitler to describe his attempt as madness if it should fail. Decaux wrote:

"In August 1943, when Hitler gave Skorzeny the job of freeing Mussolini, who was being held prisoner on the island of Maddalena, he referred to the Rudolf Hess case and said that he would have to disavow Skorzeny in the event of failure."

Here I must correct Decaux somewhat: although it is true that in August 1943, while I was preparing to free Mussolini from the island of Maddalena, Hitler made me aware that he would perhaps have to declare me mad in the event of failure, at no time did he refer to Rudolf Hess in my presence and never in any way mentioned his name or the flight made by him.

● ● ●

Toward the end of 1943 the Polish General Rowecki, head of the secret Polish army, was captured. This army was under the direct command of the Polish exile government. Minister president of this government in London was General Sikorski, who several days later was the victim of a peculiar air accident near Gibraltar. General "Grot" Rowecki's successor, General Bor-Komorowski, was also taken prisoner in early October 1944. He was received by General von Lüttwitz, commander of the German Ninth Army, who informed him that he and his general staff were considered prisoners of war and not as partisans. Toward the end of the war the German authorities handed Bor-Komorowski over to Swiss delegates of the Red Cross.

In Bor-Komorowski's *Histoire d'une Armée secrète,* published in Paris in 1955, we read that General Rowecki was supposed to be exchanged for a high-level German prisoner. "The Germans," wrote Bor-Komorowski, "were only willing to exchange Rowecki for Rudolf Hess, but Great Britain refused to agree."

At the beginning of my stay in Nuremberg the eighteen main accused were still in the same wing of the prison as the witnesses. I was therefore able to observe Hess almost every day walking in the prison courtyard, when chanced to receive my fifteen minutes "exercise" at the same time. The ban on talking was draconian in its strictness, and it was impossible for me to talk to him in order to at least offer him a word of encouragement. He appeared to me not in the least mentally ill. Quite the contrary.

While walking he was chained to an American soldier. When it came time to change direction, he made use of his prerogative as "mentally unstable" to make sudden, unexpected movements, which were only intended to upset his guard and force him to walk about in a comic fashion. It was then not so easy to tell which of the two was the actual prisoner.

On the straight sections Hess walked calmly and with firm steps, very worthy and head held high, without concerning himself with the soldier, who followed him under compulsion and appeared to be his servant.

Notes

1. The details of this intrigue and the final refusal by Cordell Hull were revealed in April 1966 by Professor C. Tansill in an article published in the weekly magazine *The Weekly Crusader*. The weekly's director is the Reverend B.J. Hargis of Tulsa, Oklahoma. Tansill's work was cited and commented on by J. de Launay in his *Histoire de la diplomatie secrète* (1966).

2. Compare to this complex the description by Ilse Hess in *Ein Schicksal in Briefen*. Leoni, 1974.

3. After halting our panzers, which could have reached Dunkirk *before* the British Expeditionary Corps, in May 1940, Hitler spoke to his generals about the significance of the British Empire to the western world. (Otto Skorzeny considered this order to be a great military-political mistake.) Sir Basil Liddell Hart related that Field Marshall Rundstedt confided the following to him after the war: "Hitler surprised us on May 24, 1940 by speaking with admiration of the British Empire, of the necessity of its existence and of the civilization England had brought to the world... His conclusion was that an honorable peace should be concluded with England."

4. Thanks to the negotiating skill of J. Benoist-Méchin, France in fact achieved a restoration of French authority in the north and at the Pas-de-Calais, concessions in the drawing of boundaries, the return of 83,000 prisoners of war, the rearming of 13 warships and a reduction in occupation costs. In return France gave Germany permission for German and Italian aircraft to overfly French territory for a limited period of time. In Syria and Iraq, Rashid Ali called for an uprising against his country's pro-British government and asked Germany for help. Admiral Canaris was unenthusiastic and the assistance he provided was inadequate.

5. The article, which the magazine carried in May 1943, included a picture captioned "The Vision of Rudolf Hess": long rows of coffins and German and English bodies. Hess also spoke about this vision in a two-and-a-half-hour talk with Lord Simon on June 10, 1941, which, if I'm not mistaken, was first acknowledged at Nuremberg on March 25, 1946. On that day Hess' defense attorney, Dr. Seidl, entered the text of the discussion with Lord Simon on June 10, 1941 into the case record. One can ask oneself, whether the writer of this fantastic article received his information at least from a person who had dealt with Hess. Why did *The American Mercury* publish this piece when it did (in the middle of the war), and how was it possible that no official or unofficial protests were raised on account of it?

7

BARBAROSSA

Pitiful condition of the equipment after the Balkan Campaign – The Persian Gulf or Egypt? – Lawrence and The Seven Columns – "Soldiers of the Eastern Front..." – What would Europe be today if Hitler hadn't attacked? – Hitler erred and was deceived – Strength and tactics of the enemy – The stubborn legend of Stalin's "surprise" – He received intelligence about our attack in December 1940. At that time Roosevelt was already sending him aircraft and placed training officers for them at his disposal.

In December 1940 our SS-Verfügungstruppe Division was renamed the SS-Division Das Reich. Our unit was retrained and rejuvenated, and in spring 1941 it was necessary to check overall our rolling stock, which was in a really pitiable condition. We had, in some cases more than once, crossed Germany, Holland, Belgium, France, Austria, Hungary, Romania and Yugoslavia. I have read that our general staff was "satisfied" with the state of our rolling stock after the Balkan Campaign. Besides it was the effects of nature as well as the wear and tear on the materiel that contributed to the slowing of our movements on the Eastern Front.

The tanks of Panzergruppe Kleist had to cross the roads of the Peloponnese and climb the Carpathians at a snail's pace before, 600 in number, finally attacking Budenny's 2,400 tanks. Generalfeldmarschall von Rundstedt, who commanded Army Group South when we attacked Russia, told the English military author Sir Basil Liddell Hart after the war that his "preparations had been hindered by the late arrival of Kleist's panzers." Kleist himself confirmed this: "A large part of the tanks under my command came from the Peloponnese, and the vehicles themselves as well as their crews needed a longer period for rest or repairs."

A motorized division had a total of about 2,200 vehicles, but unfortunately up to 50 different types and models; 10 to 18 types would have been more than enough. Our artillery regiment, for example, had 200 trucks of about 15 various models. In the rain, in the mud and during the Russian winter it was practically impossible for even the best specialists to carry out all the necessary repairs. I even ask myself whether our general staffs even understood this problem in all its importance: motorization required an unbroken supply of materiel and replacement parts.

Our Das Reich Division therefore spent several weeks working exclusively to put our rolling stock in working order, and at the beginning of June 1941 we received the order to entrain the division. After we had driven around Bohemia-Moravia our train reached Upper Silesia and finally Poland. Where were we going? We had no idea and gave our imaginations free reign. Several stated confidently that we would cross the Caucasus with the agreement of Russia in order to occupy the Persian Gulf oil fields. Others said that we were about to sign a friendship and assistance pact with Turkey (June 17, 1941). Accordingly, after crossing the Caucasus we could march through Turkey so as to fall upon Suez and Egypt and attack the English from behind, while the Italians and Rommel went on the offensive. None of us came up with the idea that we might attack Russia and so have to fight on two fronts.

• • •

Since August 1939 Stalin had gained enormous advantages without fighting: half of Poland, the Baltic States, which he had simply annexed contrary to the existing arrangements, and finally northern Bukovina and Bessarabia, near the Romanian oil wells. Obtaining his "neutrality" had been an expensive proposition. We knew that the USSR had tried to enter the Balkans thanks to General Simovich's coup d'état in Belgrade. But we had settled that question.

What we did not know, however, was that the Russians had sent only second-class troops and obsolete materiel to the front in Finland. We had no idea that their hard-won victory over the courageous Finnish Army was just a bluff intended to conceal the USSR's might offensive and defensive power. Canaris, the chief of the Wehrmacht's intelligence service, must have known about these strengths.

One believes what one hopes for, and the idea of a campaign in Persia, Arabia and Egypt seemed especially tempting to me. I had in my pack a copy of *The Seven Pillars of Wisdom* by Colonel Thomas Edward Lawrence, the peculiar adventurer, archaeologist, secret agent and champion of Arab independence from the Turks. Could we not also achieve with the Arabs and Turks against England what he had undertaken? Couldn't we seize this pipeline – which General Weygand wanted to cut – as we later tried to capture the railroad to Narvik?

During our rail journey we had time to think, and the account by Lawrence of Arabia, in which adventure and economic interests were so intimately mixed together, gave me material enough to let my imagination wander. This Waliser had conducted an unconventional campaign with great imagination, which resulted in astonishing practical results. The combined English and French fleets never succeeded in forcing the Dardanelles during the First World War. On the other hand Lawrence's action to a certain degree allowed England to secure the peace in this part of the world, which had such great strategic importance from an economic, political and military standpoint, to its own advantage.

The results of the blitzkrieg over London and the threat of our landing had the same effect as the halting of the advance by our panzer divisions across the plains of Picardie toward Dunkirk. I was of the opinion that Churchill would only give in to force, but when? Had we in fact succeeded in making adequate preparations for such a large war in the period since 1935/36?

So I went on reading *The Seven Pillars of Wisdom* as our train crossed the Polish flatland. I had just reached the point in my reading where, in September 1918, Lawrence was preparing to blow up a Turkish military train, when our train pulled into the station in Lvov (Lemberg). From there we drove through the night into the area south of Brest-Litovsk, less than 50 kilometers from the Bug, the river which divided the Polish Generalgouvernement, which was administered by Germany, and the former Polish territory occupied by the Soviets. Now it was no longer possible to have any sort of illusions.

All the units of the division were assembled at 10 P.M. on June 21. The company commanders solemnly read out an order from the Führer, part of which is reproduced here:

"Soldiers of the Eastern Front!

Burdened by heavy concerns, sentenced to months of silence, the hour has now come in which I can speak openly to you, my soldiers.

Today there are about 160 Russian divisions standing at our border. Violations of this border have been going on for weeks, not only against us but in the far north and in Romania as well.

At this moment, soldiers of the Eastern Front, an assembly of strength the like of which in size and scale the world has never seen is now complete. In league with Finnish divisions, our comrades are standing with the victor of Narvik on the shores of the Arctic in the north. German soldiers under the command of the Conqueror of Norway, and the Finnish heroes of freedom under their own marshall are protecting Finland. On the Eastern Front stand you. In Romania, on the banks of the Prut, and along the danube right down to the beaches of the Black Sea are German and Romanian troops united under Antonescu, the head of state.

When this, the biggest front line in history, now begins its advance it does so not just to provide the means of ending for all time this great war, or to defend those countries currently concerned, but the salvation of our entire European civilization and culture.

German soldiers! You are thus entering upon a harsh and demanding fight – because the fate of Europe, the future of the German Reich, the existence of our nation now rest on your hands alone.

May the Lord God help us all in this struggle!"

I would like to make several comments about this Führer Order which preceded Operation Barbarossa.

I am firmly convinced that the European states and most of the nations of Europe would today be bolshevized if Hitler had not then given the order to attack.

Hitler was wrong and was tricked. The armies that he sent to the attack in eastern Europe were not "the greatest in world history." The Soviet armies, superior in numbers, possessed armaments that were in some areas superior to ours. In 1941 we had three million men at the front, with 3,580 tanks and somewhat more than 1,800 aircraft.

We immediately found ourselves confronted by 4,700,000 soldiers, which were deployed in depth and occupying unequivocally offensive positions, as in the south, with approximately 15,000 tanks[1] and, in White Russia alone, 6,000 aircraft, of which 1,500 were newer models.

Of the Soviet tanks, the T-34, which appeared near Yelnya toward the end of July 1941, was outstanding. Other giants, unknown to our intelligence specialists, appeared in 1942 and 1943: the Klimenti Voroshilov of 43 and 52 tons, and in 1944 the 63-ton Stalin tank. From the beginning there were other surprises in store for us, like the famous "Stalin Organ" and the equipment carried by the engineer battalions of the enemy's tank divisions. These had the materials to construct a 60-meter-long bridge capable of supporting sixty-ton vehicles.

At dawn on June 22, 1941, a Sunday, we went over to the attack to the east, just as Napoleon's Grand Army had done against the same foe on June 22, 1812.

The Barbarossa plan (which as we will see Stalin had lying before him) was divided as follows:

Army Group North, under the command of Feldmarschall Ritter von Leeb, consisted of two armies and a panzer group; its objective was to advance through the Baltic States and take Leningrad.

Army Group South, commanded by Feldmarschall von Rundstedt, with its three German armies and two Romanian armies under the command of General Antonescu and its panzer group, was supposed to advance south of the Pripyat Marshes, occupy the western Ukraine and take Kiev.

Army group Center, under the command of Feldmarschall von Bock, was the strongest. It was to advance between the Pripyat Marshes and Suvalki in the direction of Smolensk. It consisted of two armies and had two panzer groups: the first, under the command of General Hoth, and the second, under the command of General Guderian. The SS-Division Das Reich marched with Guderian's Second Panzer Group. Guderian was already referred to by us as "Fast Heinz."

On the preceding day, before 1 P.M., all the general staff officers waited for one of two code words" Altona or Dortmund. The first meant that Barbarossa had been postponed. But Dortmund was the code word that was issued.

The crossing of the Bug and the battles for Brest-Litovsk were marked by three special points. At dawn I was at my post with the light artillery of my new battalion, the second, which opened fire at 3:15 A.M. then moved its positions forward and opened fire on the second line of Russian positions. At five in the morning I was in the top of an oak on the bank of the Bug, observing the effect of our fire. I was forced to agree with our forward observers, who had crossed the deep river in inflatable boats and on their return advised us that we were firing at nothing. The Russians had pulled back beyond the range of our artillery and were now concealed in the swamps and forests, from which they had to be driven out.

The first point: the enemy did not appear to have been taken by surprise. He had carried out all his maneuvers according to plan.

Second point: He was however perplexed. Before his eyes the eighty tanks of the 18th Panzer Regiment submerged beneath the waters of the Bug, only to emerge on the Russian bank several moments later. They were in fact underwater tanks which had been prepared for Operation Otario. They were completely watertight tanks which were equipped with a snorkel like that used by our U-boats years later.

Third point: This was uncomfortable for us: even though the city of Brest-Litovsk itself fell quickly into our hands, the old fortress, which was built on a rock and had once been conquered by the Teutonic Knights, put up bitter resistance for three days. Even the heavy artillery and the Luftwaffe had no visible effect. I approached the fortress with a platoon of assault artillery. The Russians fought all day from their casemates and bunkers, which were under our direct fire. We had heavy casualties and many good comrades fell beside me. The Russians fought heroically to the last round, including at the station, whose basement we finally had to flood with water, until resistance collapsed.

Our losses at Brest-Litovsk were more than 1,000 wounded and 482 killed, 80 of them officers. To be sure we took 7,000 prisoners, including about 100 officers, but the German losses at Brest-Litovsk made up five percent of the total figure on the Eastern Front during the first eight days of the war. The determined resistance put up by this fortress got me to thinking.

I believe I am speaking from experience when I say that the Russians tried to employ a double tactic throughout the entire campaign. Special units fought to the bitter end and the last man in prepared positions. While we were forced to slow our advance to master this resistance – and later partisan groups – the main body of the Soviet armies tried to escape encirclement.

I might also mention here that Stalin, in his speech of July 3, 1941, recommended the retreat by the large masses of troops and simultaneously instituted the policy of scorched earth and ordered the immediate formation of partisan groups. The latter were not considered combatants as per the valid international rules of war. Russia had not signed these agreements.

Since 1945 and to the present day they have not ceased to claim that Stalin in 1941 was "completely peaceful and faithful," that he was only interested in building socialism in Russia and had fulfilled to the letter every clause of the agreement signed with Ribbentrop in August 1939. He was "treacherously attacked," they tell us, "completely surprised," and it was this surprise which made the German success possible. After Stalin's death Khrushchev, the Soviet Minister President and First Secretary of the Central Committee of the Communist Party, even accused his predecessor of having "allowed himself to be taken by surprise."

As proof of Stalin's friendly attitude toward Germany we are offered the telegram found in the archives of the German Foreign Ministry, which originated from our ambassador at the time, Graf von der Schulenburg.

On May 12, 1941 he telegraphed Ribbentrop:

"Policy statements by the Stalin government are ... aimed at ... reducing tensions in the relationship between the Soviet Union and Germany and creating a better atmosphere for the future. In particular we may assume that Stalin has always personally been in favor of a friendly relationship between Germany and the Soviet Union."

A diplomat can always have a limited intelligence. He can also play a double game, and it is difficult to say when Schulenburg took the latter path. However, thanks to the papers of our former ambassador in Rome, Ulrich von Hassel, which were published in Zurich (*Vom anderen Deutschland*, 1946) we know that in 1943 Schulenburg, who was already retired, proposed to the anti-Hitler conspirators that they send a suitable, secret emissary to Moscow to propose peace negotiations to Stalin in the name of a new "east-oriented" German government. All he asked was to be named foreign minister.

• • •

Operation Barbarossa in no way came as a surprise to the Soviet dictator, who on May 6, 1941 had taken Molotov's place as chairman of the Council of People's Commissars.

As early as June 1939 the brothers Erich and Theo Kordt, senior officials in the German Foreign Office informed (in agreement with Canaris, Oster and General Beck) Sir Robert Vansittart that Germany and the USSR were going to sign a treaty. It is therefore natural that the allies were informed just as soon about Hitler's hostile intentions toward the USSR.

Canaris and Oster very soon realized that Hitler, like Napoleon in his day, regarded the Russians as England's soldiers on the continent. I have already said that he did not want to undertake Operation Otario in the spring of 1941 as long as he ran the risk of eventually being attacked by Stalin in the rear. On September 6, 1940 Feldmarschall Keitel had the following note sent to the chief of the Abwehr:

"The forces on the Eastern Front will be strengthened in the course of the next weeks... But these movements can in no way be allowed to give the impression that we are planning an attack on Russia, rather they should point only in the direction of the Balkans, where we must defend our interests."

This was sufficiently clear, and beginning in September 1940 the German counter-espionage people could initiate measures to inform in detail their "correspondents" in the foreign ministry and in the war ministry, as well as abroad, in Italy and Switzerland. Details were not available until December 5, 1940, when General Halder, Chief of the Army General Staff, submitted to Hitler the plan it had worked out for him and which on February 3, 1941 received the name Operation Barbarossa. In that same month of February the under-secretary in the American foreign office, Sumner Welles, informed the Soviet envoy in Washington, Konstantin Usmansky, that Germany intended to attack Russia in the spring. Sumner Welles not only gave Usmansky the Barbarossa plan, but all or part of the Oldenburg plan as well, which foresaw the industrial and agricultural use of various areas of Russia by the Wehrmacht. This plan had been worked out by General Thomas, the chief of the Military-Economic and Armaments Office in the OKW, associate of Halder and friend of Canaris.

The Soviet Army was placed on alert at the end of May 1940. Marshall Timoshenko, who had been named Commissar of Defense, immediately signed the alert plan 0-20: he accelerated the orders when our panzers reached the Seine, or on June 9. Beginning in September 1940, the majority of the active divisions of the Red Army and General Bezougly's Tenth Airborne Corps moved from the central USSR toward the west. All of the officers of the Soviet Army with German-sounding names were sent to the east.

I may reveal here for the first time, that one of my postwar friends, Colonel Adam of the US Air Force, who after the war was military attache in a West-European country, told me that as the result of an appeal by Stalin, Roosevelt provided him with military assistance from *December 1940*. Adam and about 100 American pilots were sent to the USSR at that time to train the Russians on the latest American aircraft, deliveries of which had begun to Russia. Adam told me that in his opinion this pilot training was in no way associated with an eventual war between Russia and Japan. It was clear to all that it was a war against Germany that was involved. As one sees, this does not exactly agree with the history we are taught today.

Furthermore, in his last book Liddel Hart admitted that the British secret service had "to a great extent" been informed about Operation Barbarossa "long before," and that it "informed the Russians accordingly."

In April 1941 Sir Stafford Cripps, socialist member of parliament and Great Britain's ambassador in Moscow, informed the Russians of the exact date of the attack, June 22, 1941. Hitler was even told that *the Russians were informed*. By whom? Not by Canaris, but by the naval attache of the German embassy in Moscow, who on April 25 sent the following telegram to the High Command of the Navy in Berlin:

"The English envoy is giving the date of the outbreak of hostilities between Germany and the USSR as June 22."

One can only shrug one's shoulders when an "historian" like the German Gert Buchheit tells us in his book *Hitler der Feldherr*, 1961, that Stalin and Molotov "fell into a deep depression." The same view was taken by Michel Garder, who wrote in his book *Une guerre pas comme leas autres*:

"One does not know what to say about Stalin's blindness in this period from September 1940 to June 1941... The Red Army was not prepared for the unexpected blow, which was planned without its supreme commander knowing anything at all about it."

This theory of the "absolute surprising" of the Russians is still defended today, not only in the official or semi-official publications of the communist nations, but by numerous western historians as well.

Notes

1. In a telegram to Roosevelt on July 30, 1941, Stalin claimed to have 24,000 tanks, of which more than half were on his western front. In *History of the Second World War*, Liddell Hart states that Hitler attacked Russia with only 800 more tanks than were employed by the allies in their invasion of Western Europe.

8

CONTINUAL TREASON

The secret side of the war – Origin of the continual treason – Hitler does away with the military caste-spirit – He accepts the new panzer strategy of Guderian and Manstein against the opinions of Beck, Stülpnagel and Halder – Canaris and Basil Zaharoff, the "Trader with Death" – The Tukhachevsky affair: 3 million in numbered bills – The real outcome of the affair – The entire plot against the new state – Unrealistic goals of the plotters – Churchill's realistic objective – Guilt of the traitors in the outbreak of the war – The enemy despises the conspirators – The career musicians of the Red Orchestra – A Schellenberg fable – Coro, Werther and the Three Reds – Swiss neutrality.

U ntil today the various aspects of the Second World War have been considered mainly from an analytical or chronological point of view. All armed conflicts have a political, economic, strategic and tactical side. But the war of which I speak also had a secret, scarcely-known side, which was decisive. It involved events which were not played out on the battlefield, but which caused the loss of a tremendous amount of materiel, saw the death or maiming of hundreds of thousands of European soldiers and had the most tragic consequences. Manstein and Guderian bravely assessed this side of the war in their memoirs. The most conscientious historians, like Sir Basil Liddell Hart and Paul Carell have sometimes made vague references to this matter. Where Jacques Benoist-Méchin is concerned, he has not yet finished his noteworthy and monumental history of the German Army. The Second World War was however more than any other a secret war.

At this point I must mention the resistance against the national-socialist state, which became public knowledge with the failed assassination attempt of July 20, 1944, but whose effects extended beyond the collapse of the Third Reich. It is an extremely extensive theme, which will probably never be completely cleared up, even though there are numerous accounts of German, English and American origin, while the Russians have so far only admitted the role played by their master spy Sorge.

• • •

In Germany it all began on June 30, 1934. That day, or more accurately that night, Hitler quashed a rebellion by the SA, whose Chief-of-Staff was Ernst Röhm. In reality it was a large-scale plot, whose national and international connections have not yet been completely cleared up. Röhm was only an instrument. Of whom? This horrible affair was called the "Night of the Long Knives."

The Reich President, Generalfeldmarschall von Hindenburg, publicly congratulated Hitler on July 1: "You have preserved the German people from a great danger," he telegraphed him. "For this I express to you my deep appreciation and sincere esteem."

The effective strength of the SA was initially reduced from about three million men to one million. Then the law of May 21, 1935 created the Wehrmacht in place of the Reichswehr. This law, which reintroduced general compulsory military service, began with the words: "Military service is an honorable service to the German people."

Like the Kaiser before 1918, Hitler was the Supreme Commander of the armed forces. Every officer and soldier swore the following oath to him and not to the constitution:

"I swear before God to obey Adolf Hitler, the Führer of the Reich and of the German people, Commander-in-Chief of the Wehrmacht, unreservedly and commit myself as a brave soldier to always fulfill this oath, even at the cost of my life."

It would have been possible for the officers of the Reichswehr whose consciences did not allow them to agree with the principles of the national-socialist state to refuse to take this oath.

From then on everyone, from general to common soldier, fulfilled a common duty to the nation and to the German people. There were no more castes. The entire reach of such a revolution must be understood.

The majority of the officers agreed with this, the younger ones frequently with enthusiasm. But in Berlin, in the Army General Staff, the holiest of holies of the old Prussian system, a small number of generals persevered in a conflict between tradition and anachronism. While the majority of these career soldiers understood the deep sense of the national-socialist revolution, others gave up their privileges with regret. This conflict also showed itself in the military field when Hitler supported General Guderian, who spoke out in favor of the daring, completely novel use of panzers against the opinion of General Beck, the then Chief of the General Staff.

When, in 1937, Guderian explained to the Chief of the General Staff how it would be possible to pierce an enemy front and drive deep into the enemy's rear and lead the battle by radio from a fast vehicle at the front of the army, Beck shrugged his shoulders and said to Guderian, "Haven't you read Schlieffen? How can you direct a battle without table, maps and telephone?"[1]

Guderian also encountered resistance from General Otto von Stülpnagel. He was the inspector-general of motorized units and had forbidden the employment of tanks beyond the scope of the regiment. "He considered panzer divisions as utopian."[2]

Hitler named Guderian chief of the Wehrmacht's panzer units. But the mobilization order of 1939 made him commander of a reserve army infantry corps! Guderian protested and afterward received command of the 19th Army Corps, which took Brest-Litovsk and its citadel on September 19, 1939. However four days later Guderian was forced to hand over the citadel to Russian General Krivoshine, as the fortress was located in the agreed-upon Russian zone of influence.

General Halder, Beck's successor at the head of the general staff, opposed the Manstein-Guderian plan for crossing the Meuse and driving through the Ardennes, characterizing it as "absurd." Hitler pushed through the plan, whose success is well-known, in spite of Halder's opposition.

That men like Beck and his successor Halder and Generals von Fritsch, von Witzleben, von Hammerstein, Heinrich and Otto von Stülpnagel, von Brockdorff and others should have to obey a man whom certain people called "the Bohemian corporal," was for them extremely difficult, and that into the bargain that Hitler should force upon them military plans which were successful, was for them unacceptable.

What became known as the "Conspiracy of the Generals" had no other causes. When the time of victories was past, other generals and senior officers joined them, so that in 1943/44 the names of Generals Hoepner, Lindemann, Thomas, Wagner (Quartermaster General of the Wehrmacht), Stieff (Chief of the Organization Department), von Tresckow, who was Chief-of-Staff of Army Group Center in Russia, and his adjutant, Fabian von Schlabrendorff, and others appeared on their list.

Until the fall of Admiral Canaris (spring 1944) Germany had two intelligence services, which naturally were rivals. Within the Reichssicherheitshauptamt or RSHA (Reich Central Security Office), which was led by Heydrich until his death on May 30, 1942, then by Himmler himself and finally by Kaltenbrunner from January 30, 1943 to the end, four departments formed the *Sicherheitsdienst* or SD (Security Service). Department III, under the direction of Otto Ohlendorf, was the intelligence service for domestic policy, while Department VI under Schellenberg, with Offices A, B, C, D, E, S and Z acted as the intelligence service for foreign policy. In the Abwehr, which was under the command of the OKW, Department I was the military intelligence service.

These two important offices whose jurisdictions often overlapped naturally gave rise to conflicts of authority. As far as I have been informed, never has a country successfully eliminated the rivalries between the intelligence services of the various branches of the service as well as between the political and military lines. Germany was therefore no exception. Each side watched the other and took pains to prevent interference. Since many vital documents are lacking, some lost, others not made public, it is impossible to say with certainty how much the two sides knew, whether Heydrich, for example, had in his hands proof of Canaris' treason, or whether the admiral had learned anything from his "friends" of the plan to murder Heydrich in Prague.

The two men knew each other since 1920. Canaris was then an officer on the training vessel *Berlin*, on which Heydrich was an officer candidate. Canaris knew that Leutnant Heydrich had been expelled from the navy in 1929 because he refused to marry a girl he had seduced. He likewise knew that there were doubts as to the racial background of his mother, Sarah, who was said to have been a jewess. At first Canaris tried to bring about Heydrich's downfall. It turned out, however, that Heydrich was much too powerful, much too intelligent, and the little admiral, whom I called "the medusa," soon left him in peace. Otto Nelte, the lawyer for Generalfeldmarschall Keitel, was able to say (on July 8, 1946) at Nuremberg that "Canaris cooperated with Himmler and Heydrich in an astonishingly friendly way, although he was hostile to the RSHA." Was this adaptability or caution?

A secret service is obviously the ideal cover for conspirators: so it wasn't until 1962 that the English discovered that Kim Philby of the intelligence department M.I.6 had been an agent of the Soviet secret service since 1934. Conversely, the secret service is an indispensable system in a nation which is in a state of war. From 1939 to 1945 the leaders of the Abwehr, Canaris and his colleagues Oster and Dohnanyi, came into possession of highly-important intelligence which was gathered by about 30,000 agents, of whom practically none knew they were working for conspirators.

The officers and soldiers in this enormous operation did their duty. Several members of the Abwehr recorded very great successes. I am very well informed on this, as members of the Brandenburg (Special Duties) Regiment (later Division) came as volunteers to the units of the Waffen-SS and to the SS-Jagdverbänden (commando units) which I commanded. Officers of the Abwehr worked obstinately within the scope of the possibilities given them to uncover the agents of the Red Orchestra.

Canaris was clever enough to occasionally allow intelligence to reach the OKW which at least appeared to be sensational.

By the end of 1941 Hitler was tired of Canaris' reports. In the following year Hitler, and later Jodl as well, began to have doubts about Canaris. Generalfeldmarschall Keitel, who in 1917 had been the liaison officer between the Grand Headquarters and the Naval Headquarters, defended Canaris in good faith:

"A German admiral cannot be a traitor," he said to Jodl, "what you suspect is impossible."

I had conversations with Canaris three or four times. He was neither subtle, nor did he possess exceptional intelligence, as is still sometimes written today. He was evasive, crafty, baffling, which was something else altogether.

In response to the questions by Gisevius, Lahousen and other witnesses for the prosecution, Otto Nelte said everything before the Nuremberg court which could be said in front of such a court at that time (July 8, 1946):

"Canaris' activity was of extraordinary importance to the conduct of the war... His character is not only to be characterized as ambiguous, but also as deceitful and not very trustworthy... He is a typical salon conspirator whose character is difficult for others to see through, and who, if he wants to, can submerge into the crowd completely unnoticed."

It is noteworthy that neither the surveillance, or better said the hostile attitude of Department VI of the RSHA toward the heads of the Abwehr, nor the investigations begun as a consequence of the assassination attempt of July 20, 1944 completely brought to light the treachery of Admiral Canaris and General Oster, his second in command. I read, for example, in the book by Brian Murphy *The Business of Spying*, which appeared not long ago in London, that Canaris made contact with the British Intelligence Service before the war through the notorious "Dealer in Death," Sir Basil Zaharoff. That is possible: the old Zaharoff perhaps believed that Canaris was Greek. So far as I know, this is the first time that they spoke of this descent.

Our most sensational intelligence agent was Elyesa Bazna, known under the cover name of Cicero. Bazna, who was the valet of Sir Knatchbull-Hugessen, the British ambassador in Ankara, appeared spontaneously before Dr. Moyzisch, police attache at our embassy and official of the SD. From October 1943 until 1944 Cicero passed us extraordinary information, especially about Operation Overlord, the Anglo-American landing in Normandy. No one put any faith in the information provided by Cicero, neither Rommel nor the Abwehr specialists! No one appeared to give it any closer thought.

The SD was not led by conspirators. However Department VI suffered from the disadvantage of being under the leadership of a man who neither had the determined character nor was as clever or clear-seeing as he thought he was. I first met Walter Schellenberg, then an Obersturmbannführer in the SD, in April 1943 when I took command of the *Friedenthal* Special Duties Battalion. Schellenberg was a talker. He loved to tell stories and especially to talk about himself to a newcomer to the magical world of the secret service. We often ate together at noon and recalled his former chief, Reinhard Heydrich, who had been murdered in Prague the year before. Schellenberg used a prominent example to show me how an idea could be transformed into a brilliant act. He told me the circumstances under which he had taken part in the "Operation of the Century," namely destroying the General Staff of the Red Army in 1937.

The most important episodes of this strange affair are well-known nowadays. Heydrich made use of several documents procured in Paris by a certain General Sklobin, a double agent and adjutant to General Miller, chief of the White Russian veterans. These faked documents, which incriminated Marshall Tukhachevsky, who had reorganized the Red Army, were cleverly passed to Eduard Benes. In this way Stalin received the documents by way of the Czech president, an ally.

The origin of the documents was not unknown to him, and he paid three million rubles to Heydrich by way of an agent in his embassy in Berlin. It was in large banknotes, whose serials the Russians had obviously recorded. When Schellenberg's secret agents tried to use the same in Russia they were immediately arrested.

So it was thanks to the Sklobin-Heydrich documents that Stalin began numerous trials and was able to squash any opposition in the Red Army.

Stalin and Tukhachevsky had in fact hated each other for a long time, and since the end of 1935 the relationship of the party to the army had grown increasingly worse. Stalin was feared in Russia. The Kulaks, the Trotskyites, the jews, the intellectuals, the industrial saboteurs and so on had all been ruthlessly crushed, even factory workers were convicted and executed. The pitiless GPU sent millions of Russians to forced labor camps. The canals from the White Sea to the Baltic (225 km.), the Moscow-Volga canal and other major construction projects were built by hundreds of thousands of forced laborers.

Coming from a minor royalty family in the province of Smolensk, and a former officer of the famous Semeyonovski Regiment of the Kaiser's Guard, Tukhachevsky joined the Reds in 1918. He was definitely more popular than Stalin, who had made a fool of himself when he tried to play the strategist before Warsaw in 1920. At the time Tukhachevsky, with great difficulty, was just able to save several units of the completely shattered Red Army. Stalin never forgave him for that. By 1936 he knew that the majority of officers, especially the higher ranking ones, were decidedly hostile toward the Communist Party. The faked documents he received from Prague allowed him to destroy his enemies in the Red Army.[3]

Marshalls Tukhachevsky, Yegorov and Blücher, as well as 75 of the 80 generals, the members of the Supreme Defense Council, were shot; of 15 commanders of armies 13 were removed, as well as 367 other generals. More than 32,000 officers of the Soviet Army were executed from May 1937 to February 1938.

This tremendous blood-letting in the military, which followed so much political blood-letting, not only fooled Heydrich and Schellenberg, therefore our political intelligence service, who were convinced that they had achieved a decisive success, but also Hitler himself. The Red Army was not weakened, as is still believed today, on the contrary it was strengthened. From Komandarm (army commander) to company commander with the rank of captain, all officers were placed under the command of two so-called political commissars. One of the two commissars was a member of the Special Department OO (Ossobody Otdiel), while the other belonged to the *Politkoms* Regiment.

The liquidated officers were replaced at the heads of armies, army corps, divisions, regiments and battalions by younger, more political officers who were reliable communists. At the same time Stalin used Tukhachevsky's plans: from autumn 1941 he made the Red Army into a Russian national army. The officers again wore the golden epaulets of the former imperial army; national decorations were created: the Orders of Kutuzov and Suvorov. The *Politkoms* were removed and their places taken by *Zampolits*, the same men with the same goals but under a new name. From the total, brutal house-cleaning of 1937 there emerged an army that was Russian, political and national in character and which was even capable of surviving the initial destructive defeats of 1941.

By April 1943 my experience at the front had long since taught me that the Red Army General Staff had in no way been destroyed.

• • •

Even before the war our foreign office was a "nest of traitors." In Berlin Ernst von Weizsäcker and many other senior officials used the greatest part of their working hours sending emissaries, intelligence and proposals out of the country. These diplomats and the heads of the Abwehr exchanged information. In the German embassies and consulates abroad the conspirators could count on sympathetic and active participants who met with hostile legation attaches and their agents, be it in their own countries or in Switzerland, Italy, Sweden, Spain, Portugal or Japan, in order to pass them political, economic or military information as quickly as possible. The former German ambassador in Rome, Ulrich von Hassel, the German ambassador in Moscow, Graf von der Schulenburg, and his opposite number in Brussels, Bülow-Schwante, were involved in the plot; others, like Eugen Ott in Tokyo, covered up or overlooked the spying activities and the treason of their subordinates (Dr. Sorge).

Oberst Ott had belonged to the staff of General von Schleicher, who was Reich Chancellor from December 2, 1932 to January 29, 1933. Schleicher, who had tried to talk the left wing of the national-socialist party (Strasser) into a joint move against Hitler with the communist labor unions in order to break up the party, was murdered on June 30, 1934 in the course of the countermeasures. It was also Schleicher who sent Ott to Tokyo as a "military observer" in 1933. He was named attache and later general and ambassador. His behavior in Japan concerning Dr. Sorge is inexplicable.

Before the war legation advisor Theo Kordt was active in London in cooperation with his brother, Erich Kordt, who in the beginning had been a close associate of Foreign Minister von Ribbentrop. After the declaration of war Theo Kordt had himself transferred to our legation in Bern. What Heydrich called "The Black Orchestra" was nothing more than a branch of this group, which consisted of agents of the Abwehr and diplomats posted in Rome.

What was the objective pursued by all these men? They wanted to prevent the war and later to end it in order to save their country. They saw only one avenue open to them: get rid of Hitler. Their actions repeatedly contradicted their words. They claimed to be patriots who watched in desperation as their country was enslaved by national-socialism and a despicable tyranny. In this case they there were two avenues open to them.

The first would have been the simpler and could have been carried out by a single man: to murder Hitler at some point between 1933 and 1939.

The second solution would have been to replace Hitler and national-socialism with something better. That would have required a real leader personality with a superior social, political and economic program. There was no trace of this to be found among our conspirators. None of them had the courage or the will to sacrifice his life in order "to slay the tyrants." Not even Stauffenberg. He set down the bomb, started the timed fuse and disappeared. The bomb killed or injured a dozen people without killing Hitler.

Not one of the plotters appeared to be seriously concerned with the future of Germany. They declared that the death of Hitler was enough to solve all problems and eliminate all difficulties. They did not understand that even after the murder of Hitler peace could only be achieved through unconditional surrender and that this fact would have meant a terrible civil war. Furthermore the conspirators knew from the allies that they would receive no better terms than Hitler.

Nowadays it is clear that Churchill waged war not against Hitler and "his Huns" nor against national-socialism, although he then maintained the contrary. He himself later wrote in his memoirs that "English policy depends on the nation that has dominance in Europe." This nation must be destroyed. "It makes no difference," Churchill went on, "whether it is Spain, or the French monarchy, or the French imperial empire or the German Reich." "It is," he said, "the most powerful nation or the nation that is beginning to become the most powerful." Today one can calmly say that Churchill, as an Englishman, deceived himself when he allied himself with Stalin. He admitted as much after the war, when he said, "We slaughtered the wrong pig." This form of expression could be understood by every Englishman.

Roosevelt, too, had enough of German competition in the areas of industry and trade. He therefore decided in Casablanca in 1943 that Germany must accept unconditional surrender. Churchill and Stalin immediately approved this decision, which was carried out to the letter. One of Roosevelt's chief advisors, Morgenthau, had even worked out a plan whereby Germany should be transformed into a "nation of vegetable farmers." This plan was put into practice from 1945-1947, until they realized that it was a product of blind hate and that the western world needed Germany.

It is known that allied statesmen and generals actually reckoned with serious unrest and mutinies in the German Army from October 1940. The Commander-in-Chief of Allied Forces in France, General Maurice Gamelin, declared at an official banquet at Paris city hall, "That it mattered little whether the German Army had more than 10, 20 or 100 divisions, for on the day that Germany declared war the German Army would have to march on Berlin to quell the unrest which would then break out." This story was told by the French foreign minister, George Bonnet, in his book *De Munich à la guerre*. General Gamelin knew General Beck very well and had received him before the war in the company of the future General Speidel.

In 1932 the Soviet government began building a double espionage and counter-espionage organization spanning the entire world. The Comintern had its political, economic and active agents, just as the red Army had its 4th Office. These intelligence apparatuses were expanded considerably from 1928 on, to Africa, America and Europe. Diplomatic and trade missions, military attaches, trade union organizations and so on were used by Moscow as cover for their espionage nets from early on. Finally special schools for intelligence specialists were founded in the USSR. These noteworthy efforts, initiated by Stalin himself, paid extraordinary dividends which were visible from 1936/37. One of the most important agent apparatuses was the Red Orchestra.

The fixed location agents, the intelligence gatherers, the radio operators and so on of the Red Orchestra were all veteran professional spies. Many of them are known today. The identity of their real chief inside Germany is still a mystery however. He worked in Führer Headquarters under the name Werther, and it was he who directly informed the Swiss net. Consequently a decision made by

Hitler or the OKW at noon was sometimes known to Moscow within five or six hours.

The amount of intelligence sent by the so-called "Comintern Net" in the Weimar Republic climbed considerably after the outbreak of the war against Russia. In the period from June 10 to July 8, 1941 the number of Red Orchestra radio stations rose from 20 to 78! In August 1942 the many listening posts of the Luftwaffe, the Kriegsmarine and the Abwehr's counter-intelligence service intercepted 425 transmissions from suspected radio stations! The Red Orchestra organized the sabotage of German monitoring stations and direction-finding equipment. It succeeded in smuggling communist agents into the central office of Abwehr signals counter-intelligence as decoders, and furthermore it delivered unusable direction-finding devices instead of serviceable ones or delivered the instruments to units that had no idea what to do with them. Whereas the deciphering units of the navy, air force and OKW were in business at the beginning of hostilities, the deciphering devices of the Abwehr signals counter-intelligence service were not operationally ready until mid-April 1942! In autumn 1941 the specialists of the Abwehr still had no vehicles equipped with direction-finding equipment.

The Red transmitters in Berlin and Brussels were known as early as June 24, 1940, but it took until December 1941 before all the agents of the Brussels group of the Red Orchestra were arrested by the SD.[4] In Marseille and later in Paris the Russian Sokolov, alias Kent, and Leopold Trepper, alias Gilbert, were arrested. The latter was known to the Polish and French police, whose spy net was used for some time by German signals counter-intelligence (July and November 1942).

In Moscow the intelligence sent by members of the Red Orchestra was received by specialists, who decoded the material immediately under the leadership of General Fyodor Kuznetsov, alias Director. After the information was decoded and evaluated it was passed on to Stalin, who at the end of 1941 had taken over the leadership of the State Committee for Defense and under whose command the General Staff of the Red Army (STAVKA) was.

In Berlin the Director's operatives were at first paralyzed, but at the same time protected, by their incompetence: they broadcast to no one and could not receive Moscow, ceased to transmit and passed their intelligence to Kent, who was in Brussels at that time. Moscow instructed Sokolov to go to Berlin, put the radio stations in order and gave him the addresses. But this message from Russia was deciphered on July 14, 1942 and the chief of the Berlin Orchestra was exposed. It was Luftwaffe Oberleutnant Harro Schulze-Boysen, alias Coro, grand-nephew of Admiral von Tirpitz. He had been working for the Soviets since 1933. He was not short on ambition: he wanted to become minister of war in the future German government. Why not?

Numerous opponents of the regime from within his circle of acquaintances and several communist spies were arrested with Coro, men who were active in the Ministry of Economics, the Ministry of Labor, the Air Ministry, the Foreign Ministry and the Abwehr. In total 81 persons (August-September 1942).

The radio transmissions by the Red Orchestra were to be heard from all over Europe, from Antwerp, Amsterdam, Namur, Lüttich, Lilles, Lyon, Nizza, Annecy, Marseille and Paris, but also from Barcelona, Prague and Belgrade.

In the period 1943-1945 I learned that significant Red Orchestra spy rings existed in areas occupied by the Wehrmacht, and not just in the west, but in Copenhagen, Warsaw and Athens as well. There were more in Russia, behind our front. A net of sixty stations was in operation in the Don region, a second, with twenty stations, in the Kuban, and further stations were located near Stalino and Voroshilovgrad. The net in the Don region alone sent an average of 3,000 words a day to Moscow. Hence the STAVKA had only to make the right choice.

Keitel on the other hand was able to state to the Nuremberg court on April 4, 1946:

"The intelligence service of the OKW under Admiral Canaris provided the army and me with very little material about the strength of the Red Army..."

The first Red Orchestra transmitter in Switzerland, in Lausanne, began broadcasting after the arrests in Berlin, Brussels, Marseille and Paris. The man in charge was a Hungarian jew, Alexander Radolfi, alias Rado or Dora, a career agent of the Russian MGB and an outstanding geographer and director of the Géo-Presse Society in Geneva; furthermore he seems to have been an officer of the Red Army. His contact man to the German General Staff was a certain Rudolf Roessler, alias Lucy. He was a Bavarian, a former officer of the Reichswehr, who became a traitor out of "patriotic hate" for national-socialism. Roessler appears to have been in the service of the Communist Internationale for a long time. In his book *Geheime Reichssache*, the American Victor Perry established that Roessler had been an agent of Kurt Eisner, Minister President of the Bavarian Soviet Republic in 1919. From 1940 he worked in the Swiss Special Service with a Czech, Colonel Sedlacek, alias Uncle Tom, who belonged to the British intelligence service.

Lucy did not spy for fame alone. He received 7,000 Swiss francs a month, in addition to bonuses and expenses. I have read that he wanted to "root out nazism in Germany."

However he continued his activities in Switzerland after the fall of the Third Reich and in 1953 was arrested and sentenced to a year in prison for spying on behalf of the Soviet Union. Herr Roessler therefore worked not just against the Third Reich. He was just a career spy who worked for whoever paid him best.

Roessler died in 1958, but it is known that he received the intelligence he passed on to Rado from two groups of senior German officers. The Werther group was active in the OKH and OKW and the Olga group in the Luftwaffe general staff. We know that Coro was in the air ministry in Berlin. If Werther was a group in the OKW, then who was its leader? That we do not know. We do not know who provided Lucy with the first means of radio communication and thus enabled contact with Rado. The Rado group had three radio sets, known as the Red Three (radio operators: Foote, Hamel and Margit Bolli).

The Red Three utilized the protection of an allegedly neutral country to there work for the triumph of a political system which since 1917 had made its objective the destruction of all the western powers. On the other hand it is true that they all found them beneficial, the Swiss, English, Americans and especially the Soviets, to whom the accrued material was of vital importance.

From the summer of 1940 Director received hundreds of pieces of intelligence from Werther via Lucy and Dora, and the Troika sent him several hundred radio messages each month during the course of the war in the east. Director queried the Red Three about every point of possible interest to the war effort: new weapons, supply, troop movements, creation of new divisions, personal acts by the most important army chiefs and their attitude toward Hitler, the effect of the allied bombing, political events, intelligence received from the Abwehr, production of war materiel, but especially the offensive and defensive plans of the OKW, differences of opinion at Führer Headquarters and so on.

Even though the decoding service of signals counter-intelligence could decipher the messages sent by Kent in Brussels and Coro in Berlin from the end of May 1941, the code used by Dora was much more difficult to crack, and therefore these supremely important radio communications remained a mystery to us for a long time. It was a Finnish colonel, whom I later met, who discovered the double encoding being used by the latter. I believe he's still alive in South Africa. He did not inform the German authorities in Finland of hid discoveries, rather gave them to a diplomatic representative of a neutral country, whom I also met after the war and with whom I became good friends. He gave me all the details of the affair. In this way the German Foreign Ministry learned of the discovery by way of the senior diplomats of this neutral country, and the foreign ministry passed the information on to the OKW.

When I took over command of the sabotage school in the Hague at the end of March 1943, and under Schellenberg of Office 6 assumed responsibility for this school and thus the command of Department VI S, my new duties and problems were still a great secret. I had to become familiar with the activities of Office VI and especially with the questions of the political intelligence service. It was then that I learned of the existence of the Red Orchestra.

Naturally I could then not yet appreciate its full significance. I would like to say that I immediately recognized the dangerousness of the Red Orchestra but it was not until later that I learned how decisively important these radio reports by this group were to the Eastern Front.

Many hundreds of radio messages of the various nets which made up the Red Orchestra were eventually deciphered. If many historians do not want to or cannot take this matter into account, their work gives a completely false picture of the war. Let us take a simple example. Reproduced here are four signals from the Red Orchestra, which are mentioned by Hauptmann V.F. Flicke (who during the war was a conscientious officer of the Abwehr) in his book *Spionagegruppe Rote Kapelle* (1949:

"July 2, 1941 – To Director No. 34 – RDO.
Most urgent.
The valid operations plan is Plan No. I with the objective of the Urals via Moscow and diversionary maneuvers on the wings. – Main attack in the center. Rado."

"July 3, 1941 – To Director No. 37 – RDO.
Present Stuka production is 9 to 10 daily. Average Luftwaffe losses on the Eastern Front 40 units. Source: German Air Ministry. – Rado."

"July 5, 1941 – To Director No. 44 – RDO.
The Luftwaffe currently has a total strength of 21,500 first-and second-line aircraft and 6,350 Ju 52 transport aircraft.
– Rado."

"July 27, 1941 – To Director No. 92 – RDO.

In the event that Plan I should run into difficulties, it will be immediately replaced by Plan II. It foresees an attack on Arkhangelsk and Murmansk. In the event of a change of plan I will receive details within 48 hours. – Rado."

On July 27, 1941, therefore, the STAVKA had received 92 messages from Rado alone and knew about the German attack plan and its variants.

The Swiss authorities allowed the Red Three to radio Moscow until the end of September 1943. They didn't arrest Roessler until May 19, 1944, in order to protect him from an eventual German commando action. But on September 8, 1944 the Helvetians set him free again and likewise his most important agents and helpers in Switzerland. This was one of the consequences of the assassination attempt of July 20.

Several chroniclers maintain that Roessler reestablished contact with Werther on September 16, 1944. That is unlikely. By this time Guderian had been named Chief of the Army General Staff (OKH). Many traitors were exposed and the opportunity for them to do further damage was removed. But very late. Too late.

Thanks to a single Swiss group, the Red Orchestra, for thirty months the STAVKA learned about many plans of our general staff.

Stalin was informed daily of the attack objectives of the German Army, as well as our attack strength, the chain of command of our large and medium-size units, our strategic plans, the state of our reserves of men and materiel, German defensive intentions, German losses in men and materiel, and so on.

One must ask oneself how, in spite of this permanent treason, the Wehrmacht was able to achieve its great victories, which according to Feldmarschall von Manstein's book were *Lost Victories*. Today we know how and why this was. Three hundred years before Christ the Chinese military theorist Ou-Tse said tellingly: "An enemy whose intentions one knows, is already half beaten."

The following seems clear to me: there were two basic reasons why we were able to hold off the Red Army for so long in spite of this tremendous betrayal. First the Russians were not immediately in a position to halt the blitzkrieg, which was conducted according to the principles of Guderian, Manstein and Hitler and which had yielded such good results in Poland and in the west. Without the mud and the absence of roads the war in Russia would have been won in spite of the Red Orchestra. But the Russian commanding officers, from division generals down, were good, younger and more determined than ours. Besides the Russian soldier was outstanding. Finally Stalin very soon received tremendous quantities of materiel from his capitalist allies: in total 22,500 aircraft, 13,000 tanks, 700,000 trucks, 3,786,000 tires, 11,000 railroad cars, 2,000 locomotives, without adding in the 18 million pairs of boots, 2,500,000 tons of steel and hundreds of thousands of tons of aluminum, copper, zinc and so on.

Although they were informed about all our plans, the commanders of the Soviet Army were initially forced to watch as their armies were defeated, encircled and destroyed. In cases where Hitler and our general staff made sudden changes of plan which Werther did not learn of, the situation for the Russian armies became catastrophic.

Notes

1. and 2. See Guderian: *Erinnerungen eines Soldaten*, Heidelberg 1951.

3. The affair came from Sklobin, who was instigated by the NKVD. The falsified documents came from Heydrich, however, not from Paris. Heydrich merely played the role of a helper to the NKVD in this matter, for the decision to liquidate the Tukhachevsky group had been made in January (minutes Radek trial) while the documents did not show up in Moscow until April-May.

4. This was only a first action. The Brussels group worked again from March until July 1942.

9

WHY WE DIDN'T
TAKE MOSCOW

With Panzergruppe Guderian – "Fast Heinz" and Feldmarschall Rommel – We cross the Beresina and the Dniepr – The new, almost invincible T-34 appears – The hell of Yelnya – The sad fate of the Russian farmer – Stalin without information from the Red Orchestra: victory in the Ukraine, 1,328,000 prisoners – The Battle of Borodino – The army group that disappeared – The capture of Istra – Cold – The liquid-air rockets – We fire on the suburbs of Moscow – The order to retreat – The reasons for our setback – Inexperience, limited knowledge and sabotage – One cannot win with odds of 6 to 1 – Richard Sorge: he knew the future Frau Ott in Munich – Unusual guarantors: Agnes Smetley and Dr. Zeller – The real identity of envoy Eugen Ott – He encouraged and covered up the activity of the spy – The Lyuchkov file delivered to Moscow – Why Stalin was able to almost completely denude his front against Japan (Korea) – Was Sorge exchanged like Abel? – Were his activities and perhaps his existence incompatible with the "miracle of Moscow"? – Thoughts on the retreat

From June 22-29, 1941 our Panzergruppe Guderian advanced from the Bug to the Beresina. An outstanding infantry unit, the Grossdeutschland Regiment (later a division) supported us; we found ourselves at the forefront of the Eastern Front. We lacked artillery and ammunition for a crossing of the river and radio contact could not be established with the rear: our sentries were not strong enough. I was given the task of searching for our reinforcements, which were more than 120 kilometers to the west, and return with them as quickly as possible. I left with five men and oriented myself by compass alone. I had found that our maps were inaccurate and wanted to avoid the roads we had already taken. I knew that the enemy had taken possession of them again behind us.

I found my artillery battalion and the commander, Hauptmann Rumohr – one of the best officers I ever knew – immediately gave the order to depart, direction east.

On July 3 a battalion of the SS-Division Das Reich and a battery of our artillery battalion, soon followed by a second infantry battalion, established a bridgehead near Brodets, 70 km. south of the Beresina. When "Papa" Hausser informed General Guderian of this, he was congratulated by "Fast Heinz."

Before I met Generaloberst Guderian personally in the OKH, I saw him often, even at the height of a battle, standing in his armored command vehicle, and I observed him when he discussed the situation with the commander of the Das Reich Division. He was a man in his late fifties, of medium height, but slim and very lively. He always listened most attentively to whoever he was talking to with. He was very much liked by us, significantly more so than Feldmarschall von Bock, the commander of Army Group Center. Guderian had read and studied the prophetic theories of all the tank specialists like Martel, Fuller, Estienne, Liddel Hart and the book *Der Kampfwagenkrieg* (1934) by the Austrian General von Eimannsberger before he wrote his book *Achtung! Panzer*, which was greeted skeptically by our general staff. However as soon as Hitler saw tanks, armored cars with machine-guns or 20mm cannon and fully motorized infantry in joint maneuvers, he immediately understood the views represented by General Guderian but also by General von Manstein.

Neither Beck nor Halder or Keitel or even Jodl wanted to believe that the Russians had, "more than 10,000 armored vehicles," as claimed by Guderian, who was much better informed than Canaris. On August 4, 1941 in Novy-Borisov Hitler said to the commander of Panzergruppe II:

"If I had believed that the number of Russian tanks you named in your book corresponded to the facts, I probably wouldn't have started this war in June 1941."

It is rare that a military theorist is able to transform his ideas into a victorious battle. Guderian was one of these. He was one of the three or four commanders in the German Army who spoke their opinions openly to Hitler to the very end.

It is not justified when certain people compare Guderian with Rommel. The latter was undoubtedly an outstanding tactician, but he never commanded more than four or five divisions of the Africa Corps and the Italian divisions. Guderian, who maneuvered more than thirty divisions in Russia, was a notable strategist as well as a first-class tactician. Would he, had he been at Rommel's side in July 1942, have been able to turn the tide at El Alamein? No one can say. One thing is for certain though; the fall of Alexandria would have opened the way to the oil and would have resulted in Turkey joining the Axis powers. With the Suez Canal closed and the help of the Arab oil-producing countries the war would have taken a different course.

It must be said that the Africa Corps and the Italian divisions were also victims of the permanent treason. An Italian admiral, Maugeri, betrayed us often and very effectively from the start. He did so well that he was decorated by the allies after the war. It is thanks to him that 75% of the supplies destined for the Africa Corps were sunk. Carell said in his book *Afrikakorps* that Maugeri was not the only informant the English had. "From Berlin," he wrote, "intelligence of great importance was transmitted to the Anglo-American spy centers via Rome." The Red and Black Orchestras were busily at work. Feldmarschall Kesselring, the Commander-in-Chief in Italy, told me in 1943 that the allies were well-informed about the sailing times and routes of German-Italian convoys to North Africa and even knew exactly what the individual ships were carrying as cargo. General Bayerlein, one of Rommel's closest associates, even wrote in 1959 that he was firmly convinced that, "Rommel's plans had been betrayed to the English." (See Carell, *Afrikakorps*).

It sounds almost unbelievable and like a cheap excuse when one traces the failure of a campaign back to treason. But in this case one is justified in saying, and it is proved, that the betrayal played a great role in Africa and in Russia from 1941, something which should no longer be allowed to go unsaid in the present day.

It rained in streams during our advance from the Beresina to the Dniepr and our first enemy was the mud, from which we repeatedly had to free our vehicles. Making repairs on the many vehicles was very difficult, almost impossible. But it was to become worse yet. Our division crossed the Dniepr south of Skov in spite of the mud after a brief but intense battle and a lively reaction by the Soviet Air Force.

The pincers of the two armored groups – Hoth in the north and Guderian in the south – closed on July 3, and far to the east the great pocket was closed behind Minsk. According to a report by Feldmarschall von Bock on July 8 the result was as follows: 287,704 prisoners, 2,585 vehicles destroyed or captured, including tanks of the heaviest type.

In spite of everything the Russian campaign was not "won in 14 days," as Generaloberst Halder had written so hopefully in his diary (July 3). Another error repeatedly committed by historians is to maintain that "at the beginning of the campaign the Soviet troops had received orders to resist to the death." Quite to the contrary; they received orders to withdraw as quickly as possible when threatened with encirclement. Only certain units were sacrificed. More than half a million Soviet soldiers escaped the Minsk pocket. Hitler was aware of this. After we had fought off a heavy counterattack on July 13, the following day we drove south of Gorki and together with General Schaal's 10th Panzer Division advanced toward the Smolensk – Stodoliste road. On July 18 and 19 we took Yelnya in very heavy fighting.

We fought on, fully convinced of final victory. The tactical superiority enjoyed by the panzers marked with a "G" (Guderian) was outstanding. However if the enemy had known then how to concentrate his T-34 tanks en masse in an orderly counterattack, it is likely that our difficulties would have been more than our forces could have coped with. Our anti-tank guns, which stopped the Russian T-26 and BT tanks on the spot, were ineffective against the new T-34. They drove through the unharvested wheatfields and there was little we could do against them with our 50mm anti-tank guns or the guns of the Panzer III and IV. Our soldiers, well concealed by the tall grain, ran after the tanks to put them out of action with molotov cocktails. These were simply bottles filled with gasoline with a fuse running through the stopper. The cocktail had to be thrown onto the hot engine cover plates. In this way the tanks were sometimes set afire. Also effective was a hand grenade placed in the gun barrel, a sufficient quantity of plastic explosive on the turret hatch or Teller mines on the tank's tracks. It wasn't until much later that the *Panzerfaust* was introduced, and several Russian tanks were stopped by direct artillery fire at the start of the campaign.

Fighting on a 1,000-kilometer-long front, on July 24 we found ourselves at the leading tip of the offensive. At that time several German units were still more than 100 kilometers to the west.

Yelnya on the Desna, 75 km. southeast of Smolensk, was one of the most important strategic points and a significant railway junction. Together with the 10th Division our division established a bridgehead and a hedgehog-shaped defensive position. It had a radius of about 8 kilometers and our battalion was on the southern flank.

Paul Carell was right when he characterized the battles which were played out near Yelnya as frightful. Marshall Timoshenko, who had been named Commander-in-Chief of the Russian central front, tried for six weeks to crush our hedgehog, committing reserve divisions under the command of the future Marshall Rokossovsky.

On July 30 alone thirteen Russian attacks against the hedgehog position held by the Grossdeutschland Regiment and the Das Reich Division were beaten back. On that day our Hauptsturmführer Rumohr saw T-34 tanks appear in front of the 2nd Artillery Battalion's 6th Battery. He jumped onto a motorcycle and directed the defense, cold-bloodedly driving around between our artillery and the enemy tanks. The last was destroyed from a distance of 15 meters by a 105mm howitzer. And it was high time by then! That was a really extraordinary episode. Shortly thereafter Rumohr was promoted to Obersturmbannführer.

We were relieved by two infantry divisions at the beginning of August. However we had no time to reach our rest positions and had to occupy a position north of the hedgehog position, where enemy infantry were undertaking massive counterattacks.

They suffered fearful losses. The enemy came at us in wave after wave, only to allow themselves to be massacred, always at the same spot where our artillery had the exact range. It was impossible to fathom, heart-breaking and sickening to watch. Why were thousands of brave soldiers stupidly sent to their deaths in this way? At about the same time I was decorated with the Iron Cross, Second Class.

We could understand the Russian soldier defending the soil of his fatherland, for we were the invaders. But in the name of what social order were they sacrificed? What we had seen in the Russian villages and towns we passed through had opened our eyes about the "Soviet paradise." People and animals lived together in a, for the people, degrading fashion, and men and animals had little to eat. North of Kobrin I visited a *kholkhoz* (collective farm): the Russian farmer was little more than a wretched slave from the time of Gogol's *Dead Souls*. Alexander Solzhenitsyn is still correct today; but what we saw and experienced in the USSR has been expressed for us by Kravchenko and the courageous Solzhenitsyn.

We are criticized for having considered the Russians subhumans. This does not correspond to the facts. From the first year on I employed Russian prisoners as auto mechanics. I found them to be intelligent and inventive; for example the Russians found out that a certain spring from a T-34 could be installed in our Horch cars, whose front and rear springs had all broken in a short time. Why should I treat these Russians like subhumans? Even though I was and still am anti-bolshevik, I was and am not anti-Russian.

If Hitler underestimated the Russian soldiers in the beginning, as some maintain, he made a serious mistake. We had a superior strategy and our generals were significantly better in dealing with the problems of mobile warfare and were more innovative than the Russian. But from common soldier to company commander the Russian soldiers were the equal of the German. Brave, tough, and with an outstanding sense for camouflage, they put up astonishingly bitter resistance and walked en masse and with unbelievable fatalism into certain death.

In the hell of Yelnya we were convinced that we were fighting not for Germany but for all of Europe. But the division was at the end of its strength. Like many others, I had contacted a severe case of dysentery. I refused to go to hospital and simply pitched my tent at the edge of our camp. Fortunately the Das Reich Division was sent to rest position in the Roslavl sector: the men and vehicles badly needed a rest.

At this time Hitler made a decision about which opinion is still divided today. The offensive toward Moscow was suddenly interrupted and ordered south in the direction of Kiev. The reason behind this move was not just the capture of the Ukraine and its wheat and of the Donets Basin industrial region. Prisoners capture near Yelnya had spoken of a great concentration of forces to defend the capital city of the Ukraine. "The art of war," wrote Napoleon, "consists of having the greater strength at the point at which one is attacking or being attacked."

Those German generals and historians who since the war have criticized Hitler's decision, taken in the night of August 20-21, to attack in the south while Feldmarschall von Rundstedt was supposed to attack toward the north, have apparently forgotten the activities of the Red Orchestra in Switzerland. Let us examine the situation in detail.

On August 10 Werther transmitted details of the attack plans of the greater part of Feldmarschall von Bock's army group to Lucy: primary objective Moscow. This was Directive Number 34 by the OKW of the same date. Rado immediately sent the information to Director. Stalin, Shaposhnikov, Chief-of-Staff of the Red Army, and Timoshenko, commander of the Western Front, made their decisions accordingly. Stalin summoned General Yeremenko, armor specialist, and on August 12 ordered him to fortify the sector in front of Moscow and to expect Guderian there.

But on August 18 Halder, Chief-of-Staff of the OKH, suggested to Hitler that they not carry out the attack on Moscow frontally, rather via Briansk. Guderian wanted to give the impression of veering south, before suddenly changing direction toward the north and advancing from Briansk to Moscow. In Moscow Director learned immediately of this change to Directive Number 34. For this reason Yeremenko was able to write in his memoirs that, "Comrade Shaposhnikov informed him on the morning of August 24 that the attack on Briansk would take place in the coming days." Yeremenko therefore concentrated the bulk of his forces there in order to parry a thrust from the west, as the Russian general staff had ordered.

But on August 21 Hitler decided, without informing Halder, that Guderian's Panzergruppe 2 would attack neither Briansk nor Moscow, but instead would veer south with Kiev as its objective, a move which would grant him great freedom of maneuver. Lucy was not informed in time and consequently neither was Moscow.

Guderian offered Hitler his point of view on August 23: "I want to head straight for Moscow." "Hitler let me speak my mind without interrupting me," wrote the general. "But I couldn't convince him."

It was Kiev and the Ukraine. The generals obeyed.

I cannot see the behavior of an "incompetent, a dilettante" in Hitler's decision, as Gerd Buchheit, a former Reichswehr officer, wrote in his book. It was this decision that fooled the enemy and allowed approximately fifteen Soviet armies to be destroyed and most important agricultural and industrial areas to be occupied. The rest period granted the Das Reich Division was brief, and it took part in the great battles of encirclement east of Kiev commanded by Generals Guderian from the north and von Kleist from the south. The result: 665,000 prisoners, 884 tanks, 3,178 guns on September 15. The same day Stalin demanded of Churchill "twenty to twenty-five divisions, which should disembark in Arkhangelsk."

We fought our way to Priluki and Romny, where the much-admired and courageous Carl the Twelfth of Sweden had established his headquarters in the year 1703. Then came the first phase of Operation Taifun, whose objective was the conquest of Moscow. The division marched north again, through Gomel to Roslavl, where we arrived at the end of September.

It is not an exaggeration to claim that up to that point the land and the climate had been our bitterest enemies. During the summer dust had worn out or engines and clogged the filters. Guderian, who had ordered 600 replacement engines, received half, and the Das Reich Division was no better supplied. It rained from September 3rd to the 20th, and instead of dust there was mud. When we reached the Desna I was lucky to be able to say that I had been able to pull about 100 of our trucks, almost all of which had bogged down, out of the mud. After the great battles of encirclement in the Ukraine, our march north was a new way of the cross.

At the beginning of October we veered northeast toward Gshatsk and Yukinov. We found that Stalin's directives had been followed: we were fired on by groups of partisans while transiting the woods through which we had to pass. They were still small units, made up of soldiers who had escaped our encirclement and escaped prisoners.

Escape was so simple! We could barely spare a single soldier to watch over 500 prisoners. Of every twenty villages we occupied two or three, while the others offered refuge to the partisans, whose leader forced the population into obedience in good or bad.

In Gshatsk we had to fight on two fronts: toward the west, in order to prevent a breakout by the encircled enemy, and toward the east, to face the divisions Timoshenko threw into battle against us on this "track" from Smolensk to Moscow.

That year winter came very early. The first snow fell during the night of October 6-7. I recalled that Napoleon, after crossing the Beresina on July 22, had entered Moscow on September 14, 1812 and that on October 19 he was forced to abandon the burning capital to begin his frightful retreat. When I saw this snow, which gave the countryside a monotone but dangerous appearance, I felt a sense of foreboding, but my own optimism soon swept it away. We had the crossroads near Gshatsk firmly in our hands and Moscow was only about 160 kilometers away on the "highway."

The "highway!" This word brings to mind a broad road of concrete or asphalt. In reality here it was nothing more than a wide, raised wall of earth. To the south, the double battle of Vyazma-Briansk (September 30-October 14) had finally ended with the destruction of nine Soviet armies. Generals Guderian, Hoth, von Arnim, von Manteuffel and Model had taken 663,000 prisoners and destroyed or captured 1,242 tanks and 5,142 guns. We attacked Moscow's first defensive line in front of Borodino. It was here on September 7, 1812 against Kutusov and the Princes Bagration, Duvarov, Barclay de Tolly and Rayevsky that Napoleon had won the battle that opened the gates to Moscow.

The Das Reich Division attacked with the Hauenschild Brigade of the 10th Panzer Division, the 7th Panzer Regiment and a battalion of the 90th Motorized Artillery Regiment and the 10th Reconnaissance Battalion. Between the "highway" and the old mail route, somewhat farther north, the enemy had erected a very strong defensive position with minefields, barbed-wire obstacles, anti-tank ditches and rifle pits as well as small, fixed strongpoints. The first strongpoints were defended by a special unit which had at its disposal flamethrowers, first-class artillery, Stalin Organs and excellent support from the air force. But there was also a very unpleasant surprise waiting for us: at Borodino we had to fight Siberian troops for the first time. They were very well-equipped, strong and determined lads, with huge fur coats and caps, fur-lined boots and automatic rifles, naturally with all manner of heavy weapons. It was the 32nd Light Infantry Division from Vladivostock, which was accompanied by two brigades of T-34 and KV tanks.

Of all the difficult battles which I had the honor of taking part in, this was undoubtedly the most murderous. It lasted two days. I saw many good comrades fall and "Papa" Hausser was badly wounded not far from me. He lost an eye. But our massed artillery under the command of Oberst Weidling opened a breach through which our assault grenadiers forced their way, and the barrier of the first of Moscow's defensive lines was cracked. On October 19 we occupied Moshaisk: it was only 100 kilometers to Moscow!

After Moshaisk the resistance became weaker. We were convinced that we would be in Moscow at the beginning of November. But then came the catastrophe: beginning on October 19 torrential rain fell on the area of Army Group Center, which in three days literally sank into the morass. I was given the task of getting the trucks on the "highway" mobile again. It was a frightful scene: for many kilometers, thousands of vehicles in three rows, sunk in the mud, some up to their hoods. There was no fuel. Supplies had to be delivered by air: on average 200 tons per day for each division. The complete stoppage of traffic extended several hundreds of kilometers to the west. In this way three precious weeks and an enormous quantity of materiel were lost. In his book *Decisive Battles of the Occidental World*, the English General J.F. Fuller wrote in 1958:

"More than by Russian resistance, which certainly was energetic, Moscow was saved by the collapse of the German supply system in the morass on the entire front."

In a tremendous effort, 15 kilometers of corduroy road had to be built from trees felled by us while the fighting was going on. In spite of counterattacks by Siberian troops and T-34s we crossed the Moskva above Rousak: we wanted to be the first to arrive at Red Square. We thought: long live the cold! It froze during the night of November 6 and 7. Slowly the supplies began to flow again. We received ammunition, fuel, some food and cigarettes. Finally the wounded could be evacuated, and preparations were made for the final offensive.

We were supposed to advance through Istra to Moscow. Rather prematurely I received orders to keep an important waterworks in Moscow from being destroyed and make sure that the facility kept running. The Church of Istra was still undamaged. Through the fog we could see the bells in its steeples shining. The small city was one of the main support bases of the capital's second defensive line.

In spite of the losses we had suffered our morale was good: we would take Moscow. Preparations were made for the final assault.

But on November 19 the temperature suddenly fell to minus 20 degrees Celsius. We had no cold-proof motor or gun oil, and the engines were almost impossible to start early in the morning. Nevertheless Oberstleutnant von der Chevallerie took Istra on November 26 and 27 with the twenty-four tanks he had been loaned by the 10th Panzer Division and the Das Reich Division's reconnaissance battalion, which was under the command of Hauptsturmführer Klingenberg, who had been the first to enter Belgrade. Istra was defended by another elite division, the 78th Siberian Light Infantry Division. The next day the Russian Air Force levelled Istra.

Ahead and to our left lay Khimki, Moscow's port, 8 kilometers from the city itself. On November 30 a motorcycle reconnaissance company of the 62nd Pioneer Battalion, which belonged to the Hoepner Panzer Corps, entered Khimki without firing a shot, causing an outbreak of panic. Unfortunately this incident was not exploited. Inexplicably our motorcycle infantry withdrew.

Here another very mysterious episode in our offensive against Moscow took place. This episode has so far not been mentioned by any historian. In order to give an appropriate response to the frightful rockets of the Stalin organs, we received rockets of a new type, whose payload consisted of liquid air. They looked like large aerial bombs and had, as far as I can tell, a frightful effect which resulted in a visible reduction in the will to resist on the part of the enemy.

Opposite our lines the enemy had powerful loudspeakers for his propaganda, which at that time was quite mediocre. Several days after the first use of our large, liquid-air-filled rockets, the Russians let us know by loudspeaker that they would employ poison gas if we continued to fire these rockets.

They were never used again in our sector, and I don't believe that they were used subsequently in other sectors of the front.

On December 2 we advanced farther and reached Nikolayev, 15 kilometers from Moscow. In the clear weather I could see the spires of Moscow and the Kremlin through my field glasses. Our battery fired on the suburbs and streetcars. But we had almost no tractors left for our howitzers. Chevallerie now had ten panzers and the temperature fell to minus 30 degrees C. From October 9 to December 5, 1941 the Das Reich Division, the 10th Panzer Division and the other units of XXXX Panzer Corps had lost 7,582 officers, NCOs and enlisted men. That was 40 % of their nominal effective strength. Six days later, when day and night we had to battle fresh Siberian divisions that had broken through on our right wing, our division's losses reached more than 75 percent.

That day we learned that Germany and Italy had declared war on the United States after Pearl Harbor. The result of this was that the morale of some of our comrades fell. The most important thing was to learn what attitude Japan, our ally, would take against the Soviet Union. But the presence of the Siberian troops, most of whom came from the northern border of Korea, and whose numbers had been growing for a month, gave no cause for optimism.

● ● ●

Why were we unable to take Moscow? Many historians have asked this question and have answered it in various ways. My division was one of those which had to give up just short of the objective and the reason for our failure is clear to me today. I will try to explain as briefly as possible.

Since 1938 the German Army had been under the command of Feldmarschall von Brauchitsch, who came from a Prussian officer family. He was a good general of the old school. In 1941 he was already over sixty. There should definitely have been a younger commander in his post, someone who had a better understanding of the principles of this "revolutionary" style of warfare directed by Hitler and proposed by Manstein and Guderian. But in the end the field marshall was a man of the old general staff and there is no doubt that a better planned and organized logistics by one of his specialists would have saved the Wehrmacht enormous losses.

We have seen that the Russian land with its swamps, its morass, with rainfall and frost defended itself. Our vehicles, trucks, guns and their tractors, as well as our tanks, sank deep into the sandy and muddy roads. The catastrophic, cloudburst-like rainfalls of September-October were followed by temperatures between minus 25 and 40 degrees Celsius, against which our machines and men were almost defenseless.

We of the Waffen-SS had absolutely no privileges. As we were under the command of the Wehrmacht, we received exactly the same food and equipment as the other soldiers. After the first snowfall our division's administrative people ordered our allotted winter equipment, and in mid-November we received warm clothing, as did our comrades of the 10th Panzer Division. We had also seen the equipment worn by the Siberians captured at Borodino. We questioned them and learned, for example, that when we had no felt-lined boots our leather shoes or boots should not be hob-nailed and most of all should not be too tight. Every skier knows these details, but they were unknown to our equipment specialists. Practically all of us wore fur-lined boots taken from dead Russian soldiers.

Toward the end of October I saw to my astonishment a panzer division approaching whose kübelwagens, trucks and tanks were painted sand-yellow and whose men wore summer uniforms. It was the 5th Panzer Division which was initially earmarked for the Africa Corps. This division was hit hard in its very first action and our division had to help restore the situation.

The officers of this 5th Panzer Division, and we too, found it shocking that in November Goebbels had to turn to the German people and ask for donations – skis, warm clothing and so on – for the Eastern Front. The meaning of this late appeal by Goebbels was clear to all of us: the general staff hadn't done its job. Since Operation Barbarossa had been planned for more than a year, they should have known that proper winter equipment was an absolute necessity in Russia. Even if we had taken Moscow at the end of October, we would still have needed the best winter clothing as occupation troops.

During the first days of the retreat I intervened and had a supply of warm clothing distributed to the troops. An officer of the administrative section had stored the clothing in a farmhouse and was reluctant to issue it to the needy soldiers, who had only a light coat over their normal uniform, without orders from a senior officer. This officer wanted to burn the clothing, which undoubtedly saved the lives of many of my comrades, *as per orders*. The army's administrative organization and its head office, which knew that it snowed and rained in winter in Russia, should have taken appropriate steps beginning in April. But the Chief of the army's Military-Economic and Equipment Office was General Georg Thomas, one of the conspirators of July 20, 1944. He was under the direct command of Generalfeldmarschall Keitel in the OKW and his task was to foresee all the army's needs in foodstuffs, equipment, rolling stock, weapons, munitions and so on. This he did in accordance with Göring, who played the role of a commissioner of the four-year plan, and with the Reich Minister for Armaments and Munitions, Todt, later Speer. Here is an example: in March Thomas informed the OKW that 3,000 guns with ammunition would be available at the beginning of May. In accordance with the OKW's plans these guns and ammunition were then supposed to be issued and sent on their way to the front. This task fell to the offices of General Olbricht. These offices were under the command of General Fromm, Commander of the Replacement Army, Bendlerstrasse, Berlin, whose chief-of-staff was von Stauffenberg. Every piece of inexact information the OKW received from Olbricht's or Thomas' offices, every unreported delay in production or transport naturally had the most serious consequences, both for the OKW in planning the war and most especially for the front.

In spite of the morass, the ice, the lack of roads, in spite of the constant betrayal by certain commanders, in spite of the confusion of our logistics and in spite of the bravery of the Russian soldiers, we would have taken Moscow at the beginning of December 1941 if the Siberian troops had not intervened.

In the month of December our Army Group Center did not receive a single division as reinforcement or replacement. In the same period Stalin committed 30 light infantry divisions, 33 brigades, 6 tank divisions and 3 cavalry divisions against us. From October 17 on the Das Reich Division faced the Siberian 32nd Light Infantry Division near Borodino and later, at the beginning of December, the 78th Division. Both units were very well equipped and like the 32nd Division at Borodino were supported by a new tank division. I have not mentioned the other units of the Red Army, which fought with equal determination to that of the troops from Siberia.

It must also be said that our air force, which was already short of aircraft in November and December, failed to destroy the Trans-Siberian railroad net, thanks to which the Siberian troops were able to save Moscow, which was already considered half lost by the Russian leadership and from which the Soviet government had already fled.

To get within 20 kilometers of Moscow our division had had to fight an enemy whose numerical superiority in October was 3 or 4 to 1 in soldiers, 5 to 1 in artillery, thanks to the Stalin Organs, and at the end of December 5 or 6 to 1 in men and 8 to 10 to 1 in materiel, munitions and fuel.

● ● ●

In October Stalin had a gigantic front which was threatened by Japan, which had signed the Anti-Comintern Pact. From Vladivostock and the Bering Strait to Amgu-Okhotsk it was more than 9,000 kilometers and there was a land boundary of about 3,000 kilometers from Lake Baikal to Vladivostock. The USSR had to worry about attack from a vulnerable, 12,000 kilometer southern and eastern flank.

Let us recall that the first confrontation between the Soviet Army and Japanese troops took place in August 1938 on the shores of Lake Kazan. In May 1939 the Japanese Army entered the Mongolian Peoples Republic. The Red Army intervened and the result was the battle at the Khalkin. The Japanese Army occupied not only Korea, but also a large part of northern China and was moving toward the Gulf of Bengal. In Manchuria its infantry had occupied the right bank of the Amure River. Cities like Kabarovsk, Vladivostock and Nakoda were difficult for the Soviets to defend. On July 1, 1941 the German Reich, Italy, Romania, Slovakia and Croatia recognized the pro-Japanese government in Nanking.

Forty or more Japanese divisions threatened the USSR along this long front and they could be reinforced quickly. What would the Japanese strategy be? Would Japan attack in the north and seize the Trans-Siberian railroad in spite of the Soviet-Japanese agreement signed in Moscow on April 13? Would Japan attack in the south? At the beginning of summer 1941 Stalin did not know yet.

At this point there appeared a man whose secret has still not been fully cleared up: Soviet master spy Richard Sorge.

Of course I never met Sorge, alias Johnson, Ramsey, Smith and so on, but my friend Dennis MacEvoy, one of the chief editors of the *Readers Digest* and other American papers, a journalist in Tokyo before the war, saw a great deal of Sorge, who as we will see was one of his newspaper colleagues. MacEvoy had absolutely no idea of Sorge's real occupation.

The most complete work to be written on Richard Sorge so far is *Shanghai Conspiracy* (1952) by General A. Willoughby. The author served as head of General Douglas MacArthur's intelligence service. Further details may be found in *The Case of Richard Sorge* (1966) by F. Deakin and Storry. The articles and books concerning the "heroic acts of Comrade Sorge" which were published in the USSR in

1964 are apologies. Serious study of the Sorge case brings surprises to light.

Richard Sorge was born on October 4, 1895 near Baku. His father was a German, an engineer with an oil company, and his mother, Nina Kopelov, was sixteen years younger than her husband.

Sorge volunteered for service in the German Army in 1914 and was twice wounded. He completed his studies in political science at the University of Hamburg in 1920. By 1922 he had already become a specialist in agitation propaganda with the German Communist Party. two years later he went to Moscow. Sorge attended courses at specialist schools until 1927. The Comintern agent became a specialist in the Red Army's 4th Office (intelligence). 1929 found him back in Germany. There is little doubt that he met the future wife of Eugen Ott, later an envoy of the Third Reich, in Munich at this time. She was then married to an architect and was said to hold radical leftist views. General Willoughby wrote: "Many assume that she was a member of the German Communist Party KPD)."

Sorge was sent to Shanghai in 1930. Three years later he was recalled to Moscow by the 4th Office, which gave him his most important assignment, in Tokyo. Oddly enough Sorge first spent two months in Germany, where Hitler was now Reich Chancellor. He had to create another good cover. A Soviet female spy, Agnes Smedley, a correspondent with the *Frankfurter Zeitung*, recommended him to the newspaper, which sent him to Tokyo as a correspondent. But Sorge needed a contact with Oberstleutnant Eugen Ott, who had come to Tokyo as a military observer in 1942. But who was to give Sorge the introduction?: Dr. Zeller, editor of the *Täglichen Rundschau.* Zeller had such progressive views that his paper was banned at the end of 1933. He introduced Sorge to his friend Ott as "completely trustworthy, personally as well as politically."

This should make the historians suspicious, for we know that Oberstleutnant Ott had previously belonged to the staff of General von Schleicher. Following the failure of the political-military alliance with the extreme left planned by Chancellor von Schleicher at the end of 1933, Ott was sent to safety in Tokyo. I don't believe that it was chance that Sorge was recommended to Ott by Zeller as "completely trustworthy." It has been claimed that Sorge made his entire career as a secret agent as the result of a sentimental relationship with Frau Ott. It is completely possible that this relationship existed, but there is no explanation as to why Ott and Sorge became "very intimate." It was however Eugen Ott, quickly promoted to Oberst and named First Military Attache and later, in April 1936, German ambassador in Tokyo, who assisted Sorge during his entire career and thus eased his work as a spy.

Ramsey was not only accepted as a member of the Tokyo branch of the National-Socialist Party (October 1, 1934), but in 1939 the envoy officially made him his press chief. In autumn 1934 Sorge accompanied Ott on a trip through Manchuria.

In 1936, with Sorge not yet an official member of the embassy staff, he encoded certain telegrams signed by Ott and addressed to Berlin! When he had to travel to Hong Kong to deliver microfilm to his Soviet agent leader, the new ambassador, the now General Ott, entrusted him with the secret diplomatic mail, in which Ramsey was able to smuggle through all his documents intended for the 4th Office.

In 1938 the embassy entrusted him with the files on an important Soviet defector, General Lyushkov. At the time of the Tukhachevsky clearing operation Lyushkov passed important data on the Soviet military organization in Siberia and the Ukraine to the Japanese along with secret codes, the names of Stalin's main military foes in Siberia and so on. The Japanese informed Ott and Canaris at once sent Oberst Greiling to Tokyo to summarize Lyushkov's information in a memorandum. Sorge learned of this and informed Moscow of the most important details.

After Sorge's arrest on October 18, 1941, Ambassador Ott sent reports to Berlin in which he at first portrayed Ramsey as the innocent victim of the Japanese secret service and declared that Sorge had played only a subordinate role in the embassy. No one can seriously believe that Ott did not know who Sorge really was, but no one expressed this fact, which however did not escape the Japanese, clearly and acted accordingly.

Sorge was of course careful not to expose Ott, who was not replaced as ambassador in Tokyo, by Dr. Heinrich Stahmer, until November 1943. Ott and his wife did not return to Germany, instead they went to Peking where they waited for the end of the war.

From April 1939 until October 14, 1941 Sorge's radio operator, Max Clausen, sent 65,421 words to the 4th Office via secret transmitter. Sorge also had at his disposal special couriers for his microfilm, and at the end his net had also established contact with the Russian embassy in Tokyo.

He employed at least 30 Japanese. His most important agent was Ozaki Hozumi, advisor and close friend of Prince Konoje, minister president in the years 1937-1939 and 1940-1941. It was due to the indiscretions of Eugen Ott that Ramsey was able to inform his 4th Office on March 5, 1941 that the German attack on the USSR would take place "mainly in the direction of Moscow" and in mid-June. In another signal deciphered by the Japanese, on May 15 Sorge gave the date of the attack as June 20, 1941. Immediately after the sitting of the Imperial Council on July 2, 1941 Ozaki informed Sorge that the Japanese government had decided to attack the USA. On August 14 Ozaki brought Sorge the important information that all Japanese war plans against the USSR had practically been abandoned, and Sorge also learned the significant points from the meeting of the Japanese high command held on August 20 or 23, 1941. Ozaki was also informed about the entire military transport on the Manchurian railroads. On September 27 he was able to assure Sorge that "Japan was preparing a great offensive in the south," aimed at Singapore, Hong Kong and the Philippine Islands: it would take place at the end of November or early December 1941. Any danger of a war against the USSR had been eliminated.

Only now, after receiving this intelligence, could Stalin send the bulk of the Siberian troops to Moscow. It was more than half a million men. Thus was Moscow saved.

Sorge transmitted several more radio messages, the last after a conversation with Clausen and Ozaki on October 4, 1941. After eight years of extremely successful activity as a spy in Tokyo he considered his mission ended and feared being discovered. On October 13 Miyagi, a member of his group, failed to appear at the agreed-upon meeting place: he had been arrested. Sorge had to become more cautious. On October 15 radio operator Clausen came to see him; Ramsey then dispatched a radio message to Moscow suggesting they dissolve the net. Too late. Sorge was arrested at his home on the morning of October 18 and was taken to Sugamo prison still in his pajamas and slippers. On his desk the Japanese police officials found a draft of the radio message which Clausen was to send to Director on the evening of October 15. Clausen was found in possession of the same half-encoded signal. That was the end.

● ● ●

Was Sorge a double agent? In the confession he made to the Japanese investigators, he claimed that in 1940-1941 Moscow had authorized him to pass certain, rather unimportant confidential information to the Germans.

In his memoirs Schellenberg claimed that until 1940 Ramsey passed secret intelligence to Director von Ritgen, head of the official press agency DNP, and that he, Schellenberg, was also fully informed.

It seems appropriate here to point out that Walter Schellenberg, a prisoner of the English in 1945, was sentenced to prison by the Nuremberg tribunal. He died in Italy in 1952; *The Schellenberg Memoirs* first appeared in 1956. It is clear that this document was carefully sanitized of any potentially dangerous revelations. Several paragraphs do not appear to have been written by Schellenberg at all.

In Office VI of the SD they knew that Sorge had a relationship with Stennes, one of the senior SA chiefs, in 1933. Stennes was very much orientated toward the left and a friend of Gregor and Otto Strasser and had fled to China. It is curious that no one mentioned the close relationships between the various people, like Schleicher, Ott and his wife, Stennes, Zeller (of whom Schellenberg said nothing) and Sorge, although these connections were naturally very important and revealing.

In 1941 the German political intelligence service recalled its representative, Franz Huber, from Japan. Huber, who apparently had lost no sleep over Sorge, was replaced by Chief Inspector Meisinger, who, as Schellenberg said, "had played a dark sinister on June 30, 1934." Josef Meisinger, who was sentenced to death and executed in Poland after the war, arrived in Tokyo in *May 1941*. He undoubtedly knew that Sorge was not clean. The Japanese *Tokko* special police arrested Sorge and Ozaki while Meisinger was in Shanghai to make enquiries about one – just one! – Abwehr agent. This German Abwehr man was Ivar Lissner, a correspondent of the *Völkischer Beobachter* (the daily newspaper of the Nazi Party) and a Soviet agent. Lissner, arrested by the Japanese military police on June 5, 1943, was, like Max Clausen, Sorge's radio operator, released in August 1945 on orders of the American authorities.

Ozaki and Sorge were tried behind closed doors by a regular Japanese court in September 1943 and hanged on November 7, 1944.

That Ozaki is dead is a fact. There is some doubt about Sorge, however. His arrest, his sentencing and especially his execution were aggravating moments for the Japanese in their negotiations with the Soviets. In October 1931 the government of Nanking had merely expelled a veteran of the asian intelligence service, Noulens, and his accomplices, who had been sentenced to death for spying. Sorge was then active in Shanghai, parallel to the Noulens net.

In a report to Ribbentrop, the new German envoy Stahmer claimed that Sorge had been exchanged for a group of Japanese agents of the Kouan-Tong Army then being held by the Russians. According to Hans Meissner (*The Man with Three Faces*, 1957), the exchange had taken place on Portuguese soil in Macao, to where Sorge had been taken by the Japanese General Doihara.

Richard Sorge was a first-class agent, in the category of a Richard Abel, who was another master spy who was accidentally uncovered in the USA. He was exchanged for Francis Gary Powers, the unlucky pilot of the U-2 spy plane, in Berlin on February 10, 1962.

Richard Sorge's life in Tokyo was, as Dennis MacEvoy told me, a very frivolous one. He drank very heavily, and his successes and failures with women ran into the dozens although he had married in Russia and the USA. He had a long-term relationship with a Japanese woman, Hanako-Tshii, who allegedly found and identified his body.

For twenty years no one in the USSR spoke of Richard Sorge. Then on November 5, 1964 the Soviet government published an laudatory obituary of their master spy and made him a "Hero of the Soviet Union." A street in Moscow was named after him, as was an oil tanker, and in 1963 a stamp was issued in his memory.

It is true that at this time about twenty works had appeared in Japan, the USA and Europe concerning Ramsey, whose decisive role slowly became known even behind the iron curtain. At the same time two of Sorge's former superiors, General Bersin and Colonel Borovich, both of whom had been executed on Stalin's order, were rehabilitated. It was the era of "de-Stalinization."

If Sorge really was exchanged, it may well be that Stalin let him live, naturally at a place chosen by the Soviet dictator. The man was dangerous, however. His activity and his network of spies had allowed the Siberian divisions to intervene decisively in the Battle of Moscow while we were bogged down in the mud and cold.

If the truth were known in Russia this would destroy the myth of the "Miracle of Moscow," which was attributed to Stalin. Even today the existence of the Red Orchestra is practically unknown in the USSR.

•   •   •

One can ask oneself why the retreat at the end of December 1941 and early January 1942 did not assume catastrophic proportions and end with the total destruction of the German armies. In the year 1812, after the lightning retreat by Napoleon, who had heard of General Malet's plot and the desertion of Prince Murat, the Grand Army practically ceased to exist.

It is thanks to Adolf Hitler that this was not the case with the Wehrmacht. Instead of ordering a general retreat, he decreed that only those units facing the greatest danger of encirclement could withdraw, while the others must hold their positions fanatically.

Cities were declared fortresses and defended as such: Novgorod, Schlüsselburg, Rzhev, Vyazma, Briansk, Orel, Kharkov, Taganrog, on these the divisions of Konev and Zhukov were broken. The Russian generals were unable to successfully counter the troops movements by Generals Hoth and Guderian behind Smolensk, although even airborne troops were committed. Their losses were very heavy.

We had to wait until 1970 until Liddel Hart, nearly alone among the historians of the Second World War, acknowledged that Hitler was right not to listen to the advice of his generals, who proposed a general withdrawal to a line from Pskov in the north and Mogilev-Gomel in the center to the Dniepr. Nothing is more dangerous than a panic during a retreat, and I have seen certain senior officers lose their heads. An Oberst used energetic gestures in an effort to keep me from pulling back with my trucks to Volokolamsk as per orders, informing me that he knew that the Russians were already there. However this news was false.

I reached Volokolamsk, which is about 60 kilometers northwest of Istra, without difficulty; nobody there had seen even a single Russian soldier and the Das Reich Division established a solid defensive line there.

Liddel Hart wrote:

"It is today certain, that Hitler's refusal to authorize a general retreat restored the confidence of the German troops and thus certainly prevented their total destruction."

PART II

10

THE "UNCONDITIONAL SURRENDER" THE TRUTH ABOUT STALINGRAD

Evacuated – In officer school for tank training – Back to Berlin to the reserve battalion of the Leibstandarte Adolf Hitler Waffen-SS Division – Roosevelt demands "Unconditional Surrender" – The true reason behind this decision – Secret negotiations in Stockholm and Ankara – Franz von Papen makes confidential reports in Madrid after the war – Without informing Hitler or Ribbentrop he informs the Americans in Ankara of the Russian proposals – Unfavorable reactions in the Reich Foreign Ministry – The Russians feel deceived – A good opportunity to achieve peace was missed – Surrender of the Sixth Army at Stalingrad – Causes of the tragedy – The "Blue Plan" on Stalin's desk since November – Timoshenko is defeated – Stalin asks the Red Orchestra: "Where is Paulus?" – Eighteen days without gasoline – "Rendezvous at Stalingrad": eleven armies against one – General Wenck's forces save 500,000 men – General von Seydlitz, Paulus' adjutant, calls for resistance – Gisevius believes Paulus did not give the signal at which Feldmarschall von Kluge was to unleash the putsch in the east – Failure of Operation "Silver Fox" – Thoughts on the war – I assume command of the "Friedenthal Special Duties Battalion"

By the seventh month of the Russian campaign I had seen so many brave comrades fall that I considered myself lucky to have escaped relatively intact. In November 1941 near Moshaisk I was caught by a salvo from a Stalin Organ, however I was fortunate to escape with a heavy blow and a head wound. On the other hand, however, I had not completely recovered from the severe case of dysentery that had so weakened me at Roslavl.

During the retreat I was struck by biliary colic and only managed to stay on my feet by relying on injections. At the beginning of 1942 I was transferred to Smolensk on a hospital train and from there to Vienna. I was in really poor shape, and I only managed to temporarily avoid an operation as the result of a stay in Karlsbad Hospital. Later, in 1946, I had to have the operation while in a POW camp.

During my convalescent leave in 1942 I was able to see my father again a week before his death. That was a comfort to both of us.

"I am convinced," he said, "that the European armies will defeat the Russians. Perhaps one day the western powers will understand that it is in their interest to put an end to bolshevism. Then the world will achieve a lasting peace and your generation will perhaps be happier than ours."

Many thought as he did – and deceived themselves. But at least my father died with this illusion.

The hospital release order classified me as "GvH" (fit for garrison duty at home), and so I was sent to the replacement unit of the Waffen-SS Division Leibstandarte Adolf Hitler in Berlin as engineering officer. The six months I spent there were terribly boring. I felt like a shirker, but I soon found ways and means to overcome the boredom: I volunteered for retraining with the panzer arm. After passing several tests I was transferred as an engineering officer to the Waffen-SS Division Totenkopf which in fully motorized form was to be reequipped as a panzer division.

Unfortunately I was not completely cured. In the winter of 1942-1943 I had a relapse of dysentery. They determined that I was "GvH" and sent me back to the Leibstandarte reserve unit in Berlin.

They undoubtedly needed engineering officers in the reserve units. But I found that I could be more useful. The thought of being no more than a conscientious working engineer did not please me. Then came two events, almost simultaneously, which gave every German to whom the future of his country lay near to his heart cause to think.

In January 1943 at Casablanca, Roosevelt, together with Winston Churchill, decided that the allies would demand an "unconditional surrender" from the Axis powers, and especially from Germany.

Roosevelt unintentionally supported Goebbels' propaganda with the words "unconditional surrender." Hitler and national socialism should not disappear, which actually would have been logical in a political-ideological war. Roosevelt wanted us to unconditionally lay down our weapons. Stalin would obviously emerge as the sole, big winner: that meant that not only Germany, but half of western Europe, would be delivered up to bolshevism.

Fundementally this decision of Roosevelt's was caused only by his real, panicky fear. Since November 1942 Peter Kleist, a member of the German Foreign Office in Stockholm, had been in contact with Edgar Klauss, a Swedish manufacturer and a confidante of the Russian embassy in Sweden, which was then led by the extremely active Madame Kollontai. At that time there existed a possibility of signing a peace treaty with Moscow within eight days.

More than anything Roosevelt, who was fully informed of the steps being taken by the Germans in Sweden, feared a renewal of the agreement between Berlin and Moscow. Above all his "unconditional surrender" was a bluff aimed at Stalin, who was supposed to be convinced by it that the United States would continue to pursue the war no matter what might happen.

Later, while at Nuremberg, I learned from Herr Sailer, German ambassador in Ankara during the war, that the efforts in Stockholm to reach a compromise in the east were taken up again at the end of 1943 by Franz von Papen, German ambassador to Turkey, and were carried on in am ambiguous fashion. After his release in 1949 I learned some highly interesting details from von Papen himself.

In 1952 the former Reich Chancellor was invited by the Spanish foreign ministry to give a lecture in the Ateneo, a known Madrid center of culture with a liberal tradition. The organizer of the lecture was an outstanding diplomat and friend of mine, the Marquis de Prat de Nantouillet. I had the opportunity to meet privately with von Papen twice, and we had long conversations about the little-known "Ankara affair."

The USSR had extended the first peace feelers, by way of the Turkish foreign ministry. Von Papen informed the Turkish minister that a peace did not appear impossible to him, "if reasonable proposals were made."

"What I anticipated and also desired then happened," von Papen told me. "The Turks lost no time in simultaneously informing the Americans and the Russians of my reply. The American ambassador immediately travelled to Washington. After his return he sought out the Turkish foreign ministry, which immediately informed me of the position taken by the US foreign ministry and the White House: Germany was to know that the USA was ready to sign a separate peace with Germany, twenty-four hours before the USSR."

Pity that Herr von Papen carried out these conversations alone without informing Hitler or Ribbentrop. Ribbentrop's reaction was extremely violent, and the Führer saw the discussions in Ankara, which came on the heels of those in Stockholm, as proof that the Russians had reached the end.

Had Papen immediately reported the Russian proposals to Hitler instead of alerting the Americans, a cease-fire would possibly, even probably been concluded. It was not in the interest of either Germany or Russia to see both sides bled white. In April 1943 Stalin feared that the allies would not land in Sicily (July 10, 1943) but in the Balkans as Churchill wanted. A cessation of hostilities in the east – I said this quite openly to von Papen during our "closed-doors " discussions – would have made any landing in Sicily and later in France impossible. "You are perhaps right," observed the former Reich Chancellor. "But believe me, Ribbentrop ruined everything."

Franz von Papen was undoubtedly a far better diplomat than Ribbentrop. However in this case it appears that everything was ruined by him, because he tried to negotiate alone and play a double game with the west. He probably did so out of conviction, and because Ribbentrop had signed the pact with Stalin in 1939. Papen wanted to go him one better. Had he replaced Ribbentrop in the Reich Foreign Ministry the Russian proposals would certainly have led to something. But it is likely that the former Reich Chancellor had plans extending beyond that.

Stalin and Molotov, who learned immediately of Papen's double game, did not believe for a moment that the Americans had been informed without Hitler's approval. They felt deceived and only now gave the Americans every assurance. In a speech delivered on May 1, 1943 Stalin also spoke of "unconditional surrender": "A separate peace with the fascist bandits is impossible."

General Franco and his foreign minister Jordana subsequently made themselves available for a contact with the west. But on May 11, 1943 Anthony Eden, head of the Foreign Office, officially rejected any proposal for compromise: thus was the fate of many European states settled.

It is difficult to believe that a new Germany-Russian treaty would have strengthened the European member parties of the Communist International (Comintern), as many thought. On the contrary. Their cadres and the comrades had made too much anti-German propaganda to be able to agree to a new turnabout. As had been the case earlier in the German Reich, in Italy, Portugal, Hungary, Spain and in France and Belgium in the years 1936-1939, the communist workers flocked to movements with a synthesis of socialism and nationalism which showed European perspectives. In this way European anti-marxist socialism could have taken form.

In Stockholm, and later in Ankara, everything was played out without Ribbentrop being advised of the discussions that had been held and contacts that had been made. Unlike the discussions held by Herr Kleist in Stockholm,[1] those in Ankara are almost unknown.

Ribbentrop's style of politics was basically negative since 1939. It was unfortunate for Germany and Europe that we did not, apart from Hitler, have any diplomats of rank who had a thorough knowledge of the English mentality. I am firmly convinced – and I am not alone in this – that England would have declared war on us in any case, although this was contrary to its vital interests. Ribbentrop convinced Hitler that the English would not declare war just on account of the reincorporation of Danzig into the German Reich. One can say with justification that a good opportunity of preserving the peace was missed then.

Roosevelt's advisors had assured him and Churchill that the threat of unconditional surrender, together with the bombing terror, which had only one – openly admitted – objective, to level every German city with more than 100,000 inhabitants, would bring about a quick end to the war. In any event the decisions made in Casablanca by Roosevelt and Churchill prolonged the war by at least a year.

● ● ●

1943 saw the surrender of the rest of the Sixth Army, which was commanded in Stalingrad by General Paulus. He surrendered with his staff on January 31, 1943. The last soldiers of General Strecker's II Army Corps fought to the last round. Many officers took their lives. Shortly before 9 A.M. the OKH received the following final radio message:

"XI Army Corps and its 10 divisions have done their duty. Heil Hitler. General Strecker."

Not everyone in the Sixth Army had done their duty; they had walked into a trap.

First of all one must realize that there exists a legend of Stalingrad – just as in 1812 there was a legend of the Beresina, where the French losses were exaggerated. At first it was conceded that about 400,000 German and allied officers and soldiers were taken prisoner at Stalingrad. Then Yeremenko revised this figure downward, first to 330,000 and finally to 300,000. The truth was something else.

According to a "situation report" which the OKH received on December 22, 1942, the exact number of soldiers in the pocket on December 18 was: 230,000 German and allied troops, including 13,000 Romanian. However in the period from January 19 to 24, 42,000 wounded, sick and specialists were evacuated by aircraft. 16,800 soldiers were taken prisoner by the Russians from the 10th to the 19th of January and another 91,000 after the surrender. The Russians therefore took a total of 107,000 prisoners. Of these only 6,000 soldiers returned home by 1964. The 101,800 missing died after the surrender at Stalingrad. We captured 19,800 officers and soldiers of the Red Army, who were released after the surrender. This was three times as many as the German soldiers who returned after ten years of imprisonment.

Hitler made serious mistakes during the war. For thirty years almost every historian has confirmed that he alone bore the responsibility for the tragedy of Stalingrad, in that he refused to give General Paulus the order to break out. One must realize that Hitler was assured that Paulus could be supplied from the air – which then turned out to be impossible and cost the lives of countless officers and soldiers, among them General Jeschonnek, the Luftwaffe's Chief-of-Staff, who committed suicide.

At the beginning of 1943, neither the German people nor the soldiers knew what the real causes of this defeat were. We all thought that the luck of arms had abandoned General Paulus and this meant for us a lost battle after many victories. In reality it was a great turning point.

Even today not everything is known about Stalingrad. But one can say openly that this horrible tragedy would not have taken place had the enemy not been informed daily of the intentions of our general staff and the weaknesses in our order of battle by the Red Orchestra. A certain hesitation of the part of Paulus also remains inexplicable. At the end of August 1942 he had not linked up with General Hoth's Fourth Panzer Army as ordered. Two of his most important associates, Generals von Seydlitz and Daniels, were members of the conspiracy against Hitler. Today we know that Paulus and Kluge were supposed to give the signal for the beginning of a military putsch against Hitler. Neither had the courage to do so, however, and meanwhile the *Red Orchestra* continued to play.

At the end of November 1941 the Red Orchestra informed STAVKA of Hitler's intention to attack toward the Caucasus in the spring in order to seize the oil fields of Batum on the Black Sea and Baku on the Caspian Sea. On a single day, November 21, 1941, STAVKA received news from Gilbert (Trepper in Paris) that "the Germans are assembling ships in Romanian ports and are planning an operation in the Caucasus,"; they learned from Anton (Holland) that "units of the Luftwaffe were moved from Greece to the Crimea"; and from Coro (Schulze-Boysen in Berlin) came the following information:

"Plan III, with Caucasus as its objective, originally planned for November, will not be carried out until next spring... Planned directions of battle: Losovaya-Balakleya-Chuguyev-Belgorod-Ahktyrka-Krasnograd-general staff in Kharkov. Details to follow."

Our battle plans were regularly and in every detail transmitted to the enemy. The entire Plan III, the later "Plan Blue," and all the associated maps, were openly handed over to the enemy on June 19, 1942, and by a member of the general staff, Major Reichel, who deserted with a Fieseler Storch.

All our plans therefore lay on Timoshenko's desk. There is no doubt about this: Paul Carell, Erich Kern and W.F. Flicke, a former officer of signals counterintelligence, prove it. Timoshenko thus dared to mass troops near Kharkov on May 12, 1942 for a major offensive, identical to the one which would later encircle General Paulus' Sixth Army. The attack was a failure. A joint counterattack by Generals von Kleist and von Mackensen inflicted losses on Timoshenko of 60,000 soldiers dead and wounded, 239,000 captured, and 2,026 guns and 1,250 tanks destroyed or captured. Timoshenko was subsequently relieved of his post on the southwest front. When Generalfeld-marschall von Bock, head of Army Group B, and Generalfeld-marschall List, head of Army Group A, went over to the counterat-tack, chaos broke out among the Russians.

Seen strategically, STAVKA was completely right to order the rapid withdrawal of its troops. Stalin's counter-plan was simple: draw Army Group A (List) as far into the Caucasus as possible and allow Army Group B (Bock) to advance to Stalingrad and tie it down there. In the meantime they would assemble an overpowering force of men and materiel on the banks of the Don and the Volga. Then when Army Group List was stuck deep in the Caucasus, the bulk of the Russian forces would drive toward Rostov, put the Sixth Army to flight and cut off the line of retreat of List's armies, which were inadequately supplied and would have no time to fight their way back over this tremendous distance.

Had the Soviet high command been more flexible, an even greater catastrophe would have befallen the Germans.

But what happened? Kleist's First Panzer Army took Rostov, where the oil line from the Caucasus ended. Afterward it struck south, took Krasnodar, Novorossisk, the oil fields of Maykop (annual pro-duction 2,600,000 tons), Pyatigorsk, reached Ordshonikidze on the road to Tbilisi and even a previously unknown railroad from Baku to Astrakhan.

According to the "Blue Plan" the primary task of Sixth Army (of Army Group B), commanded by General Paulus, was to screen the left flank of Army Group List. General Halder, Chief-of-Staff of the OKH, who in 1940 had had Paulus named Army Senior Quartermas-ter, gave him the order to advance on Stalingrad, "neutralize" the city and destroy the small enemy buildups which had been observed north of the Don bend.

At first the retreat ordered by STAVKA was a chaos and we missed our best opportunities. For example one might have released Gen-eral Hoth and the Fourth Panzer Army from Army Group List and had him march north of Stalingrad, which would have been a catas-trophe for the Russians. But Hoth got out of Kotelnikovo too late.

In June 1942 Paulus therefore continued his "pursuit race" to Stalingrad and advanced 300 kilometers with no serious fighting.

Meanwhile General Gordov became the provisional successor to General Timoshenko. He had carried out STAVKA's orders. Since the beginning of July he had stationed the 62nd Army, which was then commanded by Kolpakchi, in the area of Lopatin. This army was joined by the 63rd and 64th Armies under the command of Kuznetsov and Choumilov, exactly at the place where Paulus would have to cross the Don. According to the Russian plan other armies were to help encircle Paulus: the 1st and 4th Tank Armies of Moskalenko and Kruschenkin, Popov's 5th, Chistyakov's 21st, Galardine's 24th, Batov's 65th, Shadov's 66th, the 57th, 51st, 64th, the 2nd Guards under Malinovsky, the 5th Tank Army, Guerasimenko's 28th, the 4th Fully-Motorized Corps and so on hurried to the "rendezvous at Stalingrad."

But in July 1942 something suddenly happened that the STAVKA had not planned: General Paulus' Sixth Army did not appear where the Russians were expecting it! In Moscow they first reacted with alarm, then with panic. They feared that Hitler had once again overturned his plans without Werther learning of it. Where was Paulus then? It was characteristic of the general staff of the Red Army that it did not turn to its air force or patrols to find the answer to this question: Director asked Rado. From Rado and Werther the Russians learned that the Sixth Army was immobilized: due to a shortage of gasoline! This fuel crisis lasted eighteen days. In the meantime the defenses of Stalingrad were strengthened and the overall command entrusted to General Yeremenko. Our supply specialists posed no danger to the STAVKA!

The true story of the Battle of Stalingrad, which lasted from July 20, 1942 to February 2, 1943, must still be written. Let us hope that this one day happens. Neither the memoirs of Field Marshalls Chuikov and Yeremenko, nor B.C. Talpoukhov's work *The Great Victory of the Soviet Army in Stalingrad* (1953) are of much use: they give us only a simplified, incomplete account. Naturally the Red Orchestra is mentioned in none of these books.[2]

The heroic defense of Stalingrad in the months of September and October in the large factories called "Barricades", "Tractor Works" and "Red October," is definitely deserving of great admiration. Contrary to all the facts, however, General Yeremenko claims that the German Sixth Army, which also had Romanians, Hungarians and Italians at its side, was numerically and materially superior to the Russians – although a dozen Russian armies, Rudenko's 16th Air

Fleet, special units trained in street fighting, a tremendous artillery force, powerful anti-aircraft forces, elite troops and so on gave the Russians a superiority of 4 or 5 to 1 in November 1942.

Why did Hitler and the OKH not give Paulus the order to withdraw in October, although they saw that he could not move from the spot? Primarily because the commander of our Sixth Army had informed them that he would take the city. Carell wrote of this:

"Information supplied to the OKH, whose origin remains unclear to this day, confirmed the Führer's optimistic assessment of the situation: since September 9 the Russians no noteworthy operational reserve."

Six of the best-known Russian military commanders made their careers at Stalingrad: Voronov, Chuikov, Tolbukhin, Rokossovsky, Malinovsky and A.E. Yeremenko. As thanks for his good and loyal service Stalin sent the latter to the eastern Siberia and then to the Caucasus. His book often sounds like a song of praise to his patron Nikita Khrushchev and showing off of his own military talents.

The Russian soldiers fought remarkably in a city extending about 60 kilometers and which General Paulus had intended to take "by November 10 at the latest." At least that is what he telegraphed Hitler on October 25. At the end of November Hitler could no longer give Paulus the order to withdraw: his army was then holding eleven Russian armies in check, which otherwise would march to Rostov with 4,500 tanks in order to there cut off the avenue of retreat of our armies in the Caucasus, about half a million soldiers.

On November 9, 1942 Director demanded from Dora the order of battle of the Sixth Army. Ten days later the Russians attacked at the most vulnerable spots. In the northwest corner of the "pocket," one of our weakest spots, they achieved a deep penetration. My friend Wenck, who was then an Oberst, blocked the way with a brigade thrown together on the spot, consisting of Luftwaffe ground personnel, railroad workers, members of the labor service, office personnel, Romanians of the Third Army, Cossacks, Ukrainians, volunteers from the Caucasus and military police on leave. Together with Oberstleutnant von Oppeln-Bronikowski he formed a small panzer corps: 6 captured tanks, 12 armored cars, about 20 trucks and an 88mm flak. This then was the "Wenck Army," which at the end of

November held a front of 170 kilometers – with captured ammunition and "stolen" gasoline. Thanks to the Wenck group, which finally received some help from elements of General Hollidt's XVII Corps, the penetration point between the Chir and the Don was sealed off. Hurrying to the scene, Feldmarschall von Manstein was able to recapture the hills of the southwest bank of the Chir, establish a line of resistance and thereby prevent the encirclement of our divisions falling back from the Caucasus by the Russians.

One must cite the example of Wenck and his volunteers and not that of General von Seydlitz-Kurtzbach, the commanding general of LI Army Corps. He disobeyed the orders of the OKH and withdrew his corps on November 24. During this maneuver one of his units, the 94th Infantry Division, was completely wiped out. But this did not prevent the general, who had inherited a famous name, from calling for a revolt. Here is part of his explanation from November 25:

"If the OKH does not immediately rescind the order to hold out in the hedgehog position, then my own conscience in regard to the army and the German people will produce the commanding obligation to seize the freedom of action denied by the previous order."[3]

Later von Seydlitz and Paulus (whom Hitler, unaware of this treachery, promoted to field marshall) again turned up at the microphones of Radio Moscow, "acting according to their consciences." At the Nuremberg trial Paulus appeared as a "free witness" on behalf of the Russian indictment.[4] He implicated Generalfeldmarschall Keitel and Generaloberst Jodl and maintained that he knew nothing of Operation "Barbarossa," although he had himself worked on the plan, specifically when he was still Quartermaster General in the OKW.

During the court proceedings in Nuremberg on April 25, 1946, witness Gisevius stated:

"After trying in vain to convince the triumphant generals that they should make a putsch, we made another attempt after these generals realized that we were on the road to a catastrophe... We made our preparations for the moment, which we had predicted with almost mathematical certainty, at which the Paulus army would be forced to surrender, in order to at least organize a military putsch. They called me back to Switzerland at this moment to take part in all these discussions and preparations. I can state that this time the preparations were made very quickly. We had made contact with the marshalls in the east and in the west with Witzleben. But this time too the situation failed to develop as planned, for Feldmarschall Paulus surrendered instead of giving us the agreed-upon signal as laid down in our plan, according to which Marshall Kluge was to begin the putsch in the east after receiving the signal."

We know that the witness Gisevius worked in the service of the enemy in Switzerland.

● ● ●

At the time I knew nothing of all these proceedings. At the beginning of 1943 I was convinced that Germany was not losing this war but that the worst still lay ahead of us.

While I was lying in hospital and during my stay in Vienna and Berlin I always listened attentively to the comments by officers and soldiers back from the front. I thought a great deal about the campaigns in western Europe, the Balkans and in Russia, which I had experienced myself as an officer with the Waffen-SS Division Das Reich. As well I maintained contact by mail with Standartenführer Hansen, commander of my old artillery regiment. The Russians had certainly been surprised by the "blitzkrieg," in spite of the information they possessed; they were also surprised by the large panzer units which drove deep into their units. We had taken several million prisoners. This created a problem which, given the lack of agriculture (apart from the Ukraine), shortage of transport and poor supply of foodstuffs, was unsolvable. By the beginning of 1943 tens of thousands had already escaped. They rejoined Soviet units which had escaped our encirclements. In this way partisan groups of considerable size were formed, as called for by Stalin in his speech of July 3, 1941.

In these endless, roadless expanses our panzers could not achieve the same results they had in Poland, Holland or France. The combination of all our weapons – air force, artillery, tanks and infantry – could not take effect as they had in the previously mentioned countries. Furthermore our objectives and equipment were known in detail by the enemy. As in Napoleon's time our large formations were harried on their flanks or from behind by special counteroffensives and partisan units, which were impossible to find in the immensity of the land.

We knew that the Russians were receiving tremendous amounts of materiel from the Americans and that they possessed huge industrial complexes out of reach beyond the Urals. We would have occupied the "Soviet Ruhr" if Operation "Silver Fox," conducted in the far north by the 2nd and 3rd Mountain Infantry Divisions and the 9th Infantry Regiment of the Waffen-SS Division Totenkopf, had succeeded. But the railroad line from Murmansk, the main supply line of the Russian armies, could not be cut. After heavy fighting in the tundra the Finnish Third Army encountered superior enemy forces which compelled it to halt its offensive approximately 20 kilometers from Sall Lukhi. Farther north the well-known mountain infantry commander General Dietl succeeded in driving to within about 50 kilometers of Murmansk. On September 20, 1941 he, too, was forced to give the order to withdraw. The first nineteen convoys to arrive in Murmansk from the west delivered 520,000 trucks and other vehicles, 4,048 tanks and 3,052 aircraft.

This too we did not know. But I had the distinct feeling that we were no longer employing a revolutionary style of warfare but were fighting a conventional war of attrition.

We do not need to know the sad background of the Stalingrad catastrophe, whose result was not kept from the German people, to understand that the enemy had learned a great deal and adopted our new tactics.

For my part, I was convinced that if we wanted to achieve a decision as in the years 1939/40, we must turn to daring methods and the tactic of surprise as we had in those years. We had to consider the entire nature of the war and discover and produce new weapons; weapons which were especially useful for specific purposes.

Naturally I had too much imagination; I was only an unknown Obersturmführer. If I had had an opportunity to present my unorthodox ideas to one of the staff officers wearing the red stripes of the general staff he would most likely have smiled.

My personal files lay in the "Operational Headquarters" of the Waffen-SS, our general staff, commanded by Obergruppenführer Hans Jüttner. This former Reichswehr officer was a remarkable man. In military terms he was far superior to Himmler. I now felt totally fit and I expressed openly to him my wish to serve in a combat unit in which I could show more initiative than in a Berlin barracks. Judging by his questions, he had gone to the trouble of studying my military career. Not only did he know what happened when we were planning Otario, but about Yelnya in the Ukraine, Borodino, Rusa and the beginning of the retreat from Moscow. He was familiar with my reports containing proposals for installing caterpillar tracks over the rear axles of standard trucks. He also knew that I could fly an aircraft and drive and repair all the new German tanks flawlessly, as well as the American models and the T-34, in which one sometimes had to use a hammer to shift gears.

The conversation was friendly. Gradually I brought forward my unorthodox ideas for a more daring war, which in my opinion we could conduct. The general agreed heartily and I suddenly got the feeling that he had an "ulterior motive." I wasn't fooling myself. Jüttner had me summoned a few days later. He told me that he was looking for an officer who had experience at the front and a good technical knowledge to organize and command a "special duties unit."

I listened closely as he explained in several clear sentences the duties assigned to a certain battalion at Friedenthal near Berlin and a "Seehof" school at The Hague.

In conclusion General Jüttner said, "this is probably a new form of warfare for you and, I will not keep it a secret from you, a very responsible post. During our last conversation I had the impression that you are the man that we need. Naturally you must consider the proposal. You are also free to turn it down."

"I've already thought it over," I said to him. "I accept."

So I became an Hauptsturmführer and commander of the Friedenthal Special Duties Battalion and the "Seehof" School.

I stood up to take my leave and thank the general.

He smiled, "You accepted immediately. Very good. In order. I think that you should have a look at Seehof and Friedenthal first, however. It may be that certain difficulties will crop up that you can't shake yourself of. When you return tell me what you think and only then will your acceptance be considered final."

Jüttner obviously knew about the "unforseen difficulties" that I must overcome and wanted to give me the opportunity to back out of the matter. He was as courteous a general as he was farsighted.

Notes

1. See Kleist, Peter: *Zwischen Hitler und Stalin*, Bonn 1950.

2. An extensive German account has since been published: Manfred Kehrig, Stalingrad. *Analysis and Documentation of a Battle*, from the series of publications by the Military-Historical Research Office, Volume 15, 1974.

3. Carell, Paul: *Unternehmen Barbarossa*, Page 524.

4. As to the proceedings surrounding Paulus, compare Peter Strassner's *Verräter,* Munich 1960.

11

DON'T SHOOT!

The Friedenthal Special Duties Battalion – Why historians can make mistakes too – Why I couldn't receive any orders from W. Schellenberg – My first officers: "Chinaman" Hunke and lawyer Radl – I turn down an appointment to Oberst in the SD – Lord Mountbatten, his successor General Laycock and the British Commandos – "Fair play" by the BBC – My conversation with the "Phantom Major," David Stirling, the former chief of the Special Air Force – Acts of heroism in Africa – London decides to eliminate General Rommel – The night at Beda Littoria: comments by Sir Winston Churchill, legends and true occurrences – Lessons from the failure of the Scottish Commando – The inaccessible Wolfsschanze – Why we don't shoot – A conclusion by General von Clausewitz.

Friedenthal, which is located about 20 kilometers north of Berlin, was a former hunting lodge of the Hohenzollerns. In early 1943 a barracks camp was erected around two pavilions in a large park, where in their day the guests of the Kaiser had gathered. The barracks housed one complete company as well as half of another and elements of a transport company. The whole thing called itself "Special Duties Unit Friedenthal" and was commanded by a Dutch Waffen-SS officer and a staff which practically did not yet exist. There was little in the way of a records office, documentation, organization, telephones, teletypes or radio stations. Of the approximately 300 men I found in Friedenthal, about 85 percent were German and 15 percent Dutch, Flemish or Hungarian "ethnic Germans." All were volunteers who, like me, belonged to the Waffen-SS.

I have already explained that the members of the Waffen-SS were not, as is so often claimed, "police in Himmler's service," but *soldiers*. I should expand on this theme at this point.

On June 16, 1929 Hitler named Himmler "Reich Leader of the Protection Echelon" (*Reichsführer der Schutzstaffel,* or SS). At this point the echelon comprised 280 men. Then in 1933 the *"Allgemeine SS"* (General SS) was founded. The black uniform looked good and was a great success among young people: the SS appealed to students, diplomats, doctors, lawyers, officials and national socialists who wanted to distinguish themselves from the brown-clad SA.

On June 17, 1936 Hitler committed the momentous error of naming Himmler Chief of the German Police. He did not however relieve him of his position as "Reichsführer SS." This gave birth to a whole series of mix-ups which make it difficult to understand correctly the history of the Third Reich.

It is understandable that even a well-intentioned historian might confuse the six offices of the Reich Security Office (RSHA), something which still often happens. In the beginning they were all run by Reinhard Heydrich, who was himself under Hitler's command. In reality Offices I through VI all had quite different duties. The first two (I and II) were purely administrative services. Office IV was the "Gestapo" (*Geheime Staatspolizei* or Secret State Police), which, under the direction of Heinrich Müller, normally had to worry about political crimes committed by German citizens and which worked independently of Office V, the "Kri*po*" (*Kriminalpolizei* or Criminal Police), which was responsible for crimes according to civil law. The separation was so clear that if, for example, the *"Kripo"*, while investigating a civil crime, discovered that there were political motives involved the subsequent investigation was conducted by Office IV or vice versa.

Office III (Ohlendorf) and Office VI (Walter Schellenberg) were together a political intelligence service: however domestic (Office III) and foreign (Office VI) worked independently of one another.

The idea of combining all these offices into a "super office" naturally sprang from the desire to centralize the intelligence on which national security depended. But no one would have been capable of leading all six offices together. This task would have exceeded what was humanly possible. In such a large organization, in which the six offices worked side by side, personal initiative had free rein. Forceful personalities such as Nebe or Müller, who could normally turn directly to Himmler, thus achieved a great deal of independence.

Office VI had several departments, which were called "A", "B", "C" and so on. In April 1943 Department "S" (*Schule* or school) was added. I would have come under Schellenberg's command had I not been a member of the Waffen-SS, a *military* unit, to which Schellenberg could not give orders: we will later see the consequences associated with this fact.

Schellenberg's Office VI, the foreign *political* intelligence service, corresponded to – not to say concurred with – Admiral Canaris' military intelligence service. Under Admiral Canaris the Abwehr depended directly upon the OKW and Feldmarschall Keitel. However "Amt VI Ausland" is often confused with "Amt Ausland Abwehr", as in 1944 the *political* and *military* intelligence services were combined and fell under Schellenberg's command.

Prior to 1944 the "*Ausland Abwehr*" (called "Abwehr" for short) had a central Department "Z" (Generalmajor Oster). Department I (military espionage) was run by Oberst Piekenbrock, Oberst Lahousen directed Department II (sabotage and subversion), Department III (counter-intelligence) Oberst von Bentivegni. These two and lahousen later eagerly helped the prosecution at Nuremberg. Lahousen was summoned as a "free witness" (like Paulus), Piekenbrock and Bentivegni did not appear before the court. But General Zorya, the Soviet prosecutor, read incriminating statements by both colonels to the court on February 11, 1946. These statements had been signed in Moscow and bore the dates December 12 and 28, 1945. Both colonels were released by the Russians in 1955.

It is astonishing that the three officers gave themselves up to the Russians. Their Abwehr colleagues and all the heads of similar organizations, for example "Foreign Armies West" and "East", moved their offices and archives to the west and surrendered to the western allies.

● ● ●

Early on the Abwehr possessed a special duties unit. At the end of 1939 it was the 800th Special Duties Battalion, attached to the "Sabotage and Subversion" Department of Abwehr II. It can be confirmed that at this point in time the command and part of the staff of the

800th Battalion were in fact involved in very special duties. In November 1939 its commanding officer, Major Helmuth Groscurth, had the special task of working out the plans for the putsch against the Führer and the German government. There were negotiations between Canaris, Oster, Goerdeler, Groscurth and the unavoidable Gisevius. Halder, Chief-of-Staff of the Army, worked against this and transferred Groscurth to another position.

The 800th Special Duties Regiment then became the Brandenburg Regiment, later Division. I must emphasize that all the soldiers of the Brandenburg Division did their duty bravely and conscientiously. They ignored what Canaris, Oster, Lahousen, Groscurth and others planned over their heads. I will come back to the Brandenburg Division later.

The *Sonderverband z.b.V. Friedenthal* was formed as the result of an order from General der Waffen-SS Hans Jüttner, chief of the Operational Headquarters of the Waffen-SS. Only he had the authority to create and organize units of the Waffen-SS. They were commanded by Waffen-SS officers and in the beginning were allowed to recruit from Waffen-SS volunteers only. But a few months later General Jüttner authorized me to recruit from all four elements of the German Armed Forces, provided that they volunteered.

Like all the units subsequently formed on General Jüttner's order, this one was ready for "special employment," that meant that any chief of an element of the armed forces could call on them for special military operations. We were a unit within the armed forces in which we fought, and we received our orders from the commander of an army or army group. The operational plans were then worked out by my staff or, with my approval, by the general staff of the affected army.

I myself only worked for Schellenberg during Operation "Franz," as this operation was already under way when I took over. From July 1943 I always received my orders directly from the OKW or from Hitler personally.

• • •

In April 1943 I became familiar with the training program, which in my view was inadequate. Preparations were then being made for Operation "Franz." Although I was a beginner, it was immediately clear to me that I needed an entire battalion and first-class material for this and later operations.

I was supposed to "completely reorganize everything" as quickly as possible. That was easier said than done. I spent the nights contemplating my new mission from the most diverse points of view, and by day I sought suitable soldiers and materiel. I would like to mention two of the first officers to come to me, for they were a valuable help to me until the end. Untersturmführer Werner Hunke came to me as a "China specialist." He had in fact been born in that country but had left it at the age of two. He didn't speak any Chinese at all and he knew no more about China than one could find on a map. Of course we named him "Chinese."

Like me, Untersturmführer Karl Radl was Austrian. He became my adjutant. He was, or better is, a sturdy lad with broad shoulders , a daredevil, but one who is never lacking in sagacity: he conducted a paper war with the administrative services (army rations office, weapons office, etc.) with masterful dialectics, interpreted to our advantage, knew how to circumvent prohibitions and make apparently harmless applications which later proved to be of great advantage. Naturally they found our plans interesting, but unfortunately "in view of the state of affairs" they were unable to grant many of our requests.

When I had equipped Friedenthal as best as I possibly could, I made my way to the special school in The Hague. Located in a turn-of-the-century style villa in a park, I found about 25 students under the direction of Standartenführer Knolle of the Security Service (SD), Office VI. Theoretically I was his subordinate, but the SD ranks did not correspond to those of the Waffen-SS. Members of the SD were practically more officials than soldiers. My position could have become difficult had not Knolle declared on his own that he would gladly stay on at his post as my subordinate. He knew his job well: listening in on enemy radio transmitters, transmitting with various types of radio equipment, deciphering and encoding of secret messages and so on. He remained director of the school. Of the twenty-five students a dozen belonged to the Waffen-SS, one came from Iran and was earmarked for Operation "Franz", and the rest were agents for Office VI.

The situation appeared less than ideal to me. The SD agents were paid by Schellenberg's office and received much more than the volunteers of the Waffen-SS, who received only their soldier's pay.

Schellenberg suggested to me that I join the SD at the same rank as Knolle – Standartenführer – "in order to overcome these minor difficulties," as he put it. I rejected the suggestion succinctly: I would rather be a Reserve Hauptsturmführer with the Waffen-SS than a Standartenführer in the SD. He didn't press the issue any farther. I met with General Jüttner again and informed him of my final, positive decision.

Then I went to the school in The Hague, where I issued an order that henceforth all training was to be done separated and as well that different ciphering methods were to be used for the Waffen-SS. Very soon 90 percent of the students at the school were members of the Waffen-SS and only 10 percent civilians of the SD. I didn't concern myself much with them. Personally I wanted only volunteer European soldiers, who if possible were to come from the Waffen-SS. Like me, these volunteers wanted to fight bolshevism and prevent Europe from being taken over by it. They wished to serve their own nations in this way. It is often said today that we made a mistake. That is possible. But if we hadn't fought in 1941-1945 there would be no free Europe today.

We wanted to defend the soil of Europe and Germany – not as "nazis", but as patriots and soldiers.

●　●　●

Adolf Hitler was interested in all sorts of special missions as early as 1941. At the time these were undertaken mainly by the British commandos, which were very well-equipped and organized. In the years 1941-1943 Lord Mountbatten was chief of these "special operations." His successor, General Robert Laycock, was in charge from 1943 to 1947. It was he who wrote the foreword to the book by my friend Charles Foley entitled *Commando Extraordinary*, which was released in London in 1954 and in New York the following year. The American edition received a foreword by General Telford Taylor.

Foley's book illustrated the sort of spirit that existed in my unit in Friedenthal in 1943. He was one of the first authors, a citizen of one of the western allied nations, a former enemy, who took the trouble to seek me out in Madrid and study the documents that I made available to him.

He is completely correct when he says that the success achieved by the Special Air Service (SAS) in Africa under the brave Colonel David Stirling at first alarmed us.

In a three-month period at the end of 1941, Stirling's special commandos destroyed "more German military materiel" in North Africa than any squadron of the Royal Air Force. This yielded his nickname of "the phantom major." During the day he and his commando hid in the desert. They came out at night, struck, sometimes several hundred kilometers behind our lines, and then disappeared again in a secretive way.

In 1956 British television (BBC) filmed a series of ten, one-hour features on "the ten military men who achieved the most sensational feats of the Second World War." The ten people were selected by General Robert Laycock, and I was one of them.[1]

Then Colonel Stirling wrote to me expressing a desire that we should meet, something I also wanted. We met at London airport and talked for several hours. I told him candidly that the British special commandos were in general better than ours. I also said that the British had formed these units significantly earlier and had more means at their disposal.

"From 1941 to 1943 the Chief of Special Operations was Lord Mountbatten, a member of the Royal Family," I said to him, "that was of great importance. Then General Laycock became his successor."

I added that the well-led, better-equipped and trained British commandos had achieved outstanding success in Africa, Europe and Asia. Stirling agreed completely, but observed that the objectives of the operations carried out by my units had been of significantly greater importance politically and militarily. The single major action by the British was against General Rommel's headquarters – and was a failure. (Stirling did not personally take part in this operation.) No one could succeed at everything, I said, and then admitted that I had drawn certain conclusions from the action against the commander of the Africa Corps, which I had studied in detail. I will expand on this at the end of this chapter.

I found that Colonel David Stirling was a man of exemplary sincerity, extraordinarily sympathetic and very intelligent. When one speaks with a former enemy, who experienced the same dangerous situations, one realizes that the Second World War was madness for Europe.

The operations of the US Army Special Forces (OSS) obviously began much later. The American parachute and underwater commandos normally had considerable means at their disposal. In the Pacific theater the raider battalions commanded by Merrit A. Edson of the Marines distinguished themselves through their courage and their daring operations.

• • •

In North Africa we had detachments of the Brandenburg units, which blew up bridges and munitions and supply dumps and sabotaged railroad lines behind the British lines. Many of their acts are unknown. The Brandenburgers' reserve regiment commanded by Major Friedrich-Wilhelm Heinz was likewise stationed not far from Berlin. I eagerly studied its training program.

The Brandenburgers weren't the only ones who distinguished themselves in Africa by their bravery: Major Burckhardt's parachute battalion was their equal in every way. I would like to mention two more outstanding examples: Italian Major Roberto Count Vimercati San Severino and the German Hauptmann Theo Blaich. They succeeded, in two stages, in bombing Fort Lamy with an Heinkel 111. A regular panic broke out in Chad...2,500 kilometers away from our airfields!

One could write a book about the fantastic operations carried out by the detachment led by Count Almaszy of Operation "Condor" in early 1942. He was the descendant of an old Hungarian family, a monarchist conspirator, race driver and explorer. The detachment crossed 3,000 kilometers of desert in captured English vehicles. Its objective was to reach Cairo and set up an intelligence center for General Rommel there. The two Abwehr agents at the designated location were soon exposed by the British. In Cairo they were helped by two lieutenants of the Egyptian Army, then unknown but later revolutionaries, Anwar el Sadat and Abd el Nasser.

What especially struck me were the training methods used by our Russian and British adversaries and the way in which they tackled these missions. Obviously of prime interest to me was the attempt to eliminate or capture Feldmarschall Erwin Rommel carried out in November 1942. This attempt was not conducted as a single commando operation, but was supposed to result in a major victory within a three-part operation.

Following the failure of General Wavell's attack (Operation "Battleaxe") on June 17, 1942, in which several hundred British tanks were destroyed, Rommel intended to begin the offensive against Tobruk in November 1941. The new English commander, Sir Claude Auchinleck, therefore decided to attack *before* Rommel. He sent six divisions (including two armored divisions and a motorized unit) under the command of Sir Allan Cunningham in the direction of Tobruk. This was the so-called Operation "Crusader" which was scheduled for November 18, 1942.

In his memoirs Churchill confirmed that the English forces were superior in all branches of the service. In his book *History of the Second World War*, Liddell Hart shows that the British had more than 710 tanks (including some of the fast, new American Stuart tanks) available, not counting the 500 reserve tanks which were likewise committed. Opposing them were 174 German and 146 Italian "older type" tanks. The English had 690 aircraft against 120 German and 200 Italian. Churchill was therefore able to declare in a speech broadcast by the BBC on November 18, 1941 that "the English desert army is going to write a page in history that can only be compared to Waterloo."

But the reality was different: Rommel ordered a counterattack, perhaps somewhat rashly. In the end he was forced to withdraw, but on December 22, 1941 his forces destroyed 66 English tanks in front of El Hassiat. When Rommel attacked again in 1942 he advanced 400 kilometers.

In London it was decided at the highest level that Rommel and his general staff were to be eliminated the day before the attack (that meant on November 17, 1941). This was intended to supplement the plan for the "Crusader" offensive. It especially struck me that the British included a special commando operation in a conventional attack operation, which could have played a decisive role.

The combined operation against Rommel and his headquarters was carefully worked out by the staff of Admiral Sir Roger Keyes; his son Lieutenant-Colonel Geoffrey Keyes and Colonel Robert Laycock were to take part. About one hundred soldiers underwent special training. Keyes selected 53 men, which were to operate in three groups under Laycock. He would personally guard the return of the detachment, together with a sergeant and two men who made up the first group. The second group, consisting of six men, was supposed to operate outside the headquarters, destroy the mains supply and cut telephone and telegraph lines. The third group was to enter the building. Keyes led this group: his adjutant, Captain Campbell, spoke fluent German and Arabic. The English had sent photos and plans of the main building as well as the surrounding houses and store-rooms to London from Beda Littoria.

A whole series of fantastic reports were published in England, France and the United States: the greater part of Rommel's general staff had been "liquidated... four colonels killed for certain... terrible panic broken out among the Germans" and so on.

From the intelligence reports on file with Foreign Armies West in the OKH, the Brandenburg files and our radio monitoring service, in 1943 I was able to reconstruct most of what really happened. In the meantime Peter Young (in his illustrated book *Commando*, New York, 1969) and Paul Carell (in *Afrika-Korps*) have published details of this action. Young sometimes follows the account from Hillary St. George's *The Green Beret*, which appeared earlier. Carell gives direct eye-witness accounts, for example by Major Poeschel, medical officer Junge and adjutant Lentzen. So it is possible to provide an accurate description of this daring operation.

Young and Carell say nothing about it, however I believe that the detachment lost more than twenty men during the landing at Hamma Beach on the coast of Cyrenaica from the submarines *Torbay* and *Talisman* on the night of November 13-14, 1941. A considerable amount of materiel and explosives must also have been lost. Presumably the part of the headquarters where Rommel was believed to staying was to have been blown up. The operation could not be postponed because Cunningham wanted to attack on November 18. So the plans had to be changed. Only 29 of 53 soldiers reached the beach. To their credit Laycock, Keyes and their comrades tried to carry out the operation in spite of everything.

The group under Cook, which was responsible for the grounds around the headquarters, and the group under Lieutenant-Colonel Keyes and his adjutant Campbell hid in a cave and then later in a cypress forest until 6 P.M. on November 18. They were supplied by an arab robber band armed with Italian rifles, whose leader wore a bright red turban. They were probably spies in the pay of Captain J.E. Haselden, an officer of the British Desert Long Range Group, which likewise landed at the beach at Hamma.

While the detachment cautiously approached its objective during the night of November 17-18, an unusually strong storm broke over Beda Littoria; it rained in torrents. The bad weather, which had been such a disadvantage when they landed, was now favorable for them.

Young related that Campbell succeeded in convincing an Italian soldier and an arab that he and his people were a "German patrol," which is unlikely, for the detachment didn't look the part. They were now standing in front of the headquarters. No one had noticed them in the storm. Cook and his people interrupted the power supply and cut the telephone cable without being spotted. Everything took place in darkness.

From the first moment of the attack everything went wrong: the orderly, whom Sergeant Terry tried to knife, defended himself so energetically that he wasn't even injured.

There was fighting. Keyes and Campbell, who were now also on the scene, depended on Terry and didn't switch on their flashlights and couldn't intervene. The two commandos kicked open the door to the ante-room. The orderly called for help. Adjutant Lentzen appeared in the doorway with his pistol in his hand, fired blindly and shot Keyes in the hip. Keyes quickly threw two hand grenades over the head of Lentzen into the room. Who was in there? Keyes didn't know. The grenades exploded. There was one victim: Feldwebel Kovasic, who was killed on the spot.

At that moment Leutnant Kaufholz appeared above on the second floor steps, spotted Keyes in the flash of the grenade explosions, fired immediately and shot him through the heart. Campbell was knocked down by a burst of machine-gun fire, but in spite of his wounds he fired again and hit his opponent in the ankle.

Outside there was another burst of machine-gun fire. A member of the detachment shot down Leutnant Jauger; the grenades had blown a hole in one wall and shattered its window. Jauger, roused from his sleep, jumped out the window in his pajamas because he assumed that it was an air raid.

In the ante-room Keyes' soldiers saw both their superiors out of action and became convinced that they were under attack from outside. They began to retreat and in doing so killed soldier Boxhammer, who came running to the scene in the darkness.

The action was doomed from the minute Lentzen began firing and Keyes threw his grenades: this alerted all the Germans.

The result on the German side: four dead. Leutnants Kaufholz and Jauger, feldwebel Kosavic and soldier Boxhammer.

On the British side one officer (Keyes) was killed and the other seriously wounded (Campbell). His leg should have been amputated, but a German military doctor, Junge, was able to save it for him. Added to these losses were the twenty men missing after leaving the submarine.

Colonel Laycock gave the members of the detachment the order to hide themselves individually, for the storm prevented any orderly embarkation and the pursuit had already begun. All were taken prisoner. Only Laycock and Terry reached the English lines after, as Churchill wrote, "weeks of desperate adventure."

Members of the detachment were not treated as guerrillas, but as prisoners of war. Colonel Keyes[2] and the four German dead were buried with military honors at the small cemetery in Beda Littoria.

What was General Rommel doing during the attack? Winston Churchill only wrote: "One of the headquarters (General Rommel's) buildings was attacked and a number of Germans killed. But Rommel wasn't there." That is correct. The commanding general of the Africa Corps had left Cyrenaica at the end of August and set up his headquarters at Gambut, between Tobruk and Bardia. All that was in Beda Littoria was the headquarters of the Quartermaster General of the Africa Corps, which was run by Major Poeschel, Hauptmann Waitz and a few officers. How could the English secret service make such a mistake? After all it had a net of well-informed agents in North Africa. The first conclusion I drew from the British failure was as follows: the leader of such an operation must to the extent possible check the information which forms the basis of such an undertaking himself. I therefore made up my mind never to initiate an action of this kind without having the maximum amount of information from the most various sources. I needed "my own small intelligence service." We will soon see how I obtained this.

The second conclusion confirmed an idea that I always had: total surprise is a precondition for the success of the operation. It must last for at least several minutes. This time must be carefully taken into account.

If the Scottish Commando could not eliminate Rommel, the only task left to it was to render the quartermaster's headquarters unusable. But this had to be done absolutely quietly. The firing of weapons and the grenade explosions doomed the action to failure from the start. If this had in fact been an army headquarters, the Scottish Commando wouldn't have been able to flee, for the sentries would have intervened immediately.

Certainly it was not an act of sabotage. However this operation was planned in such a way that it appears doubtful to me that they really had any notion of taking General Rommel prisoner. He would most likely have been killed. Only this explains the method of the attack.

Properly led and with the necessary means, which the English commandos had at their disposal, the operation could have achieved its purpose against the real headquarters of General Rommel. The commander of German forces in Africa would have lost his life or been seriously injured. It would have been more difficult to take him along as a prisoner.

Assuming that the general escaped harm, a few of his staff officers would have been incapacitated in any case. When the enemy offensive began the functioning of the headquarters would have been seriously disrupted and the issuing of orders at least partially interrupted. Even a partial success by the Scottish Commando would have had a negative effect on the morale of our troops; not only in Africa, but on the other theaters and the Eastern Front. This action caused us to think about the defense of German headquarters, which were sometimes so poorly guarded that we had to fear the worst. Our quartermaster would have been well advised to be better prepared: the orderlies, who had to fight for their lives against an enemy trying to knife them, weren't even armed with revolvers.

● ● ●

I implemented strict security measures at Friedenthal. The park was surrounded by a four-meter-high wall, and alarm installations were soon installed. The area was patrolled at night, but the best protection was our trained dogs.

The Wolfsschanze, Führer Headquarters, lay in the midst of a wood near Rastenburg in East Prussia. Generaloberst Jodl described the Wolfsschanze as "a blend of barracks, monastery and concentration camp."

The geographic situation made security measures easier, and a penetration by a special commando was practically impossible. The Wolfsschanze lay within three security zones guarded by barbed wire and fences. The outer ring was five meters high. In order to get inside one had to show his pass and his papers to the officer of the first guard, who checked them closely. This first guard telephoned the sentry at the second barricade, who had to confirm that one was in fact expected and by whom. Then the visitor had to write his name, rank and purpose of his visit in a book. The time of his arrival and departure were noted precisely. In this way Oberst Stauffenberg immediately came under suspicion after his hasty departure on July 20, 1944.

After crossing a railroad track and still in the forest, one came upon the next checkpoint. Only then was one inside the third security zone, a sort of extended park with scattered buildings on whose roofs bushes had been planted. From above all that could be seen was forest, for huge camouflage nets stretched over houses and roads. This was Special Zone Number 1, to which even officers of the OKW had no free access, "apart from General Warlimont," as Generaloberst Jodl declared before the Nuremberg court on June 3, 1946.

Sentries patrolled inside the first two security zones as well as outside the third day and night. Hitler was not guarded by Himmler's police units, as is often written, but by a special army regiment, which was commanded by Oberst Rommel at the beginning of the war.[3] The Führer therefore knew him very well and had full confidence in him.

I am of the view that even if Colonel Laycock's entire Scottish Commando had attacked the headquarters in November 1941, it would have faced a very difficult task in spite of great courage and the best materiel.

Before July 20, 1944 Hitler scarcely concerned himself with his own security. "He endured the security measures," Oberst von Below, his Luftwaffe adjutant, told me, "out of a sense of duty to the German people and his soldiers." I also know that Hitler never wore a bullet-proof vest or a steel helmet, as is sometimes claimed.[4]

But when Generals Schmundt and Korten were fatally injured at his side on July 20, 1944, Hitler ordered strict security measures. For example, after July 20 each officer called to the headquarters had to surrender his pistol to the sentry at the first security zone checkpoint.[5]

I was ordered to the Wolfsschanze nine times and also flew over it; it was so very well camouflaged against air attack that one could only see trees. The guarded access roads snaked through the forest in such a way that I would have been unable to give the exact location of the Führer Headquarters.

Hitler's second residence, the Berghof in Bavaria, was visible from the air. But like the Wolfsschanze, it was guarded by a heavy concentration of anti-aircraft guns. The enemy air force attacked the Berghof twice and in each case sustained losses of about 50 percent.

The assassination attempt of July 20, 1944 was difficult to prevent. Hitler knew Oberst Stauffenberg personally. He had had several discussions with him over the organization of the new "Volksgrenadier" divisions. No one could suspect that there was a bomb in the briefcase under the table around which the discussion was being held.

● ● ●

We have seen why General Rommel was not killed or wounded and not taken prisoner in Beda Littoria.

After studying this action I made up my mind to instruct the soldiers of my special unit to shoot only when it was an absolute necessity.

We were all excellent shots, and with every type of weapon; but we also had the discipline to attack without shooting in order to achieve total surprise.

I found an effective, proven means of preventing my soldiers from firing: namely to go in first and not fire myself. This behavior on my part steeled the nerves of the men behind me and instilled confidence. This contributed greatly to our success in freeing Benito Mussolini and especially in Operation "Panzerfaust." In neither action was there any general bloodletting. The objective of "Panzerfaust" was to take military possession of the Burgberg in Budapest, seat of the government of the Hungarian Reich administrator, Admiral von Horthy.

I led both operations and did not fire a single shot in either. The soldiers who came right behind me were under orders not to shoot until I opened fire. They followed orders and did not fire, to the great astonishment of Colonel Stirling!

Psychologically it is of course easier to fire while attacking. The training of a special unit therefore focused on the massed and concentrated attack on the enemy. I must emphasize that it would have been a psychological mistake on my part to consider the Italians and Hungarians as enemies. Such behavior would not have been in keeping with the purpose of the mission entrusted to me. In reality they were not our enemies, but only our opponents, who for their part had orders to shoot. It is bewildering for the enemy when, surprised by events, he sees an enemy who logically shouldn't be there suddenly appear and come towards him. He doesn't believe his eyes. In this way the moment of surprise is extended, which is necessary for success.

Just one shot fired by the attackers is enough to awaken the self-preservation instinct of those being attacked, and they will automatically fire back. Nothing is more contagious than a shot.! I have seen front-line units during the night suddenly open fire with everything they have, simply because a sentry fired at a shadow.

Don't shoot! The most difficult moment in this is when one comes upon the enemy. For this tactic demands of the men under one's command the strongest nerves and a mutual, unshakable confidence in success.

There are few military theorists with such clear opinions as General Carl von Clausewitz. In his book *Vom Kriege* (Vol.1, Chapter 1) he wrote that, "the disarming of the enemy is the actual objective of a martial action." Afterward he investigated under what conditions such an objective can be achieved. But I believe that he, as well as Colonel Stirling, would have a hard time imagining that one could also disarm the enemy by making use of the moment of surprise and without shooting!

Notes

1. Otto Skorzeny was the only German to appear in this series of programs. When journalist Laycock was asked why he had selected a German officer for the series, and in particular Otto Skorzeny, the general simply said, "Courage does not recognize borders." (Editors' note)

2. Lieutenant-Colonel Geoffrey Keyes was awarded the Victoria Cross after his death. (Editors' note)

3. The outer guard was the responsibility of the Wehrmacht, but within Security Zone III, the Führer Escort Detachment, a formation of specially-picked SS men, was solely responsible for security. (Editors' note)

4. A claim to the contrary is contained in the memoirs of Rudolf Freiherr von Gersdorff. (Editors' note)

5. After the freeing of the Duce the formalities of passage through the first two security zones was simplified for Skorzeny. The officer of the watch never asked him whether he was armed. (Editors' note)

12

WHY HITLER DIDN'T BUILD THE ATOMIC BOMB THE REVENGE WEAPONS

The Lindemann Plan (March 30, 1942): 52 German cities with over 100,000 inhabitants must be totally destroyed – Reichsmarschall Göring is wrong – The German scientists' lead in atomic physics – Fantastic rumors about secret and ultimate weapons – Actions against the heavy water plant in Norway – Hitler, ill and confined to bed, sees me immediately: "The use of radioactive weapons would mean the end of civilized man." – Physicist Philipp Lenard's theory – The atomic bomb is designed "by mail" – "Tanum" and Speer – Operation Reichenberg: I want to build a manned V 1 – Plans and prototypes by Heinkel – Field Marshall Milch is skeptical – Failures – Hanna Reitsch explains the reasons to me – She succeeds in flying the V 1: "A very nice aircraft!" – The V 2 rocket – Hitler appoints Wernher von Braun to professor – Hitler's prophecies – Rockets and jet fighters derived from the V 2 – Operation Paperclip: the victors plunder and take our resources – The views of Winston Churchill and General Eisenhower

A soldier who is fighting for his country and who realizes that Europe is in deadly danger, obviously wants to win.

When, in early 1943, I studied the situation maps of all the theaters in Friedenthal, I saw that the eastern Front was holding. I knew from experience how dangerous the Russian Army was, with its masses of men, its courage and the fantastic quantities of materiel it was receiving from the USA, England and Canada.

In North Africa General Rommel's advance was stopped by the enemy in July 1942, about 100 kilometers from Alexandria. On November 8, 1942 the Americans landed at Casablanca, Algiers and

Oran, and the troops of the axis powers, all of whom had to fight on two fronts, succumbed to the law of superior numbers.

Germany's cities were the special targets of the British and American bombers. Since May 1942 thousands of aircraft had brought ruin and death to Cologne, Essen, Duisburg, Hamburg, Mannheim, Dortmund and many other cities. It was not just our factories that were attacked: each time the "carpets of bombs" killed tens of thousands of women and children. In July 1943 Hamburg burned like a torch. About 9,000 tons of high-explosive and incendiary bombs were dropped. What they hoped to achieve by this was, "an uprising by the German people against its government," forcing Germany to surrender through a type of internal revolution. In any case this was the view which F. Lindemann, RAF Bomber Command's psychological advisor, put forward in a report to Winston Churchill on March 30, 1942: 52 German cities with over 100,000 inhabitants should be razed to the ground.

Reichsmarschall Göring made the same psychological mistake when he ordered the "Blitz" on London in 1940. The total number of casualties inflicted by Luftwaffe bombing and by the V1 and V 2 is known: 60,227 dead and 80,900 injured. It is impossible, however, to give the number of victims of the Anglo-American attacks. The bombing of Hamburg alone resulted in 53,000 killed and 160,000 injured. The number of people who lost their lives in the bombing of Dresden is officially estimated at 250,000 to 300,000, from a population of 630,000. Eighteen square kilometers of the city stood in flames. When this tremendous funeral pyre, with flames eight to ten meters high, was finally extinguished, it was only possible to identify 40,000 bodies, from their wedding rings. At the end of February 1945 there were 420,000 refugees from the east in Dresden, mainly women and children.

I believe that Reichsmarschall Göring bears a great deal of responsibility for the course which the air war took. He considered the war won in 1940. On the basis of his illusions the jet aircraft were delayed at least one to two years, for our specialists were already working on turbojet engines in 1939. When our jet aircraft appeared in the sky they came as an unpleasant surprise to the enemy.

I met the Reichsmarschall personally, as chief of the Luftwaffe in his headquarters and as a brave soldier on the battlefield at Schwedt on the Oder. In Nuremberg prison I was assigned a cell opposite his, before they placed the accused and the witnesses in different parts of the building. I do not wish to speak badly of the dead. But one thing must be said: the Reichsmarschall bears a great burden of guilt toward the people of Germany and Europe.

Future historians will probably find it astonishing that Germany did not build the atom bomb, although theoretically and practically it possessed the means since 1938. At the end of that year Professor Otto Hahn and Professor Strassman produced the chemical proof of nuclear fission. Professor Hahn received the 1945 Nobel Prize for chemistry. He worked at the Kaiser Wilhelm Institute in Berlin and Dahlem with Professor Werner Heisenberg and a number of other first-class researchers. But Professor Heisenberg's assistant was Carl Friedrich von Weizsäcker, son of diplomat Ernst von Weizsäcker, one of the conspirators against Hitler.

Professor Frisch, who had worked in Germany and who emigrated to England early on, was the first (in January 1939) to produce the physical proof of nuclear fission. His aunt, Madame Professor Lise Meitner, one of Otto Hahn's associates, lived the entire war as a refugee in Stockholm, but remained in touch with Berlin.

Another institute in Germany also conducted early research into the atom. The institute, which I believe was located in Hamburg, was under the direction of an outstanding young physicist, Manfred von Ardenne, who worked in Russia and East Germany after the war. Goebbels took a great interest in this work. After the war many German physicists stated that they had done their best to prevent the construction of a German atomic bomb. One could think highly of their morals if this corresponded to the complete truth.

From 1939 Hitler was interested in the unbelievable potential of nuclear fission. In autumn 1940 he had a long discussion on the subject with Dr. Todt, the armaments minister. His opinion never changed: he thought that the use of atomic energy for military purposes would mean the end of humanity.

We also know today that Hitler read not only the paper that Professor Heisenberg wrote at the Kaiser Wilhelm Institute in 1942 (on *Nuclear Fission and the Construction of the Atomic Pile with Uranium and the Electron Gun [Betatron]*), but also other reports on research conducted prior to 1941. Albert Speer wrote that Hitler, "was not delighted by the prospect of seeing our planet transformed into a flame-ravaged celestial body during his period in government." He wrote this, as he said, based on a few conversations he had with Hitler "about the possibility of making an atomic bomb." That meant that for Adolf Hitler this question was no longer an issue. As well I might describe a personal experience.

In October 1944, after the Budapest operation, I flew once again to Führer Headquarters in East Prussia. Preparations were just being made for the Ardennes offensive and Hitler want to give me his instructions for Operation Greif.

At Führer Headquarters they told me that Hitler was sick in bed but that he wished to speak with me at once. I am certainly one of the few visitors, if not the only one, whom the Führer received in bed. I found him very changed, emaciated, but as always mentally alert. He asked me to forgive him for receiving me in this way, told me to sit down and explained briefly the strategic and tactical objectives of the Ardennes offensive and his thoughts on Operation Greif, which I was to carry out. Before me was a man in bed who needed no pomp and ceremony to underline his personality. While speaking in his calm, rather hoarse, but moderate voice he exuded a persuasive power which is rarely found. He assured me that the German Army would triumph in the end in spite of treason and mistakes. This offensive would be successful. Apart from that, "new, truly revolutionary weapons would take the enemy completely by surprise."

There was much talk about German "secret weapons" at this time, and Dr. Goebbels' propaganda did its best to nourish these rumors. One heard the strangest things about the construction and existence of these fantastic and deadly weapons.

One of these secret weapons was an anti-aircraft shell which exploded in the midst of an enemy formation and which was supposed to create the absolute zero point within a considerable area, that meant a temperature of -273 degrees Celsius, with the appropriate destructive consequences for the aircraft. However most talk was about another, terrible weapon that was supposed to be based on artificially-produced radioactivity.

Without being an atomic physicist, I knew that it was possible to make an explosive device using the fission energy of uranium. The English sabotage mission against the heavy water factory in Norway at the beginning of 1943 drew my attention, as did the bombing raid which followed the next autumn, which damaged the plant heavily.

Furthermore they sank our cargo ship which was transporting heavy water.

I put it together myself: Norway, Dr. Goebbels' speeches and articles, and what the Führer had just said. Spontaneously I began speaking of the rumors about artificial radioactivity and its eventual use as a weapon. Hitler looked at me with gleaming, feverish eyes:

"Do you know, Skorzeny, if the energy and radioactivity released through nuclear fission were used as a weapon, that would mean the end of our planet?"

"The effects would be frightful..."

"Naturally! Even if the radioactivity were controlled and then nuclear fission used as a weapon, the effects would still be horrible! When Dr. Todt was with me, I read that such a device with controlled radioactivity would release energy that would leave behind devastation which could only be compared with the meteors that fell in Arizona and near Lake Baykal in Siberia. That means that every form of life, not only human, but animal and plant life as well, would be totally extinguished for hundreds of years within a radius of forty kilometers. That would be the apocalypse. And how could one keep such a secret? Impossible! No! No country, no group of civilized men can consciously accept such a responsibility. From strike to counterstrike humanity would inevitably exterminate itself. Only tribes in the Amazon district and in the jungles of Sumatra would have a certain chance of surviving."

These marginal notes by Hitler lasted scarcely more than a few minutes, but I remember those minutes precisely. At the beginning of my time as a prisoner of war, in August 1945, I heard that two atomic bombs were dropped on Hiroshima and Nagasaki. Unnecessary bombs, by the way, for the Japanese emperor had already asked the Americans for their peace terms.

While a prisoner American officers constantly asked me the same question, "How did you bring Hitler out of Berlin at the end of April 1945 and where have you hidden him?"

I can still see the consternated expressions of the American officer before me, when, disgusted with the question, I answered: "Adolf

Hitler is dead, but he was right when he said that you and I would be the survivors of the Amazon."

• • •

In an interesting book *Britain and Atomic Energy* (1964), the official chronicle of the "organization of atomic research" from 1939 to 1945 in England, Margret Gowing stated that among the pioneers of the atomic bombs dropped on Hiroshima and Nagasaki were German refugees: among them Peierls, Frisch, Roblat and so on, as well as Klaus Fuchs, who was later convicted for betraying atomic secrets to the USSR. Mrs. Gowing also writes that in 1941 atomic specialists working in England "methodically studied what the best-known German scientists were engaged in." The intelligence service supported them in these activities. This work, they say, was "exploited in an advantageous way, as many of the scientists working in England had previously fled Germany."

And the great American specialists, Oppenheimer and Szilard: they were trained at the University of Göttingen.

In July 1945 Winston Churchill himself had the task of telling Stalin that an atomic bomb would be dropped on Hiroshima. Churchill stressed in his memoirs that the Soviet dictator greeted this news with indifference, and added: "He naturally had no idea of what we had just revealed to him." But thanks to the efforts of Klaus Fuchs Stalin knew just as much, if not more, than Churchill did about the atomic bomb.

Hitler's stance on this question was, I believe, determined primarily by a type of instinct, a revolt against the human nature that wants to destroy itself.

Hitler, who had been gassed during the First World War, always banned chemical warfare. Our chemists had discovered a new gas, against which, as we know today, there was no defense: the nerve gas "Tanum."

• • •

The V-1 and V-2 revenge weapons appeared more credible to us. The V-1, or "flying bomb," whose official designation was Fi 103 for

Fieseler 103, was a type of unmanned rocket aircraft. Speed: 640 kph; range: about 500 kilometers; weight: 2,500 kilograms, of which 1 ton was the explosive charge in the nose of the missile. On departure the machine's flight path was controlled by automatic gyroscope (direction and height). At the desired range the motor was switched off and the bomb fell to earth. But a wind could force the bomb from its direction of flight, and nothing could be done about it. However in 1944 its advantages were that it was cheap to manufacture and used little fuel. It also promised an incontestable psychological effect.

The V-1 was devised and designed by the Luftwaffe, in particular by the DFS (German Institute for Gliding Flight) and the Fieseler company. Tests were carried out at Peenemünde, as this base on the Baltic was suitably equipped for the job. The missile, which was mass-produced by Volkswagen, was fired from a simple launching ramp, usually three V-1s at once.

One day I had the opportunity to visit Peenemünde and witness the launching of one such V-1. I flew with an engineer colonel of the Luftwaffe, who was a specialist in these flying bombs, and on the return flight I discussed with him the question: would it not be possible, to have the V-1 flown by a pilot?

The very evening of that summer day in 1944 we set to work together with Focke-Wulf and Reich Air Ministry engineers. I had invited them to a villa on the Wannsee. A dozen engineers began drawing plans – on the billiards table and even lying on the floor: we had to find sufficient room in the V-1 to accommodate a pilot with ejection seat and parachute.

We worked the whole night and by morning we had the solution. All we had to do was build a prototype. Feldmarschall Milch, State Secretary in the RLM, gave me "clear road," provided that an RLM commission raised no objections. The chairman of the commission was a venerable admiral with a white seaman's goatee, who we were told had been around since Noah's ark. After two or three sittings we had cleared the first hurdle, but then the commission raised an objection: "Where do you intend to get the workers, foremen and engineers to build this prototype? We don't have enough labor forces as it is, especially in the aviation industry."

I replied that near Friedenthal there was an Heinkel factory that was not operating at full capacity and that Professor Heinkel had personally offered me three engineers and five mechanics and as well had placed three empty work barracks at my disposal.

"Good," said Noah, "but you can only carry out your work with already built V-1s, and you must know that we have none."

"That is not what Professor Porsche, a friend of mine, said to me. To his own astonishment there are several hundred V-1s in his VW factories waiting to be picked up. I can assure you that he would gladly let me have a dozen!"

Just no complications thought "Noah," and so in a short time I had two small workshops at Heinkel's. I had tables and beds moved in. Everyone, engineers, foremen and workers, worked at full speed, sometimes more than fourteen hours a day, in order to bring our so-called Operation Reichenberg to fruition as quickly as possible.

When I saw Feldmarschall Milch again, he smiled.

"Well then, Skorzeny, satisfied hopefully?"

"Naturally," I answered him, "in spite of the two to three week delay."

"Three weeks in such a project, that's nothing. A manned V-1! If you can roll out your prototype in four to five months I'll congratulate you again!"

"Herr Feldmarschall, I hope that I can show you the prototype in four to five weeks!"

He looked at me seriously and thought that I was making a joke. Then he shook his head.

"You're deluding yourself, my dear fellow. That's all well and good. But don't make too much of it. We'll talk about this machine again in four to five months. Until then, lots of luck!"

Our workshop at Heinkels was actually a craftsman operation, but one that worked with success. When I could I spent several hours each day in "my factory." After fourteen days I again contacted Feldmarschall Milch and informed him that we had both been wrong: I had three V-1s ready to fly.

Feldmarschall Milch was amazed. He gave me authorization to undertake three takeoff attempts at Gatow airfield. Two test pilots were chosen. The manned V-1 was not launched from a ramp, instead it was towed by a Heinkel 111 to a height of 2,000 meters and then released. Both machines made crash-landings, however, both pilots escaped with injuries.

A downright dour Feldmarschall Milch told me that a commission would be appointed to investigate the causes of the bad landings.

For the time being I was forbidden to make any further attempts. I was speechless. Had we worked too carelessly and too quickly?

Then Hanna Reitsch, our legendary female test pilot, called me. Since her serious crash in 1941 in a prototype jet fighter, from which she had recovered through strength of will alone, she had been living in the Luftwaffe House in Berlin. She told me that she had had the same idea as I several months earlier: the V-1 could be flown as a manned aircraft! But she had received the official order to drop the idea. There was no need to wait for the results of the investigation to learn the causes of our two accidents: both pilots had previously flown only propeller-driven aircraft. Our prototype, which was much lighter than a standard V-1, reached a speed of 700 kph and a landing speed of 180 kph, and this made both pilots more than uncertain when it came time to land. Hanna and two of her associates who had likewise flown jet aircraft, declared themselves ready to repeat the attempt.

I declined firmly and reminded them of the official, strict order and that they wouldn't make an He 111 available to us at Gatow airfield. Hanna Reitsch shrugged her shoulders and said, "I took you for a man who is willing to take a chance! One can always fly if only one wants to! My friends and I have visited your workshop and examined your first V-1s. I am sure that we're not fooling ourselves: they're outstanding aircraft! We will talk more about it later. Until tomorrow!"

I must admit that I couldn't close my eyes that night. A third accident would be unimaginable! Did I have the right to plunge this wonderful aviatrix into such an adventure? The next day Hanna Reitsch and her two companions were so convincing that I took it upon myself to dupe the airfield commander. I acted completely natural and told him that I had just received approval to continue Operation Reichenberg. I asked him his opinion on several questions and assigned two of my officers not to let him out of their sight, to accompany him into the mess and to take care that he didn't telephone Feldmarschall Milch's staff. When I saw the V-1 flown by Hanna Reitsch separate from the He 111 my heart pounded as never before.

She had taken full responsibility onto herself without hesitation. She knew that her airspeed on landing would be about 180 kph. I was firmly convinced, however, that she would pull it off. And she did! She landed smoothly and then repeated the flight. I congratulated her with all my heart. "That is a wonderful aircraft!" she said to me. "We'll be able to do something with it!"

The other two test pilots also flew the V-1 and landed without any difficulty. The manned V-1 was not destined to be a success however.

When the flights by Hanna and her two companions became known, we received permission to build five more prototypes with which about 30 selected pilots could be trained. We accepted sixty (from several hundred) volunteer pilots of the Luftwaffe in Friedenthal; especially daring missions would now be possible! Unfortunately only part of the 500 cubic meters of aviation fuel I requested at the beginning of summer 1944 was delivered, and we could only train the first dozen pilots. The V-1 pilots remained in my unit until the end. Most distinguished themselves through their coolness and courage.

● ● ●

The V-2 was not an aircraft but a rocket, whose dimensions in its ultimate form were 14.03 meters in length, a lower diameter of 3.564 meters and an upper diameter of 1.561 meters. Takeoff weight with 70% fuel (methyl alcohol and liquid oxygen) was 12.5 metric tons. Range was approximately 800 kilometers. Speed: 5,300 kph. Payload: one ton of explosives.

The inventor of the V-2 was a thirty-year-old engineer and the leader of a very dynamic group: Wernher von Braun. After the war he was "exported" to the USA and later became an American citizen. His name is known the world over.

Wernher von Braun worked in the army research center at Peenemünde, which was under the directorship of Walter Dornberger. The latter was an outstanding officer and as they said, "a great fellow." The first successful test of the V-2 took place on October 3, 1942 (without warhead of course), and the rocket reached its target 190 kilometers away, passing through the atmosphere at an altitude of 80 kilometers. Hitler took a personal interest in the tests at Peenemünde. He promoted Dornberger to general and had the younger engineer named professor. In early 1943 he ordered both men to Führer Headquarters. For better or worse, Speer had to admit what everyone knows today; the Führer recognized the revolutionary significance of the V-2 and after a conversation with Wernher von Braun declared, "This young scholar has produced a rocket that upsets all known ballistic laws. I am convinced that this young scientist is right when he says that in his opinion more powerful rockets would be capable of exploring the space surrounding the earth and perhaps even several planets in our solar system. We will have von Braun to thank for the uncovering of many great secrets."

I met Professor von Braun personally during the war and later exchanged letters with him. He was already a rocket specialist as a quite young engineer and from 1933 to 1936 he worked at the test center at Kummersdorf. He was already dreaming of space flight and trips to the moon.

Peenemünde is located on the island of Usedom, at the mouth of the Oder on the Baltic Sea, at the present border between East Germany and Poland. Several weeks after Hitler received von Braun the island was bombed by night and the installation almost totally destroyed; there were 800 killed. The center's research group was split up; production was decentralized. A wind tunnel was built in Kochel in Bavaria in which air reached speeds of more than 4,800 kph. This speed was far superior to anything achieved by the enemy in similar wind tunnels.

The V-1 and V-2 were manufactured according to the principle of decentralized factories, with final assembly by German workers.

Wernher von Braun and his young co-workers had great plans and were, so to speak, "far-seeing." Very far even. At the beginning of 1944 von Braun made statements which might have come from the fantastic novels in the style of Jules Verne or what one today calls science fiction – but it was no more than anticipation of what he later realized. It is known that his idea of a multi-stage rocket – derived from the V-2 – made it possible to launch satellites and reach and explore the moon. The history of aerospace owes him a great deal.

Professor von Braun's statements appeared in a German paper and were accompanied by drawings which gave an idea of the rocket's design. The article was immediately picked up by the neutral press.

Himmler had von Braun arrested and questioned. A week later Hitler ended this paradoxical situation.

Included in the V-weapons program was the construction of a rocket capable of bombarding New York or Moscow. This rocket was practically finished at the end of March 1945 and could have gone into series production beginning in July.

But the Russians came. General Dornberger, Wernher von Braun, his brother Magnus, Oberst Axter and engineers Lindenberg, Tassmann and Huzel, who were able to save some of their documents, fled to Bavaria and there surrendered to the American 44th Division. Soon afterward they signed a contract to work for the U.S. Army and in September they travelled to the USA.

On the far side of the Atlantic the Americans assembled 127 significant German specialists. They were heavily guarded, for the Americans feared that they might otherwise be abducted by the Russians. Professor Wernher von Braun became head of the Army Ballistic Missile Agency and deputy chief of the National Aeronautics and Space Administration (NASA) and thus leader of the Apollo Project, which on July 21, 1969 placed the first men on the moon (Armstrong and Aldrin).

● ● ●

I could go on and list a whole series of other new weapons which were designed and built by us during the war. There was the Natter or Bachem 8-348-A-1, which was to be guided remotely from the ground onto enemy fighter-bombers and which had a pilot on board. It was armed with 24 air-to-air rockets which were to be fired in two salvoes. The machine, which was armed with a full load of rockets, crashed on its first test flight. The aircraft's pilot, Oberleutnant Lothar Sieber, lost his life in the crash. The device was a combination of elements of the V-1 and V-2, and Sieber thus became the first pilot in the world to be catapulted vertically into the air by a rocket, which is the case today with the American and Russian astronauts.

The anti-aircraft rockets developed from the V-2 were numerous: the *Wasserfall* or C-2, a remotely-guided surface-to-air missile with a homing head was a small version of the V-2 with stub wings. It was launched vertically. The missile automatically flew in the direction of the hottest part of its target. Its speed of 2,900 kph was exceeded by the *Taifun* rocket, which reached 4,500 kph and was intended to be used as an anti-aircraft barrage rocket. One can also mention the *Rheintochter*, a two-stage rocket, the *Feuerlilie* or F-55, the *Enzian* with two jet engines, short and squat, and so on.

Its is known, or perhaps it is not known, that the first German jet aircraft, the He 178, flew at the end of August 1939. Professor Heinkel had been working on the project for three years. The Messerschmitt 262, a jet fighter armed with four 30mm cannon, reached a speed of 950 kph. The Arado 234 bomber flew at 900 kph, reached a height of 11,000 meters and had a radius of action of 1,600 kilometers.

In April 1945 the designers of the Henschel 0-122 bomber blew up the prototype, which was equipped with a turbo-reactor (1,000 kph, radius of action more than 2,000 kilometers). British experts confiscated the plans and the wreckage of the device and were more than astonished that such a German aircraft existed at all.

We will see that the new weapons, which were used or supposed to be used above or below water, compared to the weapons employed in the air, were superior to the technical inventions of the western allies and were no less revolutionary in concept.

I would like to draw the reader's attention to a fact that is perhaps not very well known: the most successful combined operation against Germany from east and west took place after our armies had already surrendered unconditionally.

The purpose of this operation was to seize all German patents and inventions. Characteristically this operation was called Paperclip.

An official plundering of the design bureaus and secret archives of the German factories took place at the same time as all the factories not destroyed by bombs were being dismantled. The Americans today freely admit that the benefits accrued from this operation more than covered the costs of the war.

Eisenhower stated after the war:

"If the Germans had had the new V-1 and V-2 weapons six months earlier, the invasion in Normandy in June 1944 wouldn't have been possible."

13

FROM THE BEST U-BOATS
TO THE NEW "SYNTHETIC MATERIALS"

Grossadmiral Raeder, a traditional commander-in-chief – The revolutionary ideas of Grossadmiral Dönitz, the "Manstein and Guderian of the sea" – Hitler names him chief-of-staff – His government neither surrendered nor gave up its office: it was only a military surrender – The one-man torpedo and the remote-control explosive boat – Successes and failures with conventional torpedoes – Prien's heroic act – Memories of the bay of Scapa Flow – The French fleet is sunk in Toulon – The role Canaris played – Three torpedoes against HMS Nelson: they fail to explode and Churchill was on board! – Acoustic and heat-seeking torpedoes – The "mini" U-boats – The snorkel and the Walter Type XXI "wonder" submarine – New sea-to-air guided weapons – "Fritz" sinks the battleship Roma – Churchill acknowledges the merit of the German U-boats – The Battle of the Atlantic.

The following sentences (whose significance did not escape Grossadmiral Dönitz) appeared in the manual of training for U.S. Air Force pilots engaged in anti-submarine duties at the end of 1943:

"If a U-boat sinks a 6,000-ton freighter and a 3,000-ton tanker, we lose, for example: 42 tanks, eight 152mm howitzers, eighty-eight 87.6mm guns, forty 40mm anti-tank guns, 24 armored vehicles, 50 heavy Bren machine-guns on self-propelled carriages, 52,100 tons of ammunition, 6,000 rifles, 428 tons of tank replacement parts, 2,000 tons of provisions and 1,000 barrels of gasoline."

In contrast to Grossadmiral Raeder, who in 1942 still believed in the supremacy of the battle cruiser, Dönitz, who was still a Fregettenkapitän in 1935, was convinced that the submarine was the more effective weapon.

Dönitz had studied the latest ideas put forward by all the international experts and had come up with attack plans employing packs of U-boats – against enemy ships and convoys, which were to be located and monitored by the air force. In vain he tried to convince Raeder of the correctness of his revolutionary concept. When he was named commander of U-boats in 1936 his desires had to become more modest. The grand admiral then told him that relations between England and the German Reich were very good and that Hitler considered a war between the two countries "out of the question." The result was that when England declared war on us in September 1939, Dönitz had only 26 of 55 operational submarines available for action. Nevertheless in September 1940 the U-29 (Leutnant von Schubart) sank the aircraft carrier *Courageous*. In October 1939 the U-47, commanded by Kapitänleutnant Prien, sailed right into Scapa Flow and sank the battleship *Royal Oak* of 29,000 tons. I will return to this extraordinary act of heroism.

Grossadmiral Raeder was a chief with too much tradition, who had served in the Imperial Fleet in 1894: Dönitz was three years old at that time. It was a serious disadvantage for Germany that Raeder failed to comprehend in 1939 that the U-boat was the most effective weapon against England. Manstein and Guderian could present their plans for the employment of the panzer arm openly to Hitler, who accepted them. Dönitz did not have the same opportunity in 1936-1940 to draw Hitler's attention to the submarine and the tactic of packs of U-boats.

The prospect of having to wage war against England was contrary to Hitler's wishes. However after Hess' daring flight he had to resign himself to the idea. The U-boat thus became a strategic weapon of the greatest significance.

In 1942, during the first phase of the Battle of the Atlantic, Dönitz should have had about 250 U-boats. He commanded 91, of which 23 were in the Mediterranean, 13 were involved in special missions, 33 were undergoing repairs and 10 were en route to their combat zones. No more than 12 U-boats actually engaged enemy ships at any one time: Dönitz's tactics would have required about 50.

When, at the end of 1942, an astonished Hitler criticized the fact that our large warships were not committed against PQ-18, a large, well-escorted Anglo-American supply convoy, he demanded explanations. Liddell Hart wrote: "Informed by radio reports, Raeder held back his largest ships out of excessive caution. These should have attempted to destroy the convoy." Afterward Hitler declared that if the battleships were of no use it would be better to scrap them. Raeder asked to be dismissed. It was accepted and Dönitz took his place. But it was already too late: January 30, 1943.

Dönitz never had enough U-boats to implement his U-boat pack tactics as he had wished. In his book *Zehn Jahre und zwanzig Tage* he also complained bitterly about the lack of cooperation between Göring's Luftwaffe and the Kriegsmarine.

Grossadmiral Dönitz was as good a strategist as he was a tactician. One could say that he was the "Manstein and Guderian of the sea."

Millions of German soldiers and civilians escaped capture by the Russians at the beginning of May 1945 thanks to his outstanding leadership. He saved their lives, or at least of a large percentage of them.

As Commander-in-Chief of the Navy, Dönitz represented the honor of the German Armed Force before the international tribunal at Nuremberg, and he succeeded in rescuing it, at least in the eyes of the western accusers. The victors accused him of deliberately killing enemy seamen, the crews of torpedoed ships. But Dr. Otto Kranzbühler, his defense attorney, was able to prove that the German Navy had acted according to international law. The written testimony by the Commander-in-Chief of the American fleet, Admiral Chester W. Nimitz, in this regard was decisive. On April 30, 1945 Hitler named Dönitz as his successor as head of the German state, which was in the middle of collapse. However Dönitz did not shirk this most difficult task, neither for himself nor for his government. On May 8 he was forced to offer the surrender of the Wehrmacht. The victors demanded that he "empower representatives of the three branches of the service to sign the document of surrender." He gave the authority. An inter-state surrender never was signed, however, and the new German government did not resign. A little later the members of the government were arrested under degrading circumstances.

Dönitz remained head of state after May 8 and was recognized as such by the allies for two weeks. That means that the German state continued to exist as before after May 8. Dönitz represented the legal national unity of Germany and everything that affected this, and so he signed no kind of declaration renouncing authority neither in his name or in the name of his government. On May 2, 1945 he formed a new government as president of the German Reich. He never resigned his office. There is a document, drawn up by Volkerrechtler, that confirms these facts. When he was arrested on May 23, 1945, he merely yielded to force. Dönitz was sentenced to 10 years in prison by the Nuremberg court.

● ● ●

In reality, what Goebbels called "the fortress of Europe" faced deadly threats in the west, south and east from the beginning of 1943. At sea Grossadmiral Dönitz had to defend himself against two of the mightiest fleets in the world.

In an effort to partly make up for the superiority of the enemy new weapons were invented and put to use, sometimes successfully, with volunteers from the navy and soldiers of my special units. I thus had the pleasure of meeting and working with Admiral Heye, chief of the "Special Attack Units of the Kriegsmarine." He was a seaman in the best sense of the word and a first-class tactician.

At the beginning of 1943 Grossadmiral Dönitz was faced with the fact that on the sea front we had practically nothing in the way of "miracle weapons." I saw manned torpedoes of three different types developed: Neger, Molch and Marder.

Neger was a double torpedo. Beneath the manned torpedo was an unmanned one loaded with 600-700 kilograms of explosives. The pilot in the upper torpedo approached as near as possible to his target and released the lower torpedo. He then turned and with "God's help" escaped. The Molch and the Marder were proper miniature U-boats manned by one or two sailors and armed with two torpedoes. I must emphasize that such "trip to heaven operations" were always carried out by volunteers.

The "explosive boat" was a high-speed motorboat about 3.5 meters long with a top speed of nearly 60 kph – which at the time was quite extraordinary. 500 kilograms of explosives were built into the bow. They were used in "troika" form, which meant that three boats took part in the attack and each had its own helmsman. Two boats loaded with explosives were preceded by a third, in which sat the attack commander. Scarcely visible on the surface of the water, the trio moved into attack position. At the proper distance the commander gave the signal to attack and the three motorboats raced toward their target. Less than a kilometer from the target the pilots of the two explosives boats were ejected from the boats with their seats. The attack commander then guided the boats to their target by remote control and, if possible, picked up the two pilots who had ejected.

The boats were supposed to strike their target amidships. They did not explode immediately however; the explosives separated and sank 6 or 7 meters beneath the water, below the water line. Only then did they explode, where it was significantly more effective. All the water was displaced from beneath the center of the ship and a vacuum was created. This vacuum caused the ship to break in two in the middle, as only the bow and stern were still supported by the water.

The first force to employ these "special attack units" with astounding success was the Italian X-MAS Flotilla, commanded by the well-known Lieutenant-Commander Prince Valerio Borghese. The X-MAS Flotilla attacked enemy ships even in the ports of Alexandria and Gibraltar and inflicted considerable losses on the British fleet.

At the beginning of the war our torpedoes were detonated by the magnetic field of the target. Detonation and the directional and depth control of the torpedoes were imprecise. During the night of October 13-14, 1939 Prien was able to enter Scapa Flow under the northern lights. It is not generally known that his U-47 first fired four torpedoes, three of which missed the target on account of faulty construction. Displaying great coolness, Prien ordered the tubes reloaded and fired another spread of three torpedoes, which exploded on reaching the target. The *Royal Oak* broke apart, rolled over to port and sank in several minutes.

In order to understand the symbolic meaning that Prien's act had in our eyes, we must recall June 21, 1919.

After the cease-fire of November 1918 the German High Seas Fleet was restricted to this very bay of Scapa Flow. It did not consider itself defeated. At the Battle of Skagerrak – or of Jutland – its 21 ships faced 38 British warships: the enemy's losses were 115,000 tons and ours were 61,000 tons. On July 20, 1919, Admiral von Reuter, who commanded the interned ships, received the news that the German High Seas Fleet had to be handed over to the English fully intact or else the war against Germany would be resumed.

With the agreement of the officers and men, von Reuter gave the order that our 21 battleships and battle-cruisers and 10 torpedo-boat flotillas should scuttle themselves. I was then 11 years old and the self-destruction of these proud, beautiful ships made a very deep impression on me. I knew that the S.M.S. *Friedrich der Grosse*, which flew Admiral Scheer's flag in the Battle of Skagerrak, was the first to go down.

Later I understood how Admiral de Laborde must have felt when, on November 26, 1942, he gave the order for the interned French fleet to scuttle itself in Toulon harbor. The policy of European cooperation, loudly heralded by German diplomacy, literally fell into the water – very deep in fact. How could one assume that a sailor – be it Admiral von Reuter or Admiral de Laborde – would hand over his vessels? The French Admiral Gensoul refused to hand over his battleships to the English at Mers-el-Kébir in July 1940. And why should de Laborde, who was not permitted to weigh anchor at Toulon, allow the Germans and Italians to take over his ships? Perhaps one day we will learn what role the Italian intelligence service, in cooperation with Canaris and his Abwehr, played in this matter.

• • •

The German intelligence service failed completely in regard to Operation "Torch", the Anglo-American landing in North Africa. Dönitz confirmed this in his book Zehn Jahre und 20 Tage. He added, "The German intelligence and counter-intelligence apparatus under Admiral Canaris failed completely in this case, just as it failed to provide the German U-boat command with *a single useful* piece of intelligence about the enemy during the entire war."

During Operation "Torch" the French Atlantic and Mediterranean Fleet, which was under the command of Marshall Pétain, had the mission of attacking the invasion fleet. The French seamen felt little sympathy for the English, since they had fired on their defenseless ships at Mers-el-Kébir.

The French lost the battleship Prim*auguet* and the new *Jean Bart* was badly damaged in these battles. The torpedo boats *Thyphon, Tornade, Tramontane, Frondeur, Fougueux, Epervier, Boullonais* and *Bretois* as well as 15 submarines and 9 other warships were also sunk. The French Air Force's losses were equally high. But in the end all these sacrifices were in vain, for our diplomacy did not understand our friends in Europe and their attitude toward a new, unified and socialized Europe. This constructive, positive attitude would have made this civil war unnecessary. I can state that it is not true that a type of racial hatred toward Germany existed in France, Belgium and even Holland in 1940. Our government neglected the psychological weapon, a weapon which is likely the most effective of all.

In the end Admiral Darlan, who was in Algeria in 1942, changed sides and went over to the western allies, before he was murdered.

● ● ●

Let us return to the first phase of the war at sea, to October 30, 1939. That day Leutnant zur See Zahn, commander of the U-boat U-56, had an unlikely piece of bad luck when he attacked the battle-cruiser *Nelson* in the Orkney Islands. Displaying unbelievable courage, Zahn worked his way through the screen of twelve destroyers. He was so close to his target that the crew heard the three torpedoes strike the flank of the warship. None exploded! On board the battle-cruiser was Churchill, at the time First Lord of the Admiralty. One can imagine the news at the beginning of November 1940: "The *Nelson* sunk with all hands, Churchill on board!" Churchill was aware of the fate of Lord Kitchener, who drowned on June 5, 1916 when the *Hampshire* was sunk off the Orkney Islands while en route to Russia.

I am firmly convinced that Europe's history would have taken a different course if the three torpedoes fired by U-56 had exploded.

The acoustic torpedoes, which homed onto the engines of enemy ships, worked significantly better. It was not a German invention, our experts only improved it: they became faster and received a highly-sensitive seeker head. We also used heat-seeking torpedoes, which moved at high speed toward the hottest part of its target, namely the engine room. These new weapons posed a great threat to the western allies.

Various "midget" submarines were also employed, from the Hai (Shark), which was flat like a sardine, to the best, the Seehund (Seal), which was crewed by two men. All were equipped with a snorkel, like the amphibious tanks that simply drove through the Bug on June 22, 1941. The Seehund also had an air filtering system, as did the Molch (Salamander) and the Marder (Marten). These "mini" U-boats, which were equipped with high-quality periscopes, were capable of reaching much more distant targets than the manned torpedoes. In this case the two torpedoes were attached on both sides of the keel.

The snorkel provided the submerged U-boat with sufficient air for crew and engine. The snorkel was a Dutch invention. The German Professor Walter improved the system greatly and as well invented a hydrogen-oxygen engine. The reaction produced only water, which could be used for other purposes on board.

Dönitz had been pushing for production of the revolutionary Walter U-boat since 1937. He found little understanding for the new concept and it wasn't until the year 1942 that Professor Walter and engineers Schürer, Bräking and Oelfken introduced the snorkel system. It was two more years until about 100 Type "Walter XXI and XXIII" submarines were built and finally put into service. From May 1944 older type U-boats were also fitted with improved snorkels. Our submarines, which had suffered heavy losses to air attack, no longer needed to surface in critical moments.

The Type XXI Walter submarines, which reached a submerged speed of 17.5 knots, possessed an extraordinary radius of action. For example they could sail to Argentina without surfacing or refuelling and could dive to a depth of 300 meters.[1]

In February 1945 at Yalta, the Americans and English insisted that Stalin start a major offensive against East Prussia and Danzig, where 30 of the Type XXI Walter boats were built, for, "the allied air forces and ships were having difficulty dealing with the new U-boats, and these represented a serious danger to our sea traffic in the North Atlantic." Winston Churchill himself wrote:

"If the new German U-boats had been committed earlier, they could have, as Dönitz said, completely changed the result of the submarine war on account of their great speed underwater."

If sufficient numbers of Walter U-boats had been committed starting in 1942, which was possible, the flow of supplies to England and Russia, as well as the enemy landings in North Africa and on the Italian and French coasts would have at least been seriously impeded.

• • •

The Bv-143 and Bv-246, flying bombs powered by solid fuel motors, were a product of V-2 research. They had to be launched from aircraft and at three meters above the water they went into horizontal flight and homed in on their targets, guided by an acoustic or heat-seeking homing head.

Other air-to-sea flying bombs included the five or six versions of the SD-1400. These weapons, which were fitted with stub wings, were called "Fritz" and were capable of piercing the thickest armor plate. In September 1943 the Italian battleship *Roma*, which was on its way to North Africa to surrender to the allies, was sunk by "*Fritz*" missiles launched by a Dornier 217.

The remotely-controlled Hs-293 flying bomb sank numerous enemy ships in 1943. The Hs-294 was 6.5 meters long compared to the 4 meters of the Hs-293. It was placed in service the following year. The flying bomb shed its stub wings on entering the water and turned into a homing torpedo.

The Hs-295, Hs-296 and Hs-298 rockets, which were of light alloy construction, were missiles which were guided to their targets by the launching aircraft. Their range was eight kilometers. They were 2.5 meters long and weighed about 125 kilograms. After various improvements thought was given to employing them as pure air-to-air rockets against enemy bomber formations. They would probably have been very effective, but the war ended before they could go into quantity production.

One can now understand better how I came up with the idea of using the V-1 as a manned aircraft. From the middle of a wave of V-1s crossing the English Channel two manned bombs suddenly dive on two large ships. Their pilots eject before the two missiles reach their targets – in contrast to the Japanese "kamikaze" pilots. For I was always of the view that each individual fighter must be left a chance of survival. Perhaps the manned V-1 could have backed up the Grossadmiral's U-boats.

They also tried to install the rocket motor of the V-1 in an anti-shipping weapon. It was given the rather bombastic name of *Tornado*. It was a sort of remotely-controlled giant torpedo – like our *Goliath* mini-tank – with 600 kilograms of explosives in its nose. This *Tornado* was supposed to fly just over the water; its speed never exceeded 65 kph, however, and in wavy conditions its stability was quite mediocre, although it was stabilized by two floats like a floatplane.

One can see that there was no shortage of good ideas where special weapons were concerned, only time. Here, too, our unlucky star was: "Too late."

● ● ●

Hitler's most fateful mistake was his belief in a localized war of limited duration. Never was a statesman as poorly advised by his diplomats as he. When he entered Poland to return Danzig to the Reich, Hitler was not aware that he was starting World War Two.

In the first six months of 1942 our submarines sank more than three-million tons out of the total of 4,147,406 tons of weapons and supplies shipped by the enemy alliance; therefore far in excess of fifty percent. 729,000 tons in November 1942 alone. The number of ships sunk exceeded the number of newly-built vessels and those under construction.

In spite of increasingly heavy air cover and the growing level of protection from surface vessels, the convoys of the western allies lost 627,000 tons of shipping to our U-boats in the Atlantic in the first three weeks of March 1943. Liddell Hart wrote:

"The U-boat offensive was finally brought to a halt. It is certain, however, that England came very close to defeat in March 1943." All of the above figures come from the archives of the British and American admiralty headquarters.

As grave as Hitler's responsibility and mistakes were, it is absurd to write that "he had been thinking of and preparing for a world war since 1930" and that he was its "planner and instigator."

In my opinion the most important reason for the outbreak of the Second World War was as follows: The First World War was never ended by a just peace treaty acceptable to all sides. The war was only interrupted and was adjourned until the outbreak of the next — Versailles just created more European problems than existed before the First World War.

Just as General Bonaparte found the French Republic's treasury empty in 1799, so had the Reichsbank's gold and foreign currency reserves fallen to zero in 1933. Hitler prescribed the only solution: invent, work more, produce more, in order to live and above all export. New products came on the market, mainly in the years 1935-1936, which became known in the international vernacular under the name "ersatz" (substitute). Our chemists distinguished themselves in all branches of the industry. They even produced synthetic food — to the excitement of the foreign press.

Through "ersatz" we were able to produce many new industrial goods, create modern homes for the workers, build the autobahns, manufacture the volkswagen, produce new synthetic fibre fabrics and so on. During the war "ersatz" was a part of our defense, which helped the fatherland in its struggle and allowed it to hold out as long as it did.

In Germany they not only produced fuel from hard coal, but foodstuffs as well, such as butter, sugar and honey. Buna was an outstanding rubber. The cellulose processing industry grew quite considerably. Plexiglass was invented; synthetic materials took the place of bronze and brass; artificial silk and other synthetic fabrics won the race. I will not claim that the liverwurst made from the byproducts of the cellulose industry could be compared to "Mainzer Schinken" or with goose liver paté. But we were happy to be able to satisfy our hunger with it.

The second and hopefully last world war was pure madness, as it spared neither soldiers nor the civilian population. I would like to repeat that I am firmly convinced that this war could have and should have been avoided. Happily at least some of the inventions to come out of the war have been used for peaceful purposes and for the good of mankind. Inventions that an ancient European people, which once again found itself facing defeat, created for its own self-defense.

Today Europe has disintegrated into three or four parts. The nations of Europe not in the Soviet block found themselves in a very serious energy crisis in December 1973 as a result of an oil shortage. As a result of restrictive measures imposed by the Arab nations after the war against Israel, gasoline, liquefied gas and heating oil became scarce commodities. There was scarcely a branch of industry that did not use oil as an energy source or as a basic material. The crisis had corresponding direct effects on the operations of the processing industries such as: dyes, plastics, soaps, paints, synthetic fabrics, rubber, fertilizers and so on. Unrest and a mood of near panic developed. Important branches of industry were thrown into total confusion, in West Germany as well as in France, Holland, Sweden, Italy and Belgium. In Great Britain many factories only worked three days per week.

Unfortunately one must say that, in this case, the cooperation in Europe of the "Common Market" was hardly glorious and that the large western states did not show the necessary solidarity.

All of a sudden the cry is for finding new energy sources and the invention of new technology. This appears to me to be an outstanding idea – one which we Europeans have been practicing for centuries.

The best energy source is not raw materials alone however, but the will of honorable men, who place their ideas and their capacity for work wholeheartedly into the service of the community.

Notes

1. Compare this to Heinz Schaeffer's account of sailing a conventional U-boat to Argentina in U-977, Wiesbaden 1974. (Editors' note)

14

FROM SICILY TO REMAGEN

Old wives' tales on an Andalusian beach – Canaris concludes that the Anglo-American landing will take place in Sardinia and Greece – "Husky" makes use of the mafia – Manned torpedoes at Anzio – Why I didn't allow the invincibility of the Atlantic Wall to be questioned – A series of astonishing coincidences help Operation "Overlord" succeed – The man who almost blew up the Rock of Gibraltar destroys the Nimwegen Bridge – The failure of Operation "Market Garden" – The Basler Bridge must be blown if... – Operation Forelle, actions on the Danube – The blockade of Budapest is broken – Leutnant Schreiber and his frogmen at the Remagen Bridge – Why the war had to be continued in the west and the east – Field Marshall Montgomery's battles and observations – Hitler says: "The day before yesterday I gave orders which must seem completely mad!" – From Lord Byron to Winston Churchill.

Even if our volunteers were unable to distinguish themselves with manned V-1s, there were other operations on the sea and in rivers. The operations in which I took part were played out under dramatic and unfavorable circumstances. The most significant took place at Anzio, a port in central Italy about 50 kilometers south of Rome.

In order to properly understand what happened at Anzio, we must think back to November 1942 – to the moment when the landing troops of Operation "Torch" encountered unexpectedly strong opposition from French forces commanded by General Noguès and Admiral Darlan. The Americans were fortunate to have a first-class agent in Algiers, Consul-General Murphy, who succeeded in "turning"

General (and later Field Marshall) Juin, whom we had released. The admiral also allowed himself to be convinced by Murphy and was later murdered by a young French fanatic, Bonnier de la Chapelle. The latter had received absolution and a pistol from a priest (on December 24, 1942). He was found guilty by a military court and shot – much to the relief of Churchill and de Gaulle.

According to the Abwehr's information the Anglo-American fleet must "land in Corsica or southern France" (See: Paul Carell, *Afrika-Korps*). The troops of the axis powers had to fight on two fronts and they resisted for six months. Rommel's place had been taken by General von Arnim. On May 13, 1943 the last two units of the axis powers still fighting acknowledged defeat: the "Young Fascists" Division and the Africa Corps' 164th Light Infantry Division. Both units were completely out of ammunition and food and surrendered to the British 8th Army in southern Tunisia.

Tunisia and its great port, Bizerte, now gave the allies an ideal springboard to the "soft spot" of the boot of Europe.

Hitler was aware of the danger the loss of Sicily would pose. He offered Mussolini five divisions. According to a statement by General Westphal, then Field Marshall Kesselring's chief-of-staff, which was quoted by Liddell Hart, "the duce assured us that he only needed three divisions." Two of these were made up of young Italian draftees and had to defend the Tunis bridgehead. The Italians looked for excuses. At the end of June two German divisions, one of them the Hermann Göring Panzer Division, were placed under the command of the Italian General Guzzoni and transferred to Sicily. But when the US 7th Army (Patton) and the British 8th Army (Montgomery) landed on Sicily on July 20, 1943, the island was only moderately defended by about ten Italian (of which six existed only in theory) and three German divisions.

Once again the Abwehr had misinformed the OKW and had assured Generalfeldmarschall Keitel that the landing in Europe would not take place in Corsica or in France, but in Sardinia or Greece. Canaris' agents in Spain received their "proof" as part of a carefully-planned operation by the British secret service.

Just off an Andalusian beach an English submarine dropped off a dead body which came straight from a London morgue. False papers were placed on the man identifying him as an English officer. Favorable currents carried the cadaver to the Spanish beach; "they" saw to it that the German secret service was informed. A wallet was found on the body containing a copy of a report sent by General Sir Archibald Nye, one of the two deputy chiefs of the Empire General Staff, to General Alexander and in which obvious references were made to an imminent landing in Greece.

This red herring was perhaps not as significant as several film directors or television programs of a few years ago tried to make it out to be. In any case – the Abwehr believed it. Reinforcements were in fact despatched to Greece and Sardinia, and what Montgomery grandly called "the Sicilian campaign" only lasted from July 10 to August 17, 1943. A few Italian units fought bravely; the others, poorly armed and badly led, surrendered quickly.

The mafia chiefs brought to Sicily from overseas in American trucks also did not play the role which many historians ascribe to them. It is quite certain that "Lucky" Luciano, the head of the New York underworld, who at the time was serving a thirty-year prison sentence, was called upon to use his influence to have the Sicilian mafia work for the "good allied objectives." Luciano was released in 1946 "for the extraordinary services he had rendered."

Seen strategically and tactically, Sicily offered the invaders advantages, but they were not in a position to exploit them. Three airborne operations, backed up by the heavy guns of the warships and almost total air superiority, could not stop Feldmarschall Kesselring from saving 60,000 Italians and 40,000 Germans from this trap. Montgomery, who had enormous resources at his disposal, could have closed "the net" earlier however, by shifting the focus of the attack to Messina. It wasn't until August 15 that he landed a commando brigade at Scaletta, but by then it was already too late to seal off the narrows.

Operation "Husky," the occupation of Sicily, could have had catastrophic consequences for the Wehrmacht. Generaloberst Jodl later confided in me that Hitler was of the opinion all along that the island would be difficult for the Duce to defend. The island was neither fascist nor anti-fascist: more than anything it was Sicilian. In the last century it had fallen prey to revolutions and counter-revolutions. Prisons and penitentiaries opened their doors, the criminals were released and soon seen as heroes. The popular slogan sweeping the island in July-August 1943 was *"Sicilia ai Siciliani"* (Sicily for the Sicilians).

When Hitler met with Mussolini at Feltre on July 19, 1943, he felt that the Duce was uncertain. During their conversation one of Mussolini's adjutants passed him a note, whereupon Mussolini said desperately: "At this moment the workers' quarter of Rome is being bombed heavily by the enemy!"

The raid by the B-24 Liberators left behind 1,430 dead and more than 6,000 injured. The Duce feared that there was little concern for defending Sicily among his entourage. General Ambrosio presented his ultimatum to Mussolini in private:

"Duce, you are a friend of the Führer's. You must make it clear to him that we must concern ourselves with our own affairs. Italy must make peace in two weeks!"

Mussolini did not have General Ambrosio arrested, and when he bade farewell to Hitler at Treviso airport he assured him once again:

"Führer, we have the same goal, and together we will prevail!"

I am sure that he firmly believed this, as did several of his supporters. But they were not very numerous.

● ● ●

On September 3rd and 8th general Montgomery's 8th Army and the American 5th Army under General Clark set foot in Italy itself – at Reggio and Salerno. This was anything but a success. Montgomery and Liddell Hart admit that both armies sustained "heavy" losses, had to literally fight their way forward foot by foot and from November faced a supply catastrophe. Later they were unable to break through the Hitler (or Gustav) Line which ran past Monte Cassino, where the Americans unnecessarily destroyed the famous abbey.

The original monastery of the Benedictine monks, founded by Saint Benedict in the year 529, it housed a wealth of artistic treasures, a valuable library and an art gallery. Luckily these treasures were moved to safety by German troops a few months before the allied bombing. general von Senger und Etterlin wrote in his book Krieg in Europa (Cologne, 1963), that Feldmarschall Kesselring gave orders to spare the abbey's great store of cultural treasures "even at the cost of a tactical advantage."

Not until January 22, 1944 did the Americans begin their Operation "Shingle." General John P. Lukas and his 6th Corps landed at Anzio. Since Anzio lay north of the "Gustav Line," Operation

"Shingle" was supposed to allow the Anglo-Saxons to attack the German armies in the rear and march on Rome. General Clark saw himself in the eternal city by November 1943. But he deceived himself: Rome did not fall until June 4, 1944. He didn't occupy Florence until the end of August and it wasn't until March 1945 that he passed Bologna.[1]

• • •

At Anzio our volunteers of the Kriegsmarine and from Friedenthal used Neger manned torpedoes against the enemy ships. The action took place a few weeks after the landing.

Early in the morning twenty manned torpedoes were brought to the water north of the beachhead. Seated under their plexiglass cupolas the men raced toward their targets. At dawn they pulled the release lever for the lower torpedo, turned the upper torpedo and returned north. Twenty explosions were heard.

The result was: one cruiser severely damaged, one torpedo boat sunk and more than 30,000 tons of transport ship capacity sunk or damaged. Seven torpedoes returned immediately to their base north of Anzio. The next day six men reached our lines after slipping through the beachhead; seven of the twenty men remained missing.

Later the element of surprise ceased to play a role as the enemy was now aware of the threat. The glass cupolas of the Neger and the Marder manned torpedoes, which were used in the Mediterranean and the English Channel, were easily spotted. When the ocean currents were favorable we therefore set out numerous empty, floating glass cupolas, so that thy could be spotted from one side of the selected target. The enemy then opened up on the suspected torpedoes, while the real ones approached from the other direction.

Grossadmiral Dönitz wanted to meet the thirteen survivors of the Anzio operation, and they received well-deserved decorations from him. He had asked that the four Friedenthal participants and I should also be present. I thus obtained an opportunity to talk at length with the man who was to be the last chief of the German Reich.

When soon afterward we studied aerial photographs of southeast English ports, it became clear to us that the invasion was not far off. We compared these photos with those that had been taken a few weeks earlier and found something that interested me greatly: long rows of rectangles, that looked like docks. Soon we pieced together all the parts of the puzzle and determined that what we were seeing were prefabricated port installations. These artificial harbors made it possible to land many soldiers on a broad front. To me the coast of Normandy appeared particularly suitable for such a landing operation. Admiral Heye told me of the conclusions reached by his naval experts; it was a list which classified probable landing sites from one to ten. The landing took place on the first three stretches of coast listed.

My small staff and I set to work in Friedenthal: we prepared a plan which was presented to the High Command West through military channels. Commander-in-Chief West was Feldmarschall von Rundstedt. They would form special units and incorporate volunteers from my commando units. These would wait in a permanent state of alert on ten different stretches of coast on the English Channel and on the Atlantic coast for the landing of enemy troops. Their mission would then be to locate the enemy's headquarters and eliminate them through commando operations against officers and communications centers.

● ● ●

Our plan slowly worked its way back through the chain of command. An accompanying letter stated that the High Command West was aware of it and considered it correct and feasible. And, to quote just the conclusion of the letter:

"It cannot be assumed that the necessary preparations for your plan can be kept secret from the German occupation troops stationed along the coast.

"But any such preparation could destroy the faith of these troops in the absolute impenetrability of the Atlantic Wall. For this reason, therefore, the entire plan must be rejected."

signature illegible

Liddell Hart, General Emil Wanty in his book *Die Kunst des Krieges* (Vol. III) and others admit that Hitler was thinking of a landing in the

Cotentin. He also ordered Field Marshalls von Rundstedt and Rommel "to keep a close eye on Normandy."

Generalfeldmarschall Rommel was unable to watch over Normandy on June 6, 1944, the day of the allied landing. The day before he had left Roche-Guyon to spend the day with his family, and did not return to his headquarters until the afternoon of the following day.

However Helmut Mayer, chief of the Fifteenth Army's intelligence service, which kept tabs on radio communications on the coast from Rotterdam to east of Caen, intercepted and deciphered the "Verlaine poem" on June 1. Transmitted twice, it was supposed to alert certain French resistance groups that the invasion was imminent:

Les sanglots longs
Des violons De l'automne
Bercent mon coeur
D'une langeur Monotone

Mayer at once notified the Commander-in-Chief of the Fifteenth Army, who informed Generalfeldmarschall von Rundstedt. But the only one not informed was the main participant: General Dollmann, Commander-in-Chief of the Seventh Army and overseer of the coast from Caen. As well on June 6 none of the corps commanders were at their posts – all had been summoned to Caen for a "situation briefing."

Only General Max Pemsel, Dollmann's Chief-of-Staff, remained at his post. At 2:15 A.M. on June 6 he telephoned Rundstedt's general staff and informed them that the enemy had landed. The field marshall called back half an hour later to let him know that he did not consider the landing a "large-scale operation." Rundstedt had in fact predicted the actual landing to come between Le Havre and Calais. So he went back to sleep.

Hitler himself wasn't told about the landing "until late morning." General Jodl, head of the OKW, agreed with Rundstedt and felt that the enemy was only carrying out a "screening maneuver." Hitler and Jodl ignored the fact that Rommel was not on watch at that moment and that a few days before he had given orders for the fighter unit assigned to defend the west coast to withdraw to the interior of the country. So on the morning of June 6 there were only two German fighters to face the hundreds of allied aircraft; one was flown by Oberst Josef Priller and the other by Feldwebel Wodarczyk.

The Seventh Army had only one panzer division available, and that was the 21st, which was stationed near Caen. Without receiving any orders whatsoever it counterattacked in the direction of Courseulles-sur-Mer, straight through the British lines, where it caused chaos. However as it received no reinforcements it was forced to turn around.

The 1st SS-Panzer Division Leibstandarte Adolf Hitler, which was commanded by Sepp Dietrich, was informed to late or not at all, as were the 12th SS-Panzer Division Hitlerjugend, which was in Liseux, the 17th SS-Panzer-Grenadier Division which was stationed in Saumur and Niort, and the Panzer-Lehr Division in Le Mans and Orléans. Von Rundstedt's general staff also made a serious error by holding back two panzer divisions in the Paris area: General von Lüttwitz's 2nd and General von Schwerin's 116th. On June 6 they were in Amiens and east of Rouen; in mid-July the 116th Panzer Division was still at Dieppe! In his book Generaloberst Guderian asked the question "whether the delays and the wide dispersement of the reserve troops didn't have political backgrounds." As well he quoted an article by General von Geyr published in the Irish magazine *An Cosantoir* in 1950. Von Geyr assured that Generalfeldmarschall Rommel "held back his divisions in anticipation of the assassination attempt against Hitler on July 20." But not only the panzer divisions, which were supposed to throw the enemy back into the sea, sat idle; two weeks after the landing, with a major battle raging in Normandy, seven infantry divisions stood "at ease" north of the Seine, waiting for the enemy.[2]

Many historians are of the opinion that Operation "Overlord" could not have been defeated. That is not my view. The first V-1 fell on England on June 21, 1944: that was too late. But referring to the allied landing General Wanty spoke "of a most improbable conjunction of a series of lucky coincidences." Liddell Hart found that Montgomery played fast and loose with the facts in his memoirs. In any case, wrote Sir Basil, "at the beginning of the landing success and failure of the operation lay close together."

It would have been enough if the German commanders had been at their posts and had actually wanted to win. That was not the case. I will explain why.

I must once again look ahead and summarize the most important operations undertaken by the members of Friedenthal on or in the water. It was agreed with Admiral Heye that the Kriegsmarine would undertake all operations at sea, while my specialists would be active inland on rivers and lakes.

I was there when our frogmen were trained – in the Diana pool in Vienna, which was closed to the public, in the Waffen-SS officer school at Bad Tölz, in South Tirol and at Venice, where we were housed in an empty monastery on an island in a lagoon. It was very hard training. We tried out various techniques, concentrating on those which had enabled Prince Valerio Borghese to blow up three tankers at the Gibraltar roadstead on September 19, 1944. That was an act of heroism by the Italian manned torpedoes. The frogmen, outfitted with watertight diving suits, breathing gear and fins, did not just use the previously-described equipment; they attached time bombs with special suction discs to the stabilizing Leiste of the enemy ships.

Leading my frogmen from 1943 was Hauptmann Wimmel, who moved over from the Brandenburg to Friedenthal. He was an officer of quite special bravery and cool-headedness. In 1940-41 he commanded a special detachment which operated in the Gibraltar area. He sank numerous British ships and with the help of Spanish workers he succeeded in smuggling a powerful time bomb into the rock's tunnels, where there was a munitions dump. They hid the bomb in a metal hull, which looked exactly like an English artillery shell. The detonation of this bomb would have set off an explosion by thousands of large shells and would have inflicted serious damage on the rock. Wimmel never learned exactly why it did not go off. One thing is certain: one of the men who helped transport the bomb was "talkative." Had they paid him off or forced him to talk? Probably. There were great interests at work.

The attempt was made on December 5, 1940 and obviously could not be repeated. It coincided with a trip which Janus and Canaris made to Madrid on December 7 and 8, 1940. Canaris had a long talk with General Franco on the 7th. He was unable to convince Franco to take part in the war at Germany's side. Granted – Hitler couldn't have chosen a worse ambassador.

• • •

Field Marshall Montgomery planned the largest airborne-landing operation of the war, called "Market Garden." On September 17, 1944 three British army corps crossed the Maas-Schelde canal in the direction of Kleve, Nimwegen and Arnheim. At the same time 9,000 aircraft and 600 gliders delivered 35,000 men, 2,000 vehicles, 568 guns and 2,500 tons of materiel to Son, Vegel, Kleve, Nimwegen and Arnheim.

Surprise was achieved and the enemy's numerical superiority was enormous. Montgomery confessed, however, that the fighting strength of Obergruppenführer Wilhelm Bittrich's II SS-Panzer Corps, which had withdrawn from Normandy, was underestimated. The corps offered the enemy bitter resistance. Very soon Field Marshall Montgomery's airborne troops fighting north of Nimwegen needed help from British units which were supposed to cross the Waal – one of the tributaries of the Rhine – over the large bridge at Nimwegen. German attempts to destroy the bridge by bombing were fruitless, for its anti-aircraft defenses were too strong. But the bridge had to be blown at all costs. On orders from Führer Headquarters I gave Hauptmann Wimmel the job of carrying out this difficult mission, which won him the Knight's Cross. This unique operation succeeded in the following way. The enemy had established a bridgehead of about seven kilometers on either side of the bridge. Wimmel first slipped into the river and carried out a risky night reconnaissance. Then he set out with his force of twelve frogmen and four explosive torpedoes, which were kept afloat by flotation devices. They attached their explosive torpedoes to the two bridge supports designated by Wimmel, set the time fuses and opened the vents of the flotation devices.

Wimmel and the detachment had 10 minutes and 10 seconds to escape downstream. The bridge blew up just as a group of about 10 enemy tanks and trucks was crossing the bridge. Immediately after both banks of the river were illuminated and searchlights swept the river. Finally the enemy spotted our people and three were wounded by machine-gun fire. Their comrades kept them above water. All reached our lines – certainly with great difficulty and totally exhausted.

Operation "Market Garden," whose objective and purpose was to conquer the Ruhr, was a total failure. After four days and nights of heavy fighting we took about 10,000 prisoners.

In addition, I would like to note that it was the German first-aid service of the SS panzer corps that evacuated the civilian population of Arnheim, which was under heavy artillery fire. There was also a brief cease-fire in order to evacuate wounded German and British soldiers. The senior medical officer of the 9th SS-Division, Egon Skalba and Medical Officer Warrack of the British 1st Airborne Division and their medics treated the numerous wounded soldiers on the spot or moved them to safety. This humanitarian action was carried out behind the German lines.

Without the crushing superiority of the artillery, infantry and especially the allied air force, "Market Garden" would have been an even costlier failure to Montgomery. In his memoirs he speaks of the "epic of Arnheim" and draws the following conclusion: "In the future it will be a great honor for any soldier to be able to say: I fought at Arnheim."

The Anglo-Saxons stood before Nimwegen until February 8, 1945 (almost five months long). In spite of all their resources their special operations code-named "Veritable" and "Grenade" failed. The objective of "Grenade" was to seize the Röhr dam, but it came too late; we had already blown the flood gate and the area had been under water for two weeks.

I would also like to recall that for a time in September 1944 the OKW feared that, on account of the solidifying of our front, the western allies would be forced to violate Swiss neutrality and drive past Basel into Germany. On the OKW's orders I made certain preparations to blow that city's Rhine bridge should Anglo-American troops set foot on the soil of the Swiss Confederation. It was purely a defensive measure which would in the meantime allow the OKW to prepare a defense of this border, as there were no troops of any kind stationed there. It was generally known that "Swiss Neutrality" also included making it as easy as possible for all secret services hostile to Germany. Allen W. Dulles, the head of the Office of Strategic Services (OSS) felt quite at home in Switzerland.

• • •

In perusing the organizational scheme of all the units commanded from Friedenthal, one will come across Jagdkommando Donau, which was commanded by Hauptmann Wimmel and Leutnant Schreiber. Since late summer of 1944 our comrades had been carrying out a daring guerilla war on the Danube. With an overall length of 2,800 kilometers, the Danube was 400 meters wide in Vienna, 950 meters in Budapest and 1,500 at the Iron Gate in Romania. It had numerous tributaries in which our boats could hide during the day.

All of my danube operations were carried out under the code name Forelle (Trout). I must admit that I was proud to defend this ancient river on which I had spent so many happy days during my childhood.

At this time the Red Army was in Romania, and we often attacked their convoys. Our frogmen did their best with their explosive boats and drifting mines. Our small "fleet" – camouflaged private yachts fitted with makeshift armor, armed with 20mm cannon and machine-guns and fitted with more powerful motors – also sank valuable enemy tanker ships. In the course of the various Forelle actions we inflicted losses on the Stalinists of 13,000 tons.

All large rivers have their own lives and the Danube was a world unto itself. The old experienced Danube sailors who had volunteered to serve with us knew the river like their vest pockets. By day they hid their boats in a quiet tributary of the river or in the bay of a small island and began their mission when darkness began to fall.

• • •

At the beginning of December 1944, as I was about to fly to the Western Front on Hitler's order, I learned that the defenders of Budapest were fighting desperately to prevent the city from being totally encircled by General Malinovski's troops. This subsequently took place when the city of Szekesfeherver was occupied. Supply by air was impossible, and so I was tasked by the OKW to deliver pharmaceuticals and ammunition over the Danube to Budapest. At the same time I learned that Jochen Rumohr, my former battalion commander who by now had been promoted to general, was leading the defense of Budapest.

I gave the order to use the fastest and most spacious of our Danube ships, which would be followed by a tug. The bulkheads were removed and the cargo space filled with 500 tons of food, medicine, ammunition and drums of fuel. The operation was carried out on New Year's Eve 1944; I could only follow its progress by radio.

The two boats had to break through two Soviet fronts. They were scarcely bothered as they passed the first enemy line, and by early morning they were between the two front lines, about 17 kilometers from Budapest. It was foggy and they used a tributary of the river. Then, suddenly, the helmsman spotted the remains of a blown bridge sticking up out of the water. His attempt to go around the obstacle failed; both boats ran aground. Two members of the detachment were able to reach Budapest in a small boat and inform the garrison. Most of the ammunition, fuel and medicine was secreted into the city in small boats during the next four nights.

On the first day the stranded boats attracted the attention of an enemy patrol. We had calculated on such a risk. A Russian volunteer, a proven anti-Stalinist, was a member of the crew. He told the leader of the patrol that the boat "was on an extremely secret mission." He produced false Russian papers and passed around Russian alcohol and cigarettes. The patrol moved on.

It proved impossible to refloat the ships, however. Sailing back downstream by boat was out of the question, so the soldiers of the Forelle operation joined their comrades in the beleaguered city and shared their tragic fate.

My friend Rumohr was wounded and then shot himself to avoid being captured by the Soviets. Of the ten thousand encircled German soldiers still capable of fighting, only 270 reached our lines. Erich Kern told of the last Forelle commando in his book. He probably met a survivor who had returned from Russian captivity.

● ● ●

In mid-March 1945 I was summoned to Führer Headquarters, where Generaloberst Jodl ordered me to blow up the Ludendorff Bridge at Remagen on the Rhine. Every Second World War historian mentions the bridge at Remagen. It was fitted with explosive charges and was supposed to be destroyed behind our withdrawing heavy artillery on March 7. However a detonator failed to work and the bridge was only slightly damaged. They should have notified me at once. However Reichsmarschall Göring assured that his Luftwaffe would take care of the matter. However our Stukas were as ineffective against the enemy's very heavy screen of anti-aircraft guns as they had been at Nimwegen. By March 10, 20,000 Americans had already crossed the Ludendorff bridge.

The destruction of the bridge was subsequently left to the Mammoth howitzer, which fired its 540mm shells at the bridge. After four or five shots the howitzer jammed. We were then called out of pure desperation. I explained to Generaloberst Jodl that there were very great difficulties associated with this mission. The enemy bridgehead was significantly larger than the one at Nimwegen: up to 16 kilometers south of the bridge. This had to be covered by swimming, and in water temperatures of only about 7-8 degrees Celsius. The action was carried out on March 17 by our "Danube" frogmen, who had been flown in from Vienna. They were under the command of Leutnant Schreiber, an officer who was as brave as he was daring.

On that cold night our comrades swam off, down the Rhine with the torpedo mines that had been used at Nimwegen. It took them about one and a half hours to reach Remagen. Schreiber realized that we were right to fear the worst: the enemy had built two further pontoon bridgeheads upstream. The detachment carried out its mission as well as possible. The Ludendorff Bridge was damaged and unusable. Schreiber wanted to destroy a pontoon bridge as well, but our swimmers were discovered by the beams of the canal defense lights, whose location could not be made out. Leutnant Schreiber lost three men, two to hypothermia. The others were captured by the Americans, completely exhausted and half frozen.

I am of the opinion that a soldier must be convinced to do his duty. Today an action like that of the Schreiber detachment must appear absurd. However when I explained the difficulties of this operation to Generaloberst Jodl I did not hesitate to look for volunteers only, who were willing to carry out the mission. Leutnant Schreiber and his people did their best.

We often ask ourselves whether it wouldn't have been better to let the Anglo-American armies advance more quickly than those of Stalin. But one always forgets that we could not call a halt to the battle in the west alone: the allies were demanding unconditional surrender – *on all fronts* – and all units had to cease fighting at the same time and surrender on the spot – in the east as well as in the west.

Millions of German soldiers and civilians would have died in March 1945, for the enemy was in no position in the west, and even less so in the east, to house or even feed millions of prisoners of war and refugees. So we had to keep fighting in the east and west, in order to defend the territory threatened by the Red Army in the east, until as many people as possible had escaped to the west. Movements by troops and civilians were possible only until midnight on May 9. After that only a very few managed to escape from Soviet captivity. A surrender two months before would have meant that millions of civilians would have died of cold and hunger and that they would have deported the armies of Weichs, Schörner and Rendulic almost completely to the east.

Grossadmiral Dönitz noted that the German Kriegsmarine had brought at least 2,404,477 people – mainly women and children – out of Courland, East Prussia, Pomerania and Mecklenburg to the western zone in the period from January 23 to May 8, 1945.

At Remagen a detonator failed to function and 20,000 then 35,000 American soldiers crossed the Rhine. What did they do then? They waited. The tanks of General Hodges in the north and of General Patton's 3rd Army in the south were to link up in Koblenz, but not until the beginning of the offensive by Field Marshall Montgomery, to whom Eisenhower had entrusted overall command of the allied forces. The allies thus failed to exploit the breakthrough at Remagen. Montgomery did not cross the Rhine until March 24, much farther to the north, with the 21st Army Group, which in reality consisted of three army groups: the 1st Canadian Army, the 2nd British and the 9th American. This meant a total of 26 divisions, two of them airborne divisions. Facing these were only five German divisions, which had already been decimated by the guns and the bombs of the Liberators. When Montgomery had forced a crossing of the Rhine near Wesel, on March 28 his offensive came to a stop. The impression was created – and not only among us – if not the certainty, that Montgomery in the north and Bradley and Patton in the south had orders to wait until the armies of Zhukov, Konev and Malinovski had broken through in the east.

In his memoirs Montgomery complained bitterly that Eisenhower had "put the brakes" on him. He shows in splendid fashion that the western allies could have taken Vienna, Prague and Berlin *before the Russians*. I underline this view. He drew the correct conclusion, "that the Americans did not understand that there was little value in winning a war militarily if one simultaneously lost it politically." For his part, Patton, who had significantly less resources than Montgomery, deplored the incredible slowness of the English field marshall. One must in fact ask why he waited until the night of March 23-24 to start the offensive on the Rhine and why he stopped again on the other side on March 28. There was practically no longer any resistance. Proof of this: the total losses of General William Simpson's 9th US Army which, as Liddell Hart wrote, "provided half the infantry of the 21st Army Group," was just 40 men killed.

As a former combatant on the Eastern Front I would like to make an observation: Hitler is often criticized for his stubbornness, refusing to order any sort of "elastic withdrawal," as his generals had been proposing since December 1941. Hitler certainly made grave errors in his appraisal of the war situation – but primarily because he was badly informed.

Almost all generals commanding divisions and commanders of corps at the front had the bad habit of understating their losses when reporting them to "above." Their reports were further "doctored" when they reached the army and then the army group. I would like to cite one example: In the summer of 1944 my friend Hans Ulrich Rudel, our best Stuka pilot (with 2,700 combat missions), was received by Hitler and subsequently by Göring, who was under express orders from Hitler to ban him from further flying. Oberst Rudel came straight from the Eastern Front. Before Göring told him of Hitler's decision (which Rudel disregarded, by the way), he let him in on some "big news":

"We have prepared a major offensive in your sector which will be supported by 300 tanks. Leading the attack will be the 14th Division with 60 panzers..."

However Rudel had spoken with the commanding general of the 14th Division the day before. The general confessed to him that *he did not have a single* operational panzer. When Göring heard this he couldn't believe it and telephoned the front. He found that what the Oberst had told him was true, and that instead of the 300 tanks they had allowed for, they could commit 40 at best.

This "major offensive" was called off.

I myself witnessed a similar scene at Führer Headquarters in September 1944. For three days I had to be present for briefings, the so-called "noon situation" and "evening situation" (10 P.M.), in order to gain an exact picture of the situation on the Eastern Front.

As always the officers of the general staff had prepared a map and drawn in the divisions available in the southeast. During the first two days of my stay I was able to observe Hitler at his "war game" and saw how he carefully considered all the information he was given.

If a sector of the front was involved that did not affect several of the officers present, these withdrew to the ante-room and waited. On the first day I was thus an involuntary witness to a discussion between two officers who wore the red stripes of the general staff on their trousers.

"You know," said one of the officers, "that of the three divisions in the east of Hungary two are only as strong as battalions and the third would have difficulty sending two battalions to the front. It won't do!..."

"That surely won't do," observed the other, "and it's not our fault!"

I walked away so as not to have to hear any more.

When, on the third day, Hitler asked exact and increasingly more uncomfortable questions about these three phantom divisions, it became clear to him that he had been deceived.

"That means then," he shouted, "that the orders I gave the day before yesterday were based on the existence of these divisions. And now I hear that these divisions no longer exist! At the front they must think that my orders are completely crazy. Why am I being lied to here, gentlemen? Why? I want to be told the truth! The lives of brave soldiers are at stake!"

Hitler did not chew the carpet and nor did he climb the drapes. Only in his voice was there indignation and desperation.

In any case it is certain that if he had ordered all the retreats recommended by his generals, there would be no Germany today and the Soviet Army would have occupied all of Europe.

The German soldier felt betrayed since July 20, 1944. We have seen, and will yet see, to what degree he was. In the west the Wehrmacht had lost its offensive spirit by March 1945, and the terrible sight of our wrecked cities certainly did not encourage the retreating troops. Our workers did not lose their courage to the end; in the Ruhr and Silesia the enemy found the workers at their workplaces. No one can deny that the German people fought bravely for five years against the mightiest nations in the world.

At the beginning of 1945 Winston Churchill drove across the Dutch border into Germany, accompanied by Field Marshalls Brooke and Montgomery. He had the car stop, so that he could urinate on the Siegfried Line, which ended there, and urged the two field marshalls to do the same. Both immediately did as Churchill asked. The photographers were forbidden to film this act, which wasn't exactly in keeping with the fame of the Viscount of Alamein. John Toland described this incident in *The Last 100 Days* and assures that it is authentic.

This brought to mind a remark by Lord Byron, which he made about Napoleon's jailkeeper in St. Helena: "If you pass by the grave of Hudson Lowe, never forget to piss on it!"

Notes

1. In a book titled *The D-Day*, published in London in 1974 (by Sidgwick and Jackson), with a foreword by Lord Mountbatten, the authors W. Tute, J. Castello and T. Hughes wrote: "The invasion was almost a washout. The Anglo-Saxons, who were tied down until May, held back the landing craft in the Mediterranean intended for D-Day, as a result of which the planned invasion of Southern France was delayed until August." (Editors' note)

2. More than anyone it was Hitler, who for days went on believing that a second invasion was going to take place somewhere else, who was responsible for the belated commitment of the German reserves. As well, allied air superiority made the movement of troops even more difficult. (Editors' note)

15

PLANNED OPERATIONS

The purpose of Operation Franz in Persia – I meet the real "Man with the Golden Gun" – Roosevelt, Churchill and Stalin in Teheran – The action against the summit conference is hindered by the lack of sufficient information – The story of the proposed Operation Weitsprung – How the Russians made the most of it: they "watch over" Roosevelt and isolate Churchill – Testimony by Averell Harriman, Sir Kenneth Strong and Lord Moran – Operation Ulm: target Magnitogorsk – Operation Zepppelin shows that organization is not the same as execution – A dangerous chimera: the Werwolf – Himmler dreams of a new operation after Magnitogorsk: New York! – Mohammed Amin-al Husaini, the Grand Mufti of Jerusalem, a figure from A Thousand and One Nights – The Iran-Mediterranean oil line – The wolf doesn't howl in Vichy – On the heels of Marshall Tito: why Rösselsprung failed – We take Churchill prisoner and Major Beck does business with the partisans – Bogus British pounds in circulation, and what we did with them in Italy – The treasure of the SS – Mussolini in Sweden – A submachine-gun demonstration in our park.

Operation Franz, which was already under way when I took over command of the Friedenthal Battalion, was no pipe dream. It involved sending military advisors and instructors to Iraq to support the Kashgai fighters and other mountain tribes that had rebelled in southern Persia since 1941 (after the forced renunciation of the throne by Emperor Reza Shah Palavi, who was well-disposed toward Germany, in favor of his son Mohammed Reza).

At this point in time Soviet troops had occupied the north of the country. Four or five British divisions, which had moved in from the south, had the south of the country in their hands. The only railroad in this vast area of 1,648,000 square kilometers was used to deliver supplies to Russia via Abadan, Teheran and Tabris, just like the rail lines of the Caucasus from Tbilisi or Baku. The Persians soon had to deal with another occupying power, namely the Americans, who did not treat them as roughly as the other two. Neither the Soviet troops nor the British occupiers were liked. There were uprisings in December 1942 and unrest in February 1943. Both were harshly suppressed.

It was not our objective to prepare uprisings in large cities like Teheran (750,000 inhabitants), Tabris (220,000) or Ispahan (200,000), but to appeal to the Kashgai chiefs, who were in a very good position to wage a guerilla war and thus tie down a certain number of enemy divisions in Iran and interrupt supply lines over which vital raw materials such as crude oil, nickel and magnesium as well as Anglo-American military supplies were delivered to Russia.[1]

A year earlier, in 1942, the advance by Feldmarschall List's army group failed at the last minute. The Austrians and Bavarians of the 4th Mountain Infantry Division were forced to halt on the north slope of the Caucasus, 20 kilometers from Sukhumi, on account of inadequate supplies of ammunition and food. Nevertheless the war flag of the Reich waved on the summit of Elbrus (5,633 meters), which had been conquered by Hauptmann Groth, Hauptmann Gömmeler, Oberfeldwebel Kümmler and the mountain infantry of the 1st and 4th Divisions. This symbolic victory by my countrymen on August 21, 1942 filled me with joy and I was very proud of them. The mountain climbers among my readers will understand.

But now it was not Elbrus, rather the Elbrus Mountains between the Caspian Sea and the highlands of Iran, on whose slope lay Teheran.

The first to parachute into Iran was a group of two officers and three NCOs of the Friedenthal Battalion, led by a Persian. We used a large Junkers 290 of the Luftwaffe's Kampfgeschwader 200, which had difficulty getting airborne from the Crimean airfield. The runway was too short; the equipment, which together with the instructors was to be dropped by parachute, had to be drastically reduced.

But we did not forget to take along hunting rifles and gold and silver inlaid Walther pistols as gifts for the Persian tribal chiefs. The drop took place on a dark night near a large salt lake southeast of Tehran. After a forty-hour wait we received a radio report that our people were safe.

My role was limited to training people for this mission, as the operation was under the command of Dr. Gräfe, department chief of Office VI (Foreign). I feared that the groups trained by me would encounter a dangerous enemy there: the joint Russian-English military intelligence services. I felt rather uncomfortable about training my soldiers only to send them into uncertainty. I have always taken responsibility for what I have done, and I must say that if I had suspected in advance all the intrigues, the narrow-mindedness and the clumsiness of the bureaucracy, I would probably never have accepted this commando post.

Unfortunately we were unable to supply Operation Franz, which achieved mixed results, with sufficient material and soldiers as we lacked Ju 290 transports with the required radius of action. A mechanical problem with one of our aircraft prevented a second group of military advisors from jumping. This was lucky for us, for a short time later we learned that our central operation in Tehran had been exposed. Only one of Schellenberg's agents managed to flee to Turkey. From there he informed us of what had happened. The new planned actions were immediately cancelled and our people remained with the rebel tribes until the end of the war. One of our officers then took his life to avoid falling into the hands of the Russians. Others were captured when they tried to make their way to Turkey. They returned to Germany in 1948.

Operation Franz nevertheless forced the enemy to keep several divisions at alert readiness. The Russians and the British feared a general rebellion by the various Persian tribes. The Persians who had fought against the Russians were pursued relentlessly. Many of them were killed. In 1956 I chanced to meet one of the Kashgai tribal chiefs in the Breidenbacher Hof Hotel in Düsseldorf. He had managed to flee to Rome at the time. He still had the gold-inlaid pistol that I had sent him: "One of the few things, apart from my life, that I was able to save," he told me over supper in the Persian Hotel.

• • •

In the first days of November 1943 I was ordered to Führer Headquarters, where I was told that a "summit conference" would possibly be held in Tehran at the end of the month: Stalin, Roosevelt and
Churchill would be staying there for three or four days.

It could be that the report was received from the valet of Sir Hugh
Knatchbull-Hugessen, the English ambassador in Istanbul, the Yugoslavian Elyesa Bazna, alias Cicero. But I also believe that Walter
Schellenberg was enthusiastic about the idea of planning an action
against the "big three" enemies of Germany.

Naturally it was a seductive idea to send a special commando to
Tehran. But could such an operation succeed? And how? First of all
one would need the most precise information on the situation, the
city of Tehran itself and naturally on the allied troops stationed there.

Our contact man in Tehran, a captain of the Abwehr, passed me
the information by radio via Istanbul: the yield was rather meager.
For certain the capital of Iran was completely in the hands of the
three powers, whose political and military intelligence services were
on guard. The action in Tehran would have required 150 to 200 of
our best-trained soldiers, aircraft, special vehicles, precise knowledge of the area and information about the enemy's security measures. I was able to learn almost nothing about this. Under such conditions of course there was not the least chance of success: the plan
was simply impracticable. I advised Hitler and Schellenberg of my
views on such an action – Hitler agreed with me.

At the end of 1956 the world press eagerly picked up parts of a
crime novel published by the Russian magazine *Ogornick*. In general terms the rather mediocre novel's plot was as follows:

"Evil nazis intend to kill or capture Stalin, Roosevelt and Stalin
in Tehran. The operation is ordered by me, Otto Skorzeny. The leader
of the detestable commando is a young Sturmbannführer named Paul
von Ortel – a fictional character. But Comrade Lavrenti Beria, the
supreme Soviet police commander, is on guard: all the nazis in Tehran
are exposed and liquidated at the end of November 1943. It was high
time!"

In December 1968 the *Tribune de Genève* drew attention to another work of fiction: a true democrat, the first-class Soviet spy Ilya Svetlov, "operating under the name Walter Schulz, a member of the National-Socialist Party – recommended by Rudolf Hess!" parachutes into Tehran and after unbelievable adventures foils the planned assassination attempt against the "big three" – code-named Operation Weitsprung (Broad Jump).

Two years later (November 17, 1970) the *International Herald Tribune* picked up this fictional account of Svetlov-Schulz again and as well published a photo of me with the caption: "Ex-SS Colonel Otto Skorzeny, who was supposed to carry out this plan conceived by the German Führer Headquarters." Neither the *Tribune de Genève* nor any other newspaper spoke to me about Weitsprung.

Finally, a book by Laszlo Havas entitled *Assassinat du sommet* (Murder at the Summit Conference) came out at the beginning of February 1968. The author at least took the trouble to make inquiries of me. I must confirm that the parts of his account that concern me are accurate: I had characterized this operation in Tehran as completely impossible, and he said so. However, Havas also wrote that a German action aimed at Tehran was in fact begun and failed. I think that if that were the case I should have at least learned about it later.

One cannot expect a historian or chronicler who has concerned himself with this question for years to be a modern Xenophon. The general in ancient Athens, who was also a writer of history and a philosopher, fought in Persia and in his *Anabasis* described the famous retreat by the 10,000 Greek soldiers which he personally led. But one asks oneself why the world press so eagerly published the Soviet magazine *Ogornick*'s figment of the imagination.

The only account of Operation Weitsprung worthy of being taken seriously was published in the *Sunday Times* on Jaunary 6, 1969. The London weekly noted that Sir Alexander Cadogan, who was state secretary in the Foreign Office in 1943, wrote in his memoirs that at the time of the conference in Tehran "the Soviets *claimed* to have uncovered a plot." The author's skepticism is obvious.

Averell Harriman, who was the American ambassador in Tehran, was interviewed by the *Sunday Times* and said: "Molotov said to me that there were many Germans in this area (flattering!!!) and a plot was possible. I saw Molotov again after the conference and asked him whether there had in fact been a conspiracy. He assured me that the strictest security measures had been taken on the basis of these rumors. But he never told me that there really was a threat."

Sir Kenneth Strong, who later led the British intelligence service S.M., seemed to have the most accurate view of the suspected Weitsprung action:

"I suspect," he observed, "that the Russians used this alleged plot as an excuse to move Roosevelt to a villa near the Soviet embassy in Tehran; and you can be sure that this villa was bristling with microphones."

Lord Moran, Churchill's physician, accompanied the prime minister to Tehran. In his memoirs, under the heading "How Stalin Found an Ally," Moran wrote on November 28, 1943 that the American legation, where the president of the United States was supposed to stay, was rather far from the British and Soviet embassy buildings in Tehran. Since Molotov was talking about a possible assassination attempt against Roosevelt, the American president moved to a villa belonging to the Russian embassy. "He certainly was well guarded there, for even all the domestic servants in the villa were members of the NKVD, which Beria led."

In conclusion Lord Moran said that, "Churchill protested furiously if any of us expressed skepticism about an alleged German plot. Winston Churchill was the only one who believed in a plot. Stalin was not in the least worried about the safety of President Roosevelt. He just wanted to keep an eye on him and prevent him from being able to conspire against him with the English prime minister."

It is known that Stalin visited the villa immediately after his arrival. On this occasion the American president expressed to the Russian dictator the hope that the Malaysian States, Burma and "the other British colonies" would soon "learn the art of governing themselves." As well Roosevelt recommended to his "little brother" that he not discuss India with Churchill yet... Lord Moran learned these details from Harry Hopkins, an advisor and intimate of Roosevelt's.

Certain journalists, who almost always defend the USSR and the NKVD out of fear, would do well to read Lord Moran's memoirs.

In reality Operation Weitsprung existed only in the imaginations of a few truth-loving scribes or for the "fellow comrades" of Bolshevism. Stalin succeeded in isolating Churchill at Tehran, and the British prime minister was forced to accept the proposals of his two interlocutors.

On July 3, 1958 Lord Halifax had tea with Lord Moran. On this occasion he told him the following anecdote: as British ambassador in Washington he was often invited by Republican senators. One of them said to him: "All those present consider Mr. Roosevelt a worse dictator than Hitler or Mussolini."

In July 1945 Churchill said to his doctor:

"I begged the Americans on my knees not to leave the Russians such a large part of Germany. But the president had already given in. I am going to ask Stalin: Do you want the whole world?"

On the theme of Weitsprung, I would like to add in closing that in all probability the Director in Moscow was advised of my visit to the OKW by the Red Orchestra. Moscow undoubtedly also learned that I declared the action in Tehran impossible. But for Stalin the opportunity was too good to pass up, to practically isolate Roosevelt in the Russian embassy using the excuse of "having to protect him from any danger" and in so doing completely isolating Churchill.

It is understandable that Operation Weitsprung became "news" again when various scandals in the western intelligence services became known in the years 1965-1968, followed by a wave of suicides. Philippe Thyraud de Vosjoli, a former official of the French secret service, made disclosures about the Soviet spy net "Sapphire." The "Sapphire" affair was so significant that President Kennedy even encouraged de Gaulle to take drastic measures. It was an opportunity for the east-oriented press to recall that their good friend Beria and the Soviet secret service had prevented "the murder at the summit," and had saved the life of Franklin Delano Roosevelt. The democratic leader was elected President of the United States – for the third time! – on November 5, 1940, after promising throughout his campaign, "not to send a single American soldier across the Atlantic."

• • •

Operation Ulm, planned by Reichsführer SS Himmler, was by its nature also not simple to carry out. Its aim was to destroy the blast furnaces and steel works of Magnitogorsk, as well as one or two power stations that provided the large metal and chemical plants with the necessary energy.

I had never been to Magnitogorsk, which lay beyond the Urals. The Luftwaffe had the best information about these remote Soviet heavy industries. In the period 1940-41, when we still had total air superiority, it had taken outstanding aerial photographs of the area.

Since 1942 Department VI-C of Office VI of the RSHA and the corresponding offices of the Abwehr had been striving to obtain technical details. Together with the Luftwaffe and the Foreign Armies East Department, whose chief was the later Generalmajor Gehlen, comprehensive information was assembled under the name Zeppelin.

From about 5 million Russian prisoners, 100,000 were selected who knew something about the Urals region: engineers, architects, teachers, intellectuals, shop foremen, and so on. They provided a tremendous amount of information. As a result we were finally able to create a faithful picture of this huge land, its industries and the mentality of the various people who lived there.

Through Zeppelin[2] I possessed many exact site plans and knew where the largest industrial collective combines were located and how they were built: I also knew what sort of security measures there were: for example dogs were largely used for the nighttime guards.

But that wasn't a great help: it was totally impossible for me to attack and destroy any sort of object in the Urals in the near future.

Walter Schellenberg, who had read Himmler's imploring cable, asked me for my opinion on this operation. I told him openly that I considered the plan pure fantasy and wrote a report in the same vein.

"Let it be," observed Schellenberg, "and let me give you some advice based on my experience: the more fantastic and grotesque a project coming to you from 'above' seems, then with all the more enthusiasm must you take it up and find it brilliant. Then go on for four or five months as if you're working on it; in any case long enough until a new, even crazier plan comes and the previous one is forgotten. In this way you will earn the reputation of a man who shrinks from nothing and on whom they can depend. That is easy, for if you don't undertake anything impossible then nothing can go wrong..."

It's no wonder that Schellenberg had such a brilliant career in the shadows of Himmler and Heydrich!

In November 1944, shortly before the Ardennes offensive, at a time when I was working day and night on the plan for this action, I was summoned by Himmler to his new headquarters at Hohenlychen. We sat around a large, round table: Himmler, Dr. Kaltenbrunner, Schellenberg, Obergruppenführer Prützmann and I. What was it about? In the east the city of Riga had fallen into Russian hands on October 13. The Soviet armies had taken Belgrade on October 21, entered Romanian Transylvania and were bombarding the suburbs of Budapest. The Reich itself was threatened.

"What is involved," explained Himmler, "is to form and organize a resistance movement that Martin Bormann has, I believe, given the unusual title of Werwolf."

What had I to do with that? Everyone around me wore serious expressions and Schellenberg, as always, agreed eagerly. They failed to convince me of the effectiveness of this Werwolf, for the good reason that a resistance movement must arise in the entire nation, have realistic and constructive political objectives and most of all be very strong materially and also be supported from the outside. The countryside must be suitable as well. The strategy of the Werwolf could certainly be used in the Balkans, or in Iran, in Russia or China. There were certainly tactical advantages to be gained there. But not in a country with a large population in a small area, with railroads, highways and roads, which could expect no help whatsoever from outside. It was completely illusory to expect Anglo-American help against the Russians in 1945.

We could certainly have made use of such a resistance movement within a limited time frame in the mountains and forests of the "Alpine fortress," had this been organized to continue the fight with a political objective: namely to gain time and bring our soldiers and civilian population from the east to the west. Elsewhere Werwolf would have in any case provoked harsh countermeasures by the occupation forces, without our nation being able to gain the least benefit from such resistance. A subversive war of this nature only makes sense if it is developed with the necessary time in the necessary area. The pure resistance action would have to be combined with an uprising by all the European peoples already under the Soviet yoke or directly threatened by bolshevism.

I had no faith in the success of Werwolf and immediately asked Himmler whether the field of action of my troops still lay outside Germany as before. He answered yes, and Obergruppenführer Prützmann was theoretically tasked with the organization of this movement. As I predicted, the Werwolf action achieved no noteworthy success, something that every reasonable German can be glad for. Fortunately Werwolf can also be placed in the category of an operation that remained nothing more than wishful thinking.

In the course of the discussion with Himmler the subject of new weapons also came up. Quite imprudently I mentioned that in the opinion of Admiral Heye, it would be possible to equip U-boats with launching ramps for V-1 weapons. When Himmler heard this he leapt from his armchair and ran to the map which covered a large part of the wall.

"Then we must bombard New York!" he cried out, "lay it in ruins!"

Schellenberg became even more enthusiastic; he really was an outstanding actor. Himmler's eyes looked him over behind his famous steel pince-nez.

"The Americans must also get a taste of the war," he went on dreaming. "We must inform the Führer at once and telephone the grand admiral! Believe me, the psychological effect would be enormous! I'm convinced that the Americans could not bear to be attacked in their own country! Their fighting morale would sink to zero! What do you think?"

Schellenberg nodded in silent agreement. Dr. Kaltenbrunner's face remained impassive; Obergruppenführer Prütmann was busy counting his werewolves. It was difficult to get a chance to speak before the higher-ranking officers present there. Himmler was lost in a study of the map of America. Certainly he was already looking for targets. Prützmann gave me a sign behind his back and Kaltenbrunner cast a knowing look my way. I broke the silence and interjected that the V-1 was a very imprecise weapon and that by firing it from a U-boat at sea it would lack any accuracy.

"The American government," I added, "uses the lie that Germany poses a direct threat to the United States to make propaganda. Bombarding New York with two or three V-1s would only confirm

Roosevelt's propaganda. I believe that the psychological effects would be negative for us in every respect, for I am convinced that the American people would not let themselves become panic stricken and would react bravely, like the British people during the 'Blitz' of 1940. Speaking frankly, I don't see what advantage such an operation could bring us. A single V-1 would have to be able to hit a certain target with one hundred percent accuracy and we would have to announce the target by radio beforehand: at such and such a time target so and so will be destroyed."

Kaltenbrunner came to my aid.

"It would in fact be wiser," he observed, "to wait until our specialists can build more accurate rockets."

Himmler looked at us irresolutely. Then he calmed himself, sat down again and declared that he wished to be kept apprised of the progress made in the area of the V-1.

Of course the USA was never bombarded with V-1s nor by German bombers. Today, however, the USA has moved very close to Asia: with today's nuclear-tipped rockets one can destroy half the globe in minutes.

● ● ●

One of the most amazing men I ever met is Mohammed Amin al-Husani, the Grand Mufti of Jerusalem. He was born in Jerusalem in the year 1895, is a learned doctor of the Koran and during the First World War fought against the Turkish Army. From the moment in 1920 when Lord Balfour achieved the existence of the jewish state in Palestine, he became a fanatical defender of arab claims, which resulted in his being sentenced to ten years in prison by the English. He fled to Trans-Jordan and was named Grand Mufti and chairman of the Supreme Islamic Council. He entered Jerusalem in triumph. The British High Commissioner in Palestine tried to reach an accommodation with him − without success. In 1929 al-Husaini declared "Jihad," the holy war, against zionist colonization, for he was political and religious leader in one man. Since the order to imprison him was still in effect, he fled to Lebanon where the French placed him in a heavily guarded residence as a precautionary measure. He fled from there too and after unbelievable adventures reached Baghdad. His friend Rashid Ali undertook a coup d'état there in 1941.

This received only weak support from Germany, for we had only limited landing rights in Syria, which was under French mandate. In spite of the praiseworthy efforts of the intelligence service, Rashid Ali's operation failed, and the Grand Mufti was again forced to flee. He shaved off his beard, put on a European suit and appeared in Rhodos in 1942 and then in Tirana. Finally he flew to Germany, where he was received by Hitler.

He was a striking man: snow-white beard, blue eyes and a white turban. He looked like what he was: a figure from "A Thousand and One Nights." He supported us in a most generous way and the Africa Corps undoubtedly benefited from the tremendous influence he had in North Africa.

In 1946 he returned to the Middle East from Germany and settled in Egypt, where he again became chairman of the Supreme Islamic Council: he found many adherents at the Islamic Conferences in Karachi (1951) and Bandung (1955) and many of his proposals were adopted.

With his support we could have carried out many interesting operations in the Near East. Three of these were under preparation: the purpose of the first was to cut the Iraq-Mediterranean oil pipeline. Arab commandos had already blown up this artery, which delivered crude oil to the large refineries of Haifa and Tripoli, several times. But each time the pipeline was quickly repaired. Each time new commandos had to be trained and sent into action.

The ideal solution would have been to put the pumping station out of action, for it would have taken two to three months to put it back into operation. Our engineers had developed a small floating mine that could be introduced into the pipeline; but this device would only have destroyed the valves. Dropping phosphorous bombs into a narrow valley where both lines ran parallel, to burn out the lines, would have achieved the same result: they would only need to replace a few sections of pipe, with an interruption of perhaps a week.

The most effective solution was still a direct action against a pumping station. All of these sites had a small airfield for use by the aircraft that patrolled the pipeline, and a small blockhouse for defense. It was therefore possible to send a small detachment against one of these stations in gliders by night. Professor Georgi, a friend of Hanna Reitsch and a great glider specialist, had designed a new glider which could accommodate a dozen soldiers with their equipment and could be towed at 400 kph. In Ainring near Passau we investigated how this heavy glider could be recovered, meaning how our commandos would get back. Progress on this question was slow, and as a result I came upon the idea of using shot-down or captured American aircraft, which our mechanics had repaired, for example the DC-4 and the DC-6.

After a long wait I was informed that a half-dozen of these machines were ready. They were to be stationed on the island of Crete or in Greece and take off from there on their missions to the Near East.

We had excellent photographs of the pumping stations and their airfields. The landing strips looked rather short, but we were told that they had been lengthened. The target was chosen, and I decided that six four-engined aircraft should land there and that our people would be covered by light cannon and machine-guns from the aircraft. We had a special device with which we could destroy the antenna of the blockhouse, preventing them from sounding the alarm. But just before we were to pick up our DC-4s and DC-6s, they were destroyed in an enemy air raid on Munich's military airfield. The operation against the Iraq-Mediterranean oil pipeline had to be called off. There was not sufficient time to make other American aircraft airworthy in time.

Another operation we had prepared, to block the Suez Canal, which was constantly overflown by our jet aircraft, also had to be called off. On a day when seven or eight ships would sail through the canal our frogmen would sink the first and the last ships in the canal – and as many as possible in between. The frogmen were supposed to be deposited in the Sinai Desert by glider and subsequently picked up again. By the time we worked out exactly how the gliders were to take off again – the English used a similar system in their Operation "Market Garden" by the way – there was no more fuel available for the mission!

Our attack on certain important elements of the oil production installations at Baku also had to be put off "until further notice." The reasons were always the same: lack of materials and, above all, lack of means of transport.

The locks of several harbors in southern England were especially weak points: all we needed to do was deliver our manned torpedoes there, by glider – but that was exactly what we lacked!

● ● ●

I am quite happy that of all these planned and prepared actions I did not in the end have to carry out *Operation Der Wolf bellt* (The Wolf Howls).

At the end of November 1943 I received orders from the OKW to make my way to Vichy via Paris with the *Friedenthal* Battalion and to wait there for further instructions. In paris I contacted the military commander, who was staying in the Hôtel Continental on the Place de l'Opéra, Rue de Rivoli. It really was astonishing how many officers from all branches of the service were staying there; but one met even more of his superiors in the Hôtel Majestic, the seat of the military commander of France. In the end I learned what this order from the OKW was about: on November 9 Brigadier-General de Gaulle had kicked his superior, Army General Giraud, out of the *"Comité Francais de Libération Nationale"* (National Committee for the Liberation of France), which was meeting in Algiers, and had named himself president of the committee. He then summoned two communists, Midol and Fajol, who were active as ministers on the committee. Reports which had to be taken relatively seriously indicated that Operation Badoglio was being prepared in Vichy. According to other information Marshall Pétain, the French head of state, in agreement with several personalities from the marshall's circle, was supposed to be abducted by an English-Gaullist parachute commando.

I therefore drove to Vichy and took stock. At my disposal were six police companies, the battalion of my special detachment and a battalion of the Hohenstaufen Waffen-SS Division. I posted these troops around the city; in the north at the airfield, which we of course occupied; near Vesse in the west, Cusset in the east and Hauterive in the south. This were in total 2,000 soldiers who could seal off the city in a very short time. I sent patrols to the Randan Forest. Not a single enemy paratrooper was found in the course of the entire week.

There were no new reports: neither from the SD or the Abwehr. My Ia Fölkersam and I obtained some completely contradictory information while in civilian clothes. It was clear to me that a serious uneasiness existed in Vichy, but that the reason for this was not the gaullist paratroopers. The meeting at Montoire in 1940 had not achieved the desired results, neither for Germany nor for France, with whom, as I have already said, a definitive peace should have been concluded long ago. We had now occupied the country for three years. The tide of war was turning against us on all fronts. Resistance movements had sprung up, almost always led by the communists, the same group whose leaders had recommended fraternization with our soldiers from July to October 1940. Hitler had so little interest in the future of Germany-France relations, which was so important for a new Europe, that he was surprised to hear in November 1943 that our ambassador Abetz had been working there since December of the previous year.

I made all the necessary preparations around Vichy, and since no further orders arrived I drove to Paris. There I telephoned the Wolfs-schanze and learned that I was to return immediately to the Auvergne and was to wait for the code-word "The Wolf Howls." Then I was to concern myself with the persons of French head of state Marshall Pétain and his physician Dr. Ménétrel. I was responsible for their safety and would receive further instructions when "the wolf howled."

Marshall Pétain lived in Vichy on the fourth floor of the Hôtel du Parc; his bodyguard, which I observed in the course of its duties, didn't look too bad. A confrontation with it could possibly become serious. But what worried me most was what time of day "the wolf" would "howl." I hoped that it wouldn't begin to howl at night. If two- or three-thousand enemy paratroops jumped around Vichy at two in the morning, and if the marshall was well informed about the action and was waiting dressed in his uniform or civilian clothes, they would surely be able to take him.

I must admit that I had great respect for this old soldier, who called to the politicians for help when nothing else worked. He was then eighty-six years old and still stood erect in his sky-blue uniform. When I saw him I couldn't help but think of Field Marshall von Hindenburg, who after the First World War likewise had to bear the burden of a lost war. Philippe Pétain was eighty-nine years old when they sentenced him to death. He died at the age of ninety-five as a prisoner in the fortress of the island of d'Yeu.

I am glad that the wolf didn't howl. We received departure orders, left Vichy and were able to begin our Christmas leave straightaway. At the invitation of the German submarine command we spent it in a rest and recovery home for U-boat crews on the Arlberg. It was my last leave of this war.

On the other hand I must admit that I would have been very happy to have captured a different marshall, namely Tito. The genealogy of the present-day head of state of Yugoslavia is a controversial question. My late friend Alexander Botzaris assured me that Tito's "Croatian grandmother" was pure invention. Josef F. Broz was officially born in Kamrovec in 1892. He was a soldier by profession and fought in the First World War with the Austro-Hungarian Army. He was promoted to sergeant in 1915 and was captured by the Russians in the Carpathians. He was then said to have fought with the communists in the Omsk area and subsequently – so it says in the official biography – worked for the communist party in Yugoslavia under the name "Walter." Was it the same Broz who turned up in Vienna in 1934 after five years in prison, was trained in the Moscow special schools in 1935-36 and who led the pro-Soviet resistance in Yugoslavia in 1941-42? It may have been.

In early 1944 I received orders from the OKW to locate Tito's headquarters, to destroy it and capture him. Tito had already replaced General Mihailovich as Churchill desired. The minister of war of the young King Peter II of Yugoslavia, who was living in London, Mihailovich was frightened of the growing influence of the communists. To his astonishment his chetniks sometimes even fought alongside Hungarian troops, the croatians of Ante Pavelich and even our soldiers against Tito's troops.

But where was Tito hiding? I had no idea. Yugoslavia, with its mountainous, wooded terrain, was ideal for partisan warfare. The information we received from the appropriate sections of the Abwehr and the SD was imprecise and contradictory. So I drove to Zagreb and organized my own intelligence service. I entrusted this to three capable officers. Each was in charge of his own intelligence net. The agents of each net worked independently of each other. I myself resolved not to undertake anything until I had received three unanimous reports. We acted quickly and with the necessary secrecy, for we couldn't afford to attract the attention of the enemy; a cunning enemy who was holding half a dozen of our divisions in check.

I had stationed a training battalion of my commando unit in the Fruska Gora, a chain of mountains parallel to the Danube Valley and south of it. The battalion's training would, in reality, be carried out "near the front": the soldiers saw action every day against Tito's forces. A military convoy would have made the partisans suspicious. I therefore drove from Belgrade to Zagreb in a normal car and escorted by two officers through the local area. After the Sawe Valley and over poor roads, we reached Brcko, then Zagreb. The commander of the German garrison was extremely surprised to see us in one piece after our trip: the roads we had used were controlled by the partisans. We had in fact encountered a group of bearded partisans, their rifles under their arms. We also had our machine pistols on the floor of the car – invisible from outside, with the safety catches on "fire." It was immediately obvious to me that we had committed an act of carelessness that could have had disastrous consequences: "Tito captures Skorzeny!", a lovely headline for the *Daily Mirror* in May 1944!

I then returned to Berlin and soon afterward learned from my three independent intelligence services that Tito and his staff were at the moment staying near Dvar in western Bosnia. I at once sent my chief-of-staff, Hauptsturmführer Adrian von Fölkersam, to the commanding general of X Army Corps, which was stationed in this area, in order to inform him that we would be carrying out Operation Rösselsprung (Knight's Move) against Tito. Just as I was about to leave to lead the operation on the spot, suddenly von Fölkersam showed up back in Friedenthal.

"Something's not right!" he said. "The general received me very coolly, and I don't believe that we can count on his support in this action."

A radio message from our small working staff in Zagreb soon gave us an explanation for this very cool reception: "X Corps preparing an operation against Tito's headquarters. Date set for June 2, 1944."

That was decidedly stupid. Had the general revealed his cards, I would gladly have placed myself under his command and left him the glory of this operation and also accepted the responsibility myself had it eventually misfired. But even worse was the fact that if I now knew that the plan was to be carried out on June 2, Tito had surely been informed as well. I immediately advised X Corps and sent another of my staff officers to corps headquarters in Banja Luka, in order to try and change the date of the action. It did no good. The operation took place on the scheduled day: the large force of German troops encountered alerted partisan units. A battalion of Waffen-SS parachute troops were encircled in the Dvar Valley and required reinforcements to be flown in by glider. A battalion of the Brandenburg

Division had to cover the withdrawal by our soldiers, who were attacked from all sides. This battalion was commanded by the brave Oberstleutnant Walther, who was wounded and in January 1945 took the place of my chief-of-staff von Fölkersham with my SS commando units. The Waffen-SS parachute battalion and the battalion of the Brandenburg Division also came under my command in September 1944. The courageous Brandenburgers were incorporated into my units as "Commando Unit Southeast," while the other companies, which were commanded by Major Otto Beck, were attached to "Commando Unit South," which was fighting in Italy. I will come back to Major Beck.

Broz had obviously fled. All they found in his headquarters were two British officers, whom he probably wanted to get rid of, and a brand-new marshall's uniform. Tito had named himself marshall on November 29, 1943 – and he dressed himself accordingly! Somewhat later I was informed that he had fled to the island of Viz. But as a result of the assassination attempt against Hitler on July 20, 1944, it wasn't possible for me to organize a "Knight's Move" against the Adriatic island. Major Otto Beck would have all to gladly attacked Tito's island headquarters. He was mad at me for a long time for refusing to give him the order to do it.

Does anyone remember that the real oppression in Yugoslavia began in April 1945? On November 11 of that same year Tito proclaimed the Federative People's Republic, declared the dynasty of the Karageorgians deposed and assumed the power of the throne. General Mihailovich and his general staff were executed on July 17, 1946. Ten-thousand Croats and Serbs were punished with death and 3,670,000 followers of the previous regime were arrested. Many of them died in prison or labor camps. Churchill contented himself with writing to Peter II in August 1945:

"I hear that many regrettable things are happening in Yugoslavia. Unfortunately it is not in my power to intervene against them."

That was the funeral speech for those who had fought against communism in Yugoslavia.

I would like to cite a personal experience at this point: it's a small world: after the war I chanced to meet in Mallorca one of the two officers who Broz had so nicely left behind when he fled. Like me, he had been invited aboard the ship of a mutual English friend, and we became friends right away. He belonged to Colonel David

Stirling's commando group and had taken part in the well-known operation against Benghazi (Libya) by the "phantom major." By the way some of the participants in this action wore German uniforms. Then my new friend joined a secret commando and was finally sent by Churchill to Tito. My former enemy and new friend, later a Briga-dier-General, told me that during his stay at the headquarters of the "marshall" he became very aware that if Tito assumed power com-munism would also triumph in Yugoslavia. He sent report after re-port to this effect to London – but there was no reaction.

"The situation appeared so serious to me," he told me, "and so detrimental to British interests in the Balkans, that I made my way with great difficulty to Gibraltar and from there personally spoke with our prime minister by telephone. I gave him a very factual re-port on what Tito had in mind for Yugoslavia. Churchill let me speak and then asked:

"What do you plan to do personally, after the war?"

"Somewhat baffled, I replied that I intended to return to my es-tate in Scotland."

"That means then, if I understand correctly, that you don't want to stay and live in Yugoslavia?"

"No sir, of course not."

"Then why should you care a damn what happens to Yugoslavia after the war!"

The American secret service (CIA) credited me with the opera-tion against Tito's headquarters, because it was of the opinion that the Waffen-SS parachute battalion had then already been placed un-der my command.

My "Commando Unit Southeast" did however make life diffi-cult for Tito's brave troops. For some time in Fruska Gora we had the same medical officer, a Serb, as the partisans, as the military doctor assigned to our unit had not yet arrived. This fact simplified the ex-change of wounded prisoners.

We started a small retaliatory action and captured a few British liaison officers. Among these was Churchill's son, Randolph. It was amusing that our soldiers reaped the benefits of the supplies sent to Tito by his father Winston Churchill. The credit is due to Major Beck. He was an outstanding man, who in the First World War had been awarded the Great Golden Medal of Bravey (Austria) as a common soldier. But Otto Beck, who was intimately familiar with the ways and customs of the Balkans, was also a man with big ideas. Almost too late they made available large quantities of five and ten pound Sterling notes, with which Major Beck's middlemen bought from the partisans whole truckloads of weapons, ammunition and assorted war materials. These materials were dropped off regularly by British submarines and small ships at certain hidden harbors on the Adriatic coast. Our soldiers took delivery of the wares directly and paid with phoney British Sterling pounds, which the partisans gladly exchanged for thousands of dinars. This "exchange" went on for months to the general satisfaction of everyone, until Marshall Tito's general staff got wind of it. Fighting broke out in the course of an exchange of goods and our useful and cheap deliveries were stopped.

The banknotes were made by professional counterfeiters, who were in concentration camps during the war. On this occasion we put them in special barracks, where they enjoyed more freedom. A certain Walter Hagen tries to describe the whole story in his book *Unternehmen Bernhardt*. Hagen is the cover name for Wilhelm Hoettl, one of Schellenberg's associates in Office VI (Foreign) of the RSHA. Before the Nuremberg Tribunal he wriggled out by bravely playing the role of witness for the prosecution. He had always been a master of the double game. Today he admits that he had been in contact with the Black Orchestra in the Vatican since 1943 and later established ties with Allen Welsh Dulles, later head of the CIA, in Switzerland. Unfortunately this takes us back into the magic circle of the secret service.

After the war Doctor Hjalmar Schacht explained to me that the Reichsbank had no idea that phoney Sterling pounds were being made. A few banknotes were sent to the Swiss Banking Association to be checked. In an accompanying phoney letter from the Reichsbank, they explained that they thought the notes were counterfeit. After close examination the Swiss replied that the banknotes were real and that the Bank of England had certified that the serial numbers and dates of issue corresponded to the bills in circulation.

The principal distributor of the phoney money was a clever businessman by the name of Friedrich Schwend, to whom they gave an honorary rank in the Allgemeine SS and who naturally earned a commission on each issue of money. After the war Schwend probably hid or burned most of the available English pounds, and for years the English secret service busied itself with the affair and made enquiries. Schwend, who certainly lost no money in this affair, had possessed considerable wealth even before. But as Cicero said in his famous speech against Verres[3]: *"in multis esse numnis"* (having his chests full of gold), always helped. And where the make-believe Cicero was concerned, he was paid in phoney English pounds, although his information was real gold. In 1954 Bazna wrote to Chancellor Adenauer to complain about the "great injustice" that had been done him and to demand the modest assistance of 2,100,000 DM against the 12 million that he had lying in a frozen Swiss bank account. Unfortunately the German chancellor did not agree to *Cicero's* request.

When we were preparing our commandos in the Near East, Walter Schellenberg revealed to me, "that we might eventually manage the affair," and "that we weren't quite so poor." In this way I learned of the existence of the counterfeit English banknotes. Office VI's paymaster gave 5,000 Pounds to my adjutant Karl Radl when we were trying to find and free Mussolini. Radl kept the bills in a small, locked case. I recommended that we only pass out these banknotes sparingly, and subsequently demanded very precise record keeping of Dr. Berger, who had to distribute this money to a dozen officers of the intelligence service. I must say that, in my opinion, Dr. Berger was too generous with it. I made it clear to him that this phoney money was as good as real money and therefore had to be used sparingly. Finally we were able to refund most of the sum entrusted to him to the Office VI paymaster.

Must I mention that neither Karl Radl nor I used this money in any way and that we defrayed our personal expenses from out of our soldier's pay? Many will probably say that we were stupid. But we were just convinced that the phoney pound notes were a weapon that allowed us to win a partial economic victory over the enemy. We were soldiers and it would never have occurred to us to make money on the side or buy on the black market. In Yugoslavia, on the other hand, I had not the least scruples about using this phoney money: the more weapons we bought, the fewer weapons the partisans had with which to fight and even kill our comrades.

After the war there were many chroniclers and journalists who claimed to have seen me in the vicinity of Toplitz Lake in Austria, "the chief-of-staff of a special detachment charged with raising the SS treasure sunk deep in the lake." Of course about 30 chests, containing "millions of counterfeit pounds," are lying in about 30 to 40 meters of water (others say 50 to 70 meters).

Anything is possible. During the war Toplitz was a navy testing and training center, and it is quite possible that there are chests on the bottom of the lake containing banknotes, documents and the like. I don't know; I have also never worried about it. In 1963 a so-called Max Gruber, former member of the SS, testified that he had been present at the sinking of the chests and had seen me on the shore of the lake... Questioned by an investigating commission of the Austrian government, Gruber was forced to admit that he was first of all not a former member of the SS; second, that he had never been to Toplitz until he went there with the commission; third, that he consequently never saw any chests being sunk; and fourth, that he had mentioned my name to lend himself credibility. He was charged with making false statements.

It is true, however, that the Austrian investigating committee had chests raised from the lake, however their contents have not been revealed to this day. Unfortunately in 1963 a young Munich diver aged nineteen drowned. Since then the Austrian government has forbidden further search operations.

The most unbelievable article ever published about this affair appeared in the Swedish paper *Vägen Framat* (on November 30, 1963). A certain Palmquist "confessed" that under my direction he had removed numerous chests of "treasure" from the lake, to where he had come by aircraft from Stockholm every night. He had taken several gold bars with him, which he kept in a safe. The same Palmquist introduced the editor of another Swedish paper, the *Aftonbladet*, to the *Vägen Framat* reporter as Benito Mussolini. The Duce had a new face, supposedly the result of an operation by a surgeon whom I had – of course – paid from the SS treasure. This money had also enabled the Duce to be brought to Sweden and there made the chief editor of the *Aftonbladet*!

I could recount many more crazy examples of this kind. But let us leave that. In any case for about fifteen years certain persons have made a profit from the alleged "treasure" of Toplitz, in that they have ruthlessly exploited human gullibility and written and written...

• • •

One can include the counterfeit money among the unconventional weapons. But the father of this idea cannot claim the glory of having invented this weapon. He was only imitating what the English did in 1794-1797, when they flooded France with phoney paper money on the pretext of supporting the civil war in the Vendée.[4]

In the years 1927 to 1932 ten million phoney banknotes of the Federal Reserve Bank of the USA were made on Stalin's order. These bills were mainly issued in China, Havana, Montreal, San Francisco, Belgrade and even Berlin. Numerous phoney 100-dollar bills, printed in the Soviet Union, were discovered in Berlin. The *Berliner Tageblatt* of January 23, 1930 and then the *New York Times* of February 24, 1933 came to the same conclusion, namely that the phoney dollars came from Russia and were put into circulation by known Soviet agents, which was of course a mistake.

It is really a shame that we couldn't have bought the Russian automatic rifle in 1941. This weapon, which then could fire ten shots automatically, was easy to use and showed how carefully the Russians had prepared for war. In the early phases of the war this weapon gave the Russian infantryman superior firepower.

The English also possessed perfect and simple weapons at that time, especially the Sten submachine-gun, to which a silencer could be fitted.

I took an interest in this type of weapon right at the beginning when I took over the Friedenthal Battalion, in part because they were delivered to us direct from London. In Holland we found several resistance organizations, which though insignificant, enabled our intelligence service to play an interesting radio game with the enemy. In this way I placed an order in London for a revolver with a silencer. Fourteen days later I received the weapon via the Dutch captain of a Swedish ship, a sort of double agent, as I suspected.[5] I opened the window of the office where we worked and fired at a group of ducks swimming in the canal. There was scarcely a hiss to be heard, and the passers-by never even raised their heads.

I was also one of the first German soldiers to receive a Sten submachine-gun fitted with a similar type of silencer. Obviously it was a great advantage to a special detachment or patrol when the soldiers, if forced to fire, could do so almost without making a sound. For the front-line soldiers such weapons would also be of great importance in patrol work, and the best results could be achieved with limited casualties.

Apart from the silencer the Sten offered several advantages: it was far superior to the German submachine-guns and for several reasons: much quicker to manufacture, it also cost significantly

less than ours, which were however more accurate. The Sten could be dropped into the water, the snow, the dirt and it still worked. Not ours. Why not produce the silent Sten in quantity?

I tried to convince two senior officers of the Military Economic and Armaments Office, whose commander was General Georg Thomas. I invited them to supper at Friedenthal: they were reluctant. It was spring, pleasant weather, and so I suggested a walk in the park after supper. They agreed. We walked part of the way. Suddenly I stopped them.

"Gentlemen," I said to them, "you are dead. And probably I too."

They collided in the darkness.

"Dead? We're dead?"

Behind us one of my people flashed his pocket lamp. He had the Sten with the silencer in his hand and pointed at the empty shell casings on the ground. He had fired an entire magazine into the air.

Our technicians of the armaments ministry were visibly very impressed by their theoretical and silent death. But the submachine-gun lecture in the park achieved nothing. The answer I received from General Thomas' colleagues was:

"You are correct in principle. But, you admit yourself: the Sten submachine-gun is no precision weapon. The Führer has repeatedly said that every German soldier has a right to the best weapons in every respect, and we could not accept responsibility for recommending the manufacture of a submachine-gun that, even if silent, is less accurate than those already under production in Germany. Heil Hitler!"

We could say the General Thomas, on the other hand, did not hesitate to accept grave responsibilities.

Notes

1. One should recall the mission given General Gardane, who was sent to Shah Fet Ali in Tehran by Napoleon in 1807. There Gardane and Major Verdier reorganized the Shah's troops, which consisted of 60,000 mediocre infantry and 140,000 outstanding cavalry. After Constantinople, Tehran was to be the second stop for the great Oriental Army, which was on its way to India. Napoleon guaranteed the Shah the reincorporation of Georgia (which had belonged to Russia since 1801) into the Persian Empire. Without the gold and the intrigues of Sir Hartford Jones, who also moved in from the Persian Gulf and foiled Operation Gardane in 1809, Stalin would perhaps have been born a Persian!

2. It appears that the author of Schellenberg's biography confused Ulm with Zeppelin. In it he speaks of Operation *Zeppelin*, which was supposed to inflict severe damage on Russian industrial targets, primarily in Magnitogorsk and Kubichev-Chelyabinsk. The strikes were to be made using V-1 weapons, which were to be carried part way to their targets by long range bombers (of which we never had enough, incidentally). This project could therefore not have been planned before June 1944, because the V-1 was not ready for series production until then. However, Operation *Ulm* was supposed to be carried out a year earlier (in 1943).

3. C. Licinius Verres, famous Roman tyrant, appointed money lender in Sicily in 74 B.C., imposed a crushing tax burden on Sicilian and even Roman citizens. He fled without waiting to be tried. (Editors' note)

4. This was an idea of British Prime Minister William Pitt. There was such a quantity of as*signats* (French bank notes), that paper money soon ceased to have any value whatsoever. The "Louis d'or", which was worth 2,500 paper francs in November 1795, rose to 6,500 in the following month. In 1797 the *Direktorium* was forced to withdraw all *assignat* from circulation. (Editors' note)

5. All British special units were in possession of this 7.65mm-caliber revolver in 1943. I was in Den Haag when they gave me one.

PART III

16

HITLER' ORDER:
YOU MUST FIND AND FREE THE DUCE!
OPERATION ALARICH

Why Hitler chose me – His talent, convincing men – His proposals – Discussions with General Student and Himmler – Illusions on the part of the Reichsführer – "You are not the right man for the job" – Illusions on the part of Field Marshall Kesselring – The double game played by the Italian king and Badoglio – Stalin, a "cousin" of Victor Emmanuel! – Betrayal, fear and flight by the royalist clique – Canaris steps onto the stage – The story of the Pope's arrest – Difficulties in our investigations – Mussolini on the island of Ponza – He is to be delivered to the English and is sought by the Americans, who want to kidnap him – Churchill's secret speech to the English House of Commons.

The six of us stood along the wall. We were six officers: an Oberstleutnant and a Major of the army, two Oberstleutnants of the Luftwaffe, an SS-Sturmbannführer and I. Since I had the lowest rank, I was last in the line, all leaders of special units.

The room had indirect lighting, so there were no shadows. Before us was a long table, with general staff situation maps and several colored pencils, a fireplace, beside the large window a desk and on the opposite wall a small painting, Dürer's Veilchen, in a silver frame.

A door opened to my left: Hitler stepped into the room, walked past us slowly and saluted us briefly with a raised hand. Then he looked at us for several moments without saying anything. This was the third time I had seen him. The first time had been at the 1936 Olympic Winter Games in Garmisch-Partenkirchen. The second time

I had been standing with my workers high above on a scaffolding on the Vienna Ring when he entered the city in triumph in March 1938.

At this moment he was only a few steps away from me. He wore a white shirt with black tie under his field-grey jacket. On his breast was the Iron Cross, First Class from the First World War and the silver badge awarded for having been wounded three times. His adjutant introduced the Oberstleutnant on the right end, then the others followed. When Hitler stopped before me he shook my hand, and his gaze did not leave me for an instant. I bowed briefly and gave a quick summary of my military career. Then he stepped back a few steps, sized us all up once again and asked:

"Who of you is familiar with Italy?"

For several seconds there was silence. I was the only one to speak up.

"I have travelled as far as Naples in two private trips by motor-cycle, mein Führer."

Quiet. Then suddenly the second question.

"What do you think of Italy?"

The army Oberstleutnant answered that Italy was our military and ideological ally, the Luftwaffe officers mentioned the Rome-Berlin axis, and my immediate neighbor spoke of the anti-Comintern pact. When Hitler was standing in front of me, I merely said, "I am Austrian, mein Führer!"

On hearing these words he looked at me long and searchingly. Was he waiting for me to say something else? I remained silent. I had said it all in three words: South Tirol, our struggle for union with the fatherland. The silence continued and I sensed that something must happen now.

"I have to speak further with Hauptsturmführer Skorzeny," he said in a calm voice. "The other officers may withdraw."

They excused themselves and left the room. We were alone. It was about 10:30 P.M., July 26, 1943, when Hitler informed me in the Wolfsschanze what sort of mission he was about to entrust me with. His approximate words were, "Mussolini was betrayed yesterday. His king has had him arrested. But the Duce is not only my ally, he is also my friend. To me he is the embodiment of the last great Roman, and I can not abandon this statesman. He was too careless. The new Italian government will surely desert us and deliver the Duce to the

Anglo-Saxons: he will be betrayed and sold. And I must prevent such a breach of faith from taking place!"

Both of us were still standing. He walked up and down the large room and appeared to be thinking. Then he stopped before me and once again looked at me long.

"We must find out where the Duce is being held and free him. That is the mission I have for you Skorzeny. And I have chosen you because I am convinced that you will succeed with this operation. And you must risk everything to carry out this action, which is now most important to the conduct of the war. Naturally this mission is to be kept absolutely secret, otherwise it will fail. Only five other people may be informed about it. You are attached to the Luftwaffe and placed under the command of General Student, who will subsequently give you the details. I don't want Italy to become a trap for our soldiers, and all false friends must be eliminated. I charge you personally with finding out as quickly as possible where Mussolini is being held prisoner and rescuing him from there. You will of course select your own people for the mission. But you must act quickly, very quickly! You will understand that the life of the Duce depends on it!"

"Jawohl, mein Führer!"

So it wasn't Franz, or Ulm, as I had assumed when I drove to the Wolfsschanze. I thought of my comrades in Berlin and Friedenthal, who were definitely worried.

"The most important thing," continued the Führer, "is that neither the German military headquarters in Italy nor our embassy in Rome is to be allowed to learn your exact mission. Understand, these gentlemen have a completely false picture of the situation and would probably act incorrectly. That means: strictest secrecy! I have full confidence in you Skorzeny. We will see one another again. In the meantime I wish you all the best!"

He shook my hand. I promised to do my best.

Much has been written about Hitler's gaze. It is said that this gaze was fascinating, hypnotic, magnetic. The only thing I can say for certain is that the Führer did radiate a real, unusual persuasive power. His gaze alone was enough to convince. His word, his bearing, the entire man radiated an extraordinary power. This conversation had lasted barely twenty minutes, and nevertheless I gained the impression that Hitler's account of events had lasted hours.

Hitler knew me no better than the other five officers. Why had he chosen me? ... "Because I am convinced that you will succeed," he had said, and he repeated it twice. From where did he have this conviction, and why was I too, when I stood before him, convinced of the success of this operation? I cannot say.

I felt hungry and was about to get something in the tea house when Hitler's adjutant Otto Günsche, then an Hauptsturmführer in the Waffen-SS, informed me that General Student was waiting for me in an adjoining room. He was a jovial-looking, somewhat rotund man, who had been badly wounded outside Rotterdam in 1940. A deep crevice on his forehead was a reminder. He greeted me warmly and I told him of the mission I had just received from the Führer. Then to my great surprise the Reichsführer of the SS also walked into the room.

This was the first time I had seen him close up, and I must admit that he didn't look especially sympathetic to me. He had a weak handshake, and his eyes shifted constantly behind his pince-nez. He got on very well with General Student and turned out to be friendly in spite of his extraordinary nervousness. He repeated to me what I had already heard from Hitler.

"But there's more than Mussolini involved!" he cried out. "You must also know what's behind it. And this is nothing less than treason: the conspiracy that has been planned for four months is not limited to Italy. Its feelers reach out to Madrid, Ankara and Lisbon. The leaders of this plot are King Victor Emmanuel and Prince Umberto. The Führer doesn't believe a word of Badoglio's declaration that Italy will stand by its treaties with us." Himmler began to develop a picture of the entire Italian conspiracy, and I had difficulty following and committing to memory all the names.

The suspicion existed since January 18, 1942, the day on which General Ambrosio, the commander-in-chief of the 2nd Army, was named chief of the general staff to succeed General Roatta. He had been preparing to arrest the Duce since April of that year in agreement with General Castellano. On orders from the king, a trap was laid by Dino Grandi and Counts Ciano, de Vecchi and Bottai for a sitting of the "Grand fascist Council."

"And that's not all!" continued the Reichsführer. "According to the latest statistics the National Fascist Party has 700,000 members and the "Dopolavoro" movement five million. There is the fascist militia as well! One can and must be able to hold a country with such forces!"

Himmler had plenty of illusions. He ignored the fact that the fascist militia had recently been incorporated into the army and that two days hence the National Fascist Party was supposed to be abolished.

He added that Cercia, the carabinieri general, was not to be trusted and that one couldn't trust General Carboni, whose troops were stationed near Rome. Fortunately the capital was declared an open city at the instigation of Generalfeldmarschall Kesselring.

This fact did not prevent the city from being bombarded by the allies, however.

Himmler went on: General Galbiati, who intended to defend Mussolini in front of the "Grand Council," did not possess the necessary ability, nor did Farinacci. Proof: the vote on Grandi's order of the day resulted in 19 votes against 7 and one abstention. Polverelli, the minister for press and propaganda was a washout and so on. But the craftiest was Umberto. He and the king had to be arrested. Also Badoglio and others...

"Do you know at least who the future foreign minister will be?" Himmler asked me.

Modestly I admitted that I did not. The Reichsführer shrugged his shoulders.

"Guariglia, the former ambassador in Ankara! That's also clear!"

For me that wasn't so clear. Who was supposed to arrest the king and the crown prince? The Führer had given me very explicit instructions where the Duce was concerned. Himmler showered us with an avalanche of names – generals, admirals, ministers... He was inexhaustible, and although I had a good memory, I pulled out my notebook to write down certain facts.

"Have you lost your mind?" the Reichsführer screamed at me. "Everything I'm saying here is strictly secret!"

He shrugged his shoulders again and ensured that Student had witnessed this unpardonable behavior. As it was almost eleven, I asked for permission to telephone Berlin and let my unit know what was happening. Outside in the hall I lit a cigarette as I waited for the long-distance call. Just then Himmler came out of the room and lit into me, "This is unbelievable! Don't you have enough willpower to stop smoking? Always these stinking cigarettes! I can see that you're not the right man for this job!"

I said nothing, and he walked away, furious.

"You're right not to take that too seriously," observed Otto Günsche. "You just can't talk to the Reichsführer when he's nervous."

Günsche kindly offered me a room to work in. I asked for a secretary, who came immediately. General Student called for me again: I would act as his operations officer in Rome and fly with him to Rome on July 27 at 8 A.M. Finally I got Untersturmführer Radl on the phone. I made it clear to him that there'd be little time for sleep that night, and gave him my instructions: select thirty volunteer soldiers and the best officers; dress them in paratrooper uniforms and provide them with the necessary papers. They were to leave from Staaken airfield at six o'clock the next morning. The destination was secret but would be given to the pilot during the flight. Ten officers of the intelligence service, who were assigned to us, must leave with us. Further instructions would come by teletype.

From midnight on, Karl Radl organized the operation in Berlin. He was speechless when I told him that I had spoken to the Führer personally. I didn't see Radl and his volunteers until they arrived at the Practica di Mare airport. They had in fact followed all the instructions, except for one (which came from the Reichsführer personally), that all participants were to dye their hair black – the most certain way to attract attention!

General Student and I landed at Rome at lunchtime on July 27 and subsequently drove the 20 kilometers southeast to Frascati, where Generalfeldmarschall Albert Kesselring, the commander-in-chief of the southern front, had his headquarters. As General Student's operations officer, I had to accompany him to dinner with the Generalfeldmarschall that same evening.

In the course of the evening I was able to ascertain that Hitler was right: Generalfeldmarschall Kesselring was convinced that the new monarchist government would continue the war at our side. Marshall Badoglio had officially assured him of this and had even given him his word of honor as a soldier.

Generalfeldmarschall Kesselring was one of the most sympathetic commanders I ever met. After supper I sat with some young officers who had spoken with senior Italian officers about the arrest of the

Duce. The latter had assured them that they didn't know where the Duce was and that Marshall Badoglio probably didn't know either. I assessed these statements extremely skeptically and made that plain to all, without noticing that Field Marshall Kesselring was standing behind me.

"Herr Hauptmann," he said positively, "I consider our Italian comrades to be honorable, and you would do well do adopt a similar attitude in future. We have no reason to doubt the word of honor of an Italian general who is serving his king. The Italian armed forces are and remain our loyal allies. They will fight at our side until the end!"

I did not respond to the field marshall, but he wasn't to hang on to his illusions much longer: General Castellano would sign the declaration of surrender with General Bedell-Smith in Syracuse on September 3, 1943.

On the evening of July 29 I waited for Radl and our soldiers. We quartered our apparently genuine paratroopers at Practica di Mare next to the airfield. I took Radl with me to Fracati. It is home to some very famous: Borghese, Aldobrandini, Monti, Bracciano, Tusculum... I had arranged our room in a villa next to Tusculum II, it was close to General Student's room. Only now did I explain to my adjutant what was involved: to find where the Duce was being held prisoner in order to free him as quickly as possible: that was the mission I had received from Hitler personally. But during the night of July 26-27 we received an additional order from the OKW, according to which we must eventually "take care of" the following personalities: the king, the crown prince Umberto, the new foreign minister Guariglia, the minister and advisor to the king Acquarone, as well as Signore Bottai, former member of the Fascist Grand Council. The paratroops of Student's corps had the job of arresting admirals and generals, and if I remember correctly general Student had the "gratifying" personal task of informing His Majesty Victor Emmanuel III that he was to consider himself a German prisoner. This was how Operation Alarich was to proceed in the event of betrayal on the part of the Badoglio government, or if we wanted to head off such a certain betrayal.

The Grand Council contained one of the most determined of the conspirators against the leaders of the fascists: Count Galeazzo Ciano, who was married to the Duce's oldest daughter, Edda, with whom he had three children. Mussolini had made Ciano his foreign minister, but took over the post himself on February 5, 1943 and appointed his son-in-law ambassador to the Vatican. Following the arrest of his father-in-law Ciano remained at his post at the King's wish. However Badoglio, who couldn't stand him, gave orders to keep him under observation – with the intention of later sending him to the penal island of Ponza. Edda Ciano alerted an unusual man she had met: Eugen Dollmann. He had lived for a long time with his mother in Rome and was known as a great art connoisseur. He was welcomed in certain circles in Rome, was courteous to the ladies present, although it was said that their charms had no effect on him. He held a high honorary rank in the "Allgemeine SS" and was Himmler's "spy" in Rome's high society.

Hitler had decided, "to save Mussolini's daughter and grandchildren and also to see to Ciano." Sturmbannführer Kappler, the police attache at the German embassy, organized the escape together with Hauptsturmführer Groebl, an Italian specialist in the SD, and Hauptsturmführer der Waffen-SS Priebke, who was later killed in action against Tito's partisans.

It has been claimed, wrongly, that I took part in this action on August 27. I didn't think that the operation would present serious difficulties and flew to Führer Headquarters with General Student while preparations were under way. Generalfeldmarschall Kesselring put a Ju 52 at the disposal of the refugees, who arrived safe and sound in Munich. I first met Count Ciano in September 1943, when I was forced to witness an extremely embarrassing conversation between the Duce and his son-in-law.

Much later Baron von Steengracht, the German state secretary in the Foreign Ministry, informed me that Ciano had gone through his "diaries" and substantially revised them: the count had crossed out or added passages according to the time and circumstances so as to achieve a sufficiently anti-Hitler version, which could serve as his alibi in dealing with the allies.

On the other hand, I was happy to have sent four of my men from Friedenthal with a truck to Rocca delle Caminate on September 12, 1943. Staying there were Donna Rachele, the wife of the Duce, and their two youngest children, Annamaria and Romano. They were flown to Munich, where they were reunited with their husband and father.

Operation Alarich was not to our taste. I had about 50 officers and NCOs at my disposal; about 40 were members of my 502nd Commando Battalion. The remaining 10 were military intelligence officers of Schellenberg's Office VI. Several of these outranked me, but were of course under my command. They were supposed to put us onto the trail of Mussolini. But how were we to proceed if they changed the place where the Duce was being held at the same time as we had to arrest a good dozen political personalities..."with appropriate respect in view of their positions?"

The object of Operation Alarich was to guard against a betrayal that was going to take place anyway. How could one tell in the midst of political confusion that a former ally, who still firmly maintained his loyalty, would commit open treason? Surely the decision would fall to the OKW. But how could they in the Wolfsschanze calculate the exact moment when an ally becomes an enemy?

After General Eisenhower's declaration (on July 29, 1943), in which he encouraged the Italian people to rise up against the German Army and promised allied help to free Italy, we received another list of suspicious persons, which brought the total to 70! This list was given to me by General Student and Sturmbannführer Kappler, the attache to ambassador von Mackensen. The latter was soon replaced by Rudolf Rahn, whose credentials were accepted by King Victor Emmanuel III, who was still "determined to wage the war to final victory at Germany's side," on September 8, 1943. At 7:30 P.M. on that same September 8 Badoglio was forced to admit in a radio report that the king's government had surrendered in Syracuse on September 3.

On September 3, in the course of an official conversation, Badoglio said to our ambassador Rahn:

"I don't understand why the German Reich is so suspicious of me. They're trying to insult me, which hurts me deeply. Don't you think that an old general like me knows what it means to give his word of honor to the Führer? Never, and you can be sure of that, never will we break our word!"

At that moment his own chief-of-staff Castellano was breaking the officer's word of honor he had given on his order.

The story contains another graphic example of double dealing. One must say that the Italian people felt only disgust toward this behavior. Later the Italian children in allied-occupied working class suburbs painted Marshall Badoglio in yellow traitor's colors and shouted loudly:

*"Badoglio,
Colore di olio..."*

I don't know who gave the name of the King of the Visigoths to this operation of Himmler's. Alarich, who threatened Constantinople following the death of Theodorich the Great and took Rome at the beginning of the Fifth Century, was definitely a symbolic figure in the eyes of the troubled Reichsführer. Viewed from the Wolfsschanze, such an operation could appear tempting. But seen up close, from Frascati and Rome, it was obvious that it would be difficult to carry out with the available means and rolled out political problems which we had no authority to solve.

The king and his retinue lived in a huge palace, "Villa Savoia," which was surrounded by a park and guarded by a battalion of the king's guard. General Student planned a ground action by two or three companies of paratroopers, which were to storm the palace under his personal command at the moment the gliders carrying the larger special commando landed in the park. At the beginning of August I feared that such an operation must entail considerable bloodshed, and that it would give our "allies" an official excuse to break our alliance, which they still officially stood by. I myself was to take care of Crown Prince Umberto, and I therefore resolved to proceed in all silence. The crown prince occupied the Palazzo Quirinale in the center of the city; a huge building with about 2,000 rooms. I knew that Prince Umberto and Princess Marie-José of Belgium occupied separate apartments, but I didn't know exactly where they were. It was impossible to obtain an up-to-date plan of the palace, and the aerial photos taken "in error" proved to be poor, as there was a cloud right over the palace. Furthermore in the second floor of the Quirinal there was a passage to the Palazzo Colonna, which was as big as a gallery and which was to be occupied first. Of course the Quirinal was also guarded by a battalion of carabinieri. Consequently, a forced entry must automatically lead to a bloody battle. I felt it more suitable to organize a small detachment which, with the help of ladders, could climb into the palace through a suitable salon window. One will understand that we weren't happy with Alarich for all these reasons.

Radl and I had set up fourteen files with situation plans of the residences of prominent persons who were to be neutralized on X-Day of the open betrayal. In the mornings Radl and I had breakfast in the officers mess dressed in paratrooper uniforms. Then we drove through Rome in civilian clothes in a car which had been placed at our disposal. It was unbelievably hot. Since we had to pay for our lunch out of our soldier's pay, we only rarely looked for expensive restaurants. We understood Italian fairly well and also spoke some of this language. The mentality of the people we had to deal with was thus less foreign to us.

The Italian people had had enough of a war which had begun eight years earlier with the difficult conquest of Ethiopia. The East African Expeditionary Corps comprised 500,000 soldiers and about 100,000 workers, engineers, sailors, road builders and masons, who built the roads and cities that have now disappeared. From 1937 to 1940 King Victor Emmanuel's far-flung empire had to be organized and equipped.

When on June 10, 1940 the Duce made the mistake of declaring war on Great Britain and France without being asked by Hitler, the king announced: "I entrust the head of the government, the Duce of fascism, the first marshall of the empire, with the command of the troops on all fronts." From 1940 the poorly-equipped, inadequately fed and badly-led Italian troops went from one catastrophe to the next, in Ethiopia, on the French border, in Greece, in Albania, in Cyrenaica, in Libya, Somaliland, Eritrea, in the Sudan and on the banks of the Don in Russia – three years filled with defeats and huge losses, with many killed, wounded, captured and missing in these far-away lands, and as well often unwarranted reproaches.

Benito Mussolini was not a good wartime leader. But whatever mistakes he may have made: he was arrested in treacherous fashion by his king, the man who after the victory in Ethiopia offered him the title of prince for himself and his heirs. "I turned it down," the Duce later explained, "as I would also have refused the title of duke. I answered the king: my ancestors were farmers, and that, majesty, is honor enough to me."

On January 9, 1944 this same king bestowed on Josef Stalin the Necklace of the Order of Annunziata, by which the Soviet dictator became a "cousin" of Victor Emmanuel III. Stalin must have laughed!

Operation Alarich, also called Operation Student by many historians, never took place. The monarchist government surrendered secretly and unconditionally to the Anglo-Americans on September 3 and imagined that it had enough time to disappear by September 9. But the secret conclusion of peace was announced by Radio Algiers on September 8. The monarchist government withdrew to the Ministry of the Interior and from there to a carabinieri barracks. Badoglio, half dead from fear, was the first to leave Rome, at 3 A.M. on September 9. The king and his retinue and almost all the generals did the same an hour later. They subsequently met in Bari, "in order to fully comply with their duty."

So the betrayal had taken place, and the new government could do what it wanted. I was now interested in where they were holding the Duce prisoner. From now on the Italian government was seen as the enemy and the situation had thus become clear.

Naievely, I must say today, I asked General Student whether our military intelligence service, namely the Canaris office in Italy, which must have numerous agents at its disposal, could not work hand in hand with us, so to speak. I didn't know then that Admiral Canaris had refused to spy in the country of an ally and that he pretended, "not to have any agents active in Italy." Nevertheless the Abwehr sent regular reports on the current situation in Italy to the OKW. These reports were circulated to the commanding generals of corps.

I got to see one of these reports at the beginning of August. In essence it said that, "the change of government in Italy was a guarantee of an invigorated employment of all forces," in order to continue the struggle at Germany's side. Radl was just as skeptical as I, and I also learned that Generalfeldmarschall Kesselring was no longer convinced of Badoglio's good will.

Messina fell on August 17. Almost simultaneously we heard that the head of the Abwehr, Admiral Canaris, accompanied by Lahousen, had met the chief of the Italian intelligence service, General Cesare Amé. The discussion took place on July 30 in the Hotel Danieli and the following day on the Lido. Radl and I concluded from this that the report was written by Canaris after checking with Amé.

I will explain in the next chapter how we discovered Mussolini's prison: on the northeast tip of Sardinia, on the island of Santa Maddalena. We informed the OKW and were supposed to free the Duce on August 28. But on the morning of the 27th Benito Mussolini was flown away to an unknown destination in a Red Cross seaplane. Bad luck, I thought. Then, on August 31 in Rome, Sturmbannführer Kappler informed me that during my absence (on August 29 I was with General Student at Führer Headquarters), the Italian foreign minister Guariglia had delivered the following official message to the German ambassador in Rome von Mackensen:

"The Italian government possesses solid proof that a German commando is planning a coup d'état for August 28 in Rome and, working with former fascists, intends to set up a new dictatorship in Italy. Furthermore, the German troops intend to arrest numerous persons, including His Holiness Pope Pius XII, the King, the Crown Prince, serving ministers, senior military men and other public figures, in order to deliver them to Germany dead or alive.

His Majesty's government, which since the arrest of Mussolini has strived, and will continue to strive, to continue the struggle at Germany's side, can only deeply regret such behavior. The Italian government insists that the German government be informed that any attempt of this type would be nipped in the bud."

I can only confirm that there was never any talk of, "kidnapping the King, the Crown Prince and so on, in order to deliver them to Germany dead or alive." Our orders in this regard were clear: the personalities were to be arrested, but "with appropriate respect in view of their position." In no case were they to be injured and were definitely not to be killed.

The arrest of Pope Pius XII was also never planned: I never heard of it, neither at Führer Headquarters or in Rome.

The inventor of this news could have been a special friend of Himmler's, SS General Wolff, who served as a sort of escort officer to the Reichsführer, who in 1945 had Dollmann as his adjutant.

All that I know is that in the autumn of 1943 the Holy See published an official communique in which the behavior of the German soldiers in Rome came in for special praise. Dr. Laternser, a defense lawyer before the Nuremberg court, brought this document to the court's attention on May 22, 1946.

Nevertheless, the following telegram from the Associated Press news agency appeared in *Stars and Stripes*, the newspaper of the American occupation forces in Germany, from Nuremberg dated January 29, 1946.

"When the Führer learned of the collapse of the Italian Army, he gave the order for the pope "to be murdered or eliminated," King Victor Emmanuel to be deposed and Mussolini freed at any price.

The Duce was, as planned, freed in the course of a glider landing at a height of 2,200 meters. But Admiral Canaris, the genius of German military intelligence, saw to it that the plan against the King failed when, in the course of a dramatic breakfast in Venice, he succeeded in informing the anti-fascist members of Italian military intelligence (General Amé) of the imminent operation."

The same account was printed by the world press. It is a fact that the Italian monarchy was not up to such a double game. The Duce told me: "I should have forced the King out of his position after the conquest of Abyssinia and proclaimed the republic."

Badoglio was forced to surrender his office on June 5, 1944. For his part the king abdicated in favor of Umberto, whose reign lasted little more than a year. Italy was proclaimed a republic on June 2, 1946 after a plebiscite. The result was 12,717,925 votes for the republic and 10,719,284 for Prince Umberto. But I am convinced that the House of Savoy brought about its own downfall on July 25, 1943 when King Victor Emmanuel had Mussolini arrested, the same man he had embraced in a brotherly fashion only a short time before.

In his protest note Foreign Minister Guariglia suggested that former fascists were involved in our preparations. We saw very few of them and none were involved in our operation. The few true fascists had been decimated at the front during the war years. Those who were left were serving in the blackshirt brigades at the front.

Many followed the example of the majority of the members of the Fascist Grand Council, which had abandoned the Duce after the last known sitting. They criticized Mussolini, especially those who had previously been members of fascist organizations. There was no more talk of whether fascism had saved Italy from chaos in 1922 and had "shored up a tottering throne." They also ceased to reflect on the moral and social aspects of fascist doctrine, or on a corporative system that enabled workers, technicians and employers to function cooperatively. We must state that these questions no longer played a role. For many only their own prosperity, their own interests and their own person was of importance. The enemy had set foot on the soil of their fatherland: this was the signal to switch from the side of the loser to the side of the victor as quickly as possible.

It was a mistake on the part of the Duce to enter the war. But in 1939, and even more so in 1936, there were few fascist leaders who clearly let it be known that they were against a war. At this point I must once again point out the fact that the memoirs of Count Ciano were "revised." Apart from that, the allies demanded an "unconditional surrender" of the Italian government. Field Marshall Montgomery's memoirs are very revealing in this respect.

Some of the remaining true followers and fascist leaders went into hiding. Many were persecuted or liquidated by "defenders of justice," who hated these old fascists. On August 23 Ettore Muti, the former general secretary of the Fascist Party, who was under house arrest, was lured to Fregene and killed. Ciano now became scared. He told Radl that Scorza of the Grand Council, who was still free, had been very badly mistreated. But he knew nothing, or "wanted to know nothing." This man was finished. Farinaccis, whose order of the day had received only one vote, namely his own, was in Germany and met with Hitler, Göring, Goebbels, Ribbentrop, Himmler and others.

Only among the Italian youth did one still find civil courage, loyalty and bravery. We knew that certain groups of young officers wanted to free Mussolini. But these groups were watched and spied on, and it would have been a gross mistake if we had made direct contact with them. I feared that they would in fact try and free the Duce and in the process act in such a way that the entire operation must end in a fiasco, and that the King, the Crown Prince and Badoglio would then hand Mussolini over to the English or the Americans immediately. We therefore had no time to lose; but as a result of Alarich we lost a great deal of time.

Charles Foley was right on the mark, when he wrote in *Commando Extraordinary*:

"Skorzeny...who kept the political developments in Italy away from his real objective, the freeing of Mussolini, learned that the latter had been arrested on July 25 at about 5 P.M. at the portal of the Villa Savoia and taken to an unidentified village. Various rumors surfaced and Skorzeny was quickly able to determine that the Badoglio government was behind this whispering campaign, in order to cover its tracks. The supposedly secret reports, which were said to originate from generals, ambassadors and certain personalities in the Vatican, were pure diversions: 'Mussolini was said to be in a sanatorium... He was being held prisoner in Rome... We know from a reliable source that he was flown to Portugal'..."

One who actually did fly to Portugal was Grandi, who went there to make contact with the allies and conclude a separate peace.

Thanks to a letter written by a love-sick carabinieri to his fiancee, we learned that the Duce was being held captive on the island of Ponza, where the ardent Italian soldier was in garrison. The Duce later told me that the population of the island, the mayor, the doctor and the chemist in particular, had prepared a moving reception. He remained locked up in a small house situated by the sea for a week.

"I was guarded heavily," he later told me, "and watched day and night. The carabinieri sent the population away and were themselves rotated often, out of fear that they would become too friendly toward me. The food was terrible, but they allowed the locals to secretly bring me fruit. By night the police patrolled with trained dogs. I myself thought of Italy, of those continuing the struggle, of my family and everyone I loved – but also of the ingratitude of man. I was convinced that you, the Germans, would not abandon me. But how were you to pick up my trail? A stairway led from the small house down to the Tyrrhenian Sea, whose waves lapped the bottom steps. The day of July 29 seemed especially long to me: it was my sixtieth birthday. I scanned the horizon, always expecting to see an enemy battleship appear..."

To which western country was the Duce to be handed over? To the English or the Americans? That remained questionable. At about 6 P.M. on September 8, 1943, Radio Algiers announced that "Mussolini, the former Duce, would be handed over to the English." There were differences of opinion between Crown Prince Umberto and Badoglio. They feared that Churchill and Mussolini might find common ground. The pro-English sentiment was undoubtedly predominant in monarchist circles and especially in the Italian Navy. This probably explains a previously unknown fact: the Americans, too, were trying to find out where the Duce was being held!

After the war I met a very sympathetic American: Johnny Ringling North, the owner of "the greatest show on earth." He told me that his brother Henry, a captain in a commando of the US Army, had on September 9 or 10, 1943 been given the job of seizing the Duce, who according to their information was to be found on the island of Ponza. Soon afterward I met Henry Ringling personally. He was just as sympathetic as his brother and described to me his adventure in detail:

"I landed on Ponza with my team on September 11. The Italians had become good friends and I hoped that I could bring everything to quick and successful conclusion. To my great surprise, however, I learned from the astonished and suspicious carabinieri that the Duce hadn't been on Ponza since the morning of August 8. He had left the island on the old French torpedo boat *Phantère* during the night of August 7-8, direction unknown.

"His destination was Santa Maddalena, but he was no longer there either. I had no idea! At first I didn't believe it, but then I had to resign myself to the facts. You can imagine what I thought of the American secret service at that point! In short, I spent the night on the island with my team and waited for further orders. The next day the carabinieri staff was informed that your commando had just freed Mussolini, who was being held on the Grand Sasso. We were at once suspicious. The carabinieri had probably been told by their superiors that I might be the commander of a German unit dressed as an American. As a result I myself was held prisoner on the island for a few hours."

This comical, unbelievable situation could have come from a comedy by Plautus or Goldoni. Henry Ringling is a witty man with a great sense of humor, and his account of these events was very well-told.

It proves that I would very probably have experienced a similar adventure had I depended on the reports sent by Canaris to the OKW. But by then Radl and I already knew that the admiral wasn't very trustworthy. And as for the American secret service, it functioned with even less precision and with considerable lateness, which is always embarrassing for an intelligence service.

Mussolini's fears were all too warranted. General Castellano denied several times that the monarchist government ever had the intention of handing Mussolini over to the enemy. Badoglio made similar statements. Today, however, we know that the Duce was simply to be got rid of to the allies. On September 21, 1943 Winston Churchill declared to a closed session of the House of Commons:

"An unconditional surrender naturally requires that the war criminals be handed over to the victors. Where Mr. Mussolini is concerned, there is a special clause in the Italian document. But it wasn't possible to announce this clause before the landing and before the cease-fire. Otherwise the enemy would have become aware of the true intentions of the Italian government. Anyway the enemy is interfering with all state business and have their hand on the tiller... We had every reason to assume that Mussolini was in a safe place and well guarded. It was in the Badoglio government's own interests to prevent his flight. Mussolini himself declared that he was convinced that he was going to be handed over to the allies. That was exactly our intention and we could have done so without difficulty. The measures taken by the Badoglio government in regard to Mussolini were precisely planned and carried out. But we had not counted on the massed action by paratroopers as carried out by the Germans at the Grand Sasso. Remarkably Hitler had the works of Nietzsche and other publications delivered to Mussolini in order to give him something to do in captivity. That meant that Hitler knew where he was being held and the conditions there. The operation was extremely daring in its planning and the Germans were magnificently equipped.

"This proves that modern warfare offers many possibilities for this type of action. I don't believe that the Badoglio government, which had its last trump card in its hand, is guilty of any negligence or treason.

"The carabinieri guards had orders to kill Mussolini immediately in the event of any attempt by the Germans to free him. The large number (70) of paratroopers landed on the Grand Sasso prevented the order from being carried out, in that they made the carabinieri responsible for the health and safety of the prisoner."[1]

Even after September 8 Churchill did not make public the secret clause of the cease-fire concerning Mussolini. Furthermore he erred in assuming that Hitler had knowledge of the Duce's whereabouts: the works of Nietzsche, which Hitler gave Mussolini on his sixtieth birthday, were delivered by the Badoglio government. We will also see that no "massed" drop by paratroops on the Grand Sasso took place. The truth is that the Duce's captivity ended when eighteen German soldiers and two pilots, who were not paratroopers, "came from the sky" and occupied the Hotel Imperatore.

Notes

1. This document was published by J. Launay in *The Last Days of Fascism* (Paris 1968) and by André Brissaud in *The Tragedy of Verona* (Paris 1971). Brissaud quoted part of a letter written by Roosevelt to Churchill on 26 July 1943: "I believe it necessary to force the handing-over of the demon chieftain (Mussolini) and his most important accomplices." Launay and Brissaud also quoted the testimony given by SD Hauptsturmführer Höttl, of whom I spoke in the previous chapter (Part II, Chapter 6). Höttl's book *Unternehmen Bernhardt*, which was published under the pseudonym W. Hagen, contains many inaccuracies. Höttl claims he was chief of Department VI in Schellenberg's office. However this department was led by SD Sturmbannführer Bruno Waneck. Hagen-Höttl made only two brief visits to Italy, and these were in connection with the departure of Count Ciano and his family. He knew about the Gran Sasso action only from hearsay. In his opinion the freeing of the Duce cost 50,000 counterfeit Pounds Sterling! Höttl simply added a zero to the sum of money that was issued to Radl, most of which we handed back to Office VI. 50,000 Pounds was a huge sum in 1943. Paying out large sums of money to buy information would have been the surest means of attracting the attention of the various Italian police services. The best part of all, is that Höttl accuses me of landing *first* and committing numerous errors that almost caused the operation to fail. In the same book, however, he claims to have recommended me for the Knight's Cross. Apart from the fact that Höttl was not entitled to make such a recommendation, I received the decoration in Vienna on the day Mussolini was freed, precisely at midnight. I was awarded the Knight's Cross as the result of an order from Hitler, who personally telephoned me at the Hotel Imperial from Führer Headquarters to inform me of the award. One wonders how Höttl managed to get his recommendation to Führer Headquarters in an hour! (The Duce and I landed in Vienna at about 11 P.M. on September 12, 1943, and at 12 P.M. that same day a General Staff Oberst handed me the Knight's Cross.)

17

SEARCHING FOR THE DUCE

Predictions and defense – Teetotaler Warger plays the drunk – I crash in a Heinkel: three ribs broken – Mussolini on Santa Maddalena – The OKW orders us, "To look on a small island near the island of Elba" – I succeed in convincing Hitler – "If your operation fails, Skorzeny, I will be forced to disapprove of your actions" – Four days lost: the Duce is no longer on Santa Maddalena – Secure information: the Duce is now on the Gran Sasso – The mission tactics are decided: General Student's staff calculates 80 percent technical losses – Confusion in the Italian armed forces – Roosevelt and Churchill call for resistance: Generalfeldmarschall prevents the success of this call – An angry interlude – On General Student's order I inform Major Mors of the operation's plan and objective – Hauptmann Mandel brings Donna Rachele, Annamaria and Romano Mussolini to Munich – The plan – General Soleti's silly dream – Student: "...I am certain that you will all do your duty" – Bombardment and departure at X-Hour.

To govern, it is said, means to foresee. Or to be clairvoyant, for the Reichsführer consulted fortune tellers. I can confirm that Hitler did not believe in such things.

I have read that President Poincaré secretly sought advice from an especially clairvoyant fortune teller who gave good advice to the famous Madame de Thèbes Daladier, and that Winston Churchill thought highly of the "magician" Louis de Wohl, an Hungarian refugee. Possibly this benefactor saw the constellations in a mostly Stalinist light.

In any case Himmler asked fortune tellers and astrologers to find out where the Duce was being held prisoner.

On August 10 or 11 we learned that Mussolini had left the penal island of Ponza on a warship – destination unknown. General Student subsequently passed on to me a telegram from the OKW, which said that Mussolini was a prisoner on the cruiser *Italia* in La Spezia harbor. Himmler sent a telegram, ordering us to free Mussolini as quickly as possible. An action against a cruiser, on which we had no confederates, seemed completely illusory to me. But more accurate information revealed the OKW's information to be false.

Radl wrote:

"On about August 15 several pieces of corresponding information made us aware of an interesting voyage north of the island of Sardinia. We heard that certain followers of fascism were prisoners on the 'isola di porco' and that a concentration camp was being prepared on the neighboring island of Caprera. Finally we learned from a reliable source that the Italian garrison on the island of Santa Maddalena, off the northeast tip of Sardinia, had suddenly been reinforced. Our informant was Commander Hunäus, the German liaison officer to the Italian harbor master of Santa Maddalena. We talked it over with General Student and it was agreed that Hauptsturmführer Skorzeny, together with our only officer who spoke perfect Italian, Untersturmführer Warger, should speak to the liaison officer personally. Otto Skorzeny ordered Warger to make the rounds of the Santa Maddalena bars and act as if he was mildly drunk. Unfortunately, and it was nearly a serious blow, Untersturmführer Warger was the only non-drinker among the Friedenthal volunteers, and so I set to work teaching him to drink. We fed him large amounts of Asti Spumanti, Grappa and Chianti. We helped a little, to give him courage. In the beginning he proved to be very averse to the effects of the various types of alcohol. But duty is duty, and Warger had to play his role as a drunken sailor perfectly!"

On August 18 Warger and I flew from Ciampino near Rome to Vieno Fiorita airfield on Sardinia in a Heinkel 111. Hunäus had sent his car for us, and we soon covered the 80 kilometers of mountain road to Palau in the north. In Palau the German commander of the two flak battalions stationed there told me that Mussolini had been brought ill to the monastery hospital of Santa Maria, a small village on the road we had just travelled. Oddly enough, I hadn't noticed a single carabinieri in this area. Hunäus himself had heard talk of a so-called Villa Weber or Webber, which lay somewhat outside of Santa Maddalena. A white red Cross seaplane had been anchored in a small bay below the villa for several days. Hunäus, whom I did not inform fully as to the nature of my mission, took in Warger as a common seaman and passed him off as his interpreter.

Back at Vieno Fiorita I asked the pilot to fly over Santa Maddalena. I wanted to get an overall view of the island and the coast from 4,000 meters and take photos. I was lying in the nose by the aircraft's cannon and was about to end my observations, when I heard the dorsal gunner's voice through the microphone.

"Attention! Two English fighters behind us!"

With my finger on the trigger of the cannon, I waited for the attack. At that moment the aircraft nosed down. The left engine had stopped. We hit the water with great force. I lost consciousness for a few seconds. Then the pilot, copilot and I clambered out through the upper escape hatch. I dove back down to retrieve the camera and the map. Meanwhile the pilot and his crew succeeded in releasing the life raft. We managed to rescue the other two members of the crew before the Heinkel went under. We swam to a small, rocky island where an auxiliary cruiser of the Italian flak picked us up several hours later. I had injured my right arm and broken three ribs. The captain of the cruiser saw to it that we were well cared for. But it wasn't until 11 P.M. that I reached Bonifacio on Corsica, which was then occupied by Italian units, and I lost a great deal more time before I finally reached Bastia in the north. My goal was to make contact there with the commander of the Waffen-SS brigade stationed on the island.

The Heinkel was not shot down by English fighters, however, rather it couldn't handle the Italian gasoline with which the pilot had refuelled, against my advice, at Vieno Fiorita: a subsequent analysis revealed that the gasoline contained thirty percent water!

Radl waited for me in Frascati. When he heard no news, on the evening of the 18th he went to General Student's headquarters, where an Oberst said to him, "Didn't you know that Skorzeny has come down in the water?"

Radl was amazed. Why hadn't they notified him immediately? The Oberst shrugged his shoulders, and Radl asked, "What do you mean, he's come down in the water? Are you trying to say that the He 111 has crashed into the sea? But where? And when? Was the crew able to escape?"

No one knew anything. It was unlikely that I had survived, for according to statistics, of hundreds of He 111s that had crashed into the sea only a few crews had been saved. Radl asked to see General Student immediately, but he knew no more than the Oberst. And if the OKW gave the order to start Operation Alarich? Then, declared the general, "everything must go one hundred percent nevertheless!"

Not until August 20 did Radl learn that we had escaped in one piece. The next day I drove to Frascati, where Kappler informed me that Edda Ciano was back from Germany and had written her father in Santa Maddalena. So the operation was planned in principle, in agreement with General Student and the Kriegsmarine, with Kapitän zur See von Kamptz, wearer of the Knight's Cross with Oak Leaves, and Korvettenkapitän Max Schulz, commander of motor torpedo boats in the Mediterranean. Two torpedo boats with Radl and me on board were to sail to Santa Maddalena on August 27. Then came news from Warger, who of course had stayed on the scene to keep an eye on the Villa Weber: he had seen Mussolini with his own eyes!

On August 23 Radl and I flew in an He 111 from Practica di Mare to Vieno Fiorita and from there reached Santa Maddalena. Warger had made a wager with a fruit seller that Mussolini was dead. In order to win the bet, the fruit seller showed him Mussolini, albeit from a distance, on the terrace of the villa. On our responsibility we told Hunäus of the plan and returned to Frascati to prepare the action – with the agreement of General Student and the cooperation of the Kriegsmarine. Then a report reached us from the OKW:

"Führer Headquarters has received reports from the Abwehr, according to which Mussolini is being held prisoner on a small island near Elba. Hauptsturmführer Skorzeny is to prepare a parachute operation against this island immediately and report the earliest possible starting date. The OKW will select the date of the action."

After this puzzling telegram I asked to be allowed to accompany General Student to Führer Headquarters on August 29, 1944 to, if possible, explain to the Führer myself that the Duce was on Santa Maddalena and not somewhere else.

And so I once again found myself in the Wolfsschanze, in the same room where two weeks earlier Hitler had instructed me to find and free his friend. Seated around the table were all the leading men of the Reich: to Hitler's right were Generalfeldmarschall Keitel and Generaloberst Jodl, to his left Foreign Minister von Ribbentrop, Himmler, General Student, then Grossadmiral Dönitz and Reichsmarschall Göring. I was assigned a place between Göring and Jodl. General Student soon gave me the word to begin my presentation.

I must admit that I had to overcome my shyness in the beginning. But since I knew the material well, I described in a simple and clear way how we had arrived at our conclusion that Mussolini was being held prisoner in Villa Weber on Santa Maddalena as of August 27. I also described the terrible adventure of our teetotaller Warger. Göring and Dönitz smiled. Himmler's gaze remained ice-cold, and Hitler wore a rather ironic look. He stood up and shook my hand.

"Good! I believe you Skorzeny. The operation on the small island near Elba is cancelled. Now please outline your plan for the action on Santa Maddalena."

I cast a quick glance at the clock and realized that I had been talking for half an hour. Then I outlined my plan of operation and made a few sketches to illustrate. Hitler, Göring and Jodl all interrupted me to ask questions: thus it was clear to me that I had won.

The plan conceived with the Kriegsmarine and Radl anticipated the action beginning in the morning; the element of surprise would decided the entire success. One day prior to the attack a motor torpedo boat flotilla – each boat armed with two torpedoes and two 20mm cannon – would anchor in Santa Maddalena harbor on the pretext of a hospitality visit. It would still be there the next morning, and our minesweepers, which arrived during the night, would join it without arousing suspicion. These vessels would have on board a detachment from Friedenthal and a company of Waffen-SS soldiers of the Brigade Korsika under my command. We would land in close formation and our torpedo boats would cover us. We were to give the impression of a peaceable group of Germans going on shore leave, for it was vital that we reach the vicinity of the villa as quickly as possible without hostilities breaking out. Afterward we would act as the circumstances dictated, for the villa was watched day and night by more than 150 carabinieri and police.

Our flak positions on Corsica and Sardinia would have to lend us help. We had to fear a reaction, even a late one, by the Italian flak. Telephone communication between the villa and a barracks in which 200 officer cadets of the *Regia Marina* were stationed would, of course, be cut, and a detachment would put out of action the two Italian fighters that escorted the Red Cross seaplane on all of its flights.

Hitler agreed to this plan. Grossadmiral Dönitz was to give the units of the Kriegsmarine the necessary orders, and the entire operation would be under my command.

Hitler took me aside:

"Something else, Hauptsturmführer Skorzeny. It's possible that at the time that you carry out your operation, the new Italian government will still, officially at least, be our ally. Therefore it the attack fails, or if Mussolini is not on Santa Maddalena, I might be forced to disapprove of your action publicly. In that case you will have acted on your own and not informed your superiors. I hope that you understand that I will have to punish you against my will in the event of failure?"

I understood completely and told him so. Then I answered several questions by Dönitz and assured Göring "that the He 111 could also be used as a U-boat," which amused him. I was about to take my leave when Hitler came up to me. He shook my hand and gazed into my eyes, "You will do it, Skorzeny," he said. "I am convinced of it."

But I was not to do it on Santa Maddalena at the end of August and the action was never begun, as we learned just in time – the evening before – that the Duce had been flown away in the Red Cross seaplane early that morning.

I have already mentioned that, following our first return from Santa Maddalena to Rome, we learned of the note of protest that Guariglia had sent to the German ambassador von Mackensen and in which he complained that the Germans were planning a coup d'état for August 28. That was the day of our mission to free the Duce and not of Operation Alarich, whose date was never fixed.

Canaris' report about the "monarchist government's everlasting loyalty to the Axis" seemed laughable to us. When we learned that the Duce had left the island of Ponza, a telegram from the OKW referred us to La Spezia and the battleship *Italia*, on which Mussolini was supposed to be – and that was wrong! The trail led us to Santa Maddalena. Then, based on reports by Canaris, the OKW declared that the Duce was to be found on a rock near the island of Elba. That too was wrong. We lost several precious days this way. I was able to convince Hitler that Mussolini was really on Santa Maddalena, from where they took him away exactly one day before the planned operation. The date had been set only a short time before, and only a few persons had knowledge of it. From where did the information seep through?

From Kappler we learned that General Amé, head of the Italian intelligence service and an old friend of Admiral Canaris, had long been known as an anti-fascist. We also heard that the chief of intelligence of the Royal Italian Navy, Admiral Maugeri, who had escorted the Duce from Gaeta to the island of Ponza on the corvette *Persefone*, was a friend of Amé and Canaris. After the war Maugeri received an American decoration for his good and faithful service.

All was not the best in General Student's staff. Radl and I were astonished to learn that there were even defeatists in the general staff of an elite corps. Right after our arrival in Frascati a major asked us ironically whether we knew that the war was lost. And after the Santa Maddalena fiasco we noticed more often that they made not the least effort to really help us. They seemed to think we were crazy people who had our eye on some insane goal. We reported this to General Student. But to our great surprise he was fully aware of the unusual concept of duty and moral attitude of his officers. But he couldn't, so he said, manage without them.

"The training of a paratrooper demands special technical training. One doesn't simply become an officer in our service. The people of whom you speak and who I know better than you, jumped at Narvik, Eben Emael, at Rotterdam and Crete. I am sure that they will continue to do their duty." Radl, who wasn't one to hold back, interjected:

"Allow me to state, Herr General, that an officer cannot give his best in a war that he already considers to be lost. That is a sentiment that we don't and will never understand."

I tried to shift the conversation onto another track. The next day I was to accompany General Student to Vigna del Valle, on Lake Bracciano, north of Rome. There we chanced to come across the trail of the Red Cross seaplane that had flown out of Santa Maddalena with the Duce on August 27.

Numerous false trails led us to hospitals, to Perugia on Lake Trasimeni; but our investigations proved that the Duce had been on a seaplane that landed at Vigna del Valle and he had then been taken away in an ambulance.

Kappler's office intercepted a radio message sent by a so-called General Cueli, which gave us definite proof that the trail from Lake Bracciano to the Gran Sasso was the right one. Cueli was the inspector general of the military police, and he reported to his superiors: "Security preparations around the Gran Sasso complete." Was not the "La Albergo Campo Imperatore," a mountain hotel at an elevation of 2,212 meters, the safest prison in the world? This hotel could only be reached by cable car. We therefore needed aerial photos.

General Student instructed his intelligence officer, Hauptmann Langguth, to make a reconnaissance flight with an automatic camera installed in each wing. But the reconnaissance He 111 was in Nancy and could not be in Rome until September 8.

All the pilot knew was that we wanted overfly Rimini, Ancona and Pescara and were supposed to return via the same route, which led over the Abruzzas and the Gran Sasso (2,900 meters). Langguth was supposed to take the photos. Scarcely had we boarded the aircraft, when he told us that the automatic cameras weren't working and that there was no time to repair them. Radl and I looked at each other in amazement. Langguth casually showed us how to use a heavy hand-held camera, on which the film also had to be advanced by means of a hand crank. He had no intention of doing it himself.

So I had to take the photographs myself, for better or worse. The aircraft flew at a height of 5,000 meters at 370 kph. The outside air temperature was minus eight degrees Celsius. I was in shirtsleeves and stuck my upper body half in the open through the dorsal turret's entry hatch. Radl sat on my legs to prevent me from falling out. The copilot had to give Radl a hand to pull me back into the aircraft. At the end of our air journey I was completely frozen through. But these photos gave us no idea of the slope of the mountain plains which were available for us to land on.

To complete our luck the automatic large-format camera, with which one could normally could make stereo exposures, was also out of order. General Student would otherwise have noted that the slope on which we planned to land had about the same gradient as an average-difficulty ski slope and was full of boulders. Student would definitely not have authorized the operation under these conditions. And so Hauptmann Langguth unintentionally came to our aid.

So on the evening of September 8 Radl and I outlined our plan of action. The ski hotel could only be reached by cable car from Assergi. It had telephone communications with the hotel and was naturally watched from above and below. If the funicular railway was attacked we would lose the vital element of surprise.

Parachute troops, who had jumped out onto the plateau, could have done this in front of the eyes of the Italians. That meant that we could neither carry out the operation successfully on foot or with the aid of the cable car. As well we feared that orders had been given to kill the Duce if a rescue attempt should be made.

A parachute drop had the same disadvantages, and in the thin air at this altitude and wind the rate of descent would have been too great and the paratroops would have come down widely scattered. Helicopters seemed the best solution, but the helicopter center in Erfurt couldn't let us have any. So all that was left was a landing by glider. Radl and I thought over this solution and then discussed it with General Student's staff – Oberst Trettner, Major Colani and Hauptmann Langguth. They were all skeptical.

We intended to land on the meadow of the Campo Imperatore with twelve DFS-230 gliders. Each glider seated nine men and a pilot. Theoretically we would therefore have 108 soldiers at our disposal. But Student and his staff objected that the thinner air above 2,000 meters would make landing the gliders much more difficult. No one had ever tried such a risky landing. They forecast technical losses in the order of eighty percent. That meant that we would have to take on about 200 carabinieri, most likely armed with machine-guns, automatic weapons, mortars and so on, with only about 20 combat-capable soldiers. General Student rated our chances of success very low, even if the pilots didn't crash on landing: "Even a crash landing would be suicide," General Student said to me. "I expressly forbid a landing in this way!"

But Hitler had given me an order, and to me that meant that I had to carry out this order no matter what. I also had no wish to wait until the Italians made their famous prisoner disappear again. As well the eighty percent losses seemed to be a very pessimistic estimate. No glider had ever landed at this altitude before. So how could they quote such figures? Following a lengthy discussion with the chief-of-staff and Hauptmann Langguth, who had landed at Eben Emael, I declared, "Very well then gentlemen. I am ready to carry out any other plan, as long as it is better than ours."

General Student finally gave his authorization to the operation that I had proposed, under the express condition that the landings by the gliders on the terrain in front of the hotel would be as smooth as possible.

At the time when we were working out our plans there was great turmoil in Rome. The joy over the announcement of the cease-fire on September 8, 1943 was followed by hostile pronouncements against us on one hand, and on the other the flight of certain persons and confusion within the armed forces. Rome had been declared an open city; the monarchist government had already fled. There were alerts every day. The English and Americans bombed the city. Fortunately neither the Italian divisions nor the civilian population listened to Badoglio, who before he fled on the morning of September 9 had instructed the army, "to energetically resist any attempts by the Germans to attack." On September 11 Roosevelt and Churchill went on the radio, calling for the Italian people to rise up against us.

On my order, during the night of September 8-9 the volunteers from Friedenthal – still in paratrooper uniforms – formed a small unit led by Untersturmführer Menzel and Untersturmführer Schwerdt. This unit reinforced Major Mors' parachute battalion in Africa.

On the morning of September 9 a detachment dropped from a Ju 52 just missed the Italian High Command, which had flown out just minutes before. Student's paratroopers were encircled by Italian troops; but everything turned out well, for the German parachute troops put up stubborn resistance. They emerged from the affair with honor, kept their weapons and returned to their quarters. The Italians had their hands full defending against the English and Americans. Why should they now suddenly fight us? Most had had enough of the war.

During his student days in Vienna, Skorzeny belonged to the "Markomannia" fencing club. He is seen in this photo (right front) after receiving a serious wound in 1928, which later earned him the name "scar-face."

A rarity: members of the Turkestan Legion at Legionovo near Warsaw. They took part in Operation "Zeppelin" in July 1942.

Friedenthal 1943: the inner circle in front of the so-called "barn": from left to right: Skorzeny, Warger, Cieslewitz, Menzel, Schwerdt, Gföller and Radl.

An SS-Untersturmführer in naval uniform. The teetotaling Untersturmführer and interpreter Robert Warger in Santa Maddalena in 1943. There he practiced until he was able to "handle a drink," so that he could obtain information as to Mussolini's whereabouts by talking to Italian sailors in the local drinking establishments.

September 1943 in Avezzano. The men in paratrooper uniforms, from left to right: Warger, Skorzeny, Hans Holzer, Werner Holzer, Himmel, Menzel and Glärner. Sitting in the foreground: Wagner, Radl and Gföller.

September 12, 1943: Mussolini with his liberators, the Italian General Soleti and his guard General Cueli.

After being freed on September 12, 1943, Mussolini climbed into a Fieseler Storch waiting on the rocky plateau of the Gran Sasso. At the controls was Hauptmann Gerlach. Seen leaning over the Duce is Otto Skorzeny (in Luftwaffe uniform), who insisted on accompanying Mussolini on his flight into the valley.

The men of Kommando Skorzeny who took part in the surprise raid to free Mussolini were feted as honored guests at the Harvest Festival in the Berlin Sports Palace on October 3, 1943. From left to right: Cieslewitz, Manns, Warger, Holzer, Schwerdt and Menzel.

After the freeing of Mussolini. From left to right: Skorzeny, Mors, Schwerdt, Mussolini, Skorzeny's adjutant Karl Radl and in civilian clothes, General Cueli, who was responsible for watching over Mussolini while he was a prisoner.

Franz Szalasi, leader of the Hungarian fascists, the Pfeilkreuzler, who took over the running of government in Budapest after Horthy's fall in November 1944. Here he is seen greeting the guard in front of the Hungarian War Ministry in Budapest on November 4, 1944. Otto Skorzeny had a hand in this turn of events.

A rare photo: the head of the Reichssicherheitshauptamt, Walter Schellenberg, and Otto Skorzeny (in steel helmet), in 1944.

Generalfeldmarschall Model, the Commander-in-Chief of Army Group B during the Ardennes offensive in December 1944, seen studying a map (right General Staff Major Behr).

German Panther tank disguised as an American tank, as used by the 150th Panzer Brigade during the Ardennes offensive.

Members of Otto Skorzeny's 150th Panzer Brigade in action during the Ardennes offensive in December 1944.

Ardennes offensive 1944: execution of members of one of Skorzeny's special detachments by US military police. Most of the English-speaking German soldiers, who spread confusion behind the American lines while wearing American uniforms over their German ones, returned to the German lines. Only about eight fell into American hands alive. They were shot immediately as per military law, although their actions were covered by the rules of warfare. The enemy carried out similar operations.

A member of Skorzeny's special unit calmly faces death by firing squad. All the members of Skorzeny's unit were volunteers; they were sent behind enemy lines on December 16, 1944. Unfortunately the names of those who met this fate are unknown to this day.

SS-Obersturmbannführer Jochen Peiper, one of the bravest and most highly-decorated armor commanders of the Second World War, at the fateful Malmedy crossroads, which became the talk of the whole world after the war. Later, in the so-called "Malmedy Trial" at Dachau, Peiper, who commanded an armored spearhead during the Ardennes offensive, and 42 generals, officers and men of the Waffen-SS were sentenced to death for having shot 71 American "prisoners." The sentences were later reduced to life imprisonment and soon afterward the men were set free. The convictions had no foundation, as the "confessions" obtained through torture at Schwäbisch Hall, proved to be false. It is certain that Jochen Peiper could not be reproached for the orders he gave or for his conduct in battle. Peiper, who lived in France after the war, was murdered by unknown assailants for political reasons on July 14, 1976, the French national holiday, at Traves, near Lyon.

Photographs of the "Malmedy Massacre," like those presented by the prosecution in the Malmedy trial at Dachau, were supposed to prove the shooting of 71 American prisoners by Battle Group Peiper of the 1st SS-Panzer Division LAH at the Malmedy crossroads. How many of these Americans were killed in an initial exchange of gunfire, how many had clearly surrendered, how many were shot and killed contrary to the rules of war, and how many were killed by machine-gun fire while running away, will never be clarified. It was a tragedy not uncommon in time of war.

In action on the Oder Front. Skorzeny and his division-sized battle group, whose backbone was made up of the Commando Units Center and Northwest and the parachute battalion, offered stubborn resistance to the superior Soviet forces in the Schwedt bridgehead on the Oder River beginning in February 1945. Our photo shows Skorzeny with SS-Hauptsturmführer Dr. Slama and a Volkssturm officer.

Otto Skorzeny as a prisoner of war.

Former SS-Obersturmbannführer Otto Skorzeny was handed the indictment against him at Dachau on June 24, 1947. In the course of the trial he and his men were cleared of all charges. Our photo shows the council for the prosecution, American Colonel Albert Rosenfeld, to Skorzeny's right. The letters on the legs of Skorzeny's trousers are an abbreviation of "Prisoner of War."

Skorzeny while in pre-trial detention at Nuremberg. The prosecuting authorities suspected Skorzeny of having attempted to abduct and murder General Eisenhower and other high-ranking officers.

In Darmstadt POW camp: Skorzeny with his adjutant Radl.

Skorzeny in private. This photo, taken in 1950, shows him with his daughter Waltraut.

A civilian again, Skorzeny acquired an estate in Curragh, Ireland, where he raised sheep half the year. The other half he spent in Madrid, where he worked as an engineer and represented a number of steel-making firms.

Generalfeldmarschall Kesselring was clever enough to disarm the confused Italian divisions. One after another they laid down their weapons, and the few monarchist officers who wanted to fight found they had no one to follow them. There were brief confrontations in Rome and about twenty kilometers southeast in Albano and Aricia, where our "paratroopers" from Friedenthal discovered two batteries of the royal artillery, which they promptly disarmed. Since Unter-sturmführer Menzel's men had come on foot, they commandeered the trucks and cars, which were found to be in excellent condition, and returned to their quarters in Frascati. This event was the cause of an unpleasant incident, which I will speak of shortly.

The next day, September 10, all Italian troops in and around Rome surrendered to Generalfeldmarschall Kesselring. The chiefs of the carabinieri units and the police were made responsible for the maintenance of order. In this he avoided bloody street battles, frightful confusion and probably destruction and plundering. I am not certain that a revolt wouldn't have broken out in Rome if another commander had taken Kesselring's place.

The field marshal was never angry with me for not revealing my mission when general Student introduced me as an officer of the paratrooper corps. He knew that in doing so I was following an order from Hitler, and when I saw him again after freeing the Duce he congratulated me in comradely fashion.

In my opinion Generalfeldmarschall Kesselring was one of the best commanders we had. Inferior to the enemy in numbers and materiel, he defended central and northern Italy in spite of the growing guerilla threat from July 1943 until May 7, 1945. He was sentenced him to death in Venice according to the statutes of the Nuremberg Tribunal. The sentence was commuted and he stayed in jail until 1952. It was clear: he was on the losing side.

When his book *Soldat bis zum letzten Tag* came out in 1953, he sent me a copy with a dedication, which helps console me over many injustices and minor offenses. I would like to repeat his dedication:

You too, my dear Skorzeny, will find much in this book worthy of remembering, associated with shared experiences – even in captivity. And one more saying that applies to you: "Deeds are the real man's true joy."

Albert Kesselring
Generalfeldmarschall (Ret.)
December 1953[1]

By September 3 I had brought my volunteers from Practica di Mare and Frascati. They took up quarters in tents on the grounds of a monastery, the Collegio Nobile Mandragone. The Student Division's instruction battalion, which was commanded by Major Harald Mors, occupied the same monastery quarters.

General Student made the final decision to carry out the Gran Sasso operation at noontime on September 11, and he told me that the valley would be taken by Major Mors' battalion to cover our rear. He therefore asked me to visit Major Mors and to brief him on the mission orders, which had already been worked out.

I reported to Major Mors at about twelve o'clock. Together with my Untersturmführer Peter Schwerdt, I looked him up in his tent. I described to him the plan worked out by the division staff, Radl and me, which had been accepted by General Student. Ninety men of his battalion's 2nd Company and four of my officers plus twelve of my NCOs would land on the Campo Imperatore under my and Leutnant Berlepsch's command. Meanwhile Mors and the rest of his unit would march into the valley at the foot of the Gran Sasso over side roads, barricade the entrance and cut the telephone and telegraph lines. Then he would advance to Assergi and occupy the cable car station in the valley. The occupation of the station had to take place at exactly the same time as the first of our gliders landed on the Campo Imperatore. The two operations had to be perfectly synchronized in order to prevent the mountain or the valley stations from sounding the alarm. The occupation of Aquila airport was planned in principle for later.

Now Major Mors learned the objective of the operation: to free Mussolini.

● ● ●

But there was more at stake than freeing the Duce: there was also his wife Donna Rachele and their two youngest children, the sixteen-year-old Romano and fourteen-year-old Annamaria.

Donna Rachele was heavily guarded in Rome from July 26 until August 2. Their villa, which the Duke of Torlnia had made available to the Duce in 1930, was surrounded by 300 soldiers armed with submachine-guns. From August 3 on, Donna rachele found herself under house arrest with her children in their house in Rocca delle Caminate.

I was worried about them even though the house was guarded by carabinieri. But an attack by some sort of revolutionary group was always possible, and the carabinieri probably wouldn't have put up any serious resistance. I knew that Donna Rachele was very brave and much loved in this province. But later in Munich she told me that she became fearful for her children when she heard of the murder of Ettore Mutis, an old and faithful friend of her husband. I succeeded in sending her a message: she was to leave the house as little as possible and to have faith in us; they were, so to speak, the scourge of the Badoglio government.

On September 9 Vittorio Mussolini, Pavolini, Ricci, Farinacci and Preziosi declared on Munich radio that "a national-fascist government had been founded," which would "work in the name of the Duce." Donna Rachele and her children were thus in great danger.

Six of my volunteers, commanded by Hauptmann Mandel, were given the task of getting Donna Rachele, Romano and Annamaria out of Rocca delle Caminate and bringing them to Forli, from where they would be flown to Munich. We were afraid for a few days, for the freeing of the Mussolini family could not take place before the Duce had been freed without alarming the Badoglio government. These operations had to be carried out simultaneously.

Hauptmann Mandel left in the truck, reached Rocca delle Caminate at noontime and was fortunately able to complete his mission.

● ● ●

The ultimate plan for Operation Gran Sasso was as follows:

In charge of the operation on the Campo Imperatore: Hauptsturmführer Otto Skorzeny.
In charge of the action in the valley: Major Harold Mors.

X-Day: Sunday, September 12, 1943.

1. *In the valley*: Major Mors will occupy the crossroads from Aquila to Bazzano and from Pescomaggiore to Paganica as far as Assergi. He will make all the necessary preparations to repulse an eventual attack on the valley by Italian troops from Aquila.

He will occupy the cable car valley station above Assergi.

X-Hour: 2 P.M.

2. On the Gran Sasso – *Campo Imperatore*:

X-Hour: (originally) 6 A.M. (The air currents are weakest at this time.) X-Hour for the landing has to be moved back, as the gliders coming from France have run into a delay. It is set for 2 P.M.

Means and unit strengths: 12 DFS 230 gliders, towed by 12 Henschel aircraft, and a reconnaissance aircraft with Hauptmann Langguth on board. Each glider transports 9 armed soldiers and the pilot.

Sequence for departure and arrival of the gliders: a theoretical interval of one minute between gliders.

Gliders No. 1 and 2: 18 soldiers of the 2nd Parachute Company under the command of Leutnant von Berlepsch, who is in Glider No. 5. The four machine-guns must be moved into position immediately after landing. The remaining soldiers are armed with 14 special paratrooper rifles and are to cover the two assault groups from Gliders No. 3 and 4.

Glider No. 3: On board are Hauptsturmführer Skorzeny together with an Italian officer (Carabinieri General Soleti), Untersturmführer Schwerdt, Untersturmführer Wagner and 5 Unterscharführer of the Waffen-SS from Friedenthal. They will storm the hotel, make their way to the Duce, neutralize the guards and protect the Duce.

Glider No. 4: On board are Karl Radl, adjutant to Hauptsturmführer Skorzeny, Untersturmführer Menzel and seven soldiers of the Waffen-SS from Friedenthal. They are to storm the hotel immediately after landing and support Hauptsturmführer Skorzeny and his group.

Glider No. 5: Parachute troops of 2nd Company under Leutnant von Berlepsch. Task: support the special group from Friedenthal inside the hotel.

Glider No. 6: Parachute troops of 2nd Company. Task: occupy the cable car mountain station and the tunnel which connects the station with the hotel.

Glider No. 7, 8, 9, 10, 11 and 12: Parachute troops of 2nd Company. Have heavy weapons on board: 2 heavy machine- guns, 2 light mortars, 2 light paratrooper cannon. These groups are to take up battle positions immediately. Cover for other groups advancing on the hotel.

First landing planned at 2 P.M.

Fundamental ban for all participants to fire their weapons *before* Hauptsturmführer Skorzeny. If Hpt.St.Fhr. Skorzeny is inside the hotel, Leutnant von Berlepsch assumes responsibility *outside*.

On the afternoon of September 11 I assembled all my people and said to them, "Dear comrades, for six weeks you have waited without knowing why. But now I can tell you that tomorrow we will undertake an operation that the Führer has ordered personally. The operation is not a simple one, and it may be that we will have heavy losses. But this operation must succeed under any circumstances. I will lead the action myself, and we will do our best. Anyone who wishes to volunteer, take one step forward!"

Everyone stepped forward. I had to select seventeen men, which wasn't exactly easy. A further dozen would accompany the Mors Battalion under the command of my Untersturmführer Bramfeld, a member of our pentathlon team at the 1936 Olympic Games. This group set out during the night of Saturday, September 11-Sunday, September 12.

The next morning at about five A.M. my complete commando unit was at Practica di Mare airport, ready to go. But one piece of bad news is often followed by more: the first was a lie by Radio Tunis. This station reported that the Italian warships that had sailed from La Spezia had arrived at Tunis. On one of these ships was Mussolini, "who was now a prisoner of war on African soil."

I knew, however, that the ships had not left La Spezia until the day before – the large battle-cruiser *Roma* was sunk by a remotely-controlled bomb called "Fritz," and the Duce could not at that moment have been a prisoner in Tunis or Bizerte.

The second piece of bad news: our gliders would not arrive from France for four or five hours. Last but not least, General Soleti, who was supposed to meet Radl and Warger in front of the Ministry of the Interior at 7:30 A.M., had not yet arrived and it was 8.30! Luckily, however, he showed up soon afterward.

Our twelve gliders finally landed, just as Untersturmführer Radl was dining with the general. But let us allow Radl to tell what happened:

"From the window the general watched as our twelve DFS 230s landed in front of us.

'Very interesting, very ingenious, these aircraft without motors, don't you think?'

'Yes, Herr General. The DFS 230 is an outstanding machine. *Excellentissima macchina!*'

'You are a paratrooper and surely you have flown this machine often?'

I was neither a paratrooper nor were gliders my specialty. The general wasn't aware that he was going along, in fact in the third glider with Hauptsturmführer Skorzeny. I had to reassure the general somehow or other:

'Yes, very often, Herr General. It makes an extremely comfortable impression, not only because there's no engine noise, which makes it difficult to talk, but also because one in fact feels like a bird-man; *uomouccello!*'

'Really, what are these machines for?'

I looked at my watch. The moment I had feared had now arrived.

Simple, Herr General. Later we will take off in these gliders and land on the massif of Gran Sasso and free the Duce.

At first General Soleti looked at me in incredulously and probably thought that I was making a bad joke.

'I hope that you're saying that in jest! The Duce is being held prisoner at an elevation of 2,000 meters, in the high mountains! You really intend to land there? That is impossible, my friend: that would be a really idiotic operation, plain suicide! A proper massacre! And you think that I, Soleti...'

When Warger finally managed to convince him that he was part of this 'mad operation,' he first protested, then pure desperation seized him. He actually became sick, and we had to put out an urgent call for Doctor Brunner to come."

Speaking honestly, I understand General Soleti's behavior. He was an outstanding cavalryman who had proved himself magnificently while leading his cavalry regiment. But our operation appeared to him senseless and impossible. After talking with Sturmbannführer Kappler, who remained unshakable, and a brief conversation with General Student, he was forced to agree to come with us for better or worse, "in order to avoid a bloodbath." He had no other choice: Radl and Warger didn't let him out of their sight on the morning of on September 12.

Before General Student took his leave of us, he assembled all the pilots, officers and group leaders taking part in the action in the airport administration office:

"Gentlemen," he said, "very soon you will take off on a really extraordinary mission. All present were selected from the best pilots and officers, accustomed to looking danger in the eye. This operation will go down as unique in military history, not only because you have enormous technical difficulties to overcome, but because this operation is of quite considerable political significance. Before you receive your final instructions from Hauptsturmführer Skorzeny, I would like to wish you all the best for a complete success. I am sure that every one of you will do his duty."

Using a large-scale map of the Campo Imperatore which was pinned on the wall, I explained to each pilot and each group leader his mission. I had made a close study of the attack on the fortress of Eben Emael on May 10, 1940, and I knew that *three minutes* elapsed between the time when the first paratroopers and special engineers "fell" out of the sky onto the cupola of the fortress and the moment at which the Belgians opened fire.[2]

I estimated that I and the people in my glider (No. 3) would have more than four minutes to reach the Duce before they would fire at us. Then we would receive cover from the crews of Gliders Nos. 1 and 2, while Radl, Menzel and the soldiers of Glider No. 4 would be only a minute behind us.

But, as the Italians say, there were "imponderables": beginning with the bombing of our small airfield by a few English aircraft about fifteen minutes prior to our departure. When I emerged from cover I saw that miraculously none of our gliders had been hit. Only the runway had been partially destroyed by bombs. At X-Hour for take-off, at 1 P.M., our operation began, and the glider with Langguth on board took the lead and set course to the northeast toward the mountain massif of the Gran Sasso.

Notes

1. Generalfeldmarschall Kesselring of course mentioned Hitler's order to free the Duce in his book. On Page 223 he wrote: "Generaloberst Student and Sturmbannführer Skorzeny, his executive, were chosen for this mission." (Editors' note)

2. In *Sixty Days that Shook the World* (1956), J. Benoist-Méchin wrote that Hitler had personally worked out the plan for the taking of Eben-Emael. (Editors' note)

18

THE FREEING OF THE DUCE

*The lead aircraft and Glider Number One return to Practica di Mare!
– I order a steep approach and the capture of the hotel – "I knew that
my friend Adolf Hitler would not leave me in the lurch!" – The
carabinieri surrender – Gerlach's act of heroism – The Knight's Cross
– With the Mussolini family in Munich – Neo-fascism – The conver-
sation between Mussolini and Ciano – In Führer Headquarters –
The midnight tea – Mussolini's diary – The Duce a prisoner
again...this time of the Germans – Conversation with Admiral Canaris
– Consequences of this action: Adrian von Fölkersam comes to us –
April 18, 1945: the Duce's Waffen-SS guard unit is withdrawn –
"There's nothing we can do..."*

One could see practically nothing of the landscape from
the inside of a DFS 230 glider. Its tubular steel frame was
covered only with canvas. Our formation climbed through
dense clouds to a height of 3,500 meters.

Brilliant sunshine came through the tiny plastic windows, and I
saw that several of my people, who had already eaten all their emergency rations, were now very ill. I could also see that the face of
General Soleti, who was sitting in front of me between my knees,
was taking on the grey-green hue of his uniform.

The pilot of the Henschel glider tug kept the pilot of our glider,
Leutnant Meier-Wehner, the glider pilot leader, informed of our
progress. He in turn passed on to me the current position of our formation. In this way I was able to follow our flight path precisely. I
held a detailed map in my hands, which Radl and I had drawn using
the photographs we took from Langguth's machine on September 1.

I thought of General Student's words: "...I am sure that each of you will do his duty." Then Leutnant Meier-Wehner told me that the pilot of our tow plane had informed him that Langguth's lead aircraft and Glider Number 1 were no longer in sight. I later learned that these aircraft had quite simply turned around and returned to Practica di Mare!

That meant that my and Radl's assault teams now had no one to cover their rear, and I would have to land first if I wanted to carry out the operation at all. I didn't know that two of the gliders behind me were also missing. I believed I had nine gliders behind me, when in fact I had only seven! I called to Meier-Wehner: "We're taking over the lead!" and cut two openings in the skin with my paratrooper's knife. In this way I could orientate myself to some degree and give the two pilots instructions, first to Meier-Wehner, who then passed the order on to the "locomotive" pulling us. Finally I sighted beneath us the small city of Aquila in the Abruzzis and its small airfield, then somewhat farther on the Mors column on the winding road to the cable car valley station. It had just passed Assergi and was trailing a dense cloud of dust. They were on time; down below everything was going according to plan. It was almost X-Hour, 2 P.M., and I shouted, "Fasten steel helmets!"

The hotel appeared beneath us. Leutnant Meier-Wehner gave the order: "Release tow cable!", and soon afterward he made a flawless turn over the plateau. I realized that the gently-sloping meadow on which we intended to land – as General Student had instructed – was little more than a short, steep meadow which was also littered with boulders.

I immediately shouted, "Steep approach! Land as close behind the hotel as possible!" The other seven gliders flying behind me would surely do the same. Radl, who reported our maneuver to the pilot of machine number four, later admitted to me that he thought I had gone mad.

In spite of the braking parachutes, our machine landed much too fast. It bounced several times and there was a frightful din, but finally it came to a stop about 15 meters from the corner of the hotel. The glider was almost completely destroyed. From then on everything happened very quickly. Weapon in hand, I ran as quickly as I could toward the hotel. My seven Waffen-SS comrades and Leutnant Meier followed. An astonished sentry just stared at us. To my right there was a door: I forced my way in. A radio operator was at work in front of his set. I kicked the stool out from under him and the radio operator fell to the floor. A blow from my submachine-gun destroyed the radio set. Later, I learned that at that very moment the man was supposed to send a report from General Cueli that aircraft were approaching to land. The room had no other doors, and so we dashed along the back side of the hotel looking for an entrance: but there was none, just a terrace at the end of the wall. I climbed on to the shoulders of Scharführer Himmel. I climbed up and found myself standing at the front side of the hotel. I ran on and suddenly caught sight of Mussolini's striking profile in a window frame.

"Duce, get away from the window!" I shouted as loud as I could.

There were two machine-guns in front of the main entrance to the hotel. We kicked them aside and forced the Italian gun crews to back away. Behind me someone shouted: "Mani in alto!" I pushed against the carabinieri who were bunched up in front of the entrance and fought my way against the stream in a not too gentle fashion. I had seen the Duce on the second floor to the right. A set of stairs led upward. I raced up them, taking three steps at a stride. On the right there was a hallway and a second door. The Duce was there, and with him two Italian officers and one person in civilian clothes. Untersturmführer Schwerdt bundled them into the hall. Unterscharführer Holzer and Benzer appeared at the window: they had climbed the facade using the lightning conductor. There Duce was in our hands and under our protection. The entire action had been played out in barely four minutes – without a single shot being fired.

I had no time to say anything to the Duce. Through the open window I saw Radl and his group approaching at the run: their glider had landed in front of the hotel. Weapons in hand, they rushed to the entrance where the carabinieri were just beginning to set up their machine-guns again. I called to Radl: "Everything in order here! Secure below!"

A few shots were fired in the distance: the Italian sentries had come to life. I stepped out into the hall and asked to speak to the Italian commander immediately. The carabinieri now had to be disarmed as quickly as possible. Their leader, a colonel, wasn't far away.

"Any resistance is pointless," I said to him in French. "I demand your immediate surrender!"

"I need some time to think it over!...Must speak with General Soleti..."

"You have one minute! Go!"

Just then Radl walked into the room; he had been able to push his way through. I left two of our soldiers to guard the door and stepped into Mussolini's room. Schwerdt was still there.

"Duce, the Führer has given me orders to free you!"

He shook my hand and hugged me, with the words, "I knew that my friend Adolf Hitler would not leave me in the lurch!" Benito Mussolini was extremely moved and his black eyes glistened. I must confess that this was one of the greatest moments in my life.

• • •

The minute had elapsed and the colonel had thought things over. He came back into the room, surrendered, then passed me a glass of red wine. He bowed and said, "To the victor!"

I drank to his health and passed the glass to the thirsty Radl, who emptied it immediately.

Once out of the aircraft, General Soleti became his old self again. He hadn't, of course, been able to follow us in storming the terrace, but he was spotted by the Radl group from glider number four and picked up. Since he was anxious that no one shoot at him, like all my people he repeated my order: "Mani in alto!" A bed sheet hung from a window replaced the white flag. When Leutnant von Berlepsch spied the sheet at the window, he followed my instructions to the letter and surrounded the hotel with his paratroopers. Through the open window I gave him instructions to immediately ordered him to disarm the numerous troops guarding the Duce, and added, "Gently, but as quick as you can!"

Leutnant von Berlepsch saluted and clamped his monocle firmly in his eye. He had understood. At the request of General Soleti, who knew Mussolini well, the officers were allowed to retain their sidearms. The Duce told me that the carabinieri captain Faviola, who had been badly wounded at Tobruk, and the other officers had treated him well. Nevertheless, on September 11 Faviola had taken away everything sharp that he owned, like knives, razor blades and so on: Mussolini was determined not to fall into allied hands alive.

I learned that we had also captured a general. Then a man in civilian clothes, who was with Captain Faviola and the other officers in the Duce's room, introduced himself: he was General Cueli! Later I heard that this man was supposed to have spirited Mussolini away that afternoon and handed him over to the allies! I decided that Soleti and Cueli should also be taken to Rome.

One of our gliders crashed on a scree about 800 meters away. The ten men inside were immediately recovered by our medics and Italian soldiers and treated by Dr. Brunner and the Italian medics. None of those aboard the glider were seriously hurt. We had undoubtedly been extremely lucky; we sustained nowhere near the 80 percent losses predicted by the regimental staff of the parachute regiment.

There was a brief skirmish in the course of occupying the cable station in the valley, and the Italians suffered minor casualties. But both stations had fallen into our hands intact. Major Mors telephoned and asked if he might come up; I consented.

My mission was not yet over, however. How could we get the Duce to Rome? Three possibilities had been planned. The first involved seizing the airfield at Aquila di Abruzzi. Three Heinkel 111s would land there. I would escort Mussolini to the airfield and accompany him in one of the aircraft. This machine would be escorted by the others during the flight.

I had our radio truck, which had arrived in the valley, transmit the agreed-upon signal "Operation successfully carried out." I set the attack on the airfield by the paratroopers for 4 P.M. But as I waited for confirmation that the three Heinkel 111s would land, it proved impossible to reestablish contact with the parachute corps' radio station. To this day I do not know why.

Second possible option: a Fieseler Storch aircraft was to land near Assergi, site of the valley station. Unfortunately the pilot of the aircraft, whose hard landing I had witnessed through my field glasses, radioed that his machine's undercarriage had been damaged.

So all that was left to us was the third solution: Hauptmann Gerlach, General Student's personal pilot, would land another Storch on the Campo Imperatore. Carabinieri and parachute troops worked quickly to clear a narrow landing strip, for Gerlach was circling overhead waiting for the signal that he might land, a green flare.

He landed with consummate skill, to the amazement of all. But he had to take off again, with the Duce and me aboard! I had received an order from Hitler. The takeoff would be very difficult; if I let Benito Mussolini fly away alone with Gerlach and he then perhaps crashed with the Duce, there would have been nothing left for me to do but put a bullet in my head. It would have meant that I was unwilling to risk the dangerous takeoff with Mussolini and pilot Gerlach.

Since I was forced to opt for Plan C, I informed the Duce that we would take off in the Storch in half an hour. As he was a pilot himself, he knew what a takeoff at this elevation and without a proper runway involved. I was grateful to him that he didn't waste any words over the takeoff. Mussolini at first wanted to go to Rocca delle Caminate. But he changed his mind when he learned that his wife and children were no longer there and that they had already arrived in Munich with one of my commando units under the command of Hauptsturmführer Mandel.

He gave his luggage to Radl and stepped out of the hotel into the open. Just then Major Mors arrived with two of his lieutenants. Major Mors asked "Fliegerhauptmann Skorzeny" to introduce him to the Duce. This was a fortunate moment for war correspondent von Kayser of the Student Division, who had come up to the Campo Imperatore in the cable car with Mors.

At this point I would like to mention that, although I was aware of the presence of an Italian division near Aquila, I did not know that it had moved toward Assergi. The Duce's presence in the valley and the trip from the valley station to Assergi and from there to Aquila airfield via Camarda and Bazzano would have been dangerous. I had destroyed the radio set in the hotel, the one Cueli used to send his reports. But it was possible that the commander of the Italian division might wonder about the loss of communications and seize the initiative, which would be uncomfortable for us. The Duce had to be gotten to safety as quickly as possible, however there were serious risks associated with Plan C. But let us allow Karl Radl to speak once again:

"When we saw Gerlach, Mussolini and Skorzeny squeezed together inside the small aircraft we were all seized by fear. The aircraft glided down the sloping 'runway,' where we had removed all the large stones. But a water drainage ditch ran through the second third of the strip. Gerlach tried to miss it. He tried to pull the aircraft up and then lift off. The Storch in fact jumped over the obstacle, but then it tipped to the left and almost seemed to flip over. Then it touched down again...the last few meters, and then it disappeared into the chasm.

My legs went weak; I had the feeling they had been cut off. Suddenly I sat on one of the Duce's cases. Luckily no one saw me. It was a reaction to the tremendous activity and tension of the last few days. Now it's all for nothing, I thought: the Duce will die; I will shoot myself in the head. We all stared at the aircraft, which disappeared into the valley. But we could still hear the motor. Suddenly the Storch appeared on the other side of the chasm. It was still flying...flying in the direction of Rome!"

Several years ago I was introduced to a carabinieri at Rome's international airport. He was one of those who was supposed to have defended the entrance to the hotel with a machine-gun.

"Well," he said, "up there you gave me a lovely knock with a rifle butt, Herr Oberst!"

"I'm sorry about that..."

"But I preferred that to a bullet in the head!"

"You're not mad at me?"

"No, Herr Oberst. Afterward my comrades and I helped clear away the boulders so that the Storch could land and take off again with you and the Duce on board."

We shook hands. The aircraft had sideslipped to the left and dived into the valley. I closed my eyes and waited for the impact. But I soon opened them again and saw Gerlach slowly pulling back on the stick. The Storch pulled out of its dive: we flew over the rocks at a good thirty meters to the mouth of the valley of Arezzano. I couldn't refrain from placing my hand of the shoulder of the Duce, who was just as pale as Gerlach and I. He turned and smiled. He had been fully aware of the danger but hadn't wasted a word about it. Only now did he begin to talk, and as we were flying quite low for safety reasons, he described the area to me and stirred old memories. It struck me that he spoke excellent German.

Soon the "eternal city" was off to our right. Gerlach landed artfully on the tailwheel and the right mainwheel, as the left had been damaged on takeoff. Hauptmann Melzer was waiting for us. He greeted the Duce in the name of General Student, congratulated Gerlach and I and escorted us to the three Heinkel 111s which were supposed to have picked us up in Aquila. I introduced the Duce to the crew of our aircraft and to Dr. Reuther, 2nd Parachute Division medical officer, who accompanied us on the flight.

Soon we arrived near Vienna, in the middle of a storm. Our adventure wasn't over yet: in vain we tried to make radio contact with Vienna. Visibility was practically zero. I was sitting beside the pilot, and we rechecked our course. It was night and we were slowly getting low on fuel. We had to be close to Vienna and we descended cautiously. There was no question of trying a forced landing with the Duce on board. Then suddenly I saw a large body of water shimmering through a gap in the cloud; I was sure it was Lake Neusiedler. We dropped lower: my assumption was correct. I told the pilot to fly north. We landed at Aspern airport in total darkness. There I learned from the control tower that we hadn't been able to make radio contact "because it was Sunday" and the radio center wasn't fully manned that day. A few weeks later when Goebbels spoke of "total war," I quoted him a few examples, especially the one concerning Aspern.

The Duce was subsequently taken to the Hotel Imperial in Vienna, where they had reserved a suite for him. He had no pajamas, but in any case he considered them a waste of time, which led to a lighthearted discussion. I was glad to see an entirely different man than the one I had met on the Gran Sasso when I kicked open the door of the room in the Hotel Imperatore. He had a few more kind words for us. Then I took my leave and went to my own room next door.

Slowly I began to feel the fatigue that had accumulated in the last five days. But I was not to have any claim to rest. The phone rang: it was Himmler. He sounded very friendly, and after he had congratulated me he said:

"You are Viennese, if I'm not mistaken? Your wife isn't with you? Send a car for her, that's quite in order! Of course stay with the Duce. You will accompany him to Munich tomorrow and from there to Führer Headquarters."

I gladly accepted the Reichsführer's suggestion. Just before midnight General der Waffen-SS Querner, who had escorted us to the Hotel

Imperial from the airport, informed me that the chief-of-staff of the Vienna Corps Headquarters wished to speak with me. Soon afterward the Oberst introduced himself and declared ceremoniously:

"Hauptsturmführer Skorzeny, I come on order of the Führer, the Supreme Commander of the Wehrmacht, and it is my duty to present you with the Knight's Cross of the Iron Cross!"

He took off his own decoration and placed the band around my badly-shaved neck, over the jacket of my decidedly tattered paratrooper uniform. I regretted that my father was no longer alive: he would have been happier about this than I. Then there began a confusion of congratulations, handshakes and more questions. The telephone rang, and I wasn't paying attention when General Querner said to me: "The Führer himself wishes to speak to you!"

I took the receiver and heard Hitler's voice:

"...Not only have you successfully concluded an act unique in military history, Skorzeny, but you have also returned a friend to me. I knew that if anyone could do it, it was you. I have promoted you to Sturmbannführer of the Waffen-SS and awarded you the Knight's Cross. I know that you're wearing it already, for I gave the order that they were to present it to you immediately..."

He had a few more words of thanks, and I could sense how happy he was that the Duce had been rescued. Keitel and Göring came on the line after him and likewise congratulated me. I explained to them all that the Duce could not have been freed without the courage and imagination of everyone who had taken part in the action and its planning. In particular, I mentioned Untersturmführer Radl, Leutnant Meier-Wehner, pilot of Glider No. 3, and Hauptmann Gerlach. Shortly afterward I learned to my great joy that Hauptmann Handel's operation had succeeded and that Donna Rachele, Annamaria and Romano were safe and sound in Munich.

• • •

The next day I accompanied Mussolini from Vienna to Munich in a comfortable Junkers aircraft. The overnight rejuvenated and again vital Duce explained his plans to me during the flight. These were grandiose. His new movement, the republican-fascist party, was to restore the Italian nation to its old heights. The House of Savoy had not supported the fascist revolution in any way, instead it had sabotaged it. The king, who had no notion of government, and his courtiers had fought a constant secret war and committed treason in the end. Josef Mazzini had been right.

"When our ship passed by Gaeta at about midnight on July 27," he added, "I first thought they would bring me into the famous fortress and asked that, as a special honor, they should put me in the cell in which the hero of the Risorgimento of 1870 had been jailed. But they took me to Ponza."

At Riem airport near Munich Mussolini tenderly took his wife Donna Rachele and his two children into his arms. We stayed until September 15 in the Reich government's guest house in Munich. The Duce insisted that I was also put up there and took my meals with him and his family. We had a number of conversations. He was under no illusions and knew that the republican-fascist state would still have enormous difficulties to overcome. The neo-fascist doctrine, whose fundamentals Mussolini laid out for me, was much more than a "nationalist-monarchist" fascism. It was more than anything a call for European union. This union could not come about under the domination of a single nation or a small group of nations, rather it must embrace all the countries of Europe. The new doctrine proposed to unify all free nations – outwardly against international plutocracy, and inwardly against aggressive capitalism. The nations of Europe were to join together to manage the tremendous riches of the African continent, for the benefit of the African and European peoples.

Mussolini told me that he had given a great deal of thought to the idea of Euro-Africa. It was only to be realized when the old continent left behind the egotistical and limited nationalism and was reorganized. Otherwise the European peoples, in spite of their common culture, would not be able to survive. The era of the fratricidal war was over. It was time to unite or go under.

The Duce gave a speech in this vein at the first congress of the republican-fascist party in November 1943. I can also confirm that neo-fascism – which was totally different from "monarchist" fascism – was no invention of Hitler's, as many historians contend. Since his capture (on July 25, 1943), at Ponza, as well as on Santa Maddalena and the Campo Imperatore, the Duce had had time enough to consider these problems. I remember something he said: "We don't feel like Italians, because we're Europeans, rather we feel like Europeans to the degree in which we really feel like Italians."

During the afternoon of Monday, September 13, 1943, Edda Ciano asked her father to see the man who had so effectively betrayed the Duce in the Grand Fascist Council. Mrs. Ciano claimed that it was all "a tragic misunderstanding," and that Galeazzo was ready to offer him an explanation for what had happened. But Donna Rachele stubbornly refused to see her son-in-law. She couldn't stand the sight of him and said that "bad luck had come to the family with him." The Duce gave in to his daughter's pleas, however. He met Ciano, however he insisted that I should be present during their talk.

I feared that Donna Rachele might appear at any minute to give her son-in-law a piece of her mind. The conversation was a brief one. Ciano complemented the Duce, congratulated him and tried to vindicate himself. His behavior was so miserable that I really felt sick. Mussolini was very cool and the conversation was ended quickly. I escorted Ciano out, still fearing to see Donna Rachele suddenly appear. He took his leave. Afterward the Duce told me that he felt obliged to punish the one who had betrayed him in such a mean fashion – namely the leader of the palace revolution to which he had fallen victim.

I could help but ask, "Duce, you would therefore bring the man who was just here before a court?"

"I must!" answered Mussolini seriously. "I have no illusions as to the outcome of the trial. Even if I find it hard and if Edda's concern is great – I must act so. When I think that the worst reproach that Scorza made to me on that fateful night, was that I wasn't tyrannical enough! He dared to say in the Grand Council: "You were the man least listened to in this century!" He said that, Scorza!"

● ● ●

We arrived at Führer Headquarters during the afternoon of September 15. Hitler was waiting for the Duce at the airport and gave him a warm welcome. In reality the new fascist republic had no other basis than the friendship of these two men and several tens of thousands of followers. Italy was now even more susceptible to communism than in 1921, for this time the communists came as the allies of the great democracies.

Hitler asked me to give him a detailed account of the action. I talked for two hours. I still didn't know what had become of gliders number one and two or of those that had failed to get off the ground at Practica di Mare. I took the last two for lost and told Hitler frankly that probably thirty percent of the soldiers that took part in the operation were missing. German radio then reported a "loss of thirty percent," and I was later reproached for having exaggerated our losses "in order to represent the operation as more dangerous." Two weeks later Radl and I had the opportunity to speak for an hour on German radio and clarify everything. Our total casualties were in fact ten.

The next day, September 16, 1943, Hermann Göring arrived in a special train and asked me a multitude of questions. He awarded me the Flying Badge in Gold, but remarked that I had assumed a great responsibility when I went along with the Duce in Gerlach's machine. He did add that he understood that I wanted to take the same risk as Mussolini as I was carrying out a personal order of the Führer's. I took advantage of the opportunity and asked the Reichsmarschall to allow Hauptmann Gerlach and Leutnant Meier-Wehner to be recommended for the Knight's Cross. Hitler gave his approval to both high awards, as well as for the decoration of my volunteers and Karl Radl, who was also promoted to the rank of Hauptsturmführer.

Somewhat later I had to give another speech on the operation to a good dozen generals of the Führer Headquarters. Göring and Jodl sat in the front row. If any of them were expecting a talk in the general staff style, they were surely disappointed. I described the actions as they had happened, as we had experienced them, with our hopes and mistakes, but also our will to carry out the mission successfully in spite of everything.

The next day I spoke with Oberst Strewe, who was responsible for military security in the Wolfsschanze. He expressed his concern and wanted to know whether, in my opinion, the Führer Headquarters was adequately guarded against enemy attack. All I could say to him was, "The Führer Headquarters is undoubtedly very well camouflaged. Its entrances are well guarded. But an enemy attack on the site is always possible. Obviously any headquarters can be attacked, just like any other military target."

I took part in the "midnight tea." Hitler sat between his two secretaries, Johanna Wolff and Traudl Junge and drank tea. On this evening he talked mainly with ambassador Hewel, who represented Ribbentrop at Führer Headquarters.

"You are of course invited to midnight tea whenever you come to Führer Headquarters, Skorzeny," said Hitler. "I would like to see you here more often."

I thanked Hitler, but in future I didn't take advantage of this invitation to come to midnight tea, which often lasted until three or four in the morning. Many used the occasion to try and further their careers – through flattery and intrigues, provided that they succeeded in attracting the attention of Reichsleiter Martin Bormann, who was always present in Führer Headquarters.

Today I regret that I didn't take part in this midnight tea as often as possible. I could have made Hitler aware of realities of which I knew. It is said today that it was impossible to present one's own, contrary opinion to him. That is not true. He gladly debated with those he spoke to, provided these were well-informed about the topic under discussion and made reasonable suggestions. From 1943 his physical condition deteriorated more and more – under the influence of the "treatment" he received from Doctor Morell, a dangerous quack who was supported by Bormann.

I did not meet Martin Bormann, the Reichsleiter of the party, until the day (September 16, 1943) that he invited me to supper. I was a little late in arriving, which was not to the taste of Reichsführer Himmler, who was also present. Even before I could apologize he made several malicious comments about me. Today I can't recall even one of the insignificant topics which Bormann chose to discuss. Himmler, for his part, was not talkative. In any case Bormann tried to prescribe what I should tell the Führer and what I should not. In short an icy atmosphere prevailed. Joachim von Ribbentrop, who I had visited in the afternoon for coffee, was also far from entertaining. He received me very much according to protocol, sat on a high armchair like the others and offered me Turkish cigarettes which bore his initials. I must say that our foreign minister was very poorly informed about what had happened in Italy in the past months.

When I said goodbye to the Duce at Führer Headquarters, he made me promise to visit him soon in Italy. But it wasn't until mid-June 1944 that I went to Gargnano, located on the west bank of Lake

Garda, Mussolini's new seat of government – and it was von Ribbentrop's fault.

My soldiers waited for me at Frascati. I was given permission to drive to Innsbruck via Tirol and Lake Garda, and I had just arrived in Innsbruck when I received news from Berlin relating to Generals Soleti and Cueli. Mussolini was suspicious of the former and told me so. On the other hand he had a certain degree of trust in Cueli, because he had treated him well on the Gran Sasso. One will remember that the Duce entrusted his luggage to Radl, who handed it over to the two Italian generals. Following necessary repairs, these two flew in the second Storch to Munich. There they gave the Duce back his luggage. Both men expressed a desire to return to Italy; they were in Innsbruck when their own luggage underwent a routine check. We then learned that papers apparently belonging to Mussolini were found in their bags and confiscated. I later saw with my own eyes that Mussolini's diaries were involved. I had played my own role in this adventure and consequently reported to Ribbentrop's office that these papers had been sent to the Reich Foreign Minister and should be given back to Mussolini, who was still Hitler's guest. Naturally they should explain to him that his diary had been found in the luggage of the two generals when they tried to cross the border.

From Rome and Frascati, where my volunteers had prepared an enthusiastic welcome for me, we moved up to Lake Garda, where I Panzer Corps of the Waffen-SS was located. The corps was under the command of my former chief, General Paul Hausser. The reception we received there compensated for all our labors. We forgot all the anger, the minor obstacles that had been placed in our path, and the intrigues. I also received a gift from the Duce there: a great Lancia sports convertible. It wasn't until mid-June that I was able to thank him personally. For the diary discovered in Innsbruck was held at Wilhelmstrasse for more than eight months, and I had to make several emphatic requests that they might hand it over to me, as I couldn't visit Mussolini without the diary. This was possibly taken as a sharp criticism of Ribbentrop's diplomatic skill.

In June 1944 I went to Gargnano with Hauptmann Radl. Mussolini welcomed us warmly in the Villa Feltrinelli. Prior to our visit ambassador Rahn and his office gave us numerous recommendations as to what were appropriate topics of conversation about and what were not. We were dismayed to see only a few Italian soldiers on guard outside the villa. Security was provided by a battalion of the Waffen-SS – as if Mussolini couldn't have found thousands of Italian soldiers to guard and defend him. Had we freed him from the Gran Sasso only to see him as a prisoner again? It was quite obvious: Mussolini was not a free man. I was overcome by a great sadness.

It was even worse when he greeted us in his small office: he looked like an old lion without a mane. He again accused the House of Savoy and regretted that Duke Aosta had died in captivity in Nairobi in March 1942.

"I have deceived myself, because they deceived me," he said to us. "I am happy to see that honorable socialists who had earlier refused to follow me are now supporters of the fascist republic. For example the former communist chiefs Niccolò Bombacci and Carlo Silvestri.[1] The traitors think they can save themselves – but they are wrong. They believe that our enemies will reward them for their betrayal. But they are already being treated like toadies. Badoglio was forced to resign his office three times. The King has abdicated in favor of his son. Certainly it was all the same to Umberto to pass himself off as a good leninist, just as long as he became king. But he will be thrown out by Ercoli, who came direct from Moscow."[2]

"In the House of Savoy they're convinced that they've saved the crown. But I can foretell one thing Skorzeny, this crown is lost forever."

I gave him back his diary and asked him to forgive the delay in returning it, for which I was not responsible. He replied that he was quite certain of that. Then the topic of conversation turned to another theme, namely the efforts of the republican Italians on behalf of the axis and victory.

But the enthusiasm and conviction that he had shown nine months earlier were gone. He seemed to convince only himself. I asked him to dedicate photos of himself for all the participants of the Gran Sasso operation, which he gladly did.

The Duce's dedication read:

"To my friend Otto Skorzeny, who saved my life.
We will fight for the same cause: for a united and free Europe."

In October 1943 the Duce had gold wristwatches presented to all the paratroopers and my sixteen Waffen-SS men who had landed by glider on the Campo Imperatore. The watch faces were all engraved with the famous "M." Every officer received a gold stop watch. To me the Duce sent the wristwatch and the stop watch, together with a gold pocket watch whose "M" consisted of rubies and which bore the date 12. 9. 1943. It was stolen from me by the Americans in 1945.

Other souvenirs also disappeared in this confusion! The photos, the dagger of honor of the fascist militia, as well as the "Order of the Hundred Musketeers," which was only awarded to one hundred Italian soldiers. In the meantime friends have sent me a copy of this medal.

In the course of the day I had the opportunity to speak with Prince Junio-Valerio Borghese, the commander of the famous X-MAS Flotilla.

"What madness the allies are committing," he said, "by aiding Stalin! Europe will be mortally wounded if Germany ever loses. Churchill, Roosevelt, the English and the Americans will one day regret allying themselves with militant communism. We will fight with you to the end, because we are Italian patriots and committed Europeans."

Radl and I ate our meals with the Duce and his family in the Villa Feltrinelli. A member of the German foreign ministry was likewise there and endeavored to steer the conversation toward peaceful themes. But the Duce, who had a very thorough knowledge of European, and especially German, history, enjoyed himself. He observed that Frederick the Great possessed extraordinary political and military abilities at the same time, which explained why he was self-critical. The ambassadorial advisor looked like he was sitting on hot coals when Mussolini spoke of the astonishing diplomatic virtuosity that Frederick the Great developed in the years 1740 to 1786.

One felt that the present scarcely interested the Duce any more. He was no longer chief of state, but a philosopher, historian, a far-seeing theoretician who sought the synthesis between tradition and revolution, between socialism and nationalism to the benefit of a reconciled Europe.

When we left Mussolini asked me to visit him often. He took my hand in his; I had no way of knowing that I had seen him for the last time.

• • •

"This action in the Gran Sasso massif attracted world-wide attention," wrote Charles Foley in *Commando Extraordinary*. I don't know whose silly idea it was to send a paratrooper propaganda company to the Gran Sasso to make a film that was supposed to recreate our operation and which was mediocre in every respect. The only convincing role was played by the 2,914-meter-high Gran Sasso. I would also have been happier if the German and Italian press hadn't printed so much material that was a figment of someone's imagination and hadn't published my photo as well.

This action also had psychological effects on our soldiers. Eleven officers of the Brandenburg Division requested that they be transferred to Friedenthal. This was the reason for my first discussion with Admiral Canaris, in the course of which I got to know his character. This man had something of the jelly-fish about him, like a fleeing eel. Today I ask myself why he had a portrait of Hitler on his desk: one of Roosevelt, Churchill or Stalin would have served the purpose better. The conversation lasted for hours. Oberst Lahousen appeared from time to time and declared that this or that officer was indispensable to the *Brandenburg* Division. After three hours of negotiation Canaris said to me, "Good. Very well, I will order the transfer... No, wait. I just thought of something else," and so on.

He had to begin all over again and not until four hours later did the admiral give in, albeit reluctantly.

Among the officers transferred from the Brandenbur*g* Division to Friedenthal was Oberleutnant Adrian von Fölkersam, the son of an old Baltic family. His grandfather had been an admiral in the czarist fleet and had commanded a flotilla during the Russo-Japanese War. He spoke fluent Russian, French and English and had studied economic science at the University of Berlin. As a Brandenburger he had already undertaken daring missions, such as raids behind Soviet lines, an attack on a Soviet Red Army division headquarters at the beginning of 1942 and so on. He soon became my chief-of-staff.

Fölkersam confided to me that unusual things happened in the Brandenburg Division. French- or Arabic-speaking soldiers were sent to Russia, and those who spoke English or Russian to the Balkans. By a unique coincidence he learned that the enemy had been waiting for certain commando units when they arrived in the Near East, the

USA and elsewhere (Operation Pastorius). Since certain units of the Brandenburgers were new formations and the young officers showed little initiative, Canaris decided to use the Brandenburg Division as a simple division unit within the armed forces, although the Brandenburgers could and should be used for special missions and had been trained for such.

Fölkersam and the other Brandenburg officers who transferred to Friedenthal were permitted to voluntarily join the Waffen-SS. Generals Jüttner and Jodl subsequently gave me authorization to recruit from among the soldiers of every branch of the armed forces for my commando units. On August 5 the *Sonderverband z.b.V.* Friedenthal became the 502nd SS Commando Battalion with a headquarters company and three motorized companies. Somewhat later the battalion was expanded to become Commando Unit Center (*Jagdverband Mitte*), to which four more battalions were added, the instruction battalion and others. Finally, in September 1944, additional units of the Brandenburg Division were transferred to the SS commando units and placed under my command on order of General Guderian, Army Chief-of-Staff.

I thus achieved an early departure from Schellenberg's sphere of influence and now received orders from the OKW, from General Jodl or, most commonly, direct from Hitler.

"Following the Gran Sasso operation," wrote Charles Foley, "Friedenthal became a gathering place for every dare-devil and specialist of the handiwork of war. Skorzeny had under his command soldiers of the army, the air force and the navy. At one point in time Friedenthal was literally swamped with these volunteers who wished to fight in his units: wild dare-devils, standard-bearers, idealists and the 'tough ones' who wanted to distinguish themselves in sensational actions... Hundreds of photographs from Friedenthal show how Skorzeny trained his people. One recognizes his officers by their tired appearance: Skorzeny drilled and trained them unyieldingly, so that they might be capable of overcoming expected and also unforeseen difficulties."

● ● ●

On April 28, 1945 I was on my command train in the vicinity of Salzburg. I had set up my command post in two special cars which I

had got out of Berlin with much difficulty. My mission was to organize the famous "Alpine Fortress" together with Field Marshall
Schörner. I had an excellent communications system at my disposal
with telex, telephones and a good dozen radios, and was thus able to
communicate with every front.

In the afternoon a report was received from the radio monitoring
service. Italian radio had announced that Benito Mussolini had been
captured and shot by partisans. I considered that impossible. If the
Duce was no longer alive, it was because he had taken his own life: I
was firmly convinced of that. I knew that Mussolini was guarded in
Gargnano by a battalion of the Waffen-SS. It was totally inconceiv-
able that even a large group of resistance fighters could successfully
ambush a battalion of the Waffen-SS in its quarters.

To be sure, I knew nothing of the negotiations being carried out
in Bern between General Wolff and his adjutant Dollmann and Dulles:
the Duce was not informed of this! But Himmler knew about it. I
finally succeeded in establishing contact with Major Beck, the chief
of my Jagdverband Italien (Commando Unit Italy), who had vainly
tried to get in contact with me. He explained to me a fact of which he
learned all too late: the Duce left Gargnano on April 18 to go to
Milan. Someone had withdrawn the Waffen-SS battalion assigned to
guard the Duce and sent it to the front.

"But what idiot gave that order?" I asked Dr. Beck.

"No idea," he replied. "All that we heard was that the battalion
was supposed to be replaced by a company of the Luftwaffe. And I
don't know if that was the case. I later learned that the Duce left
Milan headed north during the night of April 25-26, and this was
after a conversation with Cardinal Schuster and one of the leaders of
the resistance fighters, General Cadorna.[3] The Duce didn't want to
surrender himself..."

"To the north you say? To Switzerland or Austria?"

"I just learned that he stopped at the prefecture in Como, in order
to wait there for a strong militia column under the command of
Pavolini and then put up a fight in the Valtini Mountains. It is certain
that there were no soldiers of the Waffen-SS with him. It was too
late. There was nothing we could do..."

Nothing! And in the Valtini Mountains! We would have been quite
close, if Pavolini's 5,000 had actually existed and we had received
the order to begin the final battle in the Alps.

Our Waffen-SS was thus used to hold Mussolini prisoner and not to defend him! Generalfeldmarschall Kesselring would never have allowed such a rotten trick! But he was in Bad Nauheim, acting Commander-in-Chief of the Western Front in von Rundstedt's place.

The rest is common knowledge. Benito Mussolini was abandoned by everyone. The hangman, the communist Audisio-Valerio, a former member of the Workers International in the Spanish Civil War, said, "Duce I have come to rescue you!"

He enquired cautiously, "You aren't armed are you?"

Some have even written that the Duce did not die bravely. But according to the words of Audisio's chauffeur, the Duce's last words were, "Aim directly for the heart!"

Everyone is familiar with the horrible photographs from Loreto Square in Milan.

Notes

1. Bombacci broke with Moscow in 1927. He joined the new fascist republic and was murdered by partisans. Silvestri, a journalist, was arrested in 1924 for writing that Mussolini had given the order for the murder of socialist deputy Matteotti. Silvestri subsequently obtained proof that Mussolini had nothing to do with the murder. The Duce met with him at Gargnano and the two men made peace. (Editors' note)

2. On April 2, 1944, broadcasting over Radio Bari, communist leader Ercoli called upon the Italian people to "join the battle against fascism together with the great democracies." He also praised the heroic Soviet armies, which were going to "liberate Europe."

3. This General Cadorna was the son of a former commander-in-chief of the Italian forces whose front was broken by Austro-Hungarian troops at Carporetto in October-November 1917. The Italian Minister President Orlando had declared to Marshall Foch that Cadorno was determined "to fight to the end, even if he had to fall back all the way to Sicily." To this Foch replied: "That's out of the question. The stand must be made on the Piave!" (Marshall Foch, Memoirs, Part 2). In 1922 the Duce attempted to restore the honor of the older Cadorna. (Editors' note)

19

July 20, 1944

"...a bombing attempt at Führer Headquarters..." – Schellenberg behind his desk with a submachine-gun within reach – The supposed putsch by SS Colonel Bolbrinker, Chief-of-Staff of the Inspector of Armored Troops, is delayed – A confrontation averted – General Student doesn't want to believe it – Göring's orders – I drive to Bendlerstrasse – "The Führer is dead": Major Remer is skeptical – I speak with Adolf Hitler by telephone from Goebbels' house – The helplessness and nervousness of the conspirators – General Olbricht and Oberst von Stauffenberg, the leaders of the conspiracy – The counter-putsch by Oberst Pridun, Oberst von Heyde and others – Generaloberst Beck takes his own life; General Fromm liquidates witnesses – Speer's odd report – What Major Remer found out – My actions at Bendlerstrasse: The Walküre order is rescinded immediately – Stauffenberg's game of dice – Canaris is arrested – Hitler fears that Stauffenberg might be injured! – Field Marshalls Rommel and von Kluge commit suicide – The Red Orchestra and the 20th of July – Guderian: "The assassination attempt had devastating effects on the morale of the Führer" – The struggle continues.

"Sturmbannführer Skorzeny! Sturmbannführer Skorzeny!" An officer ran alongside the fast train standing in a Berlin station and called my name. Scarcely five minutes had passed since Radl and I had installed ourselves in our reserved sleeper car. We were about to travel to Vienna to form a new commando unit of our best frogmen. It was to visit Tito, who had fled to the island of Viz, at his new headquarters.

I rolled down the window and called out to the officer, who had already passed our compartment. He was a Leutnant from General Jüttner's staff, a liaison officer to Schellenberg's Office VI. He was quite out of breath and was scarcely able to call to me that I was most urgently expected in my office in Berlin. Radl passed my bags through the window. I told my adjutant to go on to Vienna alone and do his best there. It was 6:10 P.M., July 20, 1944.

That afternoon we had learned that Hitler had barely escaped an attempted assassination. But the seriousness of the situation was first made clear to us by a radio broadcast at 6:45 P.M. I didn't know that Himmler and Gestapo chief Müller had sent experts to the Wolfsschanze at 1 P.M. and that the entire national police force had been placed on alert at 2 P.M. Then, on the platform, I heard that there had been dead and wounded and that the situation in Berlin was still not clear.

I called Fölkersam, who was in Friedenthal, from the military office at the station. Fölkersam was to place the 502nd Commando Battalion on alert and report immediately as soon as the first company was ready to march. I then drove to the Berkaerstrasse in Berlin-Schmargendorf, where my administrative section was located. At a quarter to seven the network suddenly interrupted its broadcast and issued a special bulletin:

"A bombing attempt was made on the Führer's life today. Generalleutnant Schmundt, Oberst Brandt and colleague Berger were nearby and sustained serious injuries. Generaloberst Jodl, Generals Korten, Buhle, Bodenschatz, Heusinger and Scherff, Admirals Voss and von Puttkammer, Kapitän zur See Assmann and Oberstleutnant Borgmann escaped with minor injuries. Apart from minor burns and bruises, the Führer himself suffered no injuries. He has already gone back to work and, as planned, has received the Duce for lengthy talks. Reichsmarschall Göring joined the Führer a short time after the attempt."

The mood of the communique worried me. Who had done this thing? Had the enemy penetrated the Wolfsschanze, the Führer's H.Q.? Ten months earlier I had said to Oberst Strewe in Rastenburg Führer Headquarters was not one hundred percent secure against a surprise attack by a determined enemy with a really ingenious plan. The oddest rumors were circulating among the offices of Berkaerstrasse. The officials stood there armed to the teeth and they were waving their submachine-guns around so carelessly that I got goose-bumps and drew Oberführer Schellenberg's attention to this impossible situation.

Since February 12, 1944 the military and political intelligence services had been under a central command. Certain agents of Admiral Canaris' Abwehr were all to openly committing treason and were exposed as double agents; he himself was put on ice. However this did not stop Generalfeldmarschall Keitel from having him named "Chief of the Special Staff for the Economic War," which operated from Eiche near Potsdam. Schellenberg "inherited" the entire Ausland Abwehr organization – which was then christened "Amt Mil" – but remained chief of Office VI of the Reich Security Office.

Schellenberg was green in the face. A pistol lay on his desk.

"Just let them come," he said, "I know how to defend myself! They wont get me that easily!"

"Is someone really out to get you?"

"Skorzeny, the situation is serious. I have had submachine-guns issued to all the male employees. We will do our utmost to defend ourselves."

"You know," I said to him, "what you have ordered appears to me very imprudent. These people simply can't walk around with firearms and they will probably shoot themselves yet. I just had one of your NCOs sent to the basement: he was holding his machine-pistol like an umbrella!"

Schellenberg informed me that the center of the conspiracy was obviously located in Bendlerstrasse, and asked whether I might not order one of my companies over for "our" protection.

"Yes. Of course. I really am absent-minded! My battalion is already on alert. I should have thought of that straight away. But may I know who the enemy is?"

"I tell you everything was cooked up in Bendlerstrasse. It is a conspiracy. They won't shrink from anything!"

"And whom is it against? Who is plotting against whom?"

"A putsch is probably being prepared and tanks will roll in the streets of Berlin. Imagine that, Skorzeny, tanks!"

"Calm yourself Oberführer! I will find out what's going on while we wait for my company to arrive."

It was probably about 7 P.M. I telephoned Fölkersam and told him to send 1st Company under the command of Hauptmann Fucker to Berkaerstrasse immediately. Fölkersam and Oberjunker Ostafel were to join me as quickly as possible, which they did in record time. Fölkersam remained at Berkaerstrasse while Ostafel and I carried out a "patrol" through the government quarter. All was quiet.

"So far it seems no more than a comic opera revolt to me," I observed to Ostafel, "but let's drive over to the panzers."

I had many friends at the panzer corps and I knew Oberst Bolbrinker, the chief-of-staff of the panzer inspectorate, which was based at Fehrbelliner Square. I immediately had the impression that something wasn't right there. Two tanks sat in readiness on each of the broad streets leading into the square in a star-shaped pattern. Standing in my car, I saluted the officers; they let me pass and I found Oberst Bolbrinker. He saw me immediately and was at something of a loss. He obeyed an order from Bendlerstrasse and had all the panzers from the Wünsdorf panzer school ordered to Berlin, but he concentrated them around Fehrbelliner Square so as to keep them under his control. He was supposed to send armed patrols to Lankwitz and the Lichterfelde Barracks, the quarters of the Leibstandarte Adolf Hitler.

"What do you make of that?" said the Oberst. "Did you hear about it earlier on the radio? A bombing attempt against the Führer!... Unbelievable! Isn't it?... Oberst Gläsemer, the commander of the Krampnitz Panzer School, hasn't returned from Bendlerstrasse. The Waffen-SS planned a putsch and there have already been clashes. What do you think of it?"

"Herr Oberst, I am a member of the Waffen-SS myself and I don't believe under any circumstances that my comrades have planned a plot against the Führer and against the Reich. However, I suspect that certain people are even now trying to set off a proper civil war and play the army off against the Waffen-SS."

The Oberst was surprised.

"A civil war. How?"

I explained to Bolbrinker that the Leibstandarte would react vigorously if the panzer units, which had already moved from Wünsdorf to Berlin on his orders, were to carry out an armed reconnaissance to Lichterfelde. That had to be avoided at all costs. The order was senseless. The Oberst was of the same opinion and told me that his tanks had not yet moved any farther: he had concentrated them around

Fehrbelliner Square. Then I suggested to the Oberst that we drive to Lichterfelde with two of his officers.

He agreed. We left immediately, and as we passed by the panzer officers we recommended that they do nothing until further orders were received. Shortly thereafter Bolbrinker gave the order that the panzer units were only to obey the orders of the Inspector of Armored Troops, General Guderian.

We raced by car to my old barracks in Lichterfelde. There I had a talk with Oberführer Mohnke, who soon afterward was promoted to Generalmajor of the Leibstandarte. He saw us as heaven-sent. Goebbels had alerted him at about 7 P.M. and warned him that certain elements of the army would claim that the Führer was dead and would attempt to seize power and issue orders. Furthermore the putschists would spread the lie that the SS – and especially the Waffen-SS – had carried out the act of violence at Führer H.Q. Oberführer Mohnke had therefore brought his cannon and machine-guns into position in the Leibstandarte barracks parade square; his people were ready for battle. We discussed the situation openly.

"Dear comrades," said Mohnke, "luckily you have come. For if the panzers had showed up here there would have been shooting, and the matter would undoubtedly have taken a bloody course."

I asked him not to allow his troops to leave the barracks, for it might be that one or another panzer would show up in front of the barracks in spite of everything. The Waffen-SS was not to react to any such provocation. He agreed. One of Bolbrinker's liaison officers stayed with Mohnke; the other went to report to his commanding officer. It was about 9 P.M.

I later found out that Oberst Glasemer was captured by the conspirators. However he escaped from Bendlerstrasse and notified Oberst Bolbrinker, who then ignored any further orders from that source.

I called Fölkersam from the Leibstandarte barracks. The 1st Motorized Company had meanwhile arrived from Friedenthal. I briefed Fölkersam to stand ready for anything in front of the buildings on Berkaerstrasse. My adjutant reported to me that commander of the Berlin military district had initiated an alarm plan shortly before 4 P.M. A practice alarm of this type had been carried out by the general staff of Military District III on July 15. The exercise involved security measures in the event of an allied airborne landing against

Berlin. But the orders that had been coming from Bendlerstrasse since 5 P.M. were no practice: it was a secret mobilization for a military putsch! Who was behind it? It was clear to me that the confusion that reigned here in Berlin was linked to the attempt on Hitler's life. During the night it was confirmed to me that the conspirators had in fact attempted to camouflage their actions by giving the Walküre order: Walküre anticipated certain special measures which were to be set in motion if enemy forces suddenly broke in or in the event of a general revolt by foreign workers which might threaten state security. I also heard that the "exercise" of July 15 was merely the result of an error on the part of some of the conspirators themselves: they assumed that the attempt on Hitler's life would be made that day.

After my conversation with Fölkersam I decided to drive to Wannsee, where General Student's headquarters was located. They had not received any alert order, however. So I immediately drove to General Student's home in Lichterfelde, which I knew. The general was at home and received me. It was already past 9 P.M. He was on the garden terrace, wearing casual clothes and sitting beneath a half-darkened lamp, in front of him a mountain of files. His wife sat nearby, busy with her knitting. The general welcomed us warmly. When I explained that we were there on military business his wife excused herself and I gave the general a brief description of the day's events as I knew them. He shook his head in disbelief: "But no my dear Skorzeny, that sounds very much like an adventure novel! An attempted putsch? A military plot? That's completely impossible! It must be just a misunderstanding, that's all."

Then the telephone rang. It was Reichsmarschall Hermann Göring. He informed General Student that the attempt to kill Hitler had been carried out by a staff officer from the Bendlerstrasse, who was really convinced that his bomb had killed Hitler. Afterwards orders had come from the Bendlerstrasse, some of which had been carried out. From now on only orders that originated from Führer Headquarters or the OKW were to be followed. Göring recommended staying calm in order to avoid clashes. The Führer was unhurt and would speak to the German people during the course of the night.

The general became pale. He turned to me and said: "You are right." He reported my actions to Göring and the fact that I was there with him, hung up and said, "That is really unbelievable! Even viewed superficially the situation looks serious. I will alert our troops at once and forbid them to follow orders that do not come direct from me."

"Herr General," I said to him, "the panzers and the Waffen-SS are already taking it easy. I suggest that you establish contact with Oberst Bolbrinker and Oberführer Mohnke."

"Right! We will exchange liaison officers."

I took my leave of General Student and returned to Berkaerstrasse by the quickest route. It was already past 10:30 P.M. Fölkersam reported that the OKH had in fact been issuing orders to the military districts and the fronts since 4:30 P.M. They thought Hitler was dead! It was high treason!

Fölkersam, Fucker, Ostafel and I were disgusted. The Wehrmacht was fighting on three fronts against the strongest armies in the world. On the Eastern Front the Romania was threatened by the Red Army; it had broken into the Baltic countries and had taken Pinsk, Bialystok and Brest-Litovsk in the central sector. On the Western Front the allies commanded the air and sea and were expanding their bridgehead. The port of Cherbourg and the bomb-blasted city of St. Lô had just fallen into their hands. In Italy, after the capture of Arezzo they were already at the gates of Pisa.

I received a call from Führer Headquarters – probably on the initiative of Reichsmarschall Göring. I received the order to immediately proceed to the Bendlerstrasse "with my entire force," in order to support the watch battalion of the Grossdeutschland Division, which was commanded by Major Remer, who was already on the scene. I pointed out that I had only a single company at Berkaerstrasse at that time. I would march to Bendlerstrasse with it.

It was shortly before midnight. We rushed through the streets in great haste. The buildings had been destroyed by enemy terror attacks and looked really eerie. Our own thoughts were far from optimistic. My broad Kübelwagen led the column of about twenty vehicles. Fölkersam sat beside me, and I believe it was he who said what we were all thinking, "When I think of how many brave comrades have fallen on account of these fellows...!"

We reached the Tiergarten-Bendlerstrasse intersection. There was a car in front of us, and a second, which had just left the main entrance of the Bendler block, came toward us. Both cars stopped. I waited a moment and then got out. In the first car was Dr. Ernst Kaltenbrunner, who had taken Heydrich's place in the RSHA. In the other car sat a general. As I learned later, it was General Fromm, commander of the Replacement Army. Standing off to one side, I overheard the general say to Kaltenbrunner, "...I'm tired and am going home. I can be reached there any time."

But as it turned out General Fromm did not drive home, but to Doctor Goebbels.

Both men shook hands. The way was clear: go! I let the convoy move out, waved my pocket lamp and shouted: "Major Remer."

● ● ●

Major Hans-Otto Remer, commanding officer of the watch battalion of the Grossdeutschland Division, had been wounded eight times since the beginning of the war. A few weeks ago Hitler had decorated him with the Knight's Cross. At 4:30 P.M. he received instructions to initiate Operation Walküre. General von Kortzfleisch, commanding general of the Berlin Military District, was absent from the headquarters in Berliner Square. He had been arrested by the conspirators in the Bendlerstrasse. General von Hase, commander of the Berlin garrison, explained to Remer that Hitler was probably dead and that the Waffen-SS was attempting to seize power. Therefore the watch battalion must block off the government quarter and see to the security of the general staff of the replacement army in the Bendlerstrasse. Remer was surprised and said, "In this case, Herr General, it is up to Reichsmarschall Göring, who will replace the Führer and who must give the orders."

Below in the communications room, Untersturmführer Roehrig and Scharführer Tegeder had sensed the treachery at about 5 P.M. and at 6 P.M. transmitted the putschist's orders incoherently. At about 10 P.M. Roehrig even succeeded in taking control of the entire communications system – telephones, teletype and radio – and warned Hauptmann Schlee, one of Major Remer's officers. Remer had set up his command post in Dr. Goebbels' offices on Hermann Göring Strasse. Schlee, who was in command of the blocking force around the Bendler block, informed him of the orders given by Olbricht, Hoepner and Stauffenberg. It was now apparent that the Olbricht office was the central point of the conspiracy.

But while I was alerting Oberst Bolbrinker, Oberführer Mohnke and General Student, those inside the huge building were acting on their own and demanding explanations of the conspirators. Olbricht and von Stauffenberg were thus forced to disarm and confine General Fromm. The latter knew of the plot and was prepared to support them as soon as they were successful. But Fromm had spoken with Keitel by telephone shortly before 5 P.M. and learned from him that Hitler was not dead, but was in conversation with Mussolini and Marshall Graziani. As a result Fromm wanted nothing more to do with the conspirators. He was disarmed and locked up – together with Generals Kunze, Strecker and Specht – and was immediately replaced by General Hoepner, who had been demoted and relieved in 1942! They couldn't have made a worse choice!

It was Austrian, Oberstleutnant Pridun, who organized the counter-putsch in the Bendlerstrasse, together with Colonels von der Heyde, Kuban and Herber. But they lacked weapons. Hauptmann Fliessbach drove to the arsenal at Wünsdorf. Not until later did he succeed in bringing weapons and ammunition, submachine-guns and mortars, in a truck, and it was after 9 P.M. when these were passed out.

Oberst von der Heyde then entered Olbricht's office with twenty officers and NCOs and called on him to surrender. There was a brief exchange of fire, in which Stauffenberg was wounded. General Fromm was freed by another group and declared Generals Beck, Olbricht and Hoepner and Oberst Stauffenberg under arrest. Field Marshalls von Witzleben and Gisevius had already left. Generaloberst Beck tried to commit suicide. He only succeeded in wounding himself twice, however, and had to be finished off by an NCO.

General Fromm returned to his office and announced, "I have just convened a court martial which has sentenced General Olbricht, Oberst Mertz von Quirnheim, that Oberst there, whom I don't want to know any more (he pointed at Stauffenberg) and that Leutnant (referring to Leutnant von Haeften, Stauffenberg's adjutant) to death."

The "sentence" was carried out immediately in the courtyard of the building, which was illuminated by searchlights. The firing squad was made up of NCOs of the replacement army. It was about 11:15. General Fromm liquidated the inconvenient witnesses.

According to former armaments minister Speer's book, "the uprising was put down by Oberst Bolbrinker's panzer brigade." He, Speer, had arrived at Bendlerstrasse to try and stop the shootings, which took place shortly after midnight." He wrote, "Bolbrinker and

Remer sat in my car. In completely blacked-out Berlin the Bendler-strasse was lit brightly by searchlights: an unreal and eerie scene."

At the same time this scene was said to have had "a theatrical effect, like a movie set." Speer's car was stopped by an SS officer at the corner of Tiergartenstrasse. He saw "Skorzeny, the liberator of Mussolini, talking to Kaltenbrunner, the head of the Gestapo." Not only was Kaltenbrunner not the head of the Secret State Police (that was Müller), but it seemed that one always had to mention the Gestapo when someone was eliminated. "Their conduct had the same shadowy effect as these dark figures."

Suddenly "a mighty shadow became visible against the brightly-lit background of the Bendlerstrasse," and General Fromm came, "alone, in full uniform." He turned to Speer and "in a trembling voice" informed him of the death of Olbricht, Stauffenberg and so on.

There are so many improbable things in this book that I feel obligated to go into several: Oberst Bolbrinker's tanks put down absolutely nothing and saw no action. The reason for this is known. As well the Bendlerstrasse was not lit by searchlights. I don't remember seeing Speer that evening, and when he says that I spoke to him, I wasn't even there at the time, for General Fromm was still in the Bendler block. I also don't believe that Oberst Bolbrinker and Major Remer got into Speer's Lancia. And finally I had other things to do besides stand on the street and chat in the shadow of the trees.

It is true that the real Gestapo chief, Müller, sent a sort of investigating committee to the Bendlerstrasse at about 5:30 P.M. on Himmler's order. This commission was led by Dr. Piffrader and consisted of four people: two Gestapo officials and two members of the SS with the rank of Unterführer. General Piffrader was supposed to interrogate General Olbricht and his chief-of-staff von Stauffenberg and find out why the latter had left Rastenburg in such a hurry. Himmler, who was at Führer Headquarters at that moment, was aware that the replacement army had already issued the order for the implementation of the Walküre plan. I therefore don't understand why Müller, who must also have known about it, only sent four men. They also put Olbricht under lock and key and Dr. Kaltenbrunner, head of the RSHA, came in person to fetch him – so lightly did they take the putsch!

At that time Kaltenbrunner did not yet know that Count Helldorf, Berlin's chief of police, and Arthur Nebe, the Kripo chief, also belonged to the circle of conspirators.

In his book Speer claims that he drove to the Bendlerstrasse to protest against the executions. Apart from the fact that he did not have the authority to do so, when his book came out in 1969 that was supposed to mean that he "had offered resistance" in 1944. I asked Hans Remer, today a retired Generalmajor, what he thought of Speer's account. His reply follows:

"...Herr Speer only reached the Bendler block because I asked him to drive me there from my command post in Goebbels' official residence. I had only just received word that shootings were taking place in the Bendler block. My own car was not available at that moment, but I wanted to get to the Bendler block as quickly as possible to prevent the shootings, so I asked Speer to drive me there. He did so right away in his white Lancia sports car. If you like, Speer was no more than my driver, albeit a prominent one! No one stopped us. I met Fromm and a small party in the entrance to the Bendler block, in my opinion that was immediately after the shooting of Stauffenberg and the others.

"Fromm knew me. He said to me, 'At last a proper officer from Grossdeutschland! What do you know about the situation? ' I told him that Hitler had given me full authority in Berlin and that I was responsible for the security of the government and the restoration of legitimate order. I suggested to Fromm that if he wanted to know more about the political situation he should drive to see Goebbels, in whose residence I had set up my command post.

"I recall that Fromm and Speer spoke after this conversation. How Fromm and Speer got back to Goebbels' house I do not know. I was, however, very surprised to see SS men searching Fromm's coat, which was hanging in the hall, when I arrived there a half hour later.

"As for your question, the Bendler block was blacked out as usual. After a brief conversation with Fromm I went up to the second floor and received a quite general picture of what was happening. I subsequently spoke with Hauptmann Schlee, commander of the company on guard, in the doorman's house and gave him explicit instructions. We must therefore have met and come to our agreement at this time. In any case I subsequently drove back alone to my command post in Goebbels' residence. Himmler arrived there a short time later and I reported to him personally."

It was agreed with Major Remer that he would take over security outside the building and I the security inside. That's the way it was done.

I had often gone to the Bendlerstrasse on official business. I went up to the second floor, where Olbricht's and Stauffenberg's offices were located, with Fölkersam, Ostafel and two of my other officers. The atmosphere was still very excited. There were armed officers in every corner. I attempted to calm the mood and had Oberst Pridun and Oberst Herber, who I knew personally, describe what had happened that afternoon. Then I went into Stauffenberg's office. A Luftwaffe officer I knew told me that the chief of the radio section was waiting for orders for that night. I ordered him to cancel everything associated with Walküre *and* restore normal communications with Führer Headquarters, the military districts and the general staffs of the various fronts, as well as set up a telephone monitoring service, especially for long-distance calls. Nevertheless, I was unable to get in touch with Führer Headquarters.

I determined that the putsch and counter-putsch had been going on for a good ten hours and that all work had been forgotten in the process. The most important thing now was to get the tremendous administrative apparatus moving again, and so I had the department chief report to me. I told him:

"The main thing now is to cancel all the orders associated with the Walküre alert plan. Millions of our comrades are fighting hard. Think about them. Deliveries of food, munitions and reinforcements are needed on all fronts. Each of you must endeavor tonight to make up for lost time!"

Then an Oberst informed me that various urgent decisions about questions of supply had to be made and signed for by General Fromm or General Olbricht or Oberst von Stauffenberg. "Very well! I am assuming the responsibility for signing orders and issuing urgent instructions. You will do your part. To work gentlemen!"

I sat down at Stauffenberg's desk. In a drawer lay the real Walküre plan and two dice and a board game printed in four colors. The game showed the path that a corps of Army Group South had taken during the Russian campaign. The declarations in the various boxes were so cynical and mean that I was quite shaken.

Hitler finally spoke to the German people at about one in the morning. He stated that he was unhurt, "although the bomb planted

by Oberst von Stauffenberg exploded two meters away from me."
He then went on:

"What a fate would have befallen Germany if the attempt had
succeeded, perhaps it's better not to think about it. I myself do not
thank providence and my creator that he has preserved me – my life
is only worry and is only work for my people – rather I thank him
that he has given me the opportunity to be allowed to continue to
bear these worries and to continue my work as well as I can answer
to my conscience...

I would especially like to once again welcome you, my old comrades in arms, that I was again allowed to escape a fate that meant
nothing terrible to me, but which would have been a disaster for the
German people.

I see this as a hint from providence that I must continue, and
therefore will continue my work."

Hitler intended to speak at 9 P.M. However this was not possible as
the radio recording vehicle was in Königsberg. It was strange: on
such a day as this Führer Headquarters was unable to turn to the
German people by radio.

Two hours later, at about three in the morning on July 21, I was
finally able to get through to Generaloberst Jodl's staff by phone. He
had been wounded in the head and his friend Oberst von Below in
the neck. Generals Korten and Schmundt had been fatally injured;
Oberst Brandt was dead. I asked that they might relieve me with a
competent general. That would be done the next morning, I heard,
and until then I was to stay at my post. I stayed for more than thirty
hours – sometimes dozing in my arm-chair in spite of the coffee which
Stauffenberg's secretary made me. There were reports and telegrams
to read. I dictated to Olbricht's and Stauffenberg's secretaries and
signed outgoing orders "on behalf of."

Generaloberst Jodl himself called me from Rastenburg at about
lunchtime and instructed me to carry on for a few more hours. I was
to inform the OKW if "an especially important decision" had to be
made. I replied that in many cases it wasn't possible for me to decide
what was an important decision and what wasn't.

"Skorzeny," said Jodl, "I know that you're terrified of staff work;
but that doesn't matter. Carry on, everything will soon be straight-

ened out; you will be relieved this evening or tomorrow morning at the latest."

In the first hours of my stay at Bendlerstrasse, while there was still great excitement, Fölkersam called me from the third floor to say that they were looking for a certain Luftwaffe general. The man was sitting across the desk from me. He had just voluntarily placed himself at my disposal and requested orders.

"Please give me your pistol," I said.

He gave me his weapon. I laid it on the desk and left the room. I was told that the man was to be arrested. I waited one or two minutes. An army Hauptmann asked me where the man was.

"Stay by this door," I answered him.

I walked in. The pistol was still lying where I had left it. The general said, "Thank you. But my religious beliefs forbid me to take my own life."

"Yes, I understand."

I opened the door and the Hauptmann came in. The two men left the room.

• • •

On the morning of July 22 Himmler and General Jüttner arrived at Bendlerstrasse. Hitler had had the strange notion to name the Reichsführer commander of the Replacement Army as a replacement for Fromm. In truth Jüttner bore the entire responsibility, for Himmler was incapable of understanding military problems.

Fölkersam, Ostafel and I returned to Friedenthal. We were dog-tired and slept for fifteen hours straight. It must have been July 23 when Schellenberg called me. He still made a nervous impression and announced that he had just had two telephone conversations, one with Reichsführer Himmler and the other with Heinrich Müller, head of the Gestapo. Admiral Canaris was deeply involved in the conspiracy, and Schellenberg was to see to his arrest.

"I find myself in an uncomfortable situation," Schellenberg said. "The Reichsführer, who is following an order from above, wishes the admiral to be treated with a certain degree of respect. On the other hand I would appreciate it if you would place a detachment from your unit at my disposal. It would serve me as an escort detachment, for I have a task to carry out that I would rather dispense with. We must also expect resistance."

In 1946 in Nuremberg prison, Schellenberg told me that he would be in my eternal debt if I could testify that he had been partly on the side of the conspirators on July 20. I refused. Why should I make a false statement? Surely it was far easier to resist in 1946 than in July 1944.

But what I learned about Admiral Canaris was far too important not to pass on to my chief-of-staff Fölkersam. As we know he had been a Brandenburger and had served well and loyally there. Since coming to Friedenthal he had often expressed doubts about the performance of the Abwehr. Many commando units fell into totally inexplicable ambushes, and employing the Brandenburg Division as a normal army unit was completely unbelievable and incomprehensible. For my part, I knew what I thought of Canaris. His report about, "the firm intention to continue the war at our side," shown by the Italian royalist government (July 30, 1943), was an extremely serious matter. Luckily Generalfeldmarschall Kesselring accorded it no importance. The good admiral then wanted to send us to a small island near Elba to look for the Duce, who was certainly on Santa Maddalena. Even Generalfeldmarschall Keitel and Hitler believed him for a long time.

"Is it at all possible," said Fölkersam, "to win a modern war if the chief of the intelligence service makes common cause with the enemy?"

I asked myself that too, and posed myself another question: what would have happened if another, well-camouflaged conspirator had been sitting in my place at Bendlerstrasse?

The conspirators had demonstrated a total lack of competence in Berlin. They should have set the Walküre alert plan in motion beginning at 2 P.M. and made sure that the right units followed them. Olbricht ordered Oberst Fritz Jäger to arrest Goebbels, but they searched in vain for policemen willing to assist them. Major Remer wanted nothing to do with it. Jäger finally turned to the regional defense force, which dodged the issue, and then to the men of the firefighting school, who refused.

Meanwhile the poor Hoepner planned that 350,000 nazis should be arrested. But by whom? The firemen?

We of the Waffen-SS were to be "incorporated" into the army, that meant placed under the command of Feldmarschall von Witzleben. Any officer or soldier who refused to obey an order from a senior officer without authority to do so would be considered a traitor and stood against the wall.

Karl Goerdeler had appointed himself Reich Chancellor, while Stauffenberg promoted himself to Generalmajor and state secretary in the war ministry. There were two foreign minister aspirants: if they negotiated with the west it would have been Ulrich von Hassel, Schülenberg was responsible for the east. They had obviously never heard of unconditional surrender, which also applied to the conspirators!

It was clear that Hitler's death could only have resulted in chaos. This was the view of Grossadmiral Dönitz, Field Marshalls von Rundstedt and von Manstein, of General Guderian and all the frontline generals. Admiral Heye said to me of the 20th of July, "You know that I am a monarchist by tradition. However I have sworn loyalty and obedience to the Führer. Besides, if a navy ship runs onto a reef there is nothing in marine law that says to throw the captain overboard. He remains on board and in command until, with God's help, the crew reaches the safety of the shore. Only then does he come before a normal marine board of inquiry. Besides, one doesn't need to send twenty-three persons to the other side with a bomb just to get rid of one person."

The men of the 20th of July, whose sole, if somewhat utopian, goal it was to save Germany, certainly deserve respect, for they risked their lives. But the results of their act was catastrophic.

On one hand one must admit that Himmler was very badly informed in spite of his entire police apparatus. he didn't see until very late in the game that the assassination attempt was the starting signal for a putsch. He thought that the culprits responsible for the bombing were the workers who, during the night of July 19-20, had repaired a bunker damaged by a stray bomb. The Führer did not share this opinion. He had a search begun for Stauffenberg right after the explosion, not to interrogate or arrest him, but because he feared that the Oberst might be injured and lying unconscious somewhere. It was in this way that Stauffenberg's strange conduct was first noticed, and from then on he was under suspicion. It was thought that he could have fled behind Russian lines, which were only 100 east of Rastenburg. Himmler, who doubted this possibility, instructed Gestapo chief Müller to dispatch Dr. Piffrader to Rangsdorf airport to arrest the Oberst when he landed. However the car carrying Stauf-fenberg and Haeften passed Piffrader's on the road to the airport.

Many conspirators were drawn into this sad affair without even knowing the objectives of the leaders. The conspirators believed their ideas were realities and maintained that it would be possible to negotiate with the west after the disappearance of Hitler.

The worst thing was that Olbricht sent orders to the front, where they only increased the confusion in the east and west.

An honor court of the OKW determined which of the officers who had taken part in the conspiracy kept their rank and which did not. The court consisted of Generalfeldmarschall Gerd von Rundstedt and Generalfeldmarschall Keitel, who chaired the forum, and Generals Guderian, Schrodt, Kriebel and Kirchheim. Only those officers who had been demoted and expelled from military service came before the people's court.

The assassination attempt had wounded Hitler deeply, not physically, but morally. The mistrust he had long harbored against certain generals became open hostility. It became clear to him that Canaris, Oster and Lahousen had been committing treason since the beginning of the war, and the fact that Feldmarschall Rommel had a part in the conspiracy struck him deeply. The thought that even more traitors might be in key positions in the Wehrmacht plagued him day and night. Even the medications prescribed him by Doctor Morell failed to calm him. On the contrary: more than ever he came under the evil influence of Martin Bormann.

I myself was always received warmly by Hitler, which was not the case with many officers. General Guderian, who took over General Zeitzler's position as Army Chief-of-Staff, told me:

"The attempted on his life had the most adverse effects on the morale of the Führer. He has become excessively suspicious. It is becoming increasingly difficult to discuss matters with him. The consequences of July 20 are terrible in every respect."

One must concede that Hitler made extraordinary efforts to suppress his desperation and overcome fate. But according to Roosevelt and Morgenthau, following an unconditional surrender on all fronts Germany was to become a third-class agrarian nation with no industry whatsoever – and according to the assurances of the Soviet writer Ilya Ehrenburg "a scorched wasteland of ruin."

Did we have any other choice than to carry on the fight until the bitter end, to at least save as many German soldiers as possible from captivity in Russia?

20

OPERATION PANZERFAUST

A conspirator falls victim to Stauffenberg: General Heusinger – The Soviet partisans at work: 12,000 acts of sabotage on July 19 and 20, 1944 – Walther Girg's commando unit in the Carpathians – Hungary threatened – Inside Führer Headquarters: I scarcely recognize Hitler – It is certain that Reich Administrator Horthy is negotiating with Stalin – My mission in Budapest – Mickey Mouse is rolled up in a carpet – Bach-Zelewski and Thor – Panzerfaust: the general surrenders – Reich Administrator Horthy flees to SS General von Pfeffer-Wildenbruch – Seven dead – All Hungarian officers stay with us, to voluntarily carry on the battle – The Pfeilkreuzler in power – Grand Duke Josef and his horses – At Nuremberg with Admiral Horthy; he tries to deny the facts – Proof of his negotiations with Stalin – The German Cross in Gold – Hitler: "I will entrust you with the most important mission of your military career."

When I was summoned to the Wolfsschanze on September 10, the German armies on both major fronts in the east and west found themselves in a critical situation. The real causes of this situation were not just of a material nature, as was widely held, rather the reasons were moral and intellectual. One must examine the matter from a distance.

In May 1944 Keitel, Jodl, the Chief-of-Staff of the Wehrmacht Operations Staff, and Zeitzler, the Chief of the General Staff, asked themselves where and when the Soviet armies would attack next.

The head of the operations staff in the west, General Heusinger, had his own opinion on the subject: Stalin would continue the offensive in the south begun by Zhukov in the spring. The Soviet armies would advance between the Carpathians and the Pripyat Marshes in the direction of warsaw and the Vistula. Jodl did not quite agree, but Hitler was convinced by Heusinger's arguments.

STAVKA had in fact decided to strike in the central sector.

In his book *Verbrannte Erde* (Berlin 1966) Paul Carell wrote:

> "It should come as no surprise that the Soviet intentions remained a mystery. The Germans did not possess a smoothly- functioning espionage organization within the Soviet High Command or any-where else in Russia. No Dr. Sorge and no Werther."

On the other hand the Soviet High Command possessed detailed information about our troop concentrations in the central sector.

Military historians paint a rather superficial picture of General Heusinger. On July 20 there were twenty-four persons, including Hitler, around the large, rectangular table in the Wolfsschanze. General Heusinger stood to Hitler's right. He knew Stauffenberg very well. Nevertheless the Oberst had no scruples: he placed his brief-case containing the live bomb beneath the table and disappeared. Heusinger was lucky that nothing happened to him. But the fact that Stauffenberg set off the bomb in spite of the presence of General Heusinger proved that the assassination attempt was a completely improvised affair.

A number of diplomatic documents were made public in Washington on December 15, 1966, among them a report by General Magruder, the chief of the American intelligence service, on "all the plans of the German resistance movement." These proposals had been shown to Dulles, who was in Switzerland, in May 1944. The topic: a putsch against Hitler. General Magruder pointed out that "Zeitzler, the Chief of the General Staff, had been won over to the conspiracy by Generals Heusinger and Olbricht." The latter recommended to Dulles an airborne operation against Berlin with the support of the German Replacement Army.

Dulles replied – I am quoting the American diplomatic documents – "that he didn't think Great Britain and the USA could enter into such an agreement without consulting the USSR." General Heusinger was slightly wounded by the bomb planted by his friend and fellow conspirator and was arrested on July 24. General Guderian,

General Zeitzler's successor at the head of the OKH, then replaced him with General Wenck.

This is further proof of the futile efforts by our conspirators to negotiate with the west. Personally, I had always feared a well-organized airborne operation against Berlin. Even though I knew nothing of the plans of the resistance, I had been expressing my thoughts on the matter to members of the General Staff – Admiral Heye, General Jüttner and others – since the beginning of 1944.

• • •

At Nuremberg General Heusinger spoke out under oath against the "German fighting methods" which were used against the partisans. It is true that these police operations all too often got out of hand. They were carried out by units which usurped the designation "Waffen-SS." It was known in official circles, however, that these were in reality not members of our units. Still, it must be said that the catastrophe that followed the assault by 200 Soviet divisions against Feldmarschall Busch's 34 divisions on June 22, 1944 was prepared by the partisans and special commando units of the Red Army.

On June 19 and 20 alone more than 12,000 acts of sabotage were carried out behind Busch's lines: bridges, railway lines, power plants were blown up, telephone and telegraph lines were cut. It was the largest operation in the partisan war to that point, and as a result our units' lines of communications and supply had been almost completely cut off when the huge attack began. From a tactical and strategic point of view, it was the partisan and commando units which achieved total victory. This fact is unfairly ignored by many military historians.

The simultaneousness of the enemy offensives in the west, east and the interior was noteworthy: on June 6, 1944 the Americans and the English landed in Normandy and on June 22 took Valognes. On the same day the Soviets attacked our central front in the east. Pinsk fell on July 16; on July 20 Stauffenberg's bomb exploded two meters away from Hitler. On July 30 the Americans advanced to Avranches in Normandy, while the Russians marched into Brest-Litovsk. On the Eastern Front there were barely 10 out of the 38 German divisions manning the central sector left. The Soviet armies advanced just as rapidly as we had done in 1941: 700 kilometers in five weeks! In the north they reached the East Prussian border.

Things were no better in the south. On August 2 Turkey broke off diplomatic relations with Germany. Romania was swamped by Soviet troops, which entered Bucharest on August 31.

On instructions from Führer Headquarters I sent two platoons of my "Commando Unit East" Battalion – about 100 men – to Romania by aircraft. The units were under the command of the extremely brave Untersturmführer Walter Girg. Four months earlier he had come from the officer school at Bad Tölz, blond, daring and hardened – just twenty years old. In cooperation with V Mountain Infantry Corps of the Waffen-SS, part of Army Corps Phleps (of the Romanian Waffen-SS), Girg's soldiers, who were divided into three commando units, succeeded in advancing to the most important Carpathian passes of Kronstadt, Hermannstadt and Karlstadt. First they held the passes for a short time, then they rendered them impassable by blowing up the roads. This action enabled German units and many ethnic German Transylvanians to escape to the west. As well the observations of the enemy by Girg enabled another corps of Army Group F to escape encirclement in the Gyergyoti area. This was the so-called Operation Landfried.

After completing his mission Girg and the men of his commando unit, disguised as Romanian soldiers, entered Kronstadt with the Russian troops. Shortly thereafter they tried to reach the forward German lines. They were discovered, taken prisoner and beaten up. Girg managed to escape before he was to be shot; although a bullet struck his foot, he was able to reach a swamp and hide himself there. He reached the German lines near Morosvasachely during the night. His other two groups, which were operating farther to the south, had better luck and returned with only minor losses.

During its mission into the midst of the Soviet lines, Girg's commando unit came upon a 2,000-man-strong German flak unit. Completely surrounded in a valley, it had resigned itself to being captured by the Russians. After talking to Girg, 300 of the unit's soldiers decided to fight their way back to the German lines with his people, which they in fact did. But what became of many other units which found themselves in similar situations?

At the beginning of September 1944 Soviet troops (Russian and Romanian) marched into Transylvania. Hungary declared war on Romania. However Admiral Horthy undertook some reshuffling in his ministry that suggested a change of course politically, and indeed in a pro-Soviet sense. Although the majority of the Hungarian Army (Honvèd) was not in favor of the move, it was nevertheless very dangerous to our position in Hungary.

In Romania our allies of yesterday were now the enemy. I must state, however, that there were entire Romanian regiments that fought at our side until the end. In February 1945 at Schwedt on the Oder I had a Romanian regiment under my command, while the Russians had two Romanian regiments. A sometimes difficult situation! Marshall Antonescu was arrested on August 23, 1944, and General Zanatescu immediately asked the Russians, whose divisions were at that moment flooding Poland and Hungary, for a cease-fire. On the morning of September 10 General Jodl requested that I sit in on the Führer's situation briefings for several days, at least those where problems relating to the southeast front were under discussion.

"It is possible," he said, "that the Führer will entrust to you an important mission on this fluid and uncertain front. You must be fully informed about the strategic and tactical problems in Hungary. Please come punctually to the noon briefing." There were two situation briefings held in Führer Headquarters each day: the "midday situation" (at about 2 P.M.) and the "evening situation" (at about 10 P.M.). The most important heads of the three branches of the armed forces gathered at these briefings: army, navy and air force or their deputies and those of the OKW. Generalfeldmarschall Keitel was supreme commander of the OKW, while General Jodl was Chief of the Operations Staff.

The OKH was the High Command of the Army and was responsible only for operations on the Eastern Front: Chief of the General Staff at that point in time was General Guderian.

The Balkans usually fell into General Jodl's area of responsibility, although this area was being invaded mainly by Russian armies.

Over Keitel, Jodl, Guderian, Göring, the Commander-in-Chief of the Luftwaffe, and Dönitz, Commander-in-Chief of the Navy, stood

Hitler as Supreme Commander of the Wehrmacht and of the Army, to which the Waffen-SS belonged.

The large conference room was located in a barracks, about 50 meters from the just-completed Führer bunker. Hitler was forced to live beneath seven meters of iron-reinforced concrete. A complicated ventilation system provided fresh air. Nevertheless the atmosphere was unhealthy, as the concrete, which had not yet fully set, gave off a damp warmth.

In the situation room barracks a situation map showing every front lay on a huge table, which received light from the windows in a twelve-meter-long wall. Current troop strengths and their positions were entered in colored pencil. Two stenographers sat at the short ends of the table. Since 1942 Hitler had required that all situation briefings be recorded. By the end of the war more than 103,000 pages of notes had accumulated. These were taken out of storage near Berchtesgaden and, unfortunately, burned. The intelligence service of the 101st US Airborne Division was only able to save a fraction of the notes – scarcely one percent.[1]

When I entered the briefing room on September 10, 1944 I introduced myself to the generals and general staff officers who were already present, as I knew only a few of them. Many officers had been replaced after July 20 for reasons that are easily understood. We all stood. A stool was provided for Hitler: the colored pencils, a magnifying glass and his glasses lay on the map table.

A curt command: Hitler entered. I was shocked when I saw him up close. I scarcely recognized him. This was not the man I remembered from the previous autumn: he walked bent and dragged one leg behind him. His left hand trembled so badly that he sometimes had to hold it with his right. His voice sounded veiled and brittle. He greeted a few generals. When he spied me he had a few kind words. Then he said, "Skorzeny stay for everything that concerns the Balkans."

Generalfeldmarschall Keitel stood to Hitler's left; General Jodl was to his right and began a presentation on the general situation, which was easy to follow on the general staff map.

After General Jodl's presentation Hitler spoke. His voice had become somewhat stronger and his commentary was so clear and convincing that one had to cast aside any thoughts that the man might be suffering from Parkinson's Disease, as the rumor said. His mental activity and his still passionate reactions did not fit the symptoms of this illness or any other degenerative disease.

Both of Hitler's eardrums were burst on July 20; he also suffered injuries to his arm and back. However the moral shock was greater than the physical. As I learned from Dr. Brandt, Dr. Morell was giving him large doses of glucose, multivitamins containing caffeine, Pervitin – which the Luftwaffe gave to pilots to keep them awake – and other "wonder drugs." The pills which Hitler often took for stomach cramps contained traces of arsenic. Today we know that Morell wrote many prescriptions for rare or dangerous medications on so-called state paper, which Bormann provided. This paper bore the letterhead "The Führer and Reich Chancellor." Morell's prescriptions were thus, so to speak, transformed into "Führer Orders." The physician Professor Ernst Günther Schenk, who came home from Soviet captivity in 1955, related that in 1943 he had made Dr. Conti, the chief of the Reich Health Office, aware that in his opinion Morell was doping Hitler in a dangerous way. The nervous stability of the man on whom the lives of millions of others depended had been seriously affected. In 1966 another physician, Dr. Hans-Dietrich Röhrs, wrote in his book Hitler, *die Zerstörung einer Persönlichkeit,* that it was only due to Hitler's extraordinarily robust health that he was able to withstand "the systematic and progressive poisoning by Morell."

During my three days at the Wolfsschanze I was astonished, not only by Hitler's extraordinary memory, but by the intuitive sense he possessed for military and political situations, their possible developments and eventual solutions of the problems associated with them. General Jodl knew how to present a military situation. But when Hitler spoke afterwards, everything was much simpler and clearer.

I am convinced that the great catastrophes – especially that of Stalingrad – could have been avoided if he had always been loyally and accurately informed since 1939. I have already spoken of Hitler's outburst of rage when he learned the actual strength of certain divisions. I would like to add, that on this occasion they concealed the truth from him concerning the uprising by Polish General Bor-Komarowski's secret army in Warsaw, the cruelty of the street fighting and the ticklish situation in which several of our units in the south of the city found themselves.

The situation in Bulgaria, Romania, Yugoslavia and Hungary was gradually becoming catastrophic. Hitler was fully aware of this. The Romanian oil was lost for good; the Danube bridges had been occupied by Romanian troops on Russian orders, and we had lost 15 divisions in this trap. Bulgaria went over to the side of the enemy – with the tanks and light guns we had just delivered to them. In Yugoslavia Tito's partisans were moving north and would soon make contact with Soviet troops.

There was still Hungary. At the end of August Hitler had sent General Guderian on a secret mission to Reich Administrator Horthy. He delivered a personal letter from Hitler and was warmly welcomed. But in spite of everything Guderian came away from Hungary with a very bad impression.

On the third day, after the evening briefing, Jodl ordered me to remain in the situation barracks. Hitler had also assembled Keitel, Jodl, Ribbentrop and Himmler for this extraordinary briefing.

Hitler began to speak and declared that he was under no more illusions: the admiral-Reich administrator was in the process, not only of negotiating with the western allies, but very probably with Stalin as well. Obviously without informing us. With great effort the front had been stabilized at the Hungarian border. If the Honvéds, the Hungarian Army, now went over to the enemy too, 30 of our divisions – about 400,000 soldiers, would be trapped. And those fighting in Italy would probably also be hard pressed if the Soviets could mount an offensive from southern Hungary through Yugoslavia in the direction of Trieste.

"That's out of the question," said Hitler in a firm voice. "The Reich Administrator considers himself a great politician and he doesn't realize that in this way he would be opening the door to another Karolyi."[2]

"They really seem to have a very short memory in Budapest. They have forgotten that they extended the Anti-Comintern Pact for five years on November 25, 1941! But can they forget that you," – he turned to Ribbentrop – "made a certain arbitral award in Vienna on August 29, 1940? Through this decision Hungary got back the greater part of Transylvania that had been taken from them by the Treaty of Trianon in 1920: 45,000 square kilometers and 2,380,000 people, who today are threatened by bolshevism."

Foreign Minister von Ribbentrop declared that the political situation in Budapest was becoming increasingly clouded. Two true friends of the German Reich had been forced to step down: the acting Minister President Raasch and the Economics Minister von Imredy; a new cabinet under General Geza Lakatos had taken power.

"Power! Stalin will take power in Budapest if we are forced to leave Hungary. Can the Reich Administrator forget the solemn words he spoke on April 16 of this year: 'We will fight at the side of the German Army until we have victoriously weathered this storm.' And now they say craftily to General Guderian: 'My dear comrade, in politics one must have several irons in the fire.' The Reich Administrator said that, but no loyal ally talks that way, only a man who intends to betray us and break his solemn promises. I won't tolerate that, for our soldiers are still defending Hungarian soil too!"

"Skorzeny, I have asked you to take part in the briefings on the situation of the southeast front. You know Hungary and especially Budapest. Under no circumstances do I want a Badoglio in Hungary. If the Reich Administrator breaks his word, you are to take the Burgberg and seize all those you find in the Royal Palace and the ministries. Then seal everything off and occupy the Burgberg militarily.Begin your preparations immediately – in cooperation with Generaloberst Jodl. In forming your units there may be difficulties with other Wehrmacht offices: in order to avoid this you will receive from me a written order with far-reaching authority. We've talked about a parachute or airborne operation, but the decision is up to you."

I no longer have the order that Hitler signed for me, but I remember the words more or less exactly:

"SS-Sturmbannführer Otto Skorzeny is carrying out a personal, highly-secret order of the utmost importance. I instruct all military and state offices to support Skorzeny in every way and comply with his wishes. Signed Adolf Hitler."

For practical purposes this document was Hitler's blank cheque to me, and it will soon become obvious how useful this paper was to me. Unfortunately it was taken from me, together with the Duce's watch, when I was taken prisoner by the Americans.

● ● ●

Under the cover-name Doctor Wolff I drove to Vienna with Radl. We wore civilian clothes. One of our true allies, an Hungarian German, placed his home, with servants and cook, at our disposal. I am almost embarrassed to confess that in my entire existence I never lived as well as during these three weeks in Budapest.

Radl was urgently recalled to Friedenthal just before the action, but Adrian von Fölkersam was with me, as well as most of my men from the Gran Sasso operation.

Our host, who welcomed us like a true Magyar, was well-informed about everything being played out in the court and the entourage of the regent.

Horthy, an admiral with no fleet and a regent with no king or queen, had resisted the return of the Hapsburgs to Hungary in 1920: he quite obviously had dynastic ambitions. On February 19, 1942 he had his oldest son, Stefan Horthy, recognized by parliament as the vice-regent with the right of succession. This son, who was quite gifted by the way, fought bravely against the Soviets. He was a fighter pilot and was killed on August 19, 1942 on the Eastern Front. The character of Niklas Horthy, his younger brother, was quite different.

He was a regular customer of the Budapest night clubs and his father's worry until the day he became involved in subversive political activities. Discretion was not his strength, and when we arrived in Budapest the informers knew very well that Niklas was in communication not only with the politicians in London, but also with Stalin's and Tito's agents – and all this with his father's blessings. Our SS and police commander in Budapest, Winkelmann, knew of the dangerous associations maintained by "Nicky" – that was his nickname. Fölkersam didn't understand correctly and heard "Mickey."

From then on Niklas Horthy became to us Mickey Mouse from Walt Disney's world of wonders.

The German police knew that Nicky was supposed to meet one of Tito's agents for a conference, first on October 10, then on Sunday the 15th of October, in an office building in the middle of Budapest near the Danube. Winkelmann decided to catch Mickey Mouse "in the act," and set an appropriate trap. He asked me to provide military protection against possible intervention by the Honvéd.

Horthy Junior was suspicious. He came to the meeting place by car at about ten in the morning on October 15. A few officers of the Honvéd stayed hidden in a canvas-covered jeep parked behind Mickey's car in front of the entrance to the office building.

Then I arrived by car. I feigned engine trouble and parked my car radiator to radiator with Mickey's car, in order to prevent him from driving away suddenly. Something moved in the jeep. Two Honvéd officers were walking in the park opposite the building, but I had one of my officers and two NCOs sitting on a park bench reading newspapers. At that moment, it was 10:10 A.M., two of Winkelmann's police officials appeared. They were about to enter the building when a burst of submachine-gun fire rattled from the jeep and killed one of the men. The two Hungarian officers in the park also fired. I lay behind my car, which had been turned into a sieve, until my soldiers came from the park to help. We defended ourselves as well as we could with our pistols. My driver was shot in the thigh. Then a squad of about 30 men from Friedenthal, which had been concealed in a side street, approached at a fast run with Fölkersam in the lead.

But Mickey was well-guarded: positioned in a nearby house was a strong Honvéd unit. An explosive charge was set off immediately. It destroyed the door to this house and prevented young Horthy's guard detail from coming to his aid. Scarcely five minutes had passed.

The German police needed only to go down one flight of stairs to reach the room where the conspirators were meeting. They were four in number: Niklas Horthy, his friend Bornemisza and two of Tito's agents. For simplicity's sake, and to avoid passers-by from recognizing him, "Mickey" was bound and rolled up in a rug. The two police officers grabbed the ends. It has often been said that "Mickey" was taken away in a Persian rug. I only saw the back side of it, and if I remember correctly it was a quite ordinary rug. The rug, together with the three other men, was put into a police truck which arrived on the scene punctually. Fölkersam was in the process of withdrawing our troops, in order to disappear as quickly as possible. An inner voice advised me to follow the truck. Three Honvéd companies arrived near the Elizabeth Bridge at quick time.

Fölkersam hadn't been able to withdraw yet: I had to bluff in order to gain a few minutes. I quickly climbed out of the car, went over to an officer and called out, "Halt!...Where are you going?...Let me speak to your major...Not here?...Who's in command then? Don't go there...to the square... There's a wild mixup there!"

The Major approached. He understood German and I shouted to him, "We must avoid a fratricidal war between our peoples, which would assume quite awful proportions...quite awful."

I gained five or six minutes, and that was enough. Fölkersam had time to load all our people and the wounded into the truck. I took off, leaving the confused Hungarians behind. I arrived at the airport, where "Mickey" and his friend Bornemisza were already in a military aircraft, which soon delivered them to Vienna. And so Horthy Junior was caught in the act. He wasn't very popular and his kidnapping aroused little sympathy in Hungary. But the reaction of the Reich Administrator wasn't long in coming. I subsequently drove at once to the army corps' headquarters, where I met General Wenck. He had come from Berlin several days earlier to support and advise me if necessary. At about noon a call came from our embassy's military attache, who was housed in a small palace on the Burgberg: the Burgberg was under a state of siege and he had been turned back on every exit road. Shortly thereafter the telephone lines were cut.

At 2 P.M. Hungarian radio broadcast a special announcement by Horthy, in which he said that "Hungary had asked the Soviet Union for a separate peace." However, a communique by the Honvéd's Chief-of-Staff, Vitez Vöcröes, added that so far only "cease-fire negotiations were under way." That said it all. General Wenck and I agreed that the die had been cast and that I must now set in motion Operation Panzerfaust, for which we had made preparations.

Before I turn to the planning and execution of this operation, which involved taking and occupying the Burgberg militarily, I must mention that many briefings took place before October 15. The Police General von dem Bach-Zelewski appeared in the plan: he came straight from Warsaw and brought the gigantic "Thor" with him.

This "Thor" was not the nordic god of thunder, the son of Odin, but a 650mm howitzer whose shells each weighed 2,200 kilograms. They were capable of piercing "any thickness of concrete known today." "Thor" had only been used on two occasions: against the fortress of Sevastopol and shortly before in Warsaw at the personal request of Herr von dem Bach-Zelewski.

He was a sort of bespectacled scarecrow and didn't impress me in any way, although many officers were impressed by him. He suggested "finishing off the Burgberg without a lot of fuss," destroying the royal palace with "Thor" and with it the entire garrison. I don't believe I'm injuring the memory of poor Bach-Zelewski, when I say that he wanted to identify himself with his howitzer.

It was a waste of effort to try to explain to the man what this hill meant to me as an Austrian and a European. It was there that the Anjous, Hunyadi and the White Knights had defended the west so bravely. I simply told him that I was leading this operation and that I believed that the OKW's order could be carried out with little loss of blood – and not in so brutal a fashion as had just happened elsewhere. I didn't need to show him Hitler's letter of authority. General Wenck, who was acting as advisor from the OKW, supported my view, and "Thor" and its 2,200-kilogram shells were not used.

Shortly before midnight on October 15 a colonel of the Hungarian Ministry of Defense reported to the corps command. He showed us the letter he had been given by the minister of war, authorizing him to negotiate with the German authorities. They could give him only one answer: there was no basis for negotiation until the Reich Administrator's cease-fire declaration was withdrawn. Furthermore, our diplomats were virtual prisoners on the Burgberg. That was a typical "unfriendly act." On my suggestion the Hungarian government was given an ultimatum: If the mines and roadblocks on the Vienna Road, which led to the German embassy, were not removed by 6 A.M on October 16, to our great regret, we would be forced to draw the appropriate conclusions.

We had the definite impression that the Honvéd agent was not in agreement with the Reich Administrator's sudden about face and was certainly not alone in his opinion.

Hungarian soldiers had been battling a common enemy since June 1941, the same one which devastated Hungary in 1920-21. Tzalassy's "Pfeilkreuzler" activist party gained a great deal of support as a result of the communist threat and had many supporters among the younger officers of the Honvéd. The mood in Hungary was not for a surrender to the east. Quite the contrary.

For my part, I planned to launch a surprise attack and occupy the Burgberg, at 6 A.M. on October 16. It was a difficult mission. The hill on which sat the Burgberg, a fortification more than three kilometers long and at least 600 meters wide, towered above the Danube. I heard that the garrison had been reinforced. The Reich Administrator was guarded by 3,000 alerted men: behind the Vienna Gate lay a regimental barracks; its mortars and heavy machine-guns were in battle positions. At the other end of the hill, among the palace's terraced gardens above the Danube, were five solid positions with bunkers and machine-gun nests; tanks had been positioned in front of the citadel and in the citadel courtyard; there was a three-meter-high stone barricade in front of the gate to the citadel; behind it in the courtyard six anti-tank guns. The palace itself was occupied by a regiment which had light and heavy weapons at its disposal. Before reaching the palace one had to pass by the ministries of defense and the interior, which were defended by two battalions equipped with mortars and machine-guns. I must admit that we did not become completely aware of this distribution of forces until we had occupied the Burgberg and it was all over.

Furthermore an underground passage led from the quay on the right side of the Danube to the war ministry, which was reached by a secret set of stairs. Halfway up the stairs was the famous "treasure room," where Hungary's royal treasures were kept. This passageway was of course sealed off by several armored doors, but no matter what, we had to use this route to take the war ministry by surprise.

As I have mentioned, those in Führer Headquarters had in mind a parachute assault or an airborne operation: to attempt this would have been pure madness. The only suitable place for a landing was the "Blood Field" – it would have earned its name all over again. In the event of Hungarian resistance, this practice field beneath the Burgberg would immediately have been placed under concentrated fire by the defenders and they would have shot us down like rabbits from the walls of the fortress. Another solution had to be found.

I had the following forces at my disposal: First there was the 22nd Waffen-SS Cavalry Division Maria-Theresia (named after the Holy Roman empress and Hungarian queen). This newly-trained division consisted of 8,000 ethnic Germans (Hungarians of German descent). Beginning in the late afternoon of October 15, it formed a blocking ring around the old, medieval Burgberg. The fortress was completely encircled during the night. The Maria-Theresia Division was supported by an Hungarian regiment commanded by the courageous Lieutenant-Colonel Dr. Karl Ney. This regiment later formed the backbone of the 25th Waffen-SS Division Johann Hunyadi, one of the two Hungarian Waffen-SS divisions.[3]

As well Hitler had placed a battalion from the Wiener-Neustadt military academy under my command: about 1,000 magnificent-looking officer aspirants; two companies of Panther tanks and a battalion of Goliath tanks (remote-controlled miniature tanks which carried a powerful explosive charge). Obviously my Commando Unit Center was also present, along with a battalion of Waffen-SS parachute troops, which remained under my command until the end. A signals company and a small staff with Adrian von Fölkersam rounded out my military forces.

Fölkersam and I worked out a plan of attack, without worrying about the numerous conferences taking place at the same time. I felt it adequate that General Wenck approved of the plan.

At three in the morning I had all the officers fall in on the Blood Field and gave them my final instructions. The Burgberg had to be assaulted from four sides simultaneously. In the south the battalion from the Wiener-Neustadt military academy had to blow up the iron fence around the castle park, enter the gardens and pin down the barricading Hungarian forces. In the west, specialists of the commando units under the command of Hauptsturmführers Flucker and Hunke were to break in over the western wall, attack the front of the palace and distract the Honvéd troops. In the east the parachute battalion was supposed to force entry into the ministry of defense through the tunnel. In the meantime I would drive through the Vienna Gate directly to the palace with the bulk of our motorized units, together with the Panther tanks and two companies of Commando Unit Center.

This last action was supposed to look like a peacetime buildup. The soldiers in the trucks were all to carry weapons with safety catches on, and keep them out of sight beneath the side walls of the trucks. Not a single shot was to be fired from our side. As well there was a strict ban on replying to single shots. I just hoped that the road leading up to the Vienna Gate and the two other parallel roads on the Burgberg hadn't been mined.

As per my last detailed orders I sent another liaison officer to corps headquarters: there was nothing new. The officers went to their posts. It was one minute to six; it began to get light.

I raised my arm: "Forward march!"

I took the lead of my long column and stood in my large command car. Behind me sat Fölkersam, Ostafel and five "chums" from the Gran Sasso. All were armed with Sturmgewehr 44 assault rifles and had hand grenades hanging from their belts. Each was also armed with a "Panzerfaust," a recently-developed anti-tank weapon with a hollow-charge projectile. This was my assault squad. We were followed by four Panther tanks, the Goliath tank platoon and finally the trucks in which my troops were, so to speak, mounted, as if on an exercise.

We started from the Blood Field beneath the fortress and drove in the direction of the Vienna Gate. The engines and caterpillar tracks created a huge racket. I listened: no explosions. To my right the Vienna Gate appeared in the morning twilight: they had already opened a gateway. We drove past a few astonished Hungarian soldiers, who were even more amazed when I saluted them cordially. Then we came up to the barracks on the right. The machine-guns were in position. I saluted again, and we continued on. We drove on toward the palace, which was still one kilometer away. In driving by, the formation showed the Hungarian troops its unprotected flanks – now they could shoot us in the back. A mine could explode, a single shot fired by a sentry or a burst of machine-gun fire could be the opening act of a bloody battle.

"Drive faster!" I said to my driver. The convoy thundered up the road at 35-40 kph. I turned right, to drive by the German embassy. The other half of my group took the left, parallel side road. Another 600 meters. Nothing moved. On the left now the war ministry. Then there were two loud explosions: it was our paratroopers forcing the entrance to the secret stairs in the war ministry. Now the utmost caution was called for! In a few seconds we reached the fortress square in front of the palace and faced three Hungarian tanks. The panzerfaust anti-tank weapons were ready. But what a magnificent target we were ourselves! No: the first tank raised its gun as a signal that it didn't intend to fire. A three-meter-high stone barricade had been erected in front of the gate. Everything happened quite quickly now. I instructed my driver to pull off to the right and signalled the following tank. It headed straight for the barricade, rammed it and forced a large opening. We jumped from the car and ran through the opening into the fortress courtyard, behind me the commando unit with panzerfausts in hand. The alarm was sounded: an officer appeared in front of us; he aimed his pistol at us and shouted something. Fölkersam knocked his weapon from his hand. We spotted the six anti-tank guns in battle positions in the courtyard. But two more Panther tanks had already driven in. Another Honvéd officer made as if to stop me. I called out to him, Take me at once to the fortress commandant! We have no time to lose!"

"That way!"

He pointed to a marble stairway covered by a wonderful red carpet. We climbed up the stairs at a run, accompanied by the brave Hungarian officer. A hallway, an anteroom. A table had been pushed against the open window. On it lay a man, who opened fire on the courtyard with a machine-gun. Feldwebel Holzer simply threw the machine-gun out the window, and the gunner was so surprised that he fell onto the floor. To my right was a double door. I knocked and stepped in. A general sat at a huge desk. He stood up.

"Are you the fortress commandant?"

"Yes. But..."

"I request that you surrender the fortress immediately. There is fighting, can you hear it? Do you want to be responsible for bloodshed among allies? We have encircled all your positions. You can believe me, all resistance is now hopeless and could be very costly for you and your troops."

From outside we heard shots and a brief burst of machine-gun fire. This was the ideal moment for Obersturmführer Hunke, our "chinaman," to step in. He saluted and reported, "Courtyard and main entrances, radio station and war ministry are occupied. Request further orders."

He saluted the general, who turned to me, "I will send liaison officers with you to have the firing stopped. Must I consider myself a prisoner?"

"If you wish, Herr General. But mind you, all your officers may keep their pistols."

It was agreed that the order to cease fire should be delivered by several officer patrols, each consisting of one Hungarian officer and one of my officers.

I left the general with Ostafel and in the ante-room came upon a group of excited, hostile-looking officers. I picked out two Honvéd captains, who looked especially nervous to me, took them with me as liaison officers, and with Fölkersam and a few men from Friedenthal set out to look for the Reich Administrator.

The palace appeared to be still completely furnished. One salon followed another, with rugs, Gobelins, paintings of battles and portraits. We had studied the floor plan of the castle carefully, and I had placed a half-dozen NCOs with panzerfausts at this magnificent hall's main entrances.

I was absolutely against the use of a panzerfaust in an ornate hall, unless it was absolutely necessary. Not only was this weapon effective against tanks; it could also be used for other spectacular purposes. A single panzerfaust, fired at the junction of several halls, would surely have given the defenders cause to think, and a panzerfaust fired along the halls would have produced a terrible effect, which would surely have made a deep impression on potential defenders and reduced their desire to fight on.

We had to face the fact that the Reich Administrator was not there. I learned that he had sought protection that morning at about 5:45 in the house of General der Waffen-SS Graf Karl von Pfeffer-Wildenbruch. The latter was a good friend of Kaiser Wilhelm II, to whom he bore s striking resemblance. Horthy had left the commanding general no orders of any kind for the defense of the Burgberg.

We were now masters of the Burgberg, the seat of government. We fired several panzerfausts from the fortress without aiming. This was enough to convince the Hungarian units still fighting in the fortress garden that it was advisable to cease resisting. It was 6:30 A.M. We had lost sixteen men – four dead and twelve wounded. Losses were equally light on the Hungarian side: three dead and fifteen injured. I saw to it that the Hungarian troops of the Honvéd regiment, the guard battalion and the royal guard laid down their weapons. Then, at about 9:30, I assembled all the Hungarian officers, about 400, and gave them a short speech.

"At this historic site I would like you to remember above all that the Germans have not fought the Hungarians in centuries and that I, as a Viennese, can never forget our common liberation of 1718.[4] The situation at the moment is so serious that European soldiers, whatever their faith or their political views might be, must stand together – especially the Hungarians and the Germans! As of tomorrow any of you who wants to, may once again command his regiment, his battalion or his company. For no one has the right to force a man to fight against his will and his convictions. We must fight voluntarily!

Therefore I would like to ask that those of you who wish to continue the struggle at our side take one step forward!"

Every Hungarian officer stepped forward. I shook hands with each of them.

• • •

I forgot to mention the occasion on which Hitler's letter of authority proved useful. At the beginning of October in Vienna the motorization of our units, for example the SS-Parachute Battalion and the Wiener-Neustadt military academy, presented us with very serious problems. But I finally managed to solve it with the help of a rather fussy Oberst of the military area headquarters.

It was late and I was hungry. We went into the officers mess, where I ordered a few sausages. Then I noticed that I had forgotten my food coupons.

"Nothing can be done," observed the Oberst. "Orders are orders. You would have to be the Führer himself to get something without coupons." The good official was slowly getting on my nerves. I was hungry. Suddenly I had an inspiration: I produced the document and held it out to the Oberst, who read in astonishment. He was a man with a sensible mind: "You should have shown me this right away my dear fellow!"

He immediately gave a few instructions and they brought us two pair of sausages, which I devoured with unconcealed satisfaction, but also with the appropriate respect.

I never again had to use this document, for all those I had to deal with had been informed directly by the OKW. For better or for worse I was the military commander of the Burgberg right after the occupation and for two days afterwards. This short-lived office enabled me to finally spend two nights in a comfortable bed, in which Kaiser Franz-Josef had once slept, to enjoy a bath in his 2.5-meter-long tub and to make the acquaintance of an illustrious gentleman.

On October 16 Count Szalassy's "Pfeilkreuzler" Party took power; there was no opposition. A coalition government was formed with the former minister Imredy and President Bereghfy. The latter came to thank me for not damaging the fortress. He was pleased that losses were so low and promised that the socialist and national coalition would hold a joint service for the German and Hungarian dead. I returned to Budapest on October 20 to take part in this moving funeral ceremony.

Soon after my conversation with President Bereghfy, an older, distinguished gentleman asked to see me. He wore the uniform of an Imperial-Royal Feldzeugmeister (Colonel-General).

"Servus, servus" he greeted me in the old style. "I heard that you are a Viennese, and that didn't surprise me. I said to myself: only someone from Vienna could pull off a stunt like that. Magnificent! Daring! I am happy to meet you. It's wonderful!"

He seemed to have climbed down from one of the paintings that covered the walls of the large rococo halls, where the day before our lads had wielded panzerfausts. Fölkersam walked behind me and whispered:

"That is Archduke Josef of Hapsburg."

I asked the archduke to sit down, and asked him how I might be of help.

"Well, well. You could do me a great service. My horses are in the royal stables in the fortress. Do you think that they might stay there?"

"But of course, Your Highness. Everything is as it was before. May I have a look at the horses?"

"Please! Come with me, I'll show them to you. You'll soon see what magnificent horses they are."

They were in fact very beautiful animals. The archduke wanted to give me one as a souvenir. But I had to tell him that I had no idea what I should do with such an animal: I commanded motorized units.

"You're right," he observed sadly. "War today is not like it once was. But yesterday you handled things like in the old times, like a proper cavalier! And most of all, if you come to Buda don't forget to visit me. Servus!"

The fortress with its magnificent galleries and its horse stalls was completely destroyed by the enemy's air force and artillery in 1945. Reconstructed after the war, it was once again damaged by Soviet artillery in the course of the bloody suppression of the anti-communist uprising in 1956.

Reich Administrator Horthy had left Budapest and now lived in Hirschberg Castle in Upper Bavaria. I met him again in Nuremberg Prison in 1945. He wanted to file a protest when I was transferred from a single cell to the witness wing. This although I had had a brief, but courteous conversation with him on the train in which I had to take him and his family and their huge cache of luggage to Bavaria. In Nuremberg, however, he didn't want to have to see me every day. Generalfeldmarschall Kesselring, our spokesman with the Americans, made it clear to the former Reich Administrator that his protest – which was unprecedented, by the way – had not been accepted by the allied authorities. But if he wished to, he could take my place in the solitary cell, which I had just left and where he would be alone. The ex-Reich Administrator declined; Kesselring then arranged a conversation between us. I visited the admiral in his cell. He assured me that he had known nothing about his son's political activities, and that it was wrong to think that he had ever intended to make a pact with the Soviets and betray the Germans. His claims certainly didn't correspond to the facts, but it would have been discourteous on my part to call them untrue at this point in the conversation, for both of us were, after all, prisoners of the allies.

Admiral Horthy was released soon afterward; he lived in exile in Portugal. On November 3, 1954 he wrote to federal chancellor Konrad Adenauer from Estoril and assured again that he had never betrayed Germany or wanted to conclude a separate peace with Moscow.

In truth Horthy committed himself to a swindle. Today I would like to add that if the SD did not arrest "Mickey" on October 10, 1944, when he had his first meeting with Tito's agent, it was for the following reason: "Mickey" came that day accompanied by his father, I saw it with my own eyes – and the OKW's order said that only Horthy's son was to be arrested.

The Reich Administrator's proclamation on Hungarian radio on October 15 was also no German invention. It stated that "Hungary had asked the Soviets for a cease-fire," whereupon the commander of Hungarian troops in the Carpathians, General Miklos, went over to the enemy with several of his staff officers.

In his *Geschichte der Geheimdiplomatie (The History of Secret Diplomacy)*, J. de Launay reported that Admiral Horthy said to Hitler on March 18, 1944 in Klessheim, "Hungary has never betrayed anyone. If someday we are forced by circumstances to ask for a cease-fire, you can be assured that I will inform you openly about this intention."

He did exactly the opposite. While Hitler, who many consider all too distrustful, still believed that a betrayal was imminent, in reality it had already been committed. On October 5, 1944 the Reich Administrator sent a delegation to Moscow under the leadership of the inspector-general of police, General Faragho. During the night of October 11-12 he received radioed instructions from Horthy to accept the cease-fire terms and to sign, which he did on October 12. (in his book J. de Launay gave the date as October 11.) Later General Faragho became a member of the first coalition government under Soviet occupation.

After the war I learned that there was a secret transmitter in the cellar of the fortress, which was constantly in contact with Moscow. The responsible radio officer committed suicide when we occupied the fortress.

But Horthy sent a second group of negotiators to the Russians. An Hungarian officer, Retired Colonel Gatkiewicz, wrote me a letter dated January 15, 1945, in which he confirmed that on October 12, 1944 he accompanied his immediate superior, Oberst Roland von Utassy, to a meeting with the Soviet High Command, and that this happened on the direct order of the Reich Administrator. On the morning of October 13, after a mutually agreed upon pause in the firing (between the Russians and Hungarians), the two officers left the Hungarian lines and made their way behind the Russian lines on the other side of the Theiss in the area of Szegedin. I would also like to quote several passages from Colonel Gatkiewicz's letter:

"Finally, shortly before 10 P.M. on October 1944, we were informed that Marshall Malinovsky had arrived, and a short time later he entered our room accompanied by a small staff. He was a good-looking man, mid-fifties, blond, with a herculean physique, hands like medium-sized attache cases, a common, somewhat rough face and blue, clever, piercing eyes. The impression he gave was more that of a well-situated butcher than a senior military man. He approached us with his hand extended and welcomed us warmly."

By way of an interpreter Malinovsky first asked both negotiators about the exact course of the German-Hungarian front line. Colonel von Utassy gave false information. Malinovsky was surprised and placed a detailed, completely accurate situation map in front of the astonished colonel.

"Then he specified the main conditions for an eventual special peace: withdrawal of troops from the Debreczen area, cessation of hostilities in all sectors of the front, attack on the rear of the German troops and their forced surrender. Unfortunately I have forgotten the details. At our question, what would Hungary's fate be, he merely waved his hand casually: 'We want nothing from the Hungarians. But the Germans – and a fanatical hatred disfigured his face – we will destroy the Germans.'"

The negotiators were given a period of forty-eight hours to accept these conditions. In parting Malinovsky said that he hoped that they would soon be able to greet each other as friends and comrades in arms. Gatkiewcz wrote that the discussion was arranged on the Hungarian side by General Miklossy.

As this document shows, Rodion Malinovsky wanted the Hungarian Army to fight against us as the Romanians had done earlier, which cost us fifteen divisions. In the meantime it was proved that the USSR did not in fact want much from Hungary, just that it cease to exist as a sovereign state.

By the time Gatkiewicz and his superior were ready to return to the Hungarian front line, they found that it had moved. They were forced to walk through ten kilometers of mud to reach the battalion command post from which they had left. They arrived at the Burgberg to make their report on the morning of the 14th. Early on the morning of the 16th I took Colonel von Utassy prisoner in his uniform and slippers, for his feet had been so badly chafed by his long walk that he couldn't pull his boots on. Gatkiewciz himself escaped through the fortress garden before our arrival. In his letter he also admitted that he gave his report to the Hungarian general staff and later to a member of the SD, who interrogated him.

In any case these activities and statements by witnesses leave no doubt as to the true intentions of the Reich Administrator. On the other hand, the behavior of Marshall Mannerheim, who was elected president of the Republic of Finland on August 4, 1944, was quite different. Ribbentrop and our high command were immediately notified when it became obvious that Finland could no longer continue the war at our side if it didn't wish to be destroyed by the Soviets. The retreat by our troops began at the beginning of September; by the 14th of the month all had been evacuated from Finnish territory. Finland did not sign the cease-fire until five days later.

I would like to make just one comment at this point: Finland today is not treated worse than the Romanians – just the opposite.

On October 20 I was informed that Hitler wished me to report to him in person on the course of Operation Panzerfaust. I took Adrian von Fölkersam with me, as I knew that there was no greater treat that I could give him, and introduced him to Hitler. The latter said that he was very well informed as to Fölkersam's military career, and asked him about the daring raid he had carried out in the USSR as a Leutnant with the Brandenburgers. Hitler gave specific details, mainly about the occupation of the oil center of Maykop in the Caucasus by Fölkersam's commando unit in August 1942, for which he had been awarded the Knight's Cross. Fölkersam was deeply impressed. "Amazing," he later said to me, "one could think he was there!"

"He surely was," I answered him, "you just didn't notice it."

A day before we had driven to the Birkenwald Camp, Himmler's headquarters, which was located about 30 kilometers northeast of Rastenburg. Girg had accompanied us; Himmler wanted to hear about Romania from him. The Reichsführer had just moved; the Russians were all too close. He invited us to dinner in his special car, but he made no special impression on Fölkersam or Girg. Then we drove back to Birkenwald with two orderlies. Himmler's headquarters lay completely abandoned. The empty barracks in the middle of the forest had something eerie about them: we all sensed the coming disaster.

● ● ●

Hitler informed me through Generaloberst Jodl that he wished to speak to me alone. His warm welcome calmed me.

"From now on," he said, "you are an Obersturmbannführer of the Waffen-SS and I am awarding you the German Cross in Gold. No, don't thank me for it! All the decorations that you propose for your soldiers are approved in advance. Take them to Günsche, my adjutant. And now, tell me how it was in Budapest."

We sat in a small room in his bunker, where the air was so poor. But he seemed calmer than the last time I saw him. As well his left hand didn't tremble so much. He listened without interrupting me. He found the appearance of the archduke in imperial uniform very amusing. I was about to take my leave, but he held me back. Then he told me in every detail the plan for what is now known as the Ardennes offensive.

"I will very likely entrust you with the most important mission in your career as a soldier. In the course of this offensive, whose basic concepts I have just explained – and which is obviously top secret, I probably don't have to tell you that – you and your special commandos will occupy one or another of the Maas bridges between Lüttich and Namur. Your people will make their way behind enemy lines in English or American uniforms and there finally fight in German uniforms. I know that the Americans used the same tactic at Aachen. As well, some commandos will retain their camouflage behind the enemy lines to, where possible, misdirect enemy troops and spread confusion in the general staffs. I know that you have only a little time to organize such a large operation of this kind. But I also know that you will do your best. Generaloberst Jodl will answer your detailed questions.

Something else: I do not want you to cross the front line personally under any circumstances. You must be at the front in the course of the offensive. It would be a catastrophe if you were wounded or captured now. I have complete faith in you, my dear Skorzeny. We will see each other again soon."

And so I was tasked with Operation Greif: Griffin, the mythical animal – half eagle and half lion.

Notes

1. Those pages that were saved from destruction reside today in the library of the University of Pennsylvania. In 1964 the Albin Michel Verlag published extracts from these under the title *Hitler spricht zu seinen Generalen* (*Hitler Speaks to His Generals*). It was translated into French with a foreword by J. Benoist-Méchin. These are highly-significant documents. (Editors' note)

2. Count Michel Karolyi was a man with liberal ideals. He came from an old Hungarian aristocratic family and believed in the democratic ideal. He became president of the Hungarian Republic in 1918-1919. He took up residence in the Habsburg Palace in Buda, something that is still talked about. But soon afterward he was put to flight by Bela Kuhn's bloody Bolshevik revolution. Hitler was a good prophet: Count Karolyi in fact returned to "liberated" Hungary in 1946, but the increasing Sovietization of Hungary soon caused him to leave his homeland once again. He lived in exile in Vence on the Riveria, where he died in 1955. (Editors' note)

3. John Hunyadi (ca. 1385-1456), Hungarian general and imperial administrator, distinguished himself early on in the struggle against the Turks. The 2nd Hungarian Division, the 25th Waffen-SS Division *Gömbös* also fought at our side until the end. A third division was raised in March 1945, consisting of Hungarian volunteers and German-Hungarians.

4. Led by Prince Eugen von Savoyen-Carignan, the Austrians came to the aid of the Hungarians and defeated the Turks at Zenta (1697), thus the Peace of Passarowitz (1718). (Editors' note)

21

GRIFFIN

The Ardennes: political offensive – The objectives of Operation Greif and the opinion of Sir Basil Liddell Hart – A mistake by the OKW and a "prediction" – The offensive bogs down – I commit eight commando units and attack Malmedy in vain with the 150th Panzer Brigade – The fateful affair at the Baugnez crossroads – Colonel Willis M. Everett: a ten-year struggle for the truth – The tragedy of Malmedy – Telegram from Field Marshall Montgomery: "This time we can't embark like at Dunkirk..." Churchill calls Stalin for help – The hunt for "disguised nazis" – Bradley arrested and interrogated – Half the U.S. Army looks for Skorzeny – General Eisenhower a prisoner in his own headquarters – Raid on the Café de la Paix – Eisenhower's double or the lost illusions – Griffin as an object of study in the advanced course for American officers – Hitler's commentary – Stalin's game.

In autumn 1943 General Eisenhower, the allied commander-in-chief in the European Theater, bet General Montgomery five Pounds that Germany would surrender before Christmas 1944.

On December 15 of the same year Montgomery, by now promoted to field marshall, wrote Eisenhower to tell him that he would be spending Christmas in England and asked him to pay the five Pounds. On December 16, while playing golf, news reached him that we had launched a surprise offensive that same morning along the Luxembourg border from Monschau to Echternach.

The Ardennes offensive is still referred to as the Rundstedt offensive. But in truth the field marshall, who was seventy years old and who had again assumed command of the Western Front after the suicides of Field Marshalls von Kluge and Rommel, received the plans from Hitler.

Rundstedt, quite incapable of grasping the political objectives of the offensive, was in favor of a limited action in the Aachen area to relieve the city. That was something quite different.

In spite of their apparently comradely relationship, Eisenhower and Montgomery hated each other like poison. In his book *My Three Years with Eisenhower*, navy Captain Butcher, the allied commander-in-chief's adjutant, revealed that on December 1, 1944 Montgomery wrote the American general an extremely bitter letter in which he harshly criticized his strategic and tactical concepts and suggested to him "in a friendly way" that he resign as soon as possible.

Although Hitler wasn't aware of these details, he was certainly convinced that the western allies were far from united, and that Churchill – and consequently Montgomery – had realized that Roosevelt was insistent on playing Stalin's game in Europe. Several American generals – Patton, for example – were no longer able to comprehend Eisenhower's behavior.

The offensive's strategic objective was to take the port of Antwerp, drive a wedge between the American General Bradley's army groups and separate the British and Canadian armed forces from the American.

In the north Sepp Dietrich's Sixth Panzer Army was to reach the Maas in the direction of Lüttich, cross the river and advance on Louvain, Malines and Antwerp. In the south the Fifth Panzer Army under the command of General Hasso von Manteuffel was to advance on Dinant, reach Brabant and then, with a sudden change of direction, throw itself at Brussels and Malines.

This ambitious plan was based primarily on surprise, which meant speed. In order to fortify the element of surprise, Hitler came up with Operation *Greif* (Griffin) and made me responsible for its execution. A special unit formed for this purpose, which received the title the 150th Panzer Brigade, was placed at my disposal. I had two clearly defined missions:

1. The 150th Panzer Brigade was to exploit the breakthrough by Sepp Dietrich's Sixth Panzer Army, assume the lead and take possession of the Maas bridges at Huy, Amay and Engis, between Namur and Lüttich. These bridges had to be captured intact in order to en-

able our panzers to advance on Antwerp. Officers and men were to wear American uniforms as far as the Maas; after reaching the Maas they were to fight in German uniforms.

2. Small units, also in American uniforms, were to infiltrate behind the enemy lines and reconnoiter there, cut telephone lines, issue false orders and cause general confusion among the enemy. These units were instructed to use their weapons only in extreme emergency and to do so exclusively in German uniform.

The times when this offensive was seen by military historians as "an absurd, quite utopian operation," or as the "delusion of a sick brain," are over. It could very well have succeeded, and Patton was the first to realize this. On December 18, 1945 he said: "We could still lose this war." In his previously-mentioned book *History of the Second World War*, Sir Basil Liddell Hart expressed the same view:

"The idea, the decision and the strategic plan were Hitler's intellectual property alone. It was a brilliant concept and should have led to a brilliant success if he had possessed sufficient forces and reserves to guarantee a tolerable chance of success."

Liddell Hart made much mention of Hasso von Manteuffel's ability to maneuver his troops – Manteuffel had only just been appointed Commander-in-Chief of the Fifth Panzer Army – with particular emphasis on Operation Greif, which, as he wrote, "was commanded by another discovery of Hitler's, Otto Skorzeny." Sir Basil added that they gave me neither the time nor the means to bring Greif to fruition. I will show how very right he was.

With the full agreement of Generaloberst Jodl, to whom I had shown all the plans worked out with Fölkersam, the 150th Panzer Brigade was to consist of:

– 2 tank companies, each equipped with 10 Sherman tanks;
– 3 armored reconnaissance companies, each equipped with 10 American armored cars;
– 2 anti-tank companies;
– 3 battalions of motorized infantry (with American trucks), with reconnaissance units and a screening company;

– 1 company with a special mission;
– 1 company of light flak;
– 1 signals company;
– 1 regimental headquarters for brigade and command sections for each battalion.

This gave a total strength of 3,300 men, all volunteers of course. Theoretically they were all supposed to wear the American uniform over their German uniforms. The use of American uniforms was supposed to help them cross the battle lines; they had to be taken off before the actual hostilities. The jurists of General Winter's staff – the OKW's operations section – gave me the following instructions:

"Stratagems between combatants are not forbidden in principle. The commander-in-chief must arm himself against stratagems just as he does against force. When the ruse consists of approaching the enemy by using his uniform, regulations strictly specify that this is only permissible before actual combat begins. At the moment of coming to blows every combatant must show his colors honorably and reveal his true nationality." This can still be read today in the classic handbooks on the rules of war. In any case the Hague Convention of November 18, 1907 states in Article 23 (f):

"The misuse of flags of truce, the national flag or the military insignia or uniform of the enemy (is forbidden)..."

However in an article entitled The War Crimes Trials (Missouri Law Revue, January 1959), Max Koessler, prosecutor for the American Department of the Army, drew the attention of his readers to the fact that:

"Article 23 (f) was the most important charge in the case in which Otto Skorzeny was cleared. Unfortunately it merely forbids misuse of the uniform of the enemy, without specifying what constitutes "misuse."

I would also add that in many cases our enemies in the east and west used German uniforms, long before December 1944.

This form of warfare has remained practically unknown to this day. During the trial of my comrades and me at Dachau, our American defense lawyer, Colonel Durst, obviously did not have the American, Russian and British archives at his disposal. Nevertheless, he declared that, "all warring powers had used questionable methods in the course of the Second World War." He was able to offer as examples the operation that took place at Tobruk in September 1942 and the attacks by the American Rangers at Aachen and the Saarlouis Bridge.

Today we know the details of these three operations as well as of numerous others on all fronts.

● ● ●

In September 1942, when the Africa Corps occupied Tobruk, a unit of the Long Range Desert Group under the command of Lieutenant Katz-Grünfeld, who was born in Palestine, was assigned to blow up the defensive works and certain installations in the city; a further unit, commanded by Colonel Stirling himself, was to attack the harbor, and from the sea. A third group of volunteers under the command of Major Crewe was to use the general confusion to attack our headquarters and kidnap Generalfeldmarschall Rommel – all while wearing German uniforms. This was the second such attempt against the commander of the Africa Corps.

The operation was brilliantly prepared, but in the end it failed because of a number of coincidences which even the most carefully prepared plan could not foresee. On the eve of the three-pronged operation a member of Katz-Grünfeld's commando unit, a German emigree by the name of Grossmann, was recognized by an Africa Corps Leutnant, who was amazed to find Grossmann in Tobruk wearing a German uniform. Grossmann was taken prisoner and he talked. The surprise attack failed. Not a single member of the Stirling, Katz-Grünfeld or Crewe units was shot. They were all treated as prisoners of war.

In October 1944 Aachen was almost completely surrounded by the US 1st Army. Only in the east was a corridor, about 6 kilometers wide, still open. In order to overcome the fortified positions at the entrance to the corridor, the Americans infiltrated several detachments of Rangers into the city dressed as German soldiers, with fal-

sified papers and German weapons. On October 13 these phoney
Germans attacked the positions from behind and destroyed them.
The 1st Army was subsequently able to occupy the corridor. The city
itself resisted until October 21. None of the members of the various
commando units removed their German uniforms before the fighting
began.

Indeed it was this surprise attack that inspired Hitler to come up
with Operation Greif. The American Rangers were under the command of General Bill Donovan, just as the Brandenburg Division
was under Canaris' command. Donovan asked to see me during my
time in Nuremberg Prison. The meeting was very cordial; there was
neither victor nor vanquished, just two soldiers, both rather
daredevilish and inventive, who had served their countries to the best
of their ability.

General Donovan was supposed to be an official prosecutor in
the trial; however he was recalled to America in October 1945 and
his place as chief prosecutor was taken by Judge Jackson.

● ● ●

In 1967 Werner Brockdorff, on the basis of British and American
documents, pointed out in his book *Die Geheimkommandos des
Zweiten Weltkrieges* that there was as little doubt as to the existence
of the Rangers on the American side and of the Commandos and the
SAS on the British side, as there was to the existence of the
Brandenburg Division and my own units on the German side.

The allied military tribunal in postwar Germany finally accepted
a modification of Article 23 of the Hague Convention of 1907. The
new text read:

It may not be the mission of commando units to conduct offensive operations in the uniform of the enemy; they may only have the
task of seizing important objects behind the lines like bridges, passes,
oil refineries and so on, without fighting, defending these against
enemy attack and preventing their destruction.

The commandos may only wear the enemy uniform in non-com-
bat operations, and in order to approach their objectives behind enemy lines. As soon as they are forced to join combat they must identify themselves to the enemy before they open fire.

As long as the commandos act according to these principles, they are not breaking international law.

Every member of such a commando unit who is captured in an enemy uniform, will be considered a spy if he tried to obtain information in this uniform, or if he succeeded in doing so. If he engaged in combat in the enemy uniform or even opened fire, he is guilty of a war crime and may be sentenced accordingly.

This addition to Article 23 of the Hague Convention of 1907 was valid only under certain conditions and was provisional. The law itself was not yet modified.

I would like to recall that the convention contained an Article 31, in which it states that every spy who has returned to his own forces and is then later captured by the enemy, must be treated as a prisoner of war and may no longer be held accountable for his early activities as a spy. This paragraph is obviously applicable to all members of commando units who venture behind enemy lines and subsequently return with information about what they saw.

The high command promised me twenty Sherman tanks for this new Trojan Horse called Greif. I received two, one of which was in working order. As an interim measure we modified twelve of our Panthers to look like Shermans, so that we might perhaps be able to fool the young enemy soldiers from a distance and in conditions of poor visibility. Similar difficulties were encountered with the 23 machine-guns, the 247 jeeps, the 32 armored tracked vehicles and the 193 trucks I had requested. We had to improvise everything, using what was on hand, and furthermore hope that we could, in the course of the offensive, use captured weapons and equipment.

But I must say that I was left completely in the lurch where the 3,300 English-speaking volunteers were concerned. In Friedenthal I received an OKW order by teletype. It read:

OKW/WFSt/Op (H) West Ia no 0012759/44 – Secret –
Operation – 25. 10. 1944

All units of the Western Front are to report before the X... of October the names of those officers, NCOs and enlisted men who are willing to volunteer for a special action in the western theater. The volunteers must be in good health, have experience in hand-to-hand combat and speak fluent English. They are to be sent to Friedenthal, where they will be placed under the command of Obersturmbannführer Skorzeny.

One can be almost certain that this order was copied by the division headquarters and sent to the regiments, battalions and companies. In fact this order was in the hands of the American intelligence service eight days after it was disseminated. For the moment the Americans drew no concrete conclusions, but they should have been alerted later by the OKW order, and we shall see what the results of their belated attention were. As for me, I was almost choked with rage. At first such stupidity seemed unbelievable and I suspected sabotage. Today I think it was stupidity, which is sometimes worse than treason.

As I considered our enemies more intelligent than we, I believed that Greif was unfeasible, and it seemed to me advisable that Hitler should know why. It was here General der Waffen-SS Fegelein got involved. He was Himmler's liaison man to Hitler, a salon lion whose vanity was laughable. He was soon to marry one of Eva Braun's sisters. He deserted during the night of April 26, 1945 and was arrested in his Berlin home. He was about to flee dressed in civilian clothes with a considerable sum of foreign currency in a suitcase. Two days later he was executed by firing squad in the courtyard of the Reich Chancellery.

Fegelein intercepted my report and declared that under no circumstances could this "annoying incident" be brought to the Führer's attention. Generaloberst Jodl, who for his part was also shocked, told me that it must be passed on. Himmler, who at this time wanted to bombard New York with V-1s, shared Fegelein's view! It was typical of the Reichsführer or SS-Obergruppenführer von dem Bach-Zelewski, neither of whom were soldiers in the actual sense. Who sent Bach-Zelewski to Budapest with the monster Thor? At least Fegelein didn't bombard anything.

The experts sent 600 volunteers for testing: we found 10 who spoke fluent English, 40 who spoke it fairly well. 150 were capable of making themselves understood, 200 spoke broken English and another 200 could answer yes or no. It was therefore impossible to form an "English-speaking brigade." The OKW acknowledged this, and it was agreed that the brigade was only to advance in enemy uniform if the enemy was in full retreat. This enabled me to retain the soldiers with the best knowledge of English for the commando company, which was to carry out action number two in small units. I placed it under the command of Hauptmann Stielau.

I asked the OKW for additional units for this action, which together with the two battalions of my commando units and the rest of the 600 volunteers made a force of 2,000 men altogether. The brigade was sent to the maneuvers camp at Grafenwöhr for special training under the command of Obersturmbannführer Hardieck. In the final days they were sent to Wahn near Cologne.

One hundred and twenty volunteers were subsequently designated as talkers. All others were emphatically instructed to keep silent; if forced to join a conversation they were to murmur or speak in single syllables. All went through an intensive course of "Americanization."

Neither the 600 volunteers who assembled in Friedenthal, nor the officers and men of my own units and the additional units were told the objectives of Operation Greif. Generaloberst Sepp Dietrich, the Commander-in-Chief of the Sixth Panzer Army, was first told about Operation Greif at the end of November, the commander of I SS-Panzer Corps only a few days before the attack.

One can just imagine the imaginative and fantastic rumors that surrounded the special unit's mission. During an inspection at the beginning of 1944 Hauptmann Stielau asked me to talk about it. "I know," he said to me, "what our mission really is: we are supposed to kidnap General Eisenhower."

At that moment I slipped over to the door as if on cat's paws, opened it and assured myself that there was no one behind it or in the hall.

"My dear fellow," I said to Hauptmann Stielau, "please speak quietly. You have hit the mark. But not a word to anyone – this is most important. Here we have forbidden any contact with the outside world. However Obersturmbannführer Hardieck tells me that one of our men has succeeded in sending a letter to his fiancee. You can see the danger we're in."

"I know that, Herr Obersturmbannführer. You can count on my absolute silence. But allow me to say that I know Paris and its surroundings like my vest pocket, and I can be really useful if the need arises."

"I have no doubt of that, but have you considered all the risks of such an operation?"

"Of course, Herr Obersturmbannführer, I think of nothing else. In my opinion it's absolutely feasible."

He outlined his plan to me in detail. In his view his chances were about one in a thousand. I left him all his illusions. "My dear fellow," I said, "believe me, I will remember you when the time comes."

Stielau had surely talked about Eisenhower and Paris long before he confided in me. I am sure that he was absolutely discrete after our talk, and that he told anyone who questioned him: "You will understand that I can't say anything. But the Obersturmbannführer has promised to take me with him. We will be playing an important role in the whole affair, and so on." All this with a knowing look that couldn't fool anyone.

The rest of the 150th Brigade was divided into three battle groups – X, Y and Z. Commanding these battle groups were Hauptmann Scherff and Oberstleutnant Wolf, both army officers, as well as Waffen-SS Obersturmbannführer Hardieck. Hardieck was killed in the first hours of the battle and was replaced by Fölkersam. Each of the three groups was to take and hold one of the three bridges over the Maas. Obviously these groups could only reach their objectives if we succeeded in getting close enough to the river during the night after the first day of the offensive. Overall command of the offensive was given to Generalfeldmarschall Model, and during a conversation with his chief-of-staff, General Krebs, I got the impression that both were firmly convinced that it would succeed. I drew their attention to the masterpiece created by the American engineer units: the two oil lines which, leading from Le Havre and Boulogne, were the life-line of the Anglo-American armies. The success of Greif could put us in a position to render them useless for some time. We would then have been able to fight under less unequal conditions than at the present, where the lack of fuel was having an extremely negative effect.

The offensive, which was supposed to begin on November 20, then December 1, was postponed until December 16 for reasons of materiel and weather. I attended several briefings in Hitler's headquarters prior to X-Day. On October 22 he had assured me that we would, "soon have more than 2,000 jet fighters in the air." Göring had promised him that. Then, at the beginning of December, I heard to my astonishment that it would only be 250! I remember a lengthy conversation I had in Führer Headquarters in September prior to Operation Panzerfaust with General der Luftwaffe Ritter von Greim, to whom I was introduced by Hanna Reitsch. Greim already regretted bitterly that the jet fighter, which had been developed in 1942, was not in use on every front. Hitler intended to replace Göring with Greim, but this didn't happen until 1945 when Berlin was encircled by the Russians.

During one of the last briefings before the offensive, Hitler asked whether I had studied the aerial photos of the Huy, Amay and Engis bridges. All I could say was that I hadn't received them. Hitler then turned to the Reichsmarschall and showered him with accusations, which were undoubtedly justified. At that moment I would have liked to have been deep underground. Hitler calmed himself very quickly, and in response to his question I gave my last report on Greif. "I am sure you will do your best," he said to me when I had finished. "I also know that it is your style to be at the head of your men. In this case I expressly forbid you to cross our lines and personally take part in the operation. I will make the commander of the Sixth Panzer Army of the Waffen-SS responsible for the carrying-out of this order. You will not leave your command post and will direct Operation Greif from there by radio. I don't want you to run the risk of being captured. I still need you!"

These words acted like a cold shower. Adrian von Fölkersam, who was with me, sensed my disappointment. I informed the leaders of the three battle groups of Hitler's decision and added that if the situation of one of the groups became critical I would go to it in an instant. I had no intention of staying with the staff of the Sixth Army.

Hauptsturmführer Radl accompanied me to the last briefing prior to December 16. He had not yet met Hitler, who shook his hand and offered a few encouraging words; but our Karli was so impressed that he stood at attention as if cast in stone.

I established my command post in Schmidtheim during the night of December 15-16. No one slept that night. Our artillery went into action at five in the morning on Saturday, December 16. Groups X, Y and Z were in position, together with I Panzer Corps of the Waffen-SS, in the Losheim-Graben sector, where the effect of the artillery was mediocre. My radio operator signalled that there was heavy fighting; then a catastrophe: Obersturmbannführer Hardieck, commander of Group Z, had been killed. Fölkersam, who so far had been responsible for communications between the three groups, took over the command of Group Z. In the afternoon I drove to Losheim to get a firsthand look at the situation, and I realized why our offensive was bogged down: the narrow roads were clogged with every type of vehicle, and I had to cover ten kilometers on foot to get to Losheim. The next day was to be even worse. It was obvious that our groups could not advance. I therefore decided to wait until the next day. Not until our panzers had crossed the High Venn could we reach the Maas.

In the meantime I sent two or three squads from the special company to the southern sector of the front with orders to infiltrate between the lines. The first American prisoners arrived, and I struck up a conversation with a lieutenant. They had been taken completely by surprise; the Americans had thought they were in a quiet sector. The bad weather and the fog had prevented their air force from intervening.

Towards midnight I learned that the 1st Panzer Regiment of the Leibstandarte, commanded by the daring Jochen Peiper, had gone over to the offensive. It was he who was to smash open a breach for our battle groups. A few hours later the leading panzer units signalled: "Have taken Ronsfeld. Lively resistance by the enemy." One of our special squads returned with intelligence, which was immediately transmitted to I SS-Panzer Corps' command post.

On the morning of the 17th I made my way to the front to inspect the commando units. The roads were now completely clogged: it was impossible to get to I SS-Panzer Corps at the front and it began to suffer from a shortage of fuel on the morning of the 18th. There was no more talk of reaching the Maas bridges! Therefore, after informing the Wehrmacht operations staff (Jodl) and obtaining his consent, I placed my brigade at the disposal of I Panzer Corps.

The better roads in this area all ran in an east-west direction, which may explain the difficulties encountered by the Sixth Army, for it had to advance from east to north. On our left was the Fifth Panzer Army of General Hasso von Manteuffel, who later became a deputy in the Bundestag. He, too, had been confident of strategic success. I met him at Führer Headquarters before the offensive. During a long conference with Hitler he achieved a significant tactical amendment of the plans, which had been placed before him.

Assault battalions from his divisions were to cross the lines during the night, before our artillery preparations had alerted the enemy.
The advance by these elite units would then permit a deeper and
faster advance by our divisions. Hitler accepted this excellent plan.
In fact it was the conventional use of a tactic that had been used with
explosive effect by the 150th Panzer Brigade: the moment of surprise was used for the infiltration of troops into the enemy lines.

Farther south General von Lüttwitz's 47th Panzer Corps had the
task of taking the important crossroads at Bastogne. The unit given
the job was the Panzer-Lehr Division. But because this division became snarled in a huge traffic jam on December 16 and 17, it wasn't
able to cross the Our River until about 9 A.M. on the morning of the
18th, more than 24 hours after X-Hour. Meanwhile the 26th
Volksgrenadier Division, which was supposed to support Panzer-Lehr,
was delayed because it was forced to advance on foot due to a lack of
trucks, which were either stuck or were not available! General Fritz
Bayerlein, commander of the Panzer-Lehr, was supposed to arrive at
Bastogne on the afternoon of December 16: he didn't cross the road
from Clervaux to Bastogne until Tuesday the 19th at about 2 A.M.!
The Americans thus had time to send the 10th Armored Division
from Patton's army to Bastogne. It arrived from the south and relieved General McAuliffe, the brave commander of the 101st Airborne Division. It was only by chance that this division ended up
defending Bastogne. It had got as far as Verbomont, where it was
redirected to avoid clogged roads. Luck really was against us.

On Wednesday, December 20, I decided to attack Malmedy early
on the morning of the 21st with a dozen tanks. There was – must I
add this? – fighting, and no one wore American uniforms. Heavy
barrage fire by the enemy's artillery and a tremendous counter-of-
fensive by American tanks caused our plan to fail. The skies cleared
on the 23rd and the U.S. Air Force carried out massive attacks on
Malmedy, which was held by American troops. I couldn't comprehend it, even less when the American bombardment intensified on
the 23rd and 24th. I soon thought that Malmedy must have been taken,
but by which German units?

I knew that the town hadn't been evacuated. In fact one of our
commando units under the former Baltic naval officer Baron von
Behr was in Malmedy on the 19th. Our sailor in his black leather

coat found himself pressed by a group of civilians, who asked him: "Is it true that the Germans are coming back?" He confirmed this, as one would think, and requested the people to completely evacuate the town in order to increase the general chaos. I hoped that many of the inhabitants of Malmedy had followed his advice.

The coolness with which the commando unit carried out its role was all the greater, as it was unaware that it was behind enemy lines. "I had no idea where we were," the baron admitted to me, "nothing like that ever happened to me at sea." I advised him to equip himself with a compass and sextant.

Our attack on Malmedy resulted in heavy casualties. Leutnant Schmidthuber was wounded seven times. Fölkersam, also wounded, was just able to withdraw. We were forced to remain on the defensive. I was also hit a short time later; I received a minor wounded in the leg and a rather more serious one above my right eye, which I feared I might lose at first. After I had been seen to at the division command post they wanted to send me to the rear; however there could be no talk of that. There were many wounded, however most were not serious. One exception was the brave Untersturmführer Lochner, Fölkersam's adjutant, who was shot in the belly. Stretched out on a litter, he had lost consciousness. I spoke to him softly. He opened his eyes and recognized me. "Are you wounded too?" he asked me. I tried to comfort him. He died before they could operate.

What we lacked was heavy weapons. On December 24 they finally sent us a battery of eight mortars. But we had only 20 mortars in total. Most of our tanks had been destroyed, a new attack was quite impossible.

On December 25 I sought out Fölkersam, who had set up his command post 300 meters from the main line of resistance. There I met an American patrol that had just allowed itself to be captured by our people. The NCO in charge had a walkie-talkie with him, and one of our English-speakers began a conversation with the American unit, which amused us greatly. Our man began by reporting strong armored units to the northwest, which were obviously moving fast toward Verviers. He then went on to pass on all sorts of crazy information. When he finally declared that a formation of flying submarines was attacking, the American officer shouted: "You're drunk! Get back here immediately! It's an order!" We gave the American

NCO back his radio, and he declared, "Sorry, but I've got to go to Germany now."

On December 28 we were relieved by an infantry unit which was covering the northern flank of I SS-Panzer Corps. It was obvious that our attack, and with it Greif, had failed. We had not reached the Maas bridges. If our special units had done good work behind the enemy lines, we didn't know what benefit it might have for us.

Only eight squads, each consisting of four phoney Americans, had gone behind enemy lines, a total of 32 men. Twenty-four returned. Eight were declared missing on December 29, 1944. On that day the rest of the 150th Panzer Brigade was sent to Schlierbach, east of St. Vith, to rest. The brigade was had to be disbanded a short time later.

Later I will speak about the reports made to me by the men of the commando unit who came back. But first I would like to mention two reports spread by Radio Calais, the enemy propaganda station. The announcer declared – it must have been shortly before December 20 – that "a strong sabotage group, commanded by Colonel Skorzeny, the kidnapper (sic) of Mussolini, had been uncovered," and that "more than 100 soldiers of this unit had been exposed and taken prisoner." We will see what is to be thought of this report, which opened up various aspects of the special commando unit for me.

● ● ●

The second, somewhat later report by Radio Calais, concerned "the shooting of American prisoners and Belgian civilians by German SS troops." The American soldiers were said "to have been shot at a crossroads southeast of Malmedy on December 17." The staff of the Sixth Panzer Army instructed all commanders, "to prepare a detailed report concerning an alleged shooting of prisoners of war and civilians during the offensive." The 150th Panzer Brigade delivered a negative report.

After the war, in May 1946, Jochen Peiper and 72 members of his unit faced an American court-martial. They were accused of having shot 308 American soldiers and 111 Belgian civilians in cold blood. The charge relating to the civilians was soon dropped. The only charge that was kept was that 71 soldiers of the American 285th Field Artillery Battalion had been murdered by the unit at Baugnez crossroads southeast of Malmedy. One can summarize the accusation as follows:

At about 1 P.M. on December 17, 1944, there was a brief skirmish between the leading tanks of Peiper's 1st Panzer Regiment and the affected American company, which was commanded by Lieutenant Virgil T. Lary. The Americans surrendered and were murdered at about 2 P.M. The main accuser in May 1946 was Lieutenant Lary. The majority of the defendants had made comprehensive and identical confessions. The American tribunal handed down 42 death sentences, 23 sentences of life imprisonment, two of 20 years, one of 15 years and five of 10 years. Among those sentenced to death was Obersturmbannführer Peiper, who had already passed Ligneuville at 2 P.M. on December 17, and who was not accused of having taken part in the massacre or of having ordered it.

This judgement infuriated Colonel Willis M. Everett of Atlanta, Georgia, who had handled the defense. Convinced that this was a miscarriage of justice, he spent ten years of his life revealing the truth.

In fact Everett became convinced that, following a skirmish lasting a few minutes, Peiper had himself given the order to cease firing before he continued on his way. From an American colonel, whose name is not known and who was in the car with him, Peiper learned that there was a U.S. headquarters three kilometers south of Ligneuville. Peiper hoped to be able to take it by surprise.

It was proved that the alleged confessions of the accused had been extorted from them by means of beatings, torture and threats against their families and themselves, after they had been hooded and taken before a phoney court-martial with a phoney judge and fake priests. I am skipping over the details. The Americans set up two commissions of inquiry, one military and one senate committee. Investigations were even carried out in Germany, although the punishments were reduced in March 1948. All the death sentences were commuted in following years. In addition to other illuminating facts, in the report on the new investigations by the American judge van Hoden, one can read that the court-martial made use of the alleged confession of an eighteen-year-old member of the Waffen-SS. The confession was wrung out of him as the result of torture which he did not survive. He hanged himself in his cell – at least his guard found him hanged.

On December 22, 1956, almost twelve years to the day after the battle, all of the men convicted in the Malmedy trial were freed. Not one death sentence was carried out – *due to a lack of evidence.*

The strangest thing was that Peiper's 1st Panzer Regiment, after continuing toward the west, took prisoner 131 American officers and soldiers of the 30th Infantry Division in Stoumont on December 21, among them Major Hal McCown. In his book *The Story of the Bulge* (New York 1959) my friend John Toland related that McCown and Peiper had a long conversation and that the American officer, who was aware of the alleged massacre on December 17, was surprised to find that his captor was a cultivated, reasonable and quiet man. When he expressed concern about the fate of the 130 prisoners in La Gleize, Peiper reassured him and gave him his word of honor as a soldier that his unit respected the rules of warfare. With his supplies of fuel running low, Peiper decided to pull back. The two officers reached an agreement: the 130 American prisoners were released and the battered Waffen-SS unit could withdraw. And so it happened. McCown remained Peiper's prisoner until he managed to slip away on December 24.

Colonel Willis M. Everett had great difficulty in obtaining permission to use McCown as a witness in the trial concerning the Malmedy massacre, even though Peiper's unit was also accused of having murdered the 130 prisoners at La Gleize, some of the civilians and 250 refugee children, as well as wounded Americans and Germans in the basement of a sanatorium. Colonel Everett got his way and McCown was able to testify that none of this was true.

"His testimony," wrote Toland, "proved that the atrocities allegedly committed by the Germans in a village (La Gleize) were inventions and thus placed a large part of the indictment in doubt, which failed to prevent 42 of the accused Waffen-SS men from being sentenced to death by hanging and 23 to life imprisonment."

In any case the alleged massacre at Malmedy had further, direct consequences, which were no less tragic. When the American High Command learned what had happened there was anger and calls for revenge. This found its expression in several orders, such as that issued by the headquarters of the 328th Infantry Division on the 21st of December, which called upon its members not to take members of the Waffen-SS or German paratroopers prisoner, but to shoot them on the spot. In Chegnogne 21 German soldiers, several of whom were wounded, gave themselves up under a Red Cross flag. They were shot down on the doorstep of a house as they walked out with their hands raised.

I believe that the American High Command overreacted in this regard. Having become a victim of its own propaganda, it was convinced of the guilt of the SS units without an investigation because that is what it wanted to believe.

This is in no way an attempt to apologize for the Waffen-SS. A European force of 840,000 men, of which 360,000 were killed and 42,000 declared missing – to say nothing of the wounded – needs no apology: the numbers say it all. The wrongs committed by several Waffen-SS units, and others that helped themselves to the name, cannot be laid at the feet of the entire Waffen-SS with the notion of "collective guilt."

Generaloberst Guderian, who undeniably fought a chivalrous war, felt obliged to write the following in the forward to General Hausser's book *Waffen-SS*:

"*Our honor is loyalty*: this was the motto according to which the Waffen-SS was trained and the motto under which it fought. Whoever witnessed these units on the battlefield cannot help but confirm this fact. After the surrender this fighting force was the target of slander and outrageously serious and unjustified charges."

Generaloberst Guderian characterized the founder of the Waffen-SS, Paul Hausser, who succeeded in giving it its "esprit de corps" as "one of the most significant commanders that I know."

In a speech in Hannover in autumn 1953 Bundeskanzler Adenauer declared emphatically that "the soldiers of the Waffen-SS were soldiers like all the others." General Hasso von Manteuffel also condemned especially mean and stupid slander against the former soldiers.

Following the war the majority of the Waffen-SS were held as prisoners for many years. We were bound hand and foot and gagged as well. In spite of his serious bias, American historian George H. Stein was forced to admit in his book *The Waffen-SS* (New York 1966) that 99 percent of these men who were being held had fought a clean war: the denazification courts reached the same conclusion after lengthy investigations that were carried out in correspondence with the victors and occupying powers.

The fact remains that 71 American soldiers were killed at the Baugnez crossroads. The question is how. Most of the published reports on this theme are confused and contradictory. However it seems possible to me to give the following explanation based on the detailed reports I was able to examine:

The American artillerymen were taken prisoner during the battle with Peiper's advance guard: 3 light tracked vehicles and 3 tanks. Since the unit wanted to continue on its way quickly, the 125 prisoners were forced into a field. According to Toland and others, the first shot at one of the prisoners, from a pistol from one of the light tracked vehicles of the main body, was fired much later. The thought suggests itself that the GIs, who were left on their own, had picked up their weapons again or that at least several of them had. When the main force arrived at the crossroads it saw a group of American soldiers, some of whom were armed – and opened fire.

In 1974 the English magazine *After the Battle*, No. 4, which dealt with the battle in the Ardennes, published a photo taken by the American Army before the bodies were buried. On Page 18 one can see among the bodies stretched out on the snow-covered field one which still has a weapon in its hand, a rifle or probably a machine-gun. But a prisoner of war is not armed. This man was undoubtedly killed in battle. There was, probably as a result of a terrible misunderstanding, a *second battle*.

A misunderstanding by a chief-of-staff of General Hodges, who commanded the American 1st Army, had even worse consequences. In 1969 a book by the young Belgian historian Michel Georis, with the title *Nuts*, was released in Paris. This was the answer which General McAuliffe gave the German *parlementaire* from the 26th Volksgrenadier Division, which offered the Americans in Bastogne "an honorable surrender." One of the book's chapters is titled *The Tragedy at Malmedy*. What sort of tragedy was it?

Georis noted that I had expended "much effort for nothing" in my attempt to take Malmedy on December 21, for, he added, two days later, on December 23, the American air force bombed Malmedy and "killed more than 300 American soldiers and a good one hundred Belgian civilians." The bombing had been carried out by the U.S. 9th Air Force, and Toland related that the GI's referred to this unit as the "American Luftwaffe."

A communique by the American 1st Army said that Malmedy had been bombed because "the Germans had entered the town." "The reality was different," wrote Georis. "Apart from the brief penetration by the Fölkersam battalion, which, as we know, was immediately driven back, Malmedy was exclusively occupied by Americans for three days. This did not stop the American air force from flying more missions the next day and the day after that – Christmas – and again killing hundreds of civilians and American soldiers."

In a footnote the Belgian historian confirmed that although the exact number of soldiers killed by American bombs was not known, it was "probably 700." But what was the "probable" number of civilians killed in this senseless massacre? Georis doesn't say![1] Stubbornly bombing one's own soldiers and defenseless civilians in no way corresponds to an "obvious strategic necessity." In my view, that is the real "Tragedy of Malmedy." No one has taken note of this for a long time.

● ● ●

Let us now investigate what is true about the first report broadcast by Radio Calais about the 100 captured members of the 150th Panzer Brigade.

In Volume 4 of the English magazine After the Battle the claim is repeated that the number of special units captured behind enemy lines was fourteen. This number corresponds to the truth as little as that given by Radio Calais, for the simple reason that no more than eight units were able to advance far enough behind enemy lines to carry out their special missions.

I am not counting the units, about 20 in number, which until about January 15, 1945 carried out reconnaissance missions 2 to 3 kilometers behind the American lines on order of the army group or corps. These missions had nothing to do with Greif, and although they were carried out in American uniforms, they did not involve sabotage. Several of the units crossed the enemy lines a number of times, all returned.

Of the eight units involved in Operation Greif only two were reported missing, the other 6 came back. A previously-captured jeep was fired on while leaving the American sector by the enemy, who suspected a desertion. This was reported to us later by the opposing German division.

I received reports on the activities of six units. Two gave me reports that I thought lacked credibility, but the activities of the other four were described very precisely. The units that got the farthest reached the Maas abeam Huy, where the 150th Panzer Brigade was supposed to hold the bridge. The Hauptmann of this unit, which took up position at a crossroads, directed an American tank column into the blue. Our radio monitoring service confirmed that the headquarters of the American 1st Army searched in vain for this unit for two days. They thought that it had been destroyed or captured in the course of some mysterious battle. This unit cut telephone lines and changed roads signs intended for the American supply units.

Another command vehicle crossed the Maas near Amay with no difficulty whatsoever. Its occupants placed red banners to indicate that the roads to the front had been mined – which caused approaching enemy reinforcements to turn around and make lengthy detours. This unit also destroyed telephone lines.

Another team caused an enemy infantry unit to withdraw between Poteaux and Grand Halleux by assuring the Americans that the Germans were already farther west, in the vicinity of Lierneux.

The American officers expressed their gratitude before departing.

Unfortunately none of the units reached the large fuel depot that lay between Stavelot and Francorchamps. Peiper's column missed the same depot when it advanced on La Gleize. But one of our units captured a munitions dump and blew it up during the night.

Our eighth unit fell victim to an accident; the circumstances were as follows: as he was almost out of gas, the driver of a jeep stopped at an American supply outpost and casually said, "Petrol please."

The eyes of the GI manning the gas pump became as big as saucers, and he eyed our four comrades suspiciously; an American would ask for "gas" not "petrol," and he wouldn't say please, at least not if he was in a hurry.

"Tell me," asked the American, "do you know where you are?"

The driver thought they had been recognized. He drove away, lost control of the jeep on the icy road and rammed the first truck of a convoy coming the other way. The vehicle overturned, and when the Americans hurried to the aid of the occupants they noticed that they were wearing German uniforms under their American clothing.

Under intense questioning, one of our comrades *admitted* what he thought was true: a special unit under my command was supposed to kidnap General Eisenhower and cause the commanders of the British and American armies to disappear, as well as their staffs.

The chief of intelligence of the American army group was seen as a panic monger. They hadn't believed him when, on about December 10, General Hodge's chief of intelligence reported that new German divisions had been sighted east of St. Vith. He took out his file on OKW Order 0012759, concluded from it that 1,000 phoney Americans had mingled with the real ones and issued a general alert for the whole front against disguised Germans.

After December 18 this caused real chaos among the enemy. All the details have been described by General Omar Bradley, commander of the US 12th Army Group, and by Montgomery and Sir Basil Liddell Hart, to mention only the two most significant writers of memoirs and one of the most famous World War Two historians.

● ● ●

Let us first of all examine the offensive from a tactical point of view. One must say that on the morning of December 17 the 12th Army Group was divided into three attack columns, and that panic reigned at SHAEF (Supreme Headquarters Allied Expeditionary Force) for four or five days.

Bradley, whose headquarters were in Luxembourg, did not at all understand what was happening and sent contradictory orders into thin air. With some difficulty Eisenhower alerted Generals Hodges, Simpson and Collins, who on December 20 had seen neither Bradley nor any member of his staff. The telephones were either out or unreliable. For several days it was impossible to reach General Hodges, commander of the US 1st Army, who on December 16 had his headquarters at Spa. It was hastily transferred to Chaudfontaine without Eisenhower or Bradley being informed. Finally it was moved to Tongres.

When von Manteuffel was forced to halt six kilometers from Dinant by lack of fuel on December 23, he had only the British 29th Armored Brigade in front of him. Eisenhower, who in reality feared that Montgomery would disengage from the enemy, urged him forwards and placed all American forces on the northern flank under his command. That meant Simpson's 9th Army and Hodges' 1st, which was "fighting desperately." On the other hand the British 30th Corps remained on the west bank of the Maas until January 3, 1945, while in the south Bradley had to manage with the rest of the 3rd and the 8th US Corps.

In his memoirs Montgomery wrote that he had left the British 30th Corps on the other side of the river on December 20 just in case. His single reserve armored division had just landed and the question of whether it should be embarked again raised itself. The British expeditionary corps was "ready for anything." On that same December 20 Montgomery sent Churchill a telegram in which he characterized the situation as "extremely disturbing." Proof that he was considering a general retreat by the expeditionary corps, just like in 1940, is found in his memoirs. There he quoted a sentence from his telegram, which has never before been published:

"This time," he telegraphed, "we can't embark in Dunkirk again, for there are Germans everywhere there."

In fact Hitler had instructed that our troops were to hold certain key coastal cities at all costs: Dunkirk, Lorient, Saint-Nazaire, La Rochelle and Royan. The last named city was quite senselessly destroyed by the American air force in April 1945.

On January 6, 1945 Winston Churchill, still highly worried, called Stalin for help.

"The battles in the west are very hard," he telegraphed. I ask that you let me know whether we can count on a Russian offensive on the Vistula front or elsewhere in January."

While the tactical and strategic events of this offensive were of significance at the beginning, the political effect was no less remarkable. Churchill's call to Stalin for help betrayed real fear and worry that the result might be an unforseen agreement in the east, like that concluded in 1939.

The English had a large part of American public opinion against them. For two months the foreign press had been taking potshots at Montgomery, whose behavior and claims seemed unbearable, especially after the bloody defeat at Arnheim. But the British press certainly did not spare Eisenhower, who was criticized for lack of foresight and even incompetence.

It was on Churchill's order that Montgomery gave his famous press conference in mid-January and directed "a passionate appeal for Anglo-American solidarity." After admitting that the enemy had struck a serious blow, "which rocked the allied armies," he turned to the journalists and said, "You all know that the leader of our forces is Eisenhower. I am very attached to Ike, we are good friends. It is not without some concern that I read few flattering articles about him in the British press. I would like to ask you to do your best to change this state of affairs."

I imagine that the attending journalists were a little surprised when they heard the field marshall declare, "I have had myself issued an American pass, and so I am one of the soldiers of the US Army. My fingerprints are registered in the Pentagon, and that is better than if they were in Scotland Yard."

Such statements could only have a regrettable effect, and Montgomery admitted in his memoirs that it would have been better if he had said nothing. "I gave the impression of a loser, not to the Germans, but to the Americans." When all was said and done, the British field marshall called the battle "interesting." How could Eisenhower, Bradley, Hodges, Gerow and Simpson, who had lost 80,000 men, have agreed with Montgomery's assessment?

From 1945 to 1960 many authors characterized the Ardennes offensive as a "foolish plan of Hitler's, that was doomed to fail." Ten years later Liddell Hart, among others, recognized that the plan for the offensive was "brilliantly conceived." Furthermore he wrote that "the allies came to the brink of catastrophe at the beginning of the battle."

Operation Greif certainly impressed him. Where the 150th Brigade's action was concerned, he took into consideration the countless difficulties faced by the unit in the areas of camouflage and equipment.

"This flimsy camouflage made greater caution necessary," he wrote. "In the northern sector, where the brigade was assembled, there was no clear breakthrough; so its operation was postponed and then called off altogether. However the first stage of the plan had astonishing success, even more than expected."

Tens of thousands of military police went on the hunt, in order to ferret out the "disguised Nazis" as quickly as possible. They made a good catch. Liddell Hart offered a long and interesting list of victims; one of the first was Omar Bradley. In his book *A Soldier's Story*, Bradley drew the picture of half a million GIs playing cat and mouse whenever they met. It was quite impossible to prevent them from running into each other, and Bradley described what followed:

"Neither rank, nor identity papers, nor protests prevented the allied forces from being interrogated again at every turn."

Bradley himself had to prove three times that he was really an American, naming the capital of Illinois and the players of a famous American football team. The third time he failed, because he didn't know the name of Betty Grable's latest husband. The GI let him through nevertheless.

At least Bradley was warned. An American intelligence officer had advised him to wait until the weather improved and then take an aircraft. But in no case "should he venture onto the roads, on account of the disguised Germans." Charles Foley looked into this widespread fear in his book *Commando Extraordinary*.

"They saw enemies and spies everywhere," he wrote. "Half of the American Army was looking for Skorzeny in its ranks."

General Emile Wanty reported in his book *Art de la Guerre* that Montgomery was himself stopped several times while these dark rumors were circulating. General Eisenhower was literally held prisoner by his own guard unit. He had succeeded Feldmarschall von Rundstedt as a guest at the Chateau Saint-Germain-en-Laye. The military police picked him up there and took him to Versailles in an armored vehicle.

American military intelligence had a portrait of me drawn up in the fashion of the Chicago police. General Wanty, a Belgian, wrote that I was a *condottiere*; this was a word that the American bloodhounds, who had never seen Venice and the *Colleoni* of the Verrocchio, naturally assumed meant gangster.

Furthermore I was the "kidnapper of Mussolini," while at the same time Victor Emmanuel and Badoglio were his "liberators." A wanted poster in the best western style portrayed me as an Obersturmbannführer of the Waffen-SS:

Wanted
SKORZENY
Spy
Saboteur Murderer

Beneath the photo was the following personal description:

This man is highly intelligent (flatterer!) and dangerous. Hitler moustache or clean-shaven. He can appear in American or British uniform and so on.

All this description lacked was the false beard. Several French journalists saw in me the reincarnation of Fanthomas, although I wore no magic cap to let me come and go unseen. Charles Foley also quoted the diary of Kay Summersby, Eisenhower's secretary and loyal companion, who held the rank of Lieutenant. Her disclosures appear unbelievable today, but they correspond to the pure truth.

Once the report on my alleged "imminent arrival in Paris" became known among Eisenhower's staff, the security service transformed the area around the headquarters into a fortress with barbed wire and tanks. The guard was quadrupled and "the password became a matter of life and death."

"A simple backfire," she wrote, "caused all work in the offices to come to a halt and provoked a wave of telephone calls: 'Is the boss still there?'"

In her diary she noted on December 22 that SHAEF's intelligence service had sent a report which confirmed that the saboteurs had arrived in Paris. Fortunately their meeting place was known: the Café de la Paix.

There were of course lovely raids on the Place de l'Opéra as a result, and a number of British and American officers who had had the unfortunate idea of meeting at the Café de la Paix were arrested in spite of their protests. Peaceful Parisians, whose conduct seemed suspicious, likewise became victims of this police madness.

Eisenhower was forced to move. They found a double for him, Lieutenant-Colonel Baldwin B. Smith, who played the role of the supreme commander and served as a "decoy for Skorzeny." He risked his life each day, drove around and saluted "à la Ike." He had practiced this salute for a long time; Smith played his role so convincingly that in the end he believed that he was the big boss. After the war American friends told me that the colonel gave up his illusions with great bitterness.

They saw me everywhere in France, which was no surprise as my photo had been distributed in thousands. In Troyes a druggist had sold me aspirin, I had purchased jam jars in a grocery store in Saint-Etienne; they had sighted me in Paris, not in the Café de la Paix but in a bar on the Champs-Elysées in the uniform of an American air force commander. All this happened at the beginning of February 1945, while we were fighting the Russians at Schwedt on the Oder.

• • •

Operation Greif was investigated by many military judges and initially by those who cleared us at Dachau in October 1947. I have already cited Max Kössler, the lawyer for the American Department of the Army, in the war crimes trial of 1946 to 1949. His study was based on existing law, meaning the Fourth Hague Convention of October 18, 1907. It concludes:

"The Skorzeny affair demonstrates in striking fashion that the international law concerning the use of enemy uniforms for reasons of stratagem must be defined and explained. The word 'misuse' in Article 23(f) must be explained, in order to specify which types of use are forbidden. We hope that this submission will stimulate the United Nations to come to an agreement on new definitions."

No such agreement has been reached by the end of 1974. Captain Steven J. Abdala analyzed Operation Greif in a report for the advanced infantry officers course at the US Army Infantry School at Fort Benning, Georgia. His report, titled *The Role of Colonel Skorzeny and Operation Griffin during the Second World War*, bears the date March 3, 1972. Captain Abdalla, who made personal inquiries of me, made some interesting observations about Greif. As to the question of law, he wrote concerning the German side:

"There is discussion as to whether the commando units broke the Hague Convention of 1907. But Skorzeny received assurances that as long as the German uniform was worn under the American and the soldiers did not engage in combat, there was no breach of the law. The terms of land warfare law are far from clear where this point is concerned, and this type of stratagem will probably create the same problems in any future war."

In the chapter on success, conditions and recommendations, the captain noted:

"Special actions like Griffin deserve to be studied closely. Future military conflicts will be just as complex as the use of computers and advanced technology permit. As always, however, it will demand the military insight to appreciate that the thing will eventually be finished off by the infantry, which means that any new tactic of surprise will enjoy a certain success."

Overall the author confirmed our view of the psychological effect:

"The psychological effect of Operation Griffin was enormous, if one considers the limited means that were put into play. One can imagine a battlefield on which one of the armies no longer knows who is friend and who is foe. The psychological advantage of such an operation exceeds by far that which can be achieved by tactics and intelligence services. One only need examine the American newspapers of the time to assess the degree in which the allies were impressed by Skorzeny and Griffin."

In the foreword to his paper Captain Abdalla published the letter I wrote to him on February 28, 1972, the most important parts of which are reproduced here:

"Only sixteen of my men really operated behind the enemy lines and returned. This means that only four were captured. As they wore enemy uniforms they were shot. However in January 1945 I learned from Radio Calais that more than 100 members of the 150th Brigade had been taken prisoner. On the other hand the casualty lists reveal that only eight members of the commando company failed to return: the four who were captured near Brussels and executed, and the four who were in the overturned jeep. If Radio Calais spoke the truth, one must conclude that the allies arrested a large number of real English and American soldiers."

While interned in Darmstadt and Dachau prisoner of war camps I was in fact visited by several American officers who had been arrested under suspicion of being nazis.

One last note: it is patently obvious that we never had any intention of kidnapping or killing General Eisenhower. On the other hand the objective of the British commando unit in Beda Littoria in November 1941 under the command of Colonel Laycock and Major Keyes was admittedly to kidnap or kill General Rommel. The many members of this unit who were captured were not tried, sentenced and executed, but were considered prisoners of war and treated accordingly. Any further comment seems to me unnecessary.

● ● ●

Hitler summoned me on December 31, 1944. His headquarters was still located on the Western Front at Ziegenberg. When he saw me with a bandaged head he insisted that his doctors, one of whom was Dr. Stumpfegger, examine me before I told him anything about our operation. Wy wound had become infected and I now received proper treatment. Hitler expressed his pleasure that I hadn't lost my eye and he talked with me for half an hour. He regretted that the offensive hadn't reached its objective. Our panzers, which had been bogged down on the first two days while the enemy air forces were grounded by bad weather, could not advance quickly enough over the impossible roads. Infantry divisions on foot had advanced as fast as our panzer divisions! Nevertheless the enemy had been forced to take heavy losses, and in any case our offensive had struck a heavy blow against his morale.

"The most important thing is," he said, "that the American or British soldier believed that it was all going to be a military cakewalk. His commanders had led him to believe that. But then the mortally wounded got up and attacked! On the 17th we took 8,000 to 10,000 prisoners in the Schnee-Eifel alone. We couldn't wait for them to wring our neck, Skorzeny! The only solution for Germany is victorious battle. There is no other."

Unfortunately, I was of the opinion that neither of the two objectives of Greif had been achieved. I said this openly to Hitler and he amazed me even more:

"I have no complaints with you, Skorzeny. You had to improvise everything, with limited means, and your panzer brigade couldn't play its role in cooperation with Sixth Army. You would have been successful if I had placed you at the head of the Fifth. You would have easily been able to put Dinant behind you. You might perhaps have reached Brabant, and who knows what might have developed from that? Where your commando unit is concerned, I have the impression that its psychological effect was much greater than you might think. We shall see later."

He appeared satisfied with the advance toward Malmedy by our three battle groups after December 20 and awarded the Honor Roll Clasp of the Army to myself and the commanders of Groups X, Y and Z – namely Obersturmbannführer Wolff, Hauptsturmführer Scherff, Hauptsturmführer von Fölkersam and posthumously to the man he replaced, Obersturmbannführer Hardieck. From this moment on this army decoration was awarded generally.

When I left Hitler he said to me, "A smaller-scale offensive is beginning farther south on the Upper Rhine, along the border of the Pfalz region." Thanks to the minutes of his talk on December 28, 1944, in which he told the commanding generals of this operation, we know that he said of the Ardennes offensive.

"At last! This is the first time since autumn 1939, meaning since we have been at war, that we have been able to keep an operation secret." He was wrong. Stalin knew about it.

We must examine the game Stalin played. The western allies did not land in Normandy until June 6, 1944; he began his own offensive on the Eastern Front on June 24 in the north, on the 26th in the center and in Romania after July 20. He feared that the western allies would reach the German border very quickly. But he was very soon able to assure himself that this was not the case, and he held back his attacks in the northern and central sectors from mid-August until mid-December: this enabled Hitler to prepare his offensive in the Ardennes and Stalin his own. Eisenhower and Churchill protested in vain.

When we – Americans, British, Germans and other Europeans – had lost more than 200,000 men in the Ardennes, only then, on January 11, 1945, did Stalin throw his armies at Berlin. He was also careful not to tell his "allies" what we were preparing in the west. At the beginning of November 1945 at Yalta Stalin presented his plan for the occupation and destruction of Germany, which was curiously similar to the Morgenthau Plan, which Roosevelt and Churchill had readily accepted in September 1944. In fact both plans were written by Stalin. The actual author of the first plan, from the Quebec Conference, was the communist Harry Dexter White, a member of the powerful Soviet espionage net directed by the Silvermaster family. Cordell Hull, shocked by this "blind revenge plan," asked Roosevelt: "Why did you sign this document, which reduces Germany to an agrarian state?"

"I was tired," answered Roosevelt, "and I signed without worrying too much about what Morgenthau had written."

Not Morgenthau. Stalin.

Notes

1. According to the official statistics, which Céré and Rousseau published in their *Chronologie du conflit mondial* (Paris 1946), in the period from April 5, 1943 to July 22, 1944 approximately 7,700 Belgian civilians fell victim to Anglo-American bombing – 2,007 in Antwerp, 674 in Malines and 425 in Brussels. The number of injured is not known. The statistics end after July 22, 1944. (Editors' note)

PART IV

22

Vlasov and Bandera
Nicolai, Canaris & Gehlen

"Eye to eye" with General Vlasov again – His program and his European ideas – The danger of using Russian volunteers as divisions or corps – They turn against us in Prague in May 1945 – The English hand the cossacks of the Ataman of Pannwitz over to Stalin – Rosenberg and Koch – Operation Brauner Bär in the Ukraine – These people have been at war with bolshevism since 1918 – The UPA's stubborn struggle from 1945 to 1952 – The KGB murders Bandera in Munich – The affair of the prussic acid pistol – A bullet with a red ring – I take it from my pocket while the court is in session – A visit from Oberst Walter Nicolai, the former chief of the German intelligence service – Schellenberg doesn't want to acknowledge his actions – Character-wise, Nicolai is the exact opposite of Canaris – Conversations with General Reinhard Gehlen – The bombardment of the OKH "Zeppelin" – Gehlen, Bormann and the mysterious Werther.

Don't shoot!" The man who had just called out these words in German stepped out of the barn with his hands raised. He was a big fellow with glasses; he wore a Russian officer's jacket, was thin and unkempt. His boots and his pants were covered with dirt. Hauptmann von Schwerdtner, XXXVIII Army Corps' intelligence officer, recognized the man immediately; he had been searching for him in the Volkhov swamps near Lake Ilmen for months. He nodded to the interpreter and the man said slowly in Russian, "General Andrey Andreyevich Vlasov, give yourself up. Hauptmann von Schwerdtner asks you to hand over your weapons and military identity card."

The giant gestured with his head toward the barn door and said quickly in Russian, "The weapons are in there. I have no more ammunition."

And so General Vlasov, commander of the 2nd Guards Army, which consisted of nine rifle divisions, a tank brigade and two artillery regiments, was captured. Bitter battles had been fought against this army in this marshy Volkhov region from March to the end of May. Vlasov finally gave himself up on June 11, 1942.

I first met him two years later, shortly before Operation *Panzerfaust*. Adrian von Fölkersam, who spoke perfect Russian, had invited him to Friedenthal with several of his staff officers.

Much has been written about Vlasov and his movement, but the opinions expressed rarely correspond to the facts of the case. One must remember that General Vlasov was a career soldier. I talked to him at length, in German, which he spoke rather badly, or with the help of Fölkersam.

He was from a rural background, was born in 1900 and served in the infantry before graduating from the Frunse Academy, the Soviet general staff school, in 1930. Vlasov would most likely have been liquidated in 1937 when they arrested and did away with Marshalls Tukhachevsky and Blücher, along with 30,000 other officers who were seen as traitors, had he not been serving in the Far East at the time, more specifically under his friend Marshall Blücher in 1937-38. Blücher probably warned him in time. He also knew Konstantin Rokossovsky, the former officer candidate in the imperial army, whose background was known to Vlasov: he came from an old aristocratic family and not "from Warsaw, from a poor railroad family."

We faced each other in front of Moscow in November-December 1941: Vlasov commanded the 20th Army, which prevented us from taking the city, although we had captured Istra and Vysokovo. He related to me interesting details of Stalin's hasty flight, of the panic that then reigned in the Kremlin, and of the workers revolt that was suppressed by Beria's police units. Vlasov was then called "the saviour of Moscow!"

Fölkersam brought me the manifesto of the Vlasov movement, which the general had written in 1943: "The Russian committee calls for the following principles for the reorganization of Russia:

– Eradication of bolshevism, Stalin and his clique;

– an honorable peace with Germany;

– creation of a new Russia, without bolshevism, but also without capitalism, with the help of Germany and other peoples of the new Europe."

The committee proposed the following program for the reformation of Russia:

1. Elimination of forced labor, free right to work and labor-union organization.

2. Elimination of collective farms and return of the land to the farmers.

3. Restoration of commerce, of craftsman trade and of small industry.

4. Right of intellectuals to work freely in the interests of the people.

5. Social justice and the protection of all workers from exploitation.

6. Right to training and social insurance of all workers.

7. Elimination of terror and reintroduction of human rights.

8. Guarantee of freedom for all the peoples of Russia.

9. Amnesty and return home for all political prisoners.

10. Reconstruction of the villages and cities according to a government plan.

11. Reconstruction of the factories according to a government plan.

12. Cancellation of all debts incurred by Russia in secret agreements between Stalin and the Anglo-Saxons.

13. Guarantee of a minimum standard of living for all war-disabled and their families.

This "Manifest of Smolensk" was slightly amended in Prague on November 14, 1944.

I had the impression that Vlasov was one of those Russians who did not view Russia as an asiatic land and who wanted to see their nation take part in the building of a larger, more powerful Europe. He knew the Far East and it was clear to him what enormous power, but also what danger the still-sleeping China posed to his country and to all Europeans.

This theory scarcely fitted into certain racial theories held by Reichsführer Himmler, and which I always held to be utopian and dangerous. Vlasov told me that the officers and men of the czarist guards regiments were at least 1.8 meters tall, had blue eyes and stub noses, although they were not imported from Prussia. According to Vlasov the Russians themselves had to defeat bolshevism. Then the curse uttered by Dostoyevsky at the end of the last century would cease to have any validity.

When Fölkersam and I met him he had already ceased showing the greater Russian mentality, and he understood – even if somewhat hesitantly – that a land like the Ukraine, for example, which had its own established culture, had the right to govern itself, and that the Baltic States had never been Russian. "Socialism" was a different concept for the cossacks than for the other peoples of Russia, and the redistribution of land was a difficult problem to solve.

We had war. The Wehrmacht employed more than 500,000 Russian prisoners as auxiliary volunteers (Hiwis), who rendered great service in the rear areas. In the beginning Vlasov wanted all the Russian prisoners of war, including the Hiwis, placed under his command. He would have been able to form about 30 divisions in this way, which would have represented a great threat – not just to Germany, but to all of Europe. It was wiser to aim for smaller objectives.

I believe that Vlasov was very impressed by Stalin's speeches and by the entire Russian and British press. His general staff reinforced him in his opinion that he was an extraordinarily good politician and a great tactician and strategist.

They made very strong propaganda in favor of his ROA (Ruskaya Osvoboditelnaya Armia - Russian Army of Liberation) and numerous Russian deserters came to our troops or directly to the Vlasov battalions. Among these refugees there were of course stalinist agents, who proved to be the harshest critics of the bolshevik regime. A new committee was founded in Prague, the KONR (Komitet Osvobodydenya Naradov Russi – Liberation Committee of the Russian Peoples).

Seen from a European point of view, Vlasov's ideas and goals were extremely interesting. Besides, he held the view that, from the social point of view, the Marxist-Leninist system had been completely overtaken. The main thing for General Vlasov was to get rid of Stalin and his regime, which held the Russian people in worse slavery than in the time of the czars. His army was to be a "socialist army of liberation."

Vlasov made his best impression on me when he explained his arguments logically and precisely. He was neither mercenary nor fanatic, he was a realist. "We need you," he said to me, "because you have the weapons and are fighting Stalin – but you also need us!"

He was very critical of Stalin. He knew that the STAVKA had first-class information at its disposal, supplied by outstanding spy organizations.

"We were not in a position," he said to us, "to make full use of all this outstanding information. Stalin, Voroshilov, Budenny and his circle are mediocre strategists. Stalin has named Boris Shaposhnikov to the general staff because he had Tukhachevsky sentenced to death. But he came to the general staff in 1910 and is an officer of the old czarist school. To Stalin a regiment, a division and even an army is just cannon fodder to weaken the enemy. All that matters is the 'politruk,' the front, which the herd forces forward. It is always a mass slaughter. Our people is bleeding to death. Our captured countrymen aren't protected by the arrangements of the International Red Cross, as Russia never signed these agreements, and are seen by the party as traitors."

The problem of the Russian prisoners – we had about 5 million – was really unsolvable in many cases. It was tremendously difficult for the German supply organization to provide for these men at the front, as even our own troops weren't being supplied regularly. As well we knew that our prisoners in the USSR were being treated brutally and with systematic cruelty, which Vlasov regretted deeply.

He complained that we still weren't according him our full trust even though he had spontaneously offered to fight against Stalin. I heard from Vlasov from time to time after this long conversation. But since my activities had little in common with his, I never saw him again personally, though my staff officers later held various discussions with Vlasov's staff.

In my opinion they should have used the Russian anti-stalinist prisoners – there really were many – as soldiers and formed companies and battalions. However beyond battalion strength the use of the Russian volunteers at the front could have become very dangerous.

Toward the end of the war Vlasov commanded two divisions in the north of Czechoslovakia. The 1st Division was under the command of General Bunitshenko and the other under General Truchin. A Russian fighter squadron was commanded by Colonel Maltsev.

One recalls the sudden about-face that these two divisions made against us near Prague on May 1, 1945. The Russians played the same role as the Romanians a year before, and the situation would have become very serious had Schörner, who had just been promoted to field marshall, not ordered energetic countermeasures.

I don't believe that the very realistic Vlasov thought in all seriousness that an about-face "in extremis" could save him. He knew Stalin all too well for that. He merely wanted to use the ensuing confusion to gain several days time and make it possible for his units to escape to the west.

I was kept informed about the Prague affair, for at the request of Generalfeldmarschall Schörner, whom I met in his headquarters near Olmütz, I and what was left of my Commando Unit East II, about 100 men, were entrusted with the task of blowing up a bridge on the autobahn near Breslau, which was already in enemy hands. After carrying out its mission, our commando unit had to make its way through the Russian lines. Our "commandos" fought on grimly from April 15 to May 15, 1945 and were among the last fighters in this great war. They withdrew slowly, engaging enemy tanks until four to five days after the Wehrmacht's surrender, in order to cover the retreat of a column of refugees. The column was being pursued by the Soviet *soldateska*, who spared nothing and no one – neither there nor elsewhere.

During the retreat to Eger and the Czechoslovak-German border our volunteers saw how Vlasov's people were fighting their way to the west in small groups and in German uniforms. A certain number got through and were not handed back to the Soviets.

On the other hand, Vlasov and his staff were handed over to the Russians. It was a personal order from General Eisenhower, who consulted Washington after General Patton had issued Vlasov a letter of safe conduct. Stalin had Vlasov and his staff officers hung on August 12, 1946. Many of Vlasov's soldiers were sent to labor camps in Siberia. Several of these were fellow sufferers of Alexander Solzhenitsyn, who in his book *The Gulag Archipelago* described the suffering of these men who had wanted to put an end to Stalinism.

Solzhenitsyn admits that mass deportations and killings were begun by Lenin in 1920 and were continued by Stalin, and that concentration camps always existed in the Soviet Union. But who worries about that today?

The cossacks, whether from the Kuban, the Terek, the Don or the Urals, were always disposed to be anti-communist. In May 1918 the Don Cossacks asked for the protection of the Central Powers, who had recognized the independence of the Ukraine. Generaloberst von Eichhorn set up a military protectorate there and the cossacks took the field against bolshevik troops. At this time Oberst von Kress held the Batum – Tiblisi – Baku railway line, the transportation link to the oil region of the Caucasus.

The cossack people lived in communities in the form of clans. The entire family always followed the soldiers. During the Second World War about 30,000 cossacks fought under the command of General Helmuth von Pannwitz, whom they themselves chose to be "Ataman."

These people were completely cheated by the English after the surrender. They allowed themselves to be disarmed in the belief that they were being sent to Italy. In this way 50,000 members of the cossack "clans" were handed over to the Soviets at the end of May 1945. The English kept their horses for themselves.

General von Pannwitz and the cossack leaders were tried – soon after Vlasov and his staff. On January 16, 1947 Moscow announced that Generals T.I. Domanov and S.N. Krasnov, Lieutenant-General A.B. Skuro, the "Ataman" P.N. Krasnov, who was chief of the White Guard units during the civil war of 1918-1921, General Sultan Girej Klytsch, the commander of the "Daredevil Division," and of course General von Pannwitz, had been executed.

In this way the English finished what the cheka troops had begun in 1920-21, when they decimated, massacred and carried off cossacks from the Don to the Urals.

About 130,000 members of various Russian ethnic groups fought in the ranks of the Waffen-SS: Ukrainians, Russians, Turkmenes, Tartars, Kirghezians, Crimean Tartars, Georgians, Uzbeks and so on. But Vlasov was never seen by the soldiers of these various ethnic groups as their military commander, only the Russians did so.

Those who accuse Hitler of erring in not giving the Ukraine its freedom are undoubtedly correct. However this would first have required a credible Ukrainian government. When I was in Kiev in 1941 a dozen tiny groups were struggling for dominance: each group wanted to govern alone and in opposition to the others. One wanted a monarchy and a Romanov, the other a "solid republic," the third a democracy, and so on. Among the immigrants from the west there were certainly some good political brains, but they were unknown in the Ukraine, where a man like Gauleiter Koch, supported by Bormann, was able to do his foul work. Alfred Rosenberg supported the idea of a free Ukrainian state and wanted to reintroduce the Ukrainian language, which had been banned from books, newspapers and schools since Alexander II's "Ukas" of 1876. Himmler, Bormann and Koch were against it. After giving the matter a great deal of consideration, the Reichsführer proposed that Sevastopol should henceforth be called "Theoderichshafen" – after the Gothic king! That was what he was concerned about!

At the end of 1943 Fölkersam asked me to speak to Minister Rosenberg. Rosenberg was also of baltic origin and was Reich minister for the administration of the eastern territories. He was later burdened with all the errors and mistakes that Koch and others had committed there. At Nuremberg he was sentenced to death by hanging; his ashes were thrown into the Isar River. Fölkersam and I pointed out to Rosenberg that the real reason behind the Russian partisan movement was none other than Koch himself: through his "Commissariat of the Central Ukraine" (Kiev, Dniepropetrovsk) he had drafted 200,000 industrial and 300,000 agricultural forced laborers for Germany! The German administration also showed little understanding of the mentality of the people in the Baltic States. Rosenberg was a man of good will. He asked us to report to him all the mistakes and errors we knew of, which we did. But unfortunately he was not a good organizer, and his book *Myth of the Twentieth Century* proved that he lacked any sense of reality.

It was a great mistake to send Koch, Gauleiter of East Prussia, into the Ukraine. Strangely he was tried in Poland and was said to have been executed in 1959. On the other hand one still hears that he is alive in a Polish prison![1]

The Ukraine, a mainly agrarian land of 601,000 square kilometers and 49 million inhabitants, had suffered greatly under the Soviet system through the "collectivization" of its territory. Millions of "Kulaks," small landowners, were liquidated, first by Dzherzhinsky's

Cheka under Lenin, then by the Yagoda's and Yezhov's GPU. Solzhenitsyn places the number of farmers who were driven from their lands through "collectivization" at 15 million. About four million farmers starved to death during the great crop failures of 1932-33.

The Ukrainians have scarcely stopped fighting against communism and for their own independence since 1917. As in 1918, in 1934 they also sought the support of Germany, which then supported the "National Ukrainian Organization" (OUN) under Colonel Konovalets. This passionate man turned to the wrong man when he trusted Admiral Canaris. He was killed: on May 23, 1938 a "German secret agent," in reality a Soviet agent, gave him a package which contained a bomb.

In November 1939 we freed all the young Ukrainian nationalists languishing in Polish prisons. Among them was Stefan Bandera, who had been sentenced by the Polish government, first to death, then to life imprisonment. Bandera was about thirty years old and soon afterward became the leader of the "Ukrainska Povstanka Armia" (Ukrainian Insurgent Army). Logically Koch's "working style" was not to his taste. He and several comrades were arrested by the German police in July 1941, taken to Berlin and subsequently to Sachsenhausen concentration camp. Bandera was unjustly accused of being a minion of Canaris and Lahousen. He wasn't freed until 1944, by which time Canaris and Lahousen had been exposed. Bandera took control of the UPA and began a pitiless struggle against the Soviet armies.

● ● ●

During the summer of 1944, when the Eastern Front collapsed under the Russian offensive, it was reported to us in Friedenthal that small and medium sized units had no chance of retreating in the chaos that ensued. Without ammunition or supplies, most of them were destroyed or captured. Only small, determined battle groups succeeded in reaching our lines: about 1,000 in all, consisting of 12-15,000 soldiers.

The group which risked the most extraordinary retreat was that of Feldwebel Johannes Diercks of the 36th Infantry Regiment, a unit which supported the remnants of the 20th Panzer Division. Diercks left the Beresina on June 27, 1944. His people divided themselves into various battle groups, which included the crew of a shot-down

He 111 and a battalion of the 52nd Howitzer Regiment. They hid themselves in swamps and forests and fought like mad against the Soviet troops. When Diercks reached the area of the 107th Infantry Division in East Prussia he had just four survivors with him. All five were injured, but had hung onto their weapons. The date was August 14, 1944.

At about the same time Generaloberst Jodl informed me that another relatively large German unit was still fighting in the forest northwest of Minsk, even though the city had fallen into enemy hands on July 3. I will return to this unit in the next chapter. The German army group in Northern Ukraine was commanded by Generalfeldmarschall Walter Model. At the beginning of July 1944 Hitler also placed him in command of Army Group Center. I met Model during the Ardennes offensive. He chose to take his own life on April 21, 1945 rather than surrender to American forces, after ensuring that his officers and men, who were surrounded on the Ruhr, were able to end the battle in an honorable fashion at the end of March.

Model was an outstanding defensive commander; he was capable of improvising even in the most difficult situations. But he couldn't stop the red tide flooding over the Ukraine.

At the beginning of autumn 1944 we in Friedenthal were informed that groups of German soldiers whose retreat had been cut off had joined Bandera's partisans. Among the survivors were volunteers of the 14th Waffen-SS Division Galizien, which had been formed from Ukrainian and Ruthenian volunteers in 1943. Their insignia was the Galician lion with three crowns – the trident of the Holy Vladimir. In August 1944 the Galizien Division fought courageously in the Tarnov pocket, alongside the Waffen-SS Division Horst Wessel and a French battle group of the Waffen-SS Division Charlemagne, all of whom did their duty bravely.[2]

I decided to form a commando unit, whose mission it would be to find Bandera and negotiate with him. Our idea was to organize the German soldiers into small groups, which would do their best to reach the German front lines. In any case the UPA would receive medical supplies, weapons and ammunition from us, and the seriously wounded could be flown out from improvised airfields.

I selected Hauptmann Kern to lead the commando unit; he came from the army and had served in the Brandenburg Division. Kern spoke Russian and Polish. His team consisted of a dozen NCOs and

German soldiers and about twenty proven anti-Stalinist Russians from my Commando Unit East, altogether about thirty well-trained, determined volunteers. They were provided with Russian uniforms, boots, tobacco and false papers. With their shaved heads and two-week beards they looked like real Russian soldiers. We dubbed this operation Brauner Bär (Brown Bear).

Kern's commando unit crossed our front lines in December 1944 in eastern Czechoslovakia. Two weeks later we received the first coded radio message from Kern. He had found Bandera. He had firm control over a rather large area of forest and mountains about 50 kilometers by 20. He had organized his base of operations very quickly – thanks to the cadres he employed (among them were numerous officers of the Galizien Division) and the sympathy of the population, which was disposed to be decidedly anti-Russian and even more so anti-communist. I had a friend from Vienna among these officers, a battalion commander of the Galizien Division. Unfortunately Kern was unable to contact him and so I have no idea of his subsequent fate.

Bandera refused to release our soldiers and let them break through to our lines in the west: he needed them. The "Supreme Council of the Ukrainian Independence Movement" (*Ukrainska Holovna Vyzvolna Rada*), consisting of 25 members representing the various Ukrainian factions, had already decided that the training camps and officer schools should be run by German officers. For their part, almost all of our NCOs were placed in command of a "*sotnia*" or company.

On the other hand Bandera declared himself willing to allow our wounded to be evacuated. His people cleared a landing strip in the forest. However by the time it was ready, the Luftwaffe unit at my disposal, Kampfgeschwader 200, had no fuel left! All that we could do was drop medics with medical supplies, medicines, arms and ammunition. I instructed Kern and his commando unit to return. The "Brown Bear" came back in mid-March under extremely difficult conditions, for the unit had to pass through a combat zone held by Petrov's army. Nevertheless, Kern lost only five men. Not a single Russian deserted. Obviously at the end of the war we supplied all our foreign volunteers with the necessary papers to let them pass themselves off as forced laborers, thus preventing them from being handed over to the Russians by the allies.

Who will one day write the story of the UPA and Stefan Bandera? In my opinion the UPA faced a much more difficult task then Tito in Yugoslavia, who received every possible form of material aid from the Anglo-Saxons. In the heyday of his organization, from 1946 to 1948, Bandera had more than 80,000 soldiers under his command, of which 10-12,000 were German. But he was completely isolated: he was no longer receiving weapons, ammunition and medical supplies from us. The UPA procured new supplies by attacking Soviet convoys. This true army fought on until 1952, with no hope of help from the west.

The Ukrainian farmer worked the very fertile soil of what was known as the "black earth region," whose 1.5-meter-thick layer of humus, the *Chernosem*, extended from the Carpathians to the Urals. This "black earth" was formed by flooding at the edge of the retreating glaciers after the last ice age. The Ukrainian farmers became "kholkoze functionaries" after their frequent uprisings in the period 1922-1937 were bloodily suppressed; but they obtained a certain freedom under the German occupation – even in the central Ukraine under Koch's administration! True agrarian reform was impossible during the war years; the problems were not just of an agricultural nature. However, in those areas where Koch could not exert his authority and which were beyond Himmler's fantasies – he had not the faintest idea of what the Ukraine was like – reasonable, local solutions to the problems were found: in Northern Bukovina and in Southern Ukraine (Odessa), which were under Romanian administration, in Western Ukraine (Lvov), which was incorporated into the Polish *Generalgouvernement* under Frank, and especially in the Eastern Ukraine (Kharkov).

The complete failure of the collective farm system was obvious: for example, 7 million farmers in the United States produced more than the 40 million "farmer-workers" of the Soviet Union. The fact is that the former sometimes had to feed the USSR. It is also a fact that the Soviet "farmer-workers" now had a right to a piece of ground "for their home use." Nowadays large cities like Kiev, Kharkov and Moscow are supplied with fresh vegetables from these small "private plots."

The Ukrainians only wanted to become masters of "their" land, which they had farmed for generations and which had, in some cases, belonged to them since the times of the Austro-Hungarian monarchy and the empires of the Romanovs. That was their crime! They wanted to speak their own language, practice their own religion and follow their own customs. The Ukrainian people could only survive as an independent nation. That is what they fought for, fully aware that they would be ruthlessly opposed by the Russian *and* the Polish governments. And that is what happened. The struggle by Bandera and his partisans, which was one of the saddest and most terrible chapters in this unknown side of the war, is impossible to understand if one tries to ignore these truths. In 1946-47 Bandera had more than 200,000 partisans under his command. If they did not all fight, it was only because they lacked weapons and ammunition. But many men – and women as well – preferred to fight and possibly die than languish in a prison or concentration camp.

The press of the victorious western powers dedicated a scant few lines to the people of the Ukraine when, from May 1945 to August 1951, they fell victim to the mass destruction carried out by the Russian and Polish military police. The allies ignored the wrecked villages, the burnt-out farmhouses and other despicable acts – all carried out by Soviet troops. These cruel measures also explain the desperate resistance by the UPA. Anyone who hasn't fought in Russia will find this hard to understand.

Not until 1954 was part of the truth revealed, when a committee in New York published its first report: *The Ukrainian Insurgent Army in its Fight for Freedom.*

The persecution of the Ruthenian Catholic Church reached its climax in May-June 1946. A forcibly-held synod decided that the church should merge with the Orthodox Church after a vote by 216 priests – out of a total of 2,714. The other 2,489 priests had been arrested or killed or had chosen armed resistance with Bandera.

On January 29, 1944 a strong UPA force attacked a Soviet armored train near Kiev. The commander of the military district, General Vatutin, was killed. He was replaced by General Zhukov. Swierczewskij, another Soviet general and Marshal Rokossovsky's adjutant in the Polish war ministry, who was infamous for his ruthless suppression of Polish nationalism, was likewise killed on March 28. During the Spanish Civil War Swierczewskij had commanded the International Brigade under the name "General Walter." His adjutant was a Frenchman by the name of Marty, alias "the butcher of Albacete." The cruelty of these two men was directed not just at

Franco's troops and Spanish Nationalist civilians, but also against the militia soldiers of the International Brigade and against Republicans who "deviated from Moscow's course."

The UPA did not just fight Soviet troops, but also the military and the police of the Polish communist government, which put the 7th, 8th and 9th Infantry Divisions, a division of the KBW (Polish Internal Security Corps) police, tanks and aircraft into the field against Bandera. Stalin had previously intervened at the end of 1945 with nine infantry divisions, a tank brigade and a motorized division of the NKVD. From May to September the UPA fought more than 80 battles and lost 5,000 men (killed and wounded); the Soviet losses, however, were 7,400 killed and more than 9,000 wounded. During the night of October 31, 1945 the UPA captured Stanislavov, the former capital of Wolhynien.

From Ukrainian Christmas Day, January 7, until October 1946 the UPA was forced to fight more than 1,000 battles: bolshevik losses were more than 15,000 killed. In 1947 Stalin sent two new police divisions against Bandera. The situation became so serious that the three Soviet governments – Russian, Polish and Czechoslovakian – were forced to sign a treaty against the Bandera movement. They decided to draw up a common war plan to strike down once and for all this courageous Ukrainian who refused to accept communism. The red terror became even worse, but the west scarcely took notice. The UPA's last battles took place in July 1952 in the area of the Podolish Marshes: Stalin had despatched two police divisions and a flamethrower brigade.

● ● ●

On October 15, 1959, at about 3 P.M., the tenant of Kreittmayr Strasse Number 7 in Munich walked up the stairs leading to his second-floor apartment. He was Herr Stefan Popel, a very quiet man. Just as he was about to open his door he noticed that the key would not go into the keyhole. An individual came running up the stairs behind him, reached the landing and said, "You'd better get a locksmith!"

Popel turned around to find the man holding a pistol under his nose. There was a slight hiss and Popel fell down the stairs. He never had a chance to raise a hand in defense.

He was found dead an hour later. His body showed no signs of injury and the public-health officer concluded death by embolism. But the police knew that Herr Popel was none other than the political refugee Stefan Bandera. There was speculation that he had been poisoned or had taken his own life until 1961. That year "an agent of the KGB chose the path to freedom." He called himself Stakinsky and admitted to having killed at least two Ukrainian nationalist leaders: Lew Rebet and Bandera, who met his end the same way as Konovalets. Stakinsky used a prussic acid pistol.

Stakinsky came before a criminal court, where in defense of the acts he had committed he declared that, "he had acted on orders." He was sentenced to eight years imprisonment. Many accused Germans at Nuremberg and other military courts of the western allies, who had likewise acted on orders, were convicted and executed. But they weren't members of the KGB!

After a seven-year struggle against the UPA with military and police units, the Soviets finally overcame the Ukrainian patriots. They had Konovalets and Bandera killed, but they weren't able to eliminate the Ukrainian people. The world press stayed silent, even though from 1952 thousands of Ukrainians were arrested and deported year after year. There were bloody uprisings in Southern Ukraine in 1972. In June of that year several thousand workers went on strike in Dnieprodzherzhinsk. They attacked and set on fire several party buildings: the headquarters of the Comsomol (communist youth) and those of the KGB and the MVD (security police). The masses of people sang the anthem of the UPA. In September and October of the same year there were further, extremely violent demonstrations in Dniepropetrovsk, one of the most important industrial centers of the central Ukraine. The rebels took over some parts of the city; the police opened fire and more than 50 people were killed. The "Drujniks," auxiliary police recruited from within the ranks of the Comsomol, had to be mobilized.

There were fresh manifestations of Ukrainian discontent in 1973 – this time by the collective farmers of the Southern Ukraine. The world press remained silent.

However in 1963 I was accused by the communist press of "having had during the war a silent pistol that fired poison needles." I need not say that no such pistol ever existed in Germany. As the story went I intended to shoot Stalin with it. Furthermore, dozens of newspapers in the eastern block maintained that I had tested this "needle pistol" on inmates at the Sachsenhausen concentration camp. In what moral category do people belong who could imagine that my comrades and I were capable of shooting at defenseless people? In the war we waged, I always tried to avoid bloodshed on both sides, an undertaking in which I was successful to some degree by exploiting the elements of surprise. At the front I faced the enemy, like my comrades. I would like to repeat at this point that our opponents were very brave: this applied to Tito's partisans as well as to the Russian and American soldiers.

Is it possible then, that the people who were trying to hang evil acts on me did not notice that they were exposing their own meanness? Did these people ever fight? Did they ever face death on the battlefield? I scarcely think so.

In truth the sensation-seeking journalists raised and falsified charges against me that were the same as those which the good Mr. Rosenfeld, the American prosecutor, had brought against me sixteen years earlier at Nuremberg. He did his utmost to convict me then – but without success!

This prosecutor Rosenfeld grilled a very young soldier, who had served in my units, over and over until he finally "admitted": "they also gave us poisoned ammunition."

I asked my defense attorney, the American Colonel Durst, to have the witness state exactly how he claims to have recognized the poisoned ammunition.

"That is very easy," answered the young soldier, "there was a red ring between the casing and the bullet."

Lieutenant-Colonel Durst spoke with me briefly and then told the court that he reserved the right to question the witness the next day. I was very familiar with this round with the red ring and couldn't be angry with the boy on account of his statement; he was surely unaware of its gravity and potential consequences for me and my comrades.

It was up to me, the accused, to show proof that Mr. Rosenfeld's accusations were false. We had to act very quickly. At Dachau many prisoners left the camp under guard for daily labor service; some of my friends passed on my instructions. In court the next day Lieutenant-Colonel Durst had the young soldier called to the stand again. Then I took a red-ringed bullet, which had been smuggled in to me in a piece of bread, from my pocket. There was a moment of surprise and Mr. Rosenfeld began asking scandalous questions. Lieutenant-Colonel Durst interrupted him, "It is completely irrelevant to know *how* this bullet came into our possession. All that matters is that the court is informed about its characteristics. I ask the high court to allow the witness to examine this bullet closely and to tell us whether it is in fact one of the bullets which were issued to the officers and men on Colonel Skorzeny's order from time to time."

The witness confirmed this immediately.

"Yes. This is one of the poisoned bullets that we received in Friedenthal."

"Witness," began Durst again, "your statement is very important. Please look at the bullet again and then tell us whether you are quite certain that you haven't made a mistake. Is it really one of the special bullets that you say contained poison and which was issued to you?"

"I am absolutely certain."

"Very good! I thank you. I ask the high court to allow the accused to give several explanations."

I explained that this type of bullet was in no way poisoned and was only a so-called "waterproof" bullet. Because the bullets were completely watertight, we issued them to members of commando units who were likely to get wet in the course of their missions. The analysis requested by my attorney and the court confirmed this. The red circle prevented this ammunition from being confused with other, normal bullets. I would also like to add at this point that no unit of the Wehrmacht ever used prussic acid pistols or other weapons of this type.

In 1941-42 we found prussic acid bullets on Russian partisans. They were revolver bullets, whose tips were slit into four parts and which contained prussic acid. The previously-mentioned Arthur Nebe, the chief of Office V of the RSHA, had several hundred of these bullets manufactured in the criminal police laboratory, and I received about two-hundred of them. My officers received one of these bullets when they had missions to carry out in which they might be captured or tortured. These bullets were very easy to recognize, not by a red ring, but by a cross marked on the tip of the bullet. I myself had one, the last round in the magazine. When I voluntarily surrendered to the U.S. Army on May 22, 1945 and laid my pistol on the desk of the American officer, I warned him, "Careful! It's loaded and the last bullet is dangerous!"

I explained to him why.

Progress is unstoppable. After the war the Soviets built and perfected a battery-operated pistol which fired cyanide gas under pressure from a pulverized charge. This poison was absorbed by the mucous membranes and the skin and was spread throughout the body by the blood in minutes; the blood vessels contracted and caused death. This is how Bandera was killed.

Before the murder Stakinski took atropine pills, an effective antitoxin, as a precaution. Unfortunately this is not something from an Ian Fleming novel.

● ● ●

The Soviet intelligence service has long employed a method that is now all too well known: first they have it printed that the victim committed suicide; but an even more cunning ruse is to declare that the victim was murdered by enemies of the Soviets. Since 1942 it was known that the Polish officers killed in a mass execution in the Katyn Forest had been executed by the Soviets. However the Soviet prosecutors in Nuremberg did not hesitate to lay this mass murder at the feet of the Germans, and international historians merely "harbored doubts" until just a few years ago. Apparently they didn't want to read and cite the official reports on this mass murder (especially the Polish, American, English[3] and Swiss documents).

After the murder of Bandera, and before Stakinski came before the criminal court, General Reinhard Gehlen's intelligence service was accused of the crime. However the BND (Federal German Intelligence Service) was a powerful organization and few put much faith in this accusation. Before I evoke several memories, I would like to tell of an astonishing visit I received in Friedenthal in January 1944: the visitor was General (Special Duties) Walter Nicolai.

When they told me of the arrival of "General Nicolai," it wasn't immediately clear to me that it was the former Oberst Nicolai, the head of German military intelligence in the First World War. I had thought he was dead.

But he wasn't dead. He was no phantom, but a ghost. To this day I can still see him before me, with his blue eyes and his white hair in a brush cut and his extremely lively look. When he sat down opposite me I noticed one detail: like my father, he wore leggings over his shoes, of the type that had become popular twenty years before. We talked about the freeing of Mussolini.

"I believe," he said, "that before you freed the Duce one of the main difficulties was locating him. I had said to myself for a long time that the Italians were trying to lead you down the wrong path." I admitted that I should in fact have convinced Hitler, as they had also given him false information.

"Falsely informed," he observed with a smile, "that happens sometimes. But it shouldn't be allowed to happen too often."

I was of the same opinion, but didn't understand: Canaris hadn't yet been exposed. I explained to him what our objective was in Friedenthal: imaginative commando operations exploiting the element of surprise within the normal rules of warfare. Nicolai, who was then over seventy years old, listened with enthusiastic attention and interjected to point out that our activities needed completely accurate information as a foundation. To my amazement he also said that he would be pleased if he could be useful to me in any way and would gladly work with me. When I told Schellenberg of this he stuck his nose in the air and declared, "One can see that you're still a beginner. Nicolai is much too big a catch! Admiral Canaris can't stand him nor can the Reichsführer by the way. He knows too much about the west and even more about the east."

"One more reason," I said, "not to reject his services. Why should we not make use of his experience?"

"His former contacts in the east, made at the time of the Treaty of Brest-Litovsk, make him somewhat suspect." At my request General Nicolai gave two or three lectures to the officers at Friedenthal. He recalled past events, spoke in a witty way about his experiences and his views and about the importance of strategic information, be it of a military, political, scientific or psychological nature, and of the necessity of tactical intelligence, which relates to every single operation and eventually affects general strategy. This data must be a compilation of many and varied types of information, therefore a synthesis must be made as quickly and as accurately as possible. He considered information on the enemy the most important element in a modern war. For him the main value of a piece of information lay in its reliability and clarity. As well, however, such information could only be used at a certain time and within a certain area. It was more dangerous to use false information than to receive none at all.

Nicolai noted that a surprise advance, which was planned after careful consideration and with imagination – not contrived in the midst of a major battle – also made a great impression on the enemy. This was a new way of conducting warfare, one which general staffs unfortunately gave little thought to.

When I read today that General Nicolai had a high opinion of Admiral Canaris I can only shrug my shoulders: he was much too refined to accuse Canaris personally. But in the course of a conversation he said to me:

"You know, Skorzeny, an officer doesn't serve a regime. He serves his fatherland, whatever its political form may be. To attack the existing regime in time of war is clearly treason."

This was so obvious to me that in January 1944 I asked Nicolai why he had spoken of it. I can assure the reader that I never would have thought that Nicolai might sympathize with bolshevism; quite the contrary. He was a first-class officer of "the old school." I found him to be an upright man, whose character was an odd contrast to the ambiguous nature of a Canaris and the prevarications of a Schellenberg. In the (spurious) memoirs of Schellenberg, who placed himself completely at the service of the English, one can read that "Nicolai's small office on the Potsdamer Platz was one the most important centers working for the Soviet intelligence service" – and that was in 1943! Is so, why didn't they ever arrest General Nicolai?

In the course of the three or four conversations I had with him, I was able to ascertain that he was highly intelligent. And as far as his current reputation in international intelligence services, I can only say that it is worldwide and much greater than that of Canaris. Apart from that I had other things to do during the war besides worry about spies and counter-intelligence. I must state one thing, however: it is completely absurd for anyone to claim, as Schellenberg did, that Nicolai organized a pro-Soviet spy net on the Potsdamer Platz during the war. And when Schellenberg adds that "Gestapo chief Müller had Nicolai and his pro-Soviet net watched," it is simply laughable. If that's the case I think they should have had Müller watched too!

• • •

Not only was "Zeppelin" the name for the mass interrogations carried out by Department C of the RSHA's Office VI among the five million Russian POWs in German hands, as I described previously (Part II, Chapter 6), but it was also the code-name for OKH headquarters in Zossen, about 20 kilometers south of Berlin, at the end of 1944.

This was a small, hidden city with identical, squat, concrete buildings hidden among lawns, gardens and trees. Every building was built to the same design: the rows of rooms had a door every 10-12 meters leading to a central hallway, which had steep stairs leading to the air raid shelter.

About three-thousand officers worked in "Zeppelin" under the command of General Krebs, deputy to Generaloberst Guderian, whom Hitler had named Army Chief-of-Staff after the assassination attempt of July 20.

General Krebs' office occupied part of one building and the office of General Gehlen (Foreign Armies East) the other. Several hundred officers worked in the information department for the Eastern Front. Reinhard Gehlen was never a convinced national-socialist, although, like Heusinger, he worked under Halder as a department head in the general staff. He never really took the talk of a possible putsch seriously. General Guderian rightfully placed great stock in his information concerning the Eastern Front. He nevertheless attracted the suspicion of Hitler – who had become extremely distrustful after the 20th of July – not only because he owed his career to Generaloberst Franz Halder, but because he had married Herta von Seydlitz, a relative of General von Seydlitz, in 1931. General Seydlitz's behavior at Stalingrad is well-known. Together with Paulus, he was one of the leaders of the "National Committee for a Free Germany," based in Moscow, while a prisoner of war.

I consulted the future chief of the BND during preparations for all the operations we planned in the east as a commando unit, and I got on well with him. I would like to contribute one anecdote.

On March 13, 1945 I drove to "Zeppelin" with Oberstleutnant Walther, Fölkersam's successor. I can't recall precisely which commando unit missing behind Russian lines we were worrying about, whether it was Braune Bär or a unit involved in Operation Freischütz.

We found ourselves alone with General Gehlen in this large room with huge windows. All three of us stood bent over the staff map of the Eastern Front spread out on the table and probably overheard the air raid sirens howling. It was about twelve noon.

The first bomb fell about 100 meters from the building we were in, and the three of us quickly crawled under the table. Several seconds later the blast wave from the next bomb shattered all the windows; broken glass flew in all directions.

"That was quite close," observed Walther.

Just then General Gehlen got up without saying a word, ran to the door and disappeared. We got to our feet, stepped out into the hall and were soon standing in front of the locked armored door of the bunker. We knocked forcefully and the door was finally opened by a soldier. Inside sat the general; quite calmly he said, "Where were you then gentlemen?"

"Herr General," said Walther. "We were worried about you and looked for you everywhere. We're happy to see you here safe and sound."

It struck me that many staff officers were quite allergic to bombardments. I must admit that I wasn't especially fond of them either. Not that a general staff officer was more frightened than a mere mortal or a soldier – and General Gehlen was certainly a brave man. I merely mean to say that a general staff officer feels insulted in a certain way if he becomes a target like a common soldier. We laughed about this incident, but there were victims in the other wing of "Zeppelin." Among them was General Krebs, who was injured rather badly.

In 1971 Reinhard Gehlen published a book of recollections under the title *Der Dienst*. There one reads that the mysterious informant working for the Red Orchestra spy net was none other than...Reichsleiter Martin Bormann, the head of the party chancellery. This thesis is practically insupportable. Bormann didn't have the means to learn of Hitler's military decisions fast enough and pass them on to Rössler so quickly. The STAVKA surely turned to a highly-qualified military man, whose treachery cost the lives of thousands of soldiers – to say nothing of the civilians who were killed or carried away.

When Gehlen wrote his book – which was a disappointment by the way – it was certain that Bormann was dead, although in 1973 they were still looking for him in all of South America, even among the natives of the Amazon. The BND has now admitted that Bormann is no longer among the living. I was aware of this fact and repeated it every time I was interrogated by the allies. I always considered him to be one of the most sinister people in Hitler's entourage. peace to his ashes.

I just ask myself why Reinhard Gehlen claimed that Bormann was the "conductor" in the OKW?

Notes

1. The correctness of this speculation was confirmed to us. (Editors' note)

2. The battle group of the *Charlemagne* Division, which came from the Neweklau training camp in Bohemia, suffered the following losses from August 15 to 25: of 19 officers, 7 were killed and 9 wounded; of 1,112 soldiers, 132 were killed, 601 wounded and 59 listed as missing. 41 were taken prisoner. The last units of the French Volunteer Legion (the LVF), which had distinguished itself in front of Moscow in 1941, fought on in June 1944; they were defeated in Mogilev and fell back to Borisov on the Beresina, where Napoleon's soldiers had fought a tragic battle during their famous retreat 132 years earlier. It was II Battalion of the LVF that took part in the defense of the Borisov Bridge, across which streamed refugees and wounded and fleeing soldiers. The Soviet air force and artillery obviously concentrated their efforts on Borisov. II Battalion was ordered to blow up the bridge, as well as two munitions dumps. It was able to join the rest of the LVF and made its way through the streets of Minsk, which had been entered by the first Soviet troops. Finally, after bitter day and night fighting, it finally succeeded in reaching Greifenberg in East Prussia. (Editors' note)

3. The secret report that the former English ambassador in the Soviet Union, Sir Owen O'Malley, sent to Churchill from Moscow on May 24, 1943 was released to the public in July 1972. The report states that the massacre of Polish officers at Katyn was clearly committed by the Russians. In the margins is the notation "KCD" in Anthony Eden's hand. This meant that the report by Sir Owen was to be shown to the King, the war cabinet and the dominions. The latter never learned of the report, and the others acted as if they had never read it. (Editors' note)

23

OPERATION FREISCHÜTZ

The Soviet summer offensive 1944 – Why Rokossovsky was able to cover 270 km in nine days – 21 German generals captured – Oberstleutnant Scherhorn refuses to surrender and assembles 2,000 men – "In a forest, northwest of Minsk..." – The four paratrooper groups of Operation Freischütz – Scherhorn found! – Fähnrich R. eats in the Soviet officers mess – Kampfgeschwader 200's mission – Untersturmführer Linder is decorated with the Knight's Cross – The "long march" of the lost legion – Final report from Linder: "I just want to hear your voices..." – My fears – Dr. Zoltan von Toth, a survivor of a Soviet concentration camp, gives more precise figures – The crime of being called Skorzeny: 10 years in prison camp – The sad fate of Dr. Heller.

Before Operation Brauner Bär we were kept busy by another unit behind the Soviet lines. At the end of August 1944 I received a teletype message urgently summoning me to Führer Headquarters. There Generaloberst Jodl introduced me to two staff officers who turned out to be Eastern Front specialists. These gave me a brief account of the drama that had been played out between Minsk and the Beresina, in the sector of the front defended by Army Group Center.

Jodl could not explain how it was possible that armored and motorized troops of the 1st and 2nd White Russian Armies under Sakhorov and Rokossovsky, which had attacked north of the Pripyat Marshes, had been able to reach Stolpce, 65 kilometers west of Minsk, which fell the next day, through the seam between the Fourth and

Ninth German Armies. Rokossovsky's motorized troops advanced 270 kilometers in nine days and breached our fronts.

In his *History of the Second World War*, Sir Basil Liddell Hart notes that contradictory information and orders were given by the conspirators to the various headquarters, and that "the events of July 20 had considerable negative effects on the Eastern Front as well as in the west."

Rado and Rössler's *Red Orchestra* kept the STAVKA well informed, and by June 1944 it had in its hands a detailed plan of our central sector. It was also not to be overlooked that the movement of enemy armor, which the Soviet generals ended with a pincer movement and which uncannily struck the weakest point of our positions, bore an astonishing similarity to the attacks ordered by Hitler in 1941 based on the plans of Manstein and Guderian. It was the same plan – but in reverse. The Russian army command had been quick to learn from us.

Hitler ordered General Model to the Eastern Front in February 1943 to save the 22 divisions of the Fourth and Ninth Armies, which were threatened with encirclement in the Rzhev bridgehead. From the 1st to the 22nd of February the general withdrew the divisions, fighting in such a way that losses were reduced to a minimum in spite of ceaseless attacks by ten Soviet armies. This was the so-called Operation Büffel (Bussard).

Once again Model's mission was to save whatever there was to be saved of these two armies and bring the front to a standstill. But this time the situation was significantly different. The field marshall found complete chaos; after the 20th of July a large part of the reason was morale.

Nevertheless, and I would like to stress this once again, there was no other solution for us but to fight on.

Even the disappearance of Hitler and the national-socialist regime could not change anything about our enemies' decision. The comments of several historians, who always label Hitler's orders to "offer maximum resistance" as "absurd," are not really correct. Any German head of state who was conscious of his responsibility to history would have issued the same orders in the face of the enemy's demand for an "unconditional surrender."

• • •

At Führer Headquarters they told me that part of the Fourth Army encircled in Minsk might break out. A radio report was picked up from one of our agents who had remained behind enemy lines: "In a forest northwest of Minsk there are German units which haven't surrendered." This information was confirmed by several survivors from the Minsk pocket. Finally we received more detailed information from a small group of men who had escaped via Vilna. "A battle group of about 2,000 men, which is probably commanded by Oberstleutnant Scherhorn, has withdrawn into a forest and is determined not to surrender and to fight its way through to our lines."

"Skorzeny," Generaloberst Jodl said to me, "unfortunately we don't know exactly where Oberstleutnant Scherhorn and his group are. Do you think that we would be able to find out and make contact with the group and rescue them?"

"Herr Generaloberst," I answered, "I assure you that we will do everything humanly possible – with the means that are at our disposal."

One first becomes conscious of the true scale of the catastrophe when one realizes that seven of the forty-seven generals of the Fourth and Ninth Armies and the Third Panzer Army were killed in action, among them general Pfeiffer, the commanding general of VII Army Corps. Two generals committed suicide, one was posted missing and 21 were captured. But Scherhorn did not surrender. People of his type, who were capable of assembling 2,000 men, all prepared to sell their lives at the highest cost, in the midst of chaos deserve to have their courage praised, and not only with words.

I had the opportunity to talk to a general who managed to reach our lines in East Prussia with the remnants of his division, a mere seventy men, after a 700-kilometer march.

He told me that his division had been surrounded southwest of Smolensk with two other divisions. The highest ranking general declared offhand that in his opinion, "they ought to surrender and immediately give themselves up to the Soviets." The other two generals tried all day to talk him out of it. As a result the breakout was attempted too late, without the necessary conviction of its success. As a result only minor elements escaped from the pocket. There was no doubt that Scherhorn and his men fell victim to the irresolution and hesitation of his superiors.

What were our chances of finding these brave soldiers, who had already been fighting "in a forest northwest of Minsk" for two months? Perhaps fifteen or twenty percent. But this limited chance had to be taken advantage of. I went to work immediately, and we named the operation Freischütz. Everyone at Friedenthal exhibited the same energy and enthusiasm as one felt when listening to the overture of the famous opera of the same name composed by Carl Maria von Weber.

The recently-formed "Commando Unit East I" Battalion was given the job of carrying out this mission.[1] Four groups, each of five men, two German volunteers and three proven anti-stalinist Russian soldiers, were formed. The eight German soldiers spoke Russian and smoked the Russian machorka cigarettes. Their heads were shaven. Each group was equipped with a radio.

The first group was under the command of SS-Oberscharführer P. At the end of August 1944 the group was dropped by parachute into the Minsk area near Borisov and Gevenj, after a 500-kilometer flight in an He 111 of Kampfgeschwader 200, which had been placed at my disposal. Its mission was to march in a westerly direction and search for Scherhorn.

That same night we were able to establish contact with P., who radioed: "Difficult landing. We are trying to assemble. Under machine-gun fire." Then nothing more. Not until six to eight weeks later did I learn during Operation Panzerfaust in Budapest that P. found the Scherhorn group, but that his radio had broken down the first day.

The second group was sent into the same area, but farther south, at the beginning of September. The group, which was commanded by SS-Oberjunker (officer candidate) Linder, had the same instructions as the first group, to head west. We received a radio message on the fourth night. After the exchange of recognition code words Linder reported: "Good landing. Scherhorn group found." One can imagine our joy – especially the next day when Scherhorn sent his personal appreciation. The third and fourth groups jumped in the days following the delivery of group two, before we received the news of Linder's success, into the Dzherzhinsk and Viteyka area. Their mission was to march east.

We heard nothing from group three, although we waited by our radios for weeks. They had disappeared into the endless expanses of Russia.

The fate of the fourth group, which was under the command of young Fähnrich R., was as surprising as it was sensational. First good news: excellent landing. R. reported that all five men were together. Then he reported that they had encountered Russian deserters, who took them for the same. They got along very well with their new comrades. R. learned that special units of the Russian military police were combing the Minsk area. On the second day he informed us that he was being forced to take another route. We gave our approval. Contact again on the third day: they were receiving aid from farmers. The war-weary White Russian population in this area supported their plan: on the fourth day – nothing more.

As a Baltic German, this action was very near to Adrian von Fölkersam's heart. He feared the worst – as did I. Two weeks later we received a telephone call from a unit on the Lithuanian border: "Group R. reports itself back with no losses." The radio had broken down and the fourth group had successfully travelled many hundreds of kilometers to reach our lines.

They hadn't found Scherhorn, but the information they brought us was of great importance. The soldiers had covered more than 300 kilometers in an occupied area where the enemy was preparing a new offensive. R.'s report proved that we could still learn a lot from the Russians: they were really serious about total war. And not only did they have American war materials, the entire Russian population was mobilized. One could see women and children rolling drums of gasoline to the front and passing shells from hand to hand in their artillery positions.

Dressed in the uniform of a Red Army lieutenant, R. accepted an invitation into an officers mess. The Red Army, which was no longer an army of the proletariat but an army of the Russian nation, had just reintroduced the officer's mess. The Soviet military hymn was also no longer the Internationale.

Back in Friedenthal, R. became one of the keenest helpers in the rescue of the Scherhorn group. The most urgent priority was to drop medical supplies for his numerous sick and wounded. The first drop went badly: our volunteer doctor broke both legs on landing. His death was reported to us several days later. A second doctor was able to reach the group with more medical supplies.

From now on an aircraft of Kampfgeschwader 200 took off for the east every two or three days to drop food, medicine and small arms ammunition. These supply flights always took place at night, and preferably when there was cloud cover. The pilots had to watch for a weak light signal, which posed a risk to those on the ground. It was not surprising that many supply containers failed to arrive.

During this time we worked on a rescue plan with the experts of Kampfgeschwader 200. The only possibility was to lay down a runway near the forest where our comrades were hiding. The He 111 was to land and gradually take out the sick and the wounded and then the soldiers. A volunteer Luftwaffe engineer parachuted in to direct the construction work. After several days of enthusiasm and general hope came the disappointing news that the strip had been discovered and that men had been killed and wounded in the constant attacks subsequently mounted by the enemy.

Then we agreed with Scherhorn that he should try to march to the lake-covered plateau on the former Russian-Lithuanian border near Dünaberg, about 250 kilometers to the north. If he arrived there at the beginning of December the frozen lakes could be used as runways. We had to make further drops of supplies: warm clothing, food and more ammunition for 2,000 men. Nine Russian volunteers expressed their willingness to join Scherhorn, each with a radio set.

At the end of November 1944 I was able to advise Linder that he had been promoted to Untersturmführer and had been awarded the Knight's Cross, which I was allowed to accept on his behalf.[2]

It was patently obvious that a march to the north through enemy territory by a group of 2,000 men must attract attention. Scherhorn was therefore instructed to split his group into two groups. The sick and wounded had to be transported in farm carts; they would move more slowly and were easier to attack. They therefore formed the rearguard under Fähnrich P., who after weeks of stumbling about had found the Oberstleutnant and our comrades and had made contact with us. The Oberstleutnant and Untersturmführer Linder would take over command of the group still capable of fighting and march as fast as possible.

It had become winter. We had more apprehensions than hopes as we followed the "long march" by our brave comrades. They had been under way since November and were occasionally spotted and attacked by Soviet special units. Both groups were forced to fight, then disappeared, changed the direction of their march, hid by day and moved by night. At night, at agreed-upon hours, they were supplied by Kampfgeschwader 200. We tried in principle to establish a grid square within which the supply containers were supposed to be dropped. But the groups advanced as fast they could, often deviating from the planned route, and it was difficult to find them again. Many supply drops, which we always had great difficulty organizing, were lost.

The groups marched constantly, taking every security measure, through swamps and forest, but scarcely made more than four to five kilometers per day. We followed this daily progress with concern, but we soon had the terrible feeling that our poor comrades would never return to Germany. We struggled to suppress these thoughts: such men deserved to stay alive.

For months we did our best to ease their misery and scrape up the fuel necessary for the supply flights. Soon there was only one flight a week. Then catastrophe struck us all. Kampfgeschwader 200's fuel supplies dried up. Although we tried everything, the supply drops had to be stopped.

In February 1945 we received a message from Untersturmführer Linder: "Lake plateau reached. Will starve if we don't soon receive supplies. Can you pick us up?" We could not. We had no more Heinkel and no fuel either. At that time I was commanding a division, which consisted of scraped-together soldiers, at Schwedt on the Oder. When I thought of how much fuel and food fell into enemy hands or was destroyed each day in the east and west, to the benefit of no one, I became furious. Back in Friedenthal our comrades sat by the radio night after night. All they could do now was receive messages; they could offer nothing to raise the hopes of the lost soldiers.

Then we had to leave Friedenthal and transfer our headquarters to southern Germany. The radio operators continued to listen wherever they were: the signals from the lost legion became ever weaker. The last message from Linder was heart-rending: he asked for nothing but some gasoline to power the motors used to charge the batteries of the radios: "I just want to stay in touch with you...hear your voices." It was April 1945. After that there was only silence.

• • •

In April and May 1945, and later as a prisoner of war, I often thought of Scherhorn and his brave soldiers and of our volunteers who had sacrificed themselves in an attempt to save 2,000 comrades. What became of them? Doubts grew in me. Of course all of the radio communications between Scherhorn and our radio operators were preceded by code-words, which were changed regularly as per our agreements. All the radio messages we received, even near the end, corresponded to these agreements. However in prison I learned a great deal about the interrogation methods of the victors, and I asked myself whether the Russian intelligence service hadn't been playing a so-called "radio game" with us the whole time. When the communist press later devoted a great deal of space to Scherhorn under the title "Soviets bluffed Skorzeny," that was for me, one familiar with Soviet methods, proof that my doubts had been completely unfounded.

At the beginning of 1973 I received a letter from a Hungarian military physician, Dr. Zoltan von Toth, from which the following extracts are taken.

Doctor Zoltan von Toth was captured by the Russians in Budapest on February 14, 1945. Sentenced by a Soviet court to twenty-five years forced labor, he was sent to several camps. In February 1946 he arrived at the camp in Pechora, about 200 kilometers south of Vorkuta in Siberia. Altogether about 30,000 prisoners lived in the camp – Germans, Hungarians, Bulgarians and so on. He "treated" about 600 seriously ill men in a barracks. Most of them were doomed to die because he had no medicines.

"Among them," wrote the doctor, "was, and I can remember him well, an officer of the Waffen-SS, Will Linder from Magdeburg. He was about twenty-six years old and was suffering from tuberculosis.

Under the prevailing conditions he was lost. He was an extremely intelligent young man."

Before he died in Pechora at the end of March 1946, Linder gave the doctor an account, which Dr. Toth repeated in his letter and which essentially said, "You were in fact in contact with Oberstleutnant Scherhorn until the end of April 1945 and provided the group with supplies. Linder was with Oberstleutnant Scherhorn in the first column, which made it to the lake plateau near Dünaburg. The second column, which was led by an officer from one of your commando units and whose name I can't recall," wrote the doctor, "arrived somewhat later. But it was February 1945, and only 800 men were left of Scherhorn's entire column; they waited in vain for rescue, then for supplies and finally for just a few words...

At the end of April 1945 the 800 officers and soldiers were surrounded and attacked by Russian police units. The fighting lasted several days, with heavy losses on both sides. Those who surrendered in the end were initially treated well and then were all sentenced to the usual twenty-five years of forced labor. Subsequently they were scattered among various camps: Scherhorn himself survived the wounds he had received in the final battle."

One can see that this account corresponds to what we learned from the radio messages.

Dr. Zoltan von Toth went on, "It will probably interest you to know that I met Generalmajor Lombart, who was also a prisoner. At the beginning of the war he served as an Oberstleutnant on the staff of Führer Headquarters. It was he who reported Rudolf Hess' flight to England to Hitler. Generalmajor Lombart met Oberstleutnant Scherhorn in one of the many prisoner of war camps he passed through. General Lombart returned to Germany in 1953 and it may be assumed that Oberstleutnant Scherhorn has returned too, provided he survived captivity. But possibly he is living in East Germany. I give you permission, Colonel Skorzeny, to make use of this letter for that purpose."

I spoke personally to Dr. Toth: he was finally released from Russian captivity in 1953. He told me again of Will Linder, of the lost legion and of the terrible years of imprisonment he had shared with other brave soldiers. Many of them died before his eyes, from bad treatment, from hunger and from cold.

What happened in the Soviet prisoner of war camps in Siberia over ten years was indescribable, he said. One to two years after Stalin's death the zeal to finish off those of us who had survived those terrible years lessened somewhat. In the end there were only 20 percent of us still alive.

Many European soldiers who had fought against bolshevism had been prisoners since 1941. My brother was arrested on a Vienna street in 1946 just because his name was Skorzeny and was held prisoner in the Soviet Union for ten years. On his release in 1954, when other prisoners were also released from the death camps of the Gulag Archipelago, he could barely stand and had lost about 30 kilograms. He couldn't be allowed to turn up in Vienna like that, and for propaganda reasons the Soviets sent him to Yugoslavia, where he was treated well and fed in semi-freedom. He suffered severe heart and lung damage as a result of his ordeal and died ten years later as a result.

Doctor Toth and I also talked about the Hungarian uprising in October and November 1956. The Soviets had to employ Siberian troops, who were of the opinion that they were fighting in the Near East and thought the Danube was the Suez Canal! During the popular uprising in Budapest in 1956 there were 25,000 dead, 8,000 of which were Red Army soldiers. Ten-thousand Hungarians were subsequently arrested and deported in the name of "progressive democracy." And Stalin had been dead three years! But many of those who presume to speak in the name of the "human conscience" forget to talk about the martyrdom of Hungary under the bolshevik yoke.

Like many hundreds of thousands of Hungarians, Doctor Toth was forced to leave his country. He wrote a book titled Prisoner in the USSR (1945 to 1955). This is a really terrible piece of evidence by a physician whose sole offense was to love his country and his fellow men. He claims that there were *more than ten million* political prisoners living in the Soviet concentration camps in the years 1948-49. Toth also met Solzhenitsyn in one of the camps.

In his book Dr. Toth tells the story of Dr. Heller, one of colleagues and a jew. Dr. Heller was arrested in Budapest in 1943 and deported to Mauthausen. To the great surprise of Dr. Toth, who thought his friend was well off in Budapest, he met Heller in a Siberian prison camp. He was "accidentally" arrested in Vienna in 1945, where he was accused of being a Gestapo agent and sentenced to twenty years in prison. Finally released, Dr. Heller bravely tended to the wounded in the streets of Budapest in the uprising of 1956 and turned his own house into a hospital. When the Red Army had crushed the national revolution the communist government had Dr. Heller arrested. He was accused of "active cooperation in the counterrevolution," sentenced to death and hanged in January 1957.

Notes

1. The following account differs in several significant aspects from an account written by the former Ic of Army Group Center, Oberst Worgitzky (later BND), which may be considered absolutely reliable. (Editors' note)

2. Skorzeny seems to have confused names here. Based on several radio messages whose texts were reprinted by Worgitzky, the man referred to by Skorzeny as Linder has been positively identified as Schiffer. (Editors' note)

24

ADRIAN VON FÖLKERSAM MISSING
WALTER GIRG & HIS LAST MISSION

How Fölkersam received the Knight's Cross – His commando unit's mission in Maykop – His speech – The faked execution of the cossacks – "...Well, you're here at last!" – With the general of the NKVD – The army intelligence center is blown up – A suspicious general – The great risk in the switchboard to the northern Caucasus – The 13th Panzer Division enters Maykop – Surrounded in Hohensalza – "Break out tonight!" – Walter Girg and his Russians – 3,500 kilometers behind enemy lines with the Knight's Cross under his neckerchief – "...You are a Russian spy!" – One of the grimmest episodes of the war – Russian roulette with five bullets in the chamber.

I would like to speak here about Adrian von Fölkersam. When the 150th Panzer Brigade, whose Battle Group Z he commanded, was disbanded, he pleaded with me for command of Commando Unit East. I objected, pointing out that this would leave me without a chief-of-staff, at a time when we had difficult missions to organize. He conceded that. But this argument ceased to be valid when 1,800 officers and men of the Brandenburg Division voluntarily transferred to our SS commando units. Among them was Oberstleutnant Walther, an outstanding chief-of-staff.

So for better or worse, and against my inner voice, on January 22, 1945 I handed command of Commando Unit East I to Fölkersam. The unit couldn't have got a better commanding officer. I had a bad feeling about the move, however, and it was with great reluctance that I signed the papers promoting him to battalion commander.

At the beginning of 1945 we were under no illusions as to the outcome of the war – we needed a miracle. The Ardennes offensive, which was followed by an attack at the Saar and in Alsace (from January 1 to 26), failed to achieve the desired success. At least the western front was holding: 68 German divisions faced 69 allied divisions, and both sides were badly weakened. As is known, the American forces did not cross the Remagen Bridge until March 8. By this point the enemy's superiority, especially in the air, had become crushing, and 79 enemy divisions were opposed by only 30 German divisions, which in terms of materiel and morale were in no position to fight with any hope of success.

But since January 8, 1945 it was clear to us all that the bitterest and most decisive battles would be fought in the east. In spite of the demand for unconditional surrender and the imperatives of the Morgenthau Plan (made worse by the "Führer Orders" written and signed by Martin Bormann, which intended the almost total destruction of German industry) we hoped that Germany would hold out in the west. However we knew for certain that this could not be the case in the east.

The Russians had stopped at the Vistula in July 1944. From that point on they formed countless new divisions and received huge quantities of was materiel from the western allies. It was agreed between Roosevelt and Stalin that a double offensive would begin in the east and west on January 20, 1945. As it turned out, Churchill was forced to ask Stalin to postpone his attack as the German Ardennes offensive had upset all the Anglo-American plans.

Stalin attacked on the 12th and 14th of January, with 225 infantry divisions and 22 tank corps. General Guderian estimated the Soviet superiority as follows:

infantry	11 : 1
tanks	7 : 1
artillery	20 : 1
air forces	20 : 1

Nevertheless our goal was to fight on and hold; it was a matter of life and death. In his book *Erinnerungen eines Soldaten*, Generaloberst Heinz Guderian, at that time Army Chief-of-Staff and responsible for operations in the east, noted that the Soviet occupation of several villages in East Prussia had shown what the fate of the German people would look like if the flood could not be stopped. Seven-hundred years of work and civilization were at stake.

He concluded, "...demanding an unconditional surrender from the German people is a crime against humanity and a disgrace."

Sturmbannführer Baron von Völkersam arrived in Hohensalza[1] northeast of Posen on January 18. This was in the precise path of the Russian assault in the middle of a 75-kilometer-wide sector between the Vistula and Warthe Rivers. Thirty-one enemy infantry divisions and five tank corps broke into this small sector of the front, supported by almost unlimited air and artillery forces.

Listening to the radio reports in Friedenthal, I followed the course of the fighting with concern. As I had no troops, I sent Fölkersam two dozen trucks with ammunition and food, which he had asked for on January 18. On the 20th I heard that the city was surrounded. I tried to find out more about the battle for Hohensalza. I trusted Fölkersam and his tactical skill. He had now assumed command of all the German units surrounded there. But the information coming in from other sectors proved that the Russian superiority really was overwhelming. There was only a handful of German soldiers – Commando Unit East and the remnants of other units – against a huge mass. And so I ordered Commando Unit East to make preparations for a break-out, to be carried out on my order; I was conscious of the fact that in doing so I was guilty of disobeying orders, but it was a responsibility I was willing to accept.

Adrian von Fölkersam was certainly the most elegant and purest war adventurer: in 1945 he was twenty-seven years old. He was tall and slim and had grey eyes. In order to paint a true picture of him it is best if he describes the operation which won him the Knight's Cross, which he described to me one night in Friedenthal, in his own words:

"It was July 1942 and we were north of the Caucasus. I was a Leutnant of the Brandenburg Division, but in this action I was Major Truchin of the NKVD, who came direct from Stalingrad with special instructions – which I only talked about very secretively – and a troop of 62 men. Most of these were Baltic Germans, who spoke fluent Russian, and a number of Sudeten Germans personally selected by me. We were not exactly proud to be in NKVD uniforms, but necessity becomes the law, especially when the enemy doesn't follow the rules of war himself. We were at the forefront of General Ruoff's Seventeenth Army, or more precisely of General Heer's 13th panzer Division, which had just reached the Rostov–Kala–Baku oil pipeline at Armavir. They sent us across the front lines at Bieloret-shanskaya, about 50 kilometers north of the oil center of Maykop during the night. We had two missions: first, to make the occupation of maykop by our panzers as easy as possible, and second, to prevent to the extent possible the destruction of the production facilities. I was the leader of the commando unit and we were all dressed and armed *à la* NKVD.

A patrol brought me the news that survivors of the retreating Soviet units were camped in a nearby village. They were cut off from their units, and there was a great diversity of people in the various groups. There were cossacks from the Kuban, through which we had just marched, Ukrainians, Khirghezian troops, Cherkessians and Turkmenes – all muslims – Georgians and finally Russian and Siberian units. All in all there were some seven to eight hundred men. Only the Russians and Siberians wanted to get back to their units, but they were in the minority; their officers became anxious. It was very interesting that they had tricks and fuel, as well as camels and horses. I soon devised a plan.

We surrounded the village at dawn and attacked, firing our weapons into the air. We woke everyone, disarmed them and herded them to the main square. There I climbed onto the hood of a truck. My faithful NKVD comrades surrounded the rostrum and I improvised a speech.

After I realized that we had caught everyone asleep in a place where the Soviet fatherland required the watchfulness of every single defender, I shouted:

'What is going on! Do you plan to desert? What you are doing is treason! Don't you understand that our great Comrade Stalin, the brilliant father of our peoples, has foreseen everything? Why do you think the fascists have come to the Caucasus? I will tell you! Because they will all die here to the last man! These mountains will become their grave...'

At this point several cossacks made sarcastic remarks and one of them couldn't help laughing. On my signal two of my NKVD men seized the man.

'Should we shoot him right here, comrade commander?'

'Later comrade. He can wait quietly. Take him away!'

I continued my stern lecture, and at the end I declared:

'Most of you deserve death! However I would like to assume that many of you were talked into this by a few slimy snakes: I know who they are, for we are well informed. You are in our debt for having prevented you from committing filthy treason against our Soviet homeland! All the cossacks – fall out to the right! The Turkmenes, Georgians and others to the left! The Ukrainians over there! All the others stay here until I return. Cossacks, step forward!'

My obedient NKVD troops immediately began sorting out the groups. I left about 30 men behind, climbed aboard the trucks with my remaining men, appropriated two cars and drove the cossacks before me. After a forced march of three-quarters of an hour we came to a ravine. I got out of the car and called to the Ataman.

'You want to desert to the Germans,' I said to him. 'I know that. Do you know that many cossack units are already serving with them? Tell me the truth!'

'Why do ask me that, comrade major?'

'Do you think your people will follow you?'

No answer.

'Listen. Stay out of sight here for one to two hours. There will only be Ukrainians in the village then. Then march in the direction of Anapa. Mingle with the Red Army refugees and you will find the Germans.'

'What kind of game are you playing?'

'In a short time you will hear a wild outburst of firing nearby. You're not to move. The others will think: they're being executing by the NKVD. Now do you get it?'

I went back to the village, where they had heard the shooting, and explained to the Russian and Siberian officers that they had better leave the Caucasians and the Ukrainians behind: another NKVD unit would 'take care of them.' The Russians and Siberians climbed into the trucks, and I followed in my now fully motorized column.

On the morning of August 2 my column came to the main road and joined the line of vehicles heading south. Terrific confusion reigned. At the spot where the road crossed the Armavir – Tuapse railroad real NKVD units were trying vainly to master the panic. I introduced myself to their decidedly ill-humored commander, a lieutenant-colonel.

'Who are you?' he asked.

'Major Tuchin of the Zhdanov Brigade, comrade colonel.'

'Where do you come from? What is your mission here?'

'We come from Stalingrad with special orders, comrade. 124th Brigade.'

The lieutenant-colonel's face brightened. He knew nothing of a 124th Brigade or of special orders; but experience had taught him to be cautious.

'Well, you're finally here! We have been waiting for you since yesterday! As you see, we're sending the cavalry and the tanks to Tuapse and the vehicles to Maykop. The infantry will be regrouped there as well. Drive with your column to Maykop, but please, look closely at the infantry! There may be German spies among them. I am depending on you!'

'You can count on me comrade!'

In Maykop I had my group stop in front of NKVD headquarters. On the steps I met a Russian officer who had departed the previously-mentioned village before me. 'I have already made a report on the matter,' he said to me in passing. 'They're waiting for you.'

Consequently the NKVD general received me very warmly. Such was my reputation that he didn't ask to see my papers or the special orders. I showed them to him nevertheless. With a wave of his hand he gave me to understand that this was not necessary. 'You were right,' he said. 'These cossacks are all traitors. You have given them an instructive lesson. You are my guest this evening and I've arranged suitable quarters for you.'

When I heard this I thought I had been spotted. But no! The general requisitioned a large, comfortable villa for us with a garage. This was lucky, for there wasn't a single vacant room in Maykop, it was packed with refugees. And so we were able to make our plans right in the enemy's midst. Six to seven days lay ahead of us before our panzers would arrive. This time had to be put to the best possible use.

Careful examination of the villa convinced us that there were no microphones; nevertheless we only talked about our plans when the radio was making sufficient noise. My two deputies, Fähnrich Franz Koudele, alias Lieutenant Protoff, and Feldwebel Landowsky, alias Lieutenant Oktshakov, played their roles perfectly. Maykop was a scene of disorder. Everyone was frightened of us and didn't look too closely at us; nevertheless the slightest lack of caution by our people could cause the whole thing to fall apart. I had to take several of my soldiers to task on the first two days for not being careful enough:

'Have you forgotten what you learned at the special school in Allenstein? Comrade Vuishkin, don't always look so benevolent. That can be the end of you and us! You are a member of the Narodny Kommissaria Vnutrenny Diel, I said, never forget that! And you, Comrade Lebedev, stop following around the girls of the Univermag department store: that's not your mission! Comrade Balamontov, I have told you over and over that you are only allowed to say the word 'fascist' together with 'stinking rat' or something similar. With several exceptions, you always say 'fascist' as if you were saying 'shoemaker' or 'garage.' When you say the word 'fascist' you must first grin most malevolently. Then you must look deep into the eyes of whoever you're speaking to and look at him suspiciously. This will make him tremble all the more, because he doesn't know what a fascist actually is. He will feel guilty and knuckle under.'

After two invitations to spend the evening with General Persholl and a large number of emptied vodka glasses I was on a fine footing with him. The two of us inspected the combat positions. The sole dangerous point was this crossing of the road and railroad. All the artillery was positioned there, arranged in three lines. As well anti-tank ditches were being dug. The general asked for my honest opinion of the preparations.

'Comrade the defensive position is excellent, provided that the fascists approach on this road and in single file. But what if they appear fanned out behind those sunflower fields, or there, or over there behind this hill?'

The general thought for a moment and then declared:

'I said exactly the same thing to the leader of the anti-tank forces!'

'The fascists were able to pass Taganrog and Rostov just because we waited for them only on the main road, comrade general! But what happened? The fascists advanced with several spearheads over a wide front. They could just as well do the same here. A spearhead here, one there, and another there, and they meet behind our rear. One must be ready for anything, comrade! An echeloned attack is always dangerous!'

'You are right! Now that I know your opinion it will be easier to defend my own point of view. The appropriate measures will have to be taken tonight.'

He was obviously happy not to have to take any responsibility on his own. We also took the necessary steps. By the morning of August 7 we had gathered all the important information and made our plans accordingly. By the end of the day all was ready.

I drove to NKVD headquarters. Persholl was away – I never saw him again. The archive had been evacuated. Plunderers were already at work in the city, there was complete chaos everywhere. We divided ourselves into three groups. The first and largest group was led by Feldwebel Landowsky. His mission was to prevent the destruction of the production facilities as best he could. Nothing had been dismantled. There were no trucks and the Armavir – Tuapse railroad was the front line.

I gave command of the second group to Koudele-Protoff; he was to stay in the city and destroy the telephone exchange and the telegraph lines to the northern Caucasus.

I wanted to take command of the first group myself, but during the night of August 8-9 I learned that two brigades of the Red Guard had arrived from Tbilisi and Baku and had taken up position at the road-rail crossing. That was stupid. Early on the morning of August 9 I received a radio message stating that patrols of the 13th Panzer Division were now 20 kilometers away and would attack the crossing in a very short time. So I despatched four cars; with armed soldiers on the running boards, I succeeded in clearing a path through the passing refugees against the flow. Finally I was out of the city. I had the men park the cars near a free-standing building that was guarded by the military: the army communications center. Shells from our 150mm howitzers were already falling in many places. The streets had become emptier. One could hear the sound of Russian guns firing. Six of our people slipped into the center with packets of explosives under their arms. When they returned we set off at top speed through the exploding shells in the direction of the front. A few minutes later we heard a loud explosion: the communications center had gone up.

On reaching the Russian artillery I summoned its commander, a lieutenant-colonel, who had been introduced to me by Persholl in the course of our inspection. I asked him at what and whom he thought he was firing with his guns.

'At the germanskis naturally!'

'The fascists have taken another direction and the front line now lies beyond Maykop. Call and see!'

He tried to telephone – in vain of course. Then he gave the order to cease fire and to initiate the retreat as quickly as possible.

'Are you coming with us,' he wanted to know.

'Duty is duty, comrade. I will inform our heroic infantry so that the trap doesn't close behind them.'

'Comrade major, do you know what you're risking by doing that?'

'I have been aware of it for some time!'

We reached the positions held by an infantry division of the Red Army. I introduced myself to the general and informed him that he was almost cut off. The fascists had already passed Maykop. he was a pedantic and suspicious general; obviously he had little sympathy for the NKVD. I immediately launched into my telephone ploy again and remarked that the artillery was already retreating. He tried in vain to telephone and then began asking me some uncomfortable questions. It became quiet. We looked into each others eyes. I didn't want to draw my pistol. At that moment a liaison officer arrived, completely out of breath, and reported that the artillery was withdrawing. I turned around. Only then did the Russian general order the retreat. The neighboring units noticed the movements and sent officers to ask whether new orders had arrived, which spared me an embarrassing conversation which could have had downright uncomfortable consequences for me.

In the remaining time before X-Hour, Koudele-Protoff and his people entered the North Caucasus Communications Center. They acted as if they had been ordered there. They spoke loudly and came upon a commander who declared at them from above: 'Just because the NKVD is running away doesn't mean that I have to do the same!'

'What!' shouted Koudele-Protoff. 'I am a lieutenant of the NKVD and I ask that you please take back what you have just said!'

The comrade major became somewhat quiet and declared that he had not yet received orders to withdraw.

'Then you aren't going to receive any! The new front line is already forming near Apshetousk. Find out for yourself!'

He called the communications center. No answer – naturally.

'I have orders to blow up this building,' said Koudele.

'And I have orders, in case...'

'Good. Stay here with your men if you can't come up with a better idea, and go up with it! In fifteen minutes the north Caucasian communications center will not exist! The fascists could show up here at any minute!'

The commander and his subordinates cleared out with astonishing speed. Then came the big number: Koudele and his people sat at the radio operator positions and answered all queries: '...impossible to connect you with X, Y or Z. The city is being evacuated and the troops are marching toward Tuapse. We have orders to blow up the center in a few minutes.'

All of the offices in Maykop still capable of action fled south as fast as they could go. Koudele and his small detachment held the North Caucasus Central for as long as they could on that August 9, 1942. But coded messages came that they couldn't answer. They were asked who they were. The best thing was to blow up everything at once. But this decision was to significantly hinder Landowsky's third group very significantly in carrying out its mission.

The Russians had calculated on the arrival of German troops in Maykop and they had taken steps – even for the possibility of an attack by parachute troops. Landowsky had the numerically strongest unit, which he divided into small groups of phoney NKVD troops. Using a field telephone which he connected to a proper telephone cable, he called the army communications center. When he received no answers to his inquiries he sent his group in all directions to the oil production facilities. They moved in as planned: they arrived at the run and had themselves taken to the factory police sentries. There they claimed to have orders 'from above' to take over the duties of the factory police immediately and destroy all the oil field installations at the approach of nazi troops.

This trick did not succeed in every case: at Makdse they arrived to late. The duty security chief had already called the army central, then the North Caucasus central. When he received no answer from both places he immediately blew up all the machines and well sites. The clouds of smoke from the explosions immediately alerted other security units, who then followed this example.

The advance guard of the 13th Panzer Division, which attacked Maykop in the north, encountered only weak resistance from small infantry units which formed the rearguard. At noon on that same

August 9, 1942 the first of General Heers' panzers rolled into the suburbs of Maykop."

This performance, which earned him the Knight's Cross, typified Adrian von Fölkersam the man and the soldier. He was at my side when we stormed the citadel in Budapest. I saw him go into action in the Ardennes. Why should a man like him die in Hohensalza?

An officer with the task of leading a unit in combat has only one desire: to reach the assigned objective. He also needs a little luck. When from a tactical point of view all the advantages are on the side of the enemy, even the best of intentions are of no use. In the course of the final months of the war the intelligence and creativity of the soldier in the east and west only played a role when he could act before he was caught by the avalanche.

Like many others, SS-Sturmbannführer von Fölkersam, at the head of his battalion and the remnants of other units, was caught and overrun by the storm flood. The news coming from the front was enough to convince me that in spite of his great skill and courage, it would be impossible for him to halt the enemy attack. The Soviet artillery had already massed more than forty guns per kilometer around Hohensalza and was showering our surrounded troops with an intensive bombardment. I knew that Fölkersam would do his utmost, but I feared that he wouldn't tell me how hopeless even the great bravery of his battle group was.

Fölkersam was my best comrade and my most loyal friend. To sacrifice him such a hopeless situation would have been too hard for me. To simply and unnecessarily let him and Commando Unit East be destroyed was to much for me. At noon on January 21, 1945 I received the following brief radio message from him: "Situation untenable. Should I try to break out? F." I took it upon myself to send the order to withdraw: "Break out tonight!" It was already too late. In the afternoon Major Heinz radioed the bad news:

"Fölkersam badly wounded while leading a scouting advance. Shot in the head.Have assumed command of the battle group. Break-out attempt tonight."

Several weeks later the survivors of Commando Unit East, just 2 officers (Balts) and 13 men out of 800, returned to Friedenthal.

The nocturnal breakthrough, made in two groups, enjoyed initial success. Sturmbannführer von Fölkersam, still unconscious, was laid on an artillery tractor after his wounds were dressed. This half-tracked vehicle was to follow the group whose breakthrough point was estimated to be the most favorable. After a successful break-out a radio message advised that the small group escorting Fölkersam and the gun tractor had made it through. From that point on there was no further news of the group. During the night of January 22-23 the main body of the battalion was surprised and wiped out in bitter fighting. The fifteen survivors wandered around between the lines for three weeks, and after their return they were unable to give us any precise information as to the fate of our other comrades.

Fölkersam's wife and his newborn daughter were in Posen, about 140 kilometers west of Hohensalza. When, on January 20, I saw that the situation on the Eastern Front was worsening hourly, I ordered the division medical officer, Dr. Slama, to Posen. He was just able to bring mother and daughter to the west. Fölkersam had a younger brother who was likewise with the Brandenburg Division. As a prisoner in the Soviet Union in 1947, he was said to have learned that Adrian had recovered from his injuries and was being held as a prisoner. I was told that he believes this to this day.

For all those who knew Adrian von Fölkersam he is not dead: he scorned death too much, ever to die and be forgotten.

● ● ●

Of the officers from Friedenthal whose conduct was marked by a total disregard for danger, Untersturmführer Walter Girg stands out. It was he, who at the end of August 1944 blocked the three most important Carpathian passes while leading an assault team in Romanian uniforms.

At the end of 1944 and in early 1945, acting on orders from the OKH and with the help of General Gehlen's "Foreign Armies East," we at Friedenthal organized numerous actions behind the Soviet lines by Commando Unit East, but also by Front Reconnaissance Unit II, which was now under my command. These long-range reconnaissance operations in Russian-occupied areas allowed the OKH to get a better picture of where the enemy's strong and weak points were. The Soviets were now committed exclusively to a policy of "offensive at any price." This posed a great risk as their supply lines became ever longer. No doubt: if the Ardennes offensive had begun in

November as Hitler originally intended it to and not in december, and if it had been successful, the Western Front would have stabilized until at least April. Has Stalin attacked as casually as he now did, his offensive might have come to a bad end.

Our missions provided proof that the enemy scarcely controlled the areas occupied by him. We were often able to make contact with cities, villages, factories or offices by way of still-intact telephone lines. On one occasion, for example, I spoke by telephone with the director of an important German factory in Litzmannstadt, present day Lodz, who asked whether they should go back to work. The enemy passed by the city without occupying it or showing any concern for it at all.

One will understand that our missions provided the OKW with interesting details, which were evaluated by the OKH.

Early in January 1945 the task fell to Obersturmführer Girg to go into the area of the former Polish Generalgouvernement. His group consisted of twelve German soldiers and twelve Russian volunteers. They were taken by ship to East Prussia, which was still in our hands but cut off from the rest of Germany. The commando unit was outfitted with several captured Russian tanks and advanced in the direction of southern Poland. There was radio contact for several days, then it was lost. Weeks passed with no news and I assumed that the unit was lost.

Fortunately this was not the case: Girg's unit disguised itself as a Red Army inspection battalion whose official task it was to check whether the positions responsible for supply were functioning correctly. In contrast to Fölkersam, however, Girg spoke not a word of Russian. Consequently all the acting officers and NCOs were Russians. They inspected everything in detail and returned at night to destroy telephone lines and railroad signal installations and, where possible, to blow up bridges, power plants and food and munitions dumps.

Of course they also collected interesting intelligence. Whenever they encountered a strong unit headed in the opposite direction, they stopped it, feigning a breakdown. As soon as the Russians were gone the radio operator, a German Feldwebel, transmitted the latest information to Friedenthal. This continued until the truck carrying the radio operator and all his equipment was lost; it broke through the ice while crossing the frozen Vistula and sank. Girg and the rest of the commando unit continued on their way, frequently sleeping and resting with the inhabitants of the villages. The more suspicious the unit appeared, the better it was treated by the villagers.

The unit's luck was extremely changeable during its six weeks behind enemy lines. On a number of occasions our Russian "officers" were invited into the mess, where they found many critical, war-weary Soviet officers who rejected the mass sacrifice of standard Stalinist tactics. Our entire commando unit owed its survival to anti-bolshevik partisans, into whose midst it had to flee on several occasions.

After an advance of 1,500 kilometers into the enemy rear, Girg managed to return to the fortress of Kolberg on the Baltic coast. The city was already surrounded by the Russians, and the German general in command there wouldn't believe a word spoken by our comrades. The only identifying symbol Girg had with him was his Knight's Cross, which he wore beneath his neckerchief.

The general said to him bitterly, "Not only are you a Soviet spy, but you also take me for an idiot!"

Unfortunately I can't remember the name of this general, although he knew me well: when I introduced Girg to him, he had come from the Oder where he had been my superior several days earlier when I was commander of the Schwedt bridgehead, which I will discuss in the next chapter.

"So you claim that you belong to Commando Unit Center from Friedenthal," the general said to Girg. "Alright then, who is your commander?"

"Sturmbannführer Otto Skorzeny, Herr General."

"Good. Where is he at the moment?"

"Probably in Friedenthal, Herr General."

"It is quite clear that you are a spy for the National Committee for a Free Germany, for three weeks ago I spoke with your chief on the Eastern Front. Bad luck!"

Girg replied that I had been in Friedenthal when I gave him the orders for this mission.

"Possible. Then surely you must know the wavelengths and the special radio codes with which to contact Friedenthal."

"Unfortunately no. My radio operator drowned in the Vistula at the beginning of our mission and all his equipment was lost."

"Really? In the Vistula! You could have come up with something more original!"

Girg and his men had to endure the indignity of being sentenced to death by their own countrymen. It was a brain wave on Girg's part that finally brought them to their senses.

"Whether I die or not is all the same to me. But what annoys me is that I am to be shot by friends, although so many enemies have failed to get me!"

Girg made one last proposal: they should radio General Jüttner in the Bendlerstrasse in Berlin and obtain the wavelengths and codewords for Friedenthal. The commander of Fortress Kolberg could then radio Friedenthal himself and confirm Girg's identity.

And so Karl Radl learned that the German soldiers in Fortress Kolberg intended to shoot Girg and other comrades! One can imagine how quickly Radl cleared up the situation. The general was then happy that he could make use of Girg and his commando unit: he had them carry out patrols and designated them the rearguard when the fortress was evacuated with the help of the navy. The general was himself the last to leave the fortress with teh rearguard.

In his book *Commando Extraordinary*, Charles Foley wrote of Walter Girg's fantastic adventure:

"The siege of Fortress Kolberg by the Russians was one of the worst episodes of this war. The French, volunteers of the Waffen-SS Division Charlemagne, fought for several weeks to hold open a narrow corridor through which the German refugees could flee to the west, while at the same time the "red" Germans of the Seydlitz Division, who had been recruited from the prisoner of war camps, did all they could to block and cut off their own countrymen's escape route.

Three French battalions under the command of Oberführer Puaux defended the city of Küstrin, and a battle group of the Charlemagne Division held out in Kolberg until March 6, 1945. Later another battalion of the French Waffen-SS took part in the final battles in Berlin near the Reich Chancellery which lasted until May 1, 1945.

What surprised Walter Girg the most during his last mission was the loyalty and willingness to sacrifice of the German population in the areas already occupied by the reds. 'It was the women in particular,' he said, 'who were ready to accept any risk to help us.'"

In the entire mission Girg lost only three men in addition to the radio operator. The Russians were convinced that the radio operator was one of theirs, and they buried him with full military honors in the nearest cemetery to the Vistula. Not a single Russian member of the commando unit committed treason. Girg was promoted to Hauptsturmführer on my recommendation and he became the 814th German soldier to receive the Knight's Cross with Oak Leaves. He was an extraordinarily clever officer who defied fate.

"The black sheep of Friedenthal" was still alive, having meanwhile forgotten how many times he had gone through the Soviet lines. Karl Radl observed that he had a very personal style of playing "Russian roulette" – he played with five bullets in the cylinder instead of only one, or put simply, "he was plain lucky."

In any case luck must have been on his side for him to carry out missions of the kind that Walter Girg did and still be alive.

___

Notes

1. Hermann von Salza was Grand Master of the Teutonic Knights, which converted the resident heathens to Christianity in the Thirteenth Century. (Editors' note)

25

SCHWEDT ON THE ODER
LAST REUNION WITH VIENNA

A regrettable decision by Hitler: Himmler becomes Commander-in-Chief of Army Group Vistula – Organization of the Schwedt bridgehead – "The Reds will never get in here!" – Our floating batteries and self-propelled guns – Tactical change – Limited in time and space – Krasnov's cossacks "lend voices" – A European division – The battles – Himmler's fits of rage – Reichsleiter Bormann beside himself with anger – Grabow is lost and is recaptured – Wilscher's sharpshooters – Speer: "The decision will soon be made concerning our new weapons" – In the Reich Chancellery – Eva Braun – Pilot Oberst Rudel – In Vienna, a dead city – Two old policemen to encircle the Russians – Baldur von Schirach's subterranean salon – Neu-Starhemberg 1683 – A farewell to the city of my birth.

Our reconnaissance missions behind the Soviet lines enabled the Army Chief-of-Staff, Generaloberst Guderian, to create an accurate picture of what was coming at us from the east. Hitler refused to believe it, however, until January 12, 1945. He was badly informed by Himmler, who claimed that "the Soviet preparations for a major offensive were just a gigantic bluff."

On January 23 Hitler received news that Fortress Lötzen, the most powerful strongpoint in East Prussia, had surrendered without a fight. "Terrible news," wrote Guderian. "The Führer called it treason." Generaloberst Reinhardt, the Commander-in-Chief of Army Group Center, was replaced with Generaloberst Rendulic. Rendulic was a fellow Austrian, an army general and a very capable man, whom I later met after he was placed in command of Army Group South. At the end of the war there was a High Command South, which was led by Generalfeldmarschall Kesselring, whose Chief-of-Staff was Generaloberst Winter.

The choice of Rendulic was a good one. But as a result of the surrender of Lötzen Hitler became even more suspicious of several generals. He now made a regrettable decision: he named Himmler to command Army Group Vistula.

As we know, after July 20 the Reichsführer took the place of Generaloberst Fromm as head of the Replacement Army. In truth it was General Jüttner, his chief-of-staff, who did all the work and did it well. Himmler was also chief of the Reich Security Office and Minister of the Interior. The exercising of any one of these posts would have been more than enough to keep busy any man with great work initiative. Furthermore Himmler was neither a tactician nor a strategist. He named SS-Generalmajor Lammerding to be his chief-of-staff. Lammerding was an honest officer who was equal to the task. Guderian was able to convince Hitler of the necessity of temporarily placing General Wenck at Himmler's side. Unfortunately Wenck fell victim to a serious car crash and so General Krebs was assigned to Himmler. In the end Himmler had to be replaced as head of Army Group Vistula by the outstanding General Heinrici, the CO of the First Panzer Army, which had most recently been fighting in the Carpathians (March 20). But it was already too late.[1]

It was therefore Himmler, the Commander-in-Chief of Army Group Vistula, who on January 30, 1945 ordered me to set out for Schwedt on the Oder immediately with all my available units. My mission was to establish a bridgehead on the east bank of the river "from which a counteroffensive would follow later." The city and bridgehead were to be held at all costs. The order further said that we were supposed to "liberate the town of Freienwalde, which was occupied by the enemy, during the advance."

Himmler seemed to ignore where the enemy actually was, and he found it an obvious matter to capture a city "in passing." A phone call to Führer Headquarters proved to me that they didn't in fact know much about the situation on the Eastern Front.

The situation in the east took an ominous turn during the night of January 28-29. The Soviet Marshall Zhukov, who commanded the 1st White Russian Army Group, sent the 1st and 2nd Tank Armies of the Red Guards, the 8th Guards Army, the 5th Elite Army and the

61st Army in the direction of the Oder. The spearheads of the 2nd Tank and the 5th Elite Armies had reached the suburbs of Landsberg (Gorzow) and there was heavy fighting in front of Lüben. It was feared that the enemy would cross the frozen Oder between Stettin in the north and Küstrin in the south – at Schwedt, only about 60 air miles from Berlin.

The old city of Schwedt, the so-called "Pearl of the Uckermark," was famous for its castle and its cavalry regiment, in which the Pomeranian aristocracy served. About 50,000 people lived in the city, whose population was now swelled by numerous refugees from the east.

At about 5 P.M. on January 30, 1945 I received the order to create a bridgehead there. I immediately informed Friedenthal and Neustrelitz, where my parachute battalion was quartered, and at 3 A.M. I despatched two patrols to Schwedt, as I didn't know how far the Russians had hot. While on the move my liaison officer informed me that the road to Schwedt was open.

It must have been about 7 A.M. on January 31 when I arrived in Schwedt. My reconnaissance troops were waiting near the big Oder bridge at the canal parallel to the river. I immediately sent them to Königsberg, Neumark, a town located on the Stettin – Küstrin railroad about 17 kilometers east of Küstrin on the Oder, to find out where the enemy was.

We had spent the whole night in Friedenthal organizing the units and making them fully motorized: there was Commando Unit Center, the battalion commanded by Hauptsturmführer Fucker; the sniper company led by Oberleutnant Wilscher; Commando Unit Northwest, which had been reduced to two companies under the command of Hauptmann Appel; and finally, in reserve, an assault company with light tanks commanded by Obersturmführer Schwerdt, a comrade from the Gran Sasso. My parachute battalion in Neustrelitz was led by SS-Hauptsturmführer Milius. In addition to these units there was the headquarters and the headquarters company under Oberstleutnant Walther, Fölkersam's successor, with Hauptsturmführer Hunke, our "chinaman," and the monitoring service, a supply company and two signals platoons, which stayed in touch with Friedenthal. Only the most important posts were manned there; a guard company of the Waffen-SS, consisting of Romanian ethnic Germans under the command of the faithful Radl, also stayed behind. Normally we were supplied by Friedenthal, but we came upon additional sources.

In Schwedt all I found was three reserve infantry battalions and a reserve pioneer battalion – all four were very incomplete, and the soldiers included sick and convalescents. But the commander of the pioneer battalion proved to be very innovative and energetic and he soon proved to be a great help to me.

On the very first day I set up my command post on the right bank of the Oder in Niederkrönig and drove to Königsberg, Neumark, which was filled with refugees from the east and soldiers separated from their units. I immediately issued the necessary orders for all the retreating stragglers to assemble in a barracks in Schwedt, where they were fed, issued equipment and assigned to one of the four battalions. Soon they didn't look all that bad. The flood of civilian refugees, coming from Königsberg in the south and from Stettin in the north, were channelled. These poor people were in very bad shape, and I saw to it that the women, children and old people were gradually evacuated by train. The city commandant of Schwedt, a colonel who had been badly wounded in the war, helped me in this, as did the mayor, an intelligent reserve officer.

● ● ●

Nothing is as contagious as the fear that always follows the greatest chaos. As far as I could tell, there was complete chaos within a radius of fifty kilometers. If two or three Soviet tanks had driven up to Schwedt before our arrival, the Russians could have crossed the river unopposed.

I had proposed a plan for the bridgehead and on February 1 I assembled the political, civilian and military authorities and said the following words to them, "I have heard several of you say or murmur: 'What's the good of all this? Everything is more or less lost. The Russians will be here tomorrow.' But I will tell you one thing: as long as I am here in Schwedt, the Russians won't be here tomorrow or any other time, rather they will never be here! You, the Ortsgruppenleiter of the NSDAP, will now order the male inhabitants to dig holes and rifle pits with shovels and hoes. You yourselves will take up shovels and hoes and provide them with an example. And you will give them a further example when you pick up a rifle after the digging is done. Then you will see how your example is followed and Schwedt will remain German."

I spent the first four days fortifying the bridgehead, assembling the stragglers, raising and establishing new units, obtaining reinforcements, locating materiel, weapons and ammunition and constantly harassing the enemy with heavily-armed patrols. I requested good staff officers to lead my newly-formed battalions; the army group sent me a few outstanding, experienced captains and majors.

The pioneer major helped me lay out the bridgehead on the right bank of the Oder, with an outer semicircle with a radius of about 8 kilometers running from the Oder to a small tributary, the Rörike. Rifle pits and strongpoints were dug on this front line by a labor service regiment from Stettin and the male population of Schwedt. A second line of fortifications was laid down within this semicircle, with strongpoints, machine-gun nests, communications trenches and small hedgehog positions. The third ring was laid down around the east end of the Oder bridge in a radius of about one kilometer, and was intended to protect the city and Niederkrönig. Troops were placed in a few of the villages outside the belt of positions to avoid surprises. A stream of confusing and contradictory orders came from the Commander-in-Chief of Army Group Vistula; I merely answered each one with a request for reinforcements and more weapons.

We lacked heavy machine-guns. The Ib, the supply officer in my staff, located a arms dump containing new MG 42 machine-guns and ammunition near Frankfurt on the Oder.

No artillery? The commander of the supply company found out that there was factory for 75mm anti-tank guns about 50 kilometers to the southwest. There were about 40 working guns there, plus ammunition. Göring sent me two flak battalions with 88mm and 105mm guns. I had six of these guns mounted on trucks – for we had also found trucks and fuel – and had these hard to locate "flying batteries" drive up and down a 20 kilometer front and fire at the enemy positions. This gave the enemy the impression that he was facing a strong enemy unit with dangerous artillery.

The Oder and the canal were frozen over. The commander of the pioneer unit blew up the layer of ice, transforming the river back into a natural obstacle. Oder barges were also refloated. I had a flak battery mounted on three of these ships, enabling my "floating artillery" to also operate from the Oder canal with constant changes of position. This brought outstanding results, and in a report to the OKW I suggested the use of the same method in Berlin, where there were numerous waterways and where they were short on artillery but not on anti-aircraft guns. No attention was paid to this proposal, however.

In the beginning I sent several detachments as far as possible to the east each day. These strong patrols drove as much as 50 to 60 kilometers behind the enemy lines and caused unrest among the enemy units. The Soviet division headquarters were surprised. Our 105mm shells exploded as much as 15 kilometers behind their lines. Farther east there were serious small battles. The Russians were disconcerted. So the fascist troops weren't on the retreat after all? Was this not the precursor of a German counteroffensive?

Armed patrols brought back prisoners and information, which allowed me to plan further actions against weakly defended positions.

I would like to mention that from February 3, 1945 the outer ring in the north was defended by the first of our newly-formed battalions, while I assigned the second battalion to defend in the south. The center was held by Commando Unit East and my parachute battalion. The parachute battalion, which had gone into position in the east of the position, had to act as a shock absorber so to speak, to intercept and brake the expected attack. Commando Unit Center took over the defense of the second inner ring in the bridgehead.

Through these tactical measures I was able to strengthen all of my positions in the briefest time and by the shortest route. This probably wouldn't have been possible if I hadn't been able to fool the enemy as to our actual strength through the commando operations deep into the enemy rear and the fire of our 88mm and 105mm guns.

The Schwedt bridgehead on the Oder River was certainly just one tiny episode in the closing story of the Second World War. It must be borne in mind, however, that we had to improvise everything in the shortest time, and that we were able to deceive the enemy, who enjoyed a fivefold superiority over us, as to our real strength for several weeks through our bold commando operations far behind the front and our mobile artillery. These tactics won us time. Seen close up, it looked as follows: east of Königsberg the parachute battalion was soon supported by two battalions of the Volkssturm, first by a battalion commanded by the district commander personally and composed mainly of farmers from Königsberg; then by a fully-equipped and armed Volkssturm battalion from Hamburg. The latter unit consisted almost exclusively of dockyard workers. Most of them had once been socialists or communists, but I never met a more determined and committed group of soldiers.

In the first weeks I received additional reinforcements in the shape of a battalion of the Hermann Göring Division; it consisted of pilots without aircraft and students from Luftwaffe schools. They were assigned to the units and received their baptism of fire two weeks later. It is true, by the way, that I also spread the cadre personnel of the officer school among the new units.

A radio unit sent by Führer Headquarters installed a direct telephone line to the Reich Chancellery. A squadron of cavalry from the 8th Regiment, a cossack unit under Captain Krasnov, the son of the famous general, and a regiment of Romanian-Germans increased our fighting strength. I must admit that Krasnov's people were true masters at "lending voices" to their patrols – captured Russian officers and NCOs who were especially talkative. The information obtained in this way was of great use to us.

My Commando Unit Northwest included men from Norway, Denmark, Holland, Belgium and France. Together with the soldiers separated from their units, on February 7 I was in command of a 15,000-man-strong division, which I – not entirely without pride – would like to call my "European division." When I arrived on January 30 there was scarcely a soldier capable of fighting to be found in Schwedt. My battle group became the Schwedt Division; they formed a corps from a Kriegsmarine division fighting on our right to the south. A commanding general and staff were appointed; I will return to this later.

• • •

The first battles took place on February 1; our reconnaissance patrols ran into enemy forces in Bad Schönfliess, 8 kilometers east of königsberg, or 25 kilometers away from Schwedt. During the first week there was an increasing amount of hostile contact with enemy units, which were steadily reinforced. Information from Russian prisoners and other secure intelligence confirmed that the Russians were planning a major offensive against the bridgehead and wanted to feel out our fighting strength.

From February 5 our reconnaissance probes deep into the rear were no longer possible; they encountered a ring of Soviets which was growing ever thicker. Bad Schönfliess was attacked. I went along on a patrol by my Commando Unit Center, all former comrades from Gran Sasso. On the road lay two dead civilians. There was a deathly silence. We met a man who could scarcely believe that we were Germans. Then he gave us some information: the Russians had set up their headquarters near the station and there was also a gathering of tanks there. The railroad had been put back in service and a steady stream of trains was arriving with supplies and fresh troops.

My three-man patrols confirmed this information and reported that they had in fact seen about thirty tanks on the grounds of the station. The Russian troops were south and east of the city. We saw still more bodies of civilians on the streets, among them an almost naked woman. Gradually several inhabitants ventured out of their homes. They were completely shattered. We had only two cars, and I was thus able to evacuate just two women and their two children. I immediately had my parachute battalion, an army battalion and two Volkssturm battalions occupy Königsberg. The enemy attack took place in the afternoon. There was heavy fighting in the streets. Our troops destroyed eleven tanks with panzerfausts. Not until after midnight was the enemy, now also attacking from the north and south, able to enter the city. I ordered our troops in the outer ring of fortifications to fall back, and amazingly our losses were light.

This first nocturnal, large-scale battle proved that the newly-formed units would hold together. The first assault was repulsed by a company of paratroopers; losses were heavy. The commander of the Volkssturm unit from Königsberg, the district commander, had run away. I will look into this in more detail.

The Russians attacked the bridgehead daily. I received further reinforcement from Friedenthal in the shape of a company of armored reconnaissance troops commanded by Obersturmführer Schwerdts. In the weeks that followed this unit formed my best, last reserve.

From February 7 on, the enemy superiority was such that we had to evacuate all the villages outside the bridgehead. Each day there were several attacks at three different places – always the same – by

Russian assault battalions, which were supported by improved T-34 tanks as well as American-supplied tanks. The Russians fought bravely, but they made the mistake of trying to break through with force. All of their attempts were stopped at heavy cost to them and beaten back. In each case we counterattacked immediately.

The Soviets nevertheless managed to breach the first defensive ring, at Grabow, which was defended by us. At 4 P.M. that day I was ordered to the headquarters of Army Group Vistula. There was no question of me leaving my soldiers alone in the midst of a battle to drive to see Himmler. I did not arrive at Hohenlychen until about 8:30 P.M., after the enemy had been thrown back out of our bridgehead; dirty and wearing the clothes I had worn in combat, I now stood in the headquarters. Himmler's toadies received me like men who had been condemned to death. The one showed pity, the other satisfaction. Himmler was in a foul mood: I heard: "...Letting me wait four hours! ... Unbelievable! ... You failed to obey an order! ... Demotion ... Court martial!"

But his greatest reproach was that I had refused to have a young Luftwaffe officer, the leader of the defense of Nipperwiese, tried because he had withdrawn into the actual bridgehead.

"Reichsführer," I said, "this unit withdrew on my orders. The officer only did his duty."

In the end Himmler agreed with me. I also pointed out that I had received a mass of senseless orders from the staff of the corps to which I was subordinate, but that they had forgotten to allocate us a minimum of supplies. We had to improvise everything. Then the reichsführer invited me to dinner – to the great astonishment of those who had just received me so haughtily. The attitude of the "courtiers" changed immediately. The whole thing was so sickening that I hurried to get back to Schwedt.

I was fully conscious that this pitiful story had been cooked up by a man who had borne a grudge against me since Budapest: the police general von dem Bach-Zelewski, who had been prominent at that time and who wanted to destroy the citadel with the "Thor" giant howitzer. Unfortunately he was now my commanding general, as his predecessor, who had been named only a few days before, had taken command of Fortress Kolberg; three weeks later he had a few good reasons to take Walter Girg for a Soviet spy.

Himmler calmed himself and even promised me a battalion of assault guns, a reinforcement that he took away from me again ten days later. Of the planned offensive that was to take place from the Schwedt bridgehead not a word was spoken. I drove back to Schwedt the same night.

For the sake of completeness I must add that I also had an enemy in the Reich Chancellery who was as tenacious as he was powerful: Martin Bormann. Before we reconnoitered to Bad Schönfield, I received an order to look in this direction for some "important state papers" that two party comrades had left in two trucks in a forest. After several inquiries I learned that they were not "state papers" but Bormann's own papers from the Reich Chancellery. I also asked the chancellery to send me in Schwedt the two officials who, in their haste to get to the west, had abandoned the two trucks. They would be helpful in the search, as they could tell us the exact location of the vehicles. But the two gentlemen didn't consider it necessary to appear and the Russians were already in Schönfliess. So I sent word back to the effect that I wouldn't risk the life of a single one of my soldiers in order to recover these files. We had more important things to do.

Then came the story of Königsberg. After the withdrawal of my troops into the bridgehead I returned to my command post and found the district party leader there: he had simply abandoned his city and his Volkssturm battalion. The excuses he made for his actions were pitiful and, unfortunately for him, also common knowledge. After his flight from Königsberg a certain panic seized the farmers – that I knew only all too well. The two groups that fled in disorder suffered some killed and wounded, for to flee in panic before an enemy almost always means heavy losses. Luckily my paratroopers and the Hamburg dock workers brought the situation under control again. But I was left with no choice but to bring the man who was supposed to have provided his people with an example in courage and coolness before a division court martial for desertion and cowardice in the face of the enemy. The court handed down the death sentence and two days later he was publicly executed.

Martin Bormann fumed and foamed: all party leaders from the rank of a district leader up were unimpeachable. In his view they could only be sentenced by a party court. I answered Gauleiter Stürtz, who visited me on Bormann's behalf, that the circuit leader had not been sentenced as a party leader, but as the responsible commander of a military unit that was under my command, and added, "I ask you to answer this question honestly: are party leaders not punished for desertion and cowardice in the face of the enemy?"

I never received an answer from the Reich Chancellery to this question. At least I could undertake a surprise counterattack in the south to Hauseberg with teh assault gun battalion and Commando Unit Center. An enemy flamethrower battalion was wiped out and its commander captured. There was a terrific haul of enemy equipment: howitzers, anti-tank guns, heavy machine-guns with ammunition, all more than welcome in Schwedt.

The enemy's superiority in soldiers, tanks, artillery and air forces was in the order of about 15 to 15 to 1. After several days of bitter fighting Grabow was stormed for the second time, and the Russians stood in front of Hohenkrönig, about 2 kilometers from the Oder. The situation was critical if not to say desperate. God knows what would happen if we were overrun and the enemy crossed the river. I was certain that my soldiers would make a superhuman effort. Obersturmbannführer Schwerdt, who soon afterward was to be promoted to Hauptsturmführer, recaptured Grabow after a surprise counterattack from the flank. Four old hands from Gran Sasso were killed in the attack. Schwerdt had them carried in front of the church and they were buried with full military honors.

I was surprised to find Reichsmarschall Göring at my command post in Schwedt. His staff had phoned regularly to see "how things were going." He came, he said, "as a neighbor": Karinhall, his famous estate, lay somewhat further to the west.

The marshall came without the usual glittering uniform and he wore no decorations on his grey jacket. He wanted to go to the front; in my opinion there was nothing standing in his way. But a general from his entourage whispered, "This is your responsibility!"

When darkness fell I instructed the cars stop on the road to Niederkrönig and we continued on our way on foot, side by side. Sometimes we had to throw ourselves down on the frozen ground when an enemy artillery round fell not far away. The Reichsmarschall was mainly interested in the enemy tanks, a number of which were still burning nearby. He especially wanted to visit a Flak 88 which had been employed in the anti-tank role in the very front line and to congratulate the crew. As well as handshakes he passed out liquor, cigarettes and cigars, with which he was very well supplied. He passed out the same at the command post of our parachute troops. It was totally dark when I escorted Hermann Göring to the big Oder bridge.

"They won't cross the Oder here tomorrow!", he said.

"Never, as long as we can fight, Herr Reichsmarschall!"

He had a few encouraging words for the "division from out of thin air." The next time we saw each other was in prison in Nuremberg. Although Luftwaffe pilots and gunners fought bravely in Schwedt, as a branch of the service the Luftwaffe itself played a rather negative role. During my first reconnaissance the strange appearance of a small, abandoned airfield caught my eye: a few slightly damaged aircraft sat at the edge of the runway. I climbed out of the armored car and discovered in the hangars and the radio room a mass of weapons and materiel – all in excellent condition. Everything suggested that here as elsewhere everyone had fled in panic. We took everything usable with us and destroyed the rest. When we returned to schwedt the airfield's commander, a Luftwaffe Oberstleutnant, was waiting for me. His conscience had plagued him, he had returned and now explained to me that he couldn't contact his superiors and was therefore without orders. The general who was his superior had disappeared.

"My dear fellow," I said to him, "it is of course a stupid thing that you acted so irresponsibly in this situation. You know the book of military law as well as I do, and I fear that a court martial will sentence you for deserting your post. Unfortunately I feel myself obliged to report this to Generaloberst von Greim, commander-in-chief of the Luftwaffe. In the meantime you may not leave Schwedt."

When the Oberstleutnant left Königsberg airfield I was not yet in command of the bridgehead. The affair was therefore a Luftwaffe matter. But I was surprised the next morning to see a Fieseler Storch land on the barracks grounds and Generaloberst von Greim climb out. He brought the Oberstleutnant before a Luftwaffe court martial. The proceedings determined that the main guilty party was the general who had disappeared. The Oberstleutnant was sentenced to a jail term but was allowed an opportunity to prove himself at the front. He immediately became a member of Battle Group Schwedt; he fought well and bravely and survived everything.

• • •

The Schwedt bridgehead was still holding on February 28, 1945. Of my 25 months as commander of Special Unit Friedenthal, I spent 14 months at the front or in action, and I can say that we really had to face a great diversity of combat situations.

In the beginning the bridgehead was established for a strategic purpose, but one that existed only in Himmler's imagination, namely to occupy a certain area for a specified period in order to allow a counteroffensive by an army corps. Battle Group Schwedt, and later the division of the same name certainly played a tactical, defensive role, but this was not in Army Group Vistula's plan. The Soviet armies did not succeed in crossing the river; as a matter of fact Zhukov's leading tank divisions gained the impression that preparations were being made for a German counteroffensive – about 60 kilometers from Berlin, in Schwedt.

As for the tactical operations carried out within and outside the bridgehead, they were of course those of a conventional war. However with the limited means at our disposal, we would never have been able to deceive the enemy for so long without the training and without the fighting strength of my own unit, which provided the backbone of the defense, without the mobile anti-aircraft guns mounted on trucks and boats, and without another unit that weakened the enemy considerably: I am referring to the company of snipers from Friedenthal, which was under the command of Odo Wilscher.

There wasn't supposed to be any shooting at Gran Sasso and in the storming of the citadel in Budapest. But there had to be shooting at Schwedt – and accurate shooting at that. I often pestered responsible generals. "Why," I asked, "didn't they systematically commit the snipers that each division possessed?" Since the first days of the Russian campaign in June 1941 we had seen the Russian snipers at work. They were dangerous and were feared, for their targets were officers and NCOs.

At Schwedt, Wilscher hid his snipers by night in groups of two in no-man's-land. I have already mentioned that we blasted away the layer of ice covering the Oder. Apart from that there was something of a thaw at the beginning of February; huge blocks of ice, some covered with wood and branches, washed ashore. The floating islands offered Wilscher's riflemen natural and mobile cover. I estimate that our 25% of our defensive success was attributable to the snipers.

• • •

I saw Himmler again during the month of February, together with Oberst Baumbach, the commander of Kampfgeschwader 200, which was assigned to me, and Armaments Minister Speer.

The latter, who always showed a great deal of sympathy for my requests, was very optimistic – in contrast to what he claimed in his memoirs: "That night (beginning of February 1945) I made the decision to do away with Hitler." Quite suddenly the thought came to his consciousness: "...I had, strictly speaking, thoughtlessly lived among murderers for twelve years..." How could one live among murderers without becoming the least bit suspicious, especially when one had been present at the apex of power as Hitler's favorite since 1933 and had occupied one of the most responsible positions of the war? (Speer, Page 437). In the first days of May 1945 certain leaders of the national-socialist state were seized by the so-called "resistance complex." There weren't many, but there were some.

The only thing I can confirm is that in mid-February 1945 Albert Speer, far from acting like "a member of the resistance," behaved like a zealous Reich minister. No doubt, they will say, he wanted to play his cards close to the vest. But then he had his cards very well concealed! To him Heinrich Himmler was a person worthy of respect. I myself was called to Führer Headquarters to be briefed on an intensification of the air war in the east. In my presence Minister Speer promised the Reichsführer new aircraft and new bombs for the beginning of April. Today Speer assures us that he then considered any hope as illusory. However on one February day I was able to speak with him alone for a moment. I wanted to learn more about the famous "secret weapons," which we had been hearing volumes about since October 1944. He could have advised me to give up any hope in this direction. However he contented himself with stating to me, "The decision will be made soon!"

This was a sentence that all soldiers heard often. I am not surprised that Speer forgot to include it in his memoirs. What does astonish me, on the other hand, is that the highly intelligent Albert Speer was seriously thinking of killing Hitler at the same moment, in

February 1945. At least that's what he claims now. Assuming that he actually intended to gas every living person in the Reich Chancellery, he must have known that the single result would have been chaos. Grossadmiral Dönitz has solemnly stated this, as have others.

Even without Adolf Hitler the German people would have had to surrender unconditionally. This demand of Roosevelt's, Stalin's and Churchill's prolonged the war by two years. Who benefited from this?

• • •

On the evening of February 28, 1945 I was summoned to Führer Headquarters in Berlin. Another Waffen-SS officer took command in the bridgehead. This time the Western Front was the topic. But the organization of combined operations was proving to be increasingly difficult. Friedenthal was bombed heavily and the BBC had reported three times that "the headquarters of Mussolini kidnapper Skorzeny had been completely destroyed." However my most important offices had already been transferred to Hof in Bavaria. This didn't exactly make my work easier when I had to improvise an action against the Remagen bridge.

The monitoring service informed me of a further BBC report, according to which Hitler had promoted me to Generalmajor, given me an important post in the defense of Berlin and that I had already begun a purge. In fact Hitler had decorated me with the Knight's Cross with Oak Leaves for the defense of Schwedt and congratulated me personally. I had just come down the long stairs of the Reich Chancellery when he left teh situation room. His appearance was shocking: bent, with grey hair – a picture of misery. The date was March 29 or 30, 1945.

"Skorzeny," he said, "I would once again like to thank you for your accomplishments on the Oder."

The bridgehead had been abandoned on March 3!

"We'll see each other again soon," he said. But I was never to see Hitler again.

I later learned that Generaloberst Jodl had in fact mentioned my name: he wanted to use me in the defense of Berlin. But how could the news reach the BBC if I didn't even know about it?

I often drove to the Reich Chancellery on official business in that terrible month of March 1945. My eye injury hurt and Doctor Stumpfegger wanted to look at it.

The examination took place in the room of Hitler's secretary. On this day I was introduced to Eva Braun, who shortly before she died was to become Hitler's wife. She was a young, very simple and extremely likeable woman, of whose existence I had previously been unaware. I had a long talk with her. She was pleased to meet me and invited me to have dinner another day. I didn't take her up on this invitation, however, for Doctor Stumpfegger told me that Fegelein, who was married to Eva Braun's sister, was always present at such receptions. I already spoke of Fegelein in a previous chapter. His boasting and arrogance were well known within the Waffen-SS. I had had something to do with him during the preparation of Operation Greif and didn't want to know him any better.

The weeks I spent in devastated Berlin, a shadow of the city I had known, and which Hitler wanted to completely rebuild in 1940, were a nightmare for me.

One evening an air raid warning had been issued, and when the 2,000-kilogram bombs began falling I fled to the large bunker near the Zoological Gardens. The Luftwaffe had installed a field hospital in this unusual structure, which the allies had great difficulty destroying after the war. I used the opportunity to visit two of my men being treated there, our "chinaman" Werner Hunke and Leutnant Holle, who had been wounded at Schwedt. I also found Flugkapitän Hanna Reitsch there – in a poor frame of mind – and Luftwaffe Oberst Hans-Ulrich Rudel, the famous Stuka pilot, who had just had a leg amputated.

My comrade and friend Rudel had flown more than 2,530 combat missions, destroyed 519 tanks and sunk the 23,000-ton battleship *Marat* in Kronstadt harbor. Hitler created a special decoration for this German soldier: the Knight's Cross in Gold with Oak Leaves, Swords and Diamonds. In spite of his injuries and a strict ban from the Führer, Rudel continued flying until May 8, 1945.

On that day Rudel and what was left of his Geschwader voluntarily surrendered to the U.S. Air Force at Kitzingen airfield in Bavaria. The pilots destroyed their aircraft after landing. They were led into the officers mess; Rudel was taken to the hospital where they casually bandaged his bleeding stump. Then Hans-Ulrich Rudel also appeared in the mess. As he walked in his men stood up and greeted him with the Hitler salute, which had been the official Wehrmacht salute since July 20, 1944. An interpreter told Rudel that the American commander wanted no further demonstrations of this kind and that he didn't care for this salute. I now quote John Toland, who wrote in *The Last 100 Days*: "We have been ordered to salute this way. And as we are soldiers we will obey this order whether you like it or not!"

He also declared that the German soldier had not been defeated by a "superior human enemy," but by overwhelming masses of materiel and said, "We have landed here on German territory, because we didn't want to stay in the Soviet zone. We are prisoners and don't wish any further discussion. We would like to wash – if that's possible."

The American commander subsequently had a very cordial conversation with the Oberst. But just as they took from me the watch the Duce had given me, so too was Rudel robbed of his Knight's Cross in Gold while he slept. Rudel was the only recipient of the decoration.

Like in Balzac's novel *Peau de chagrin*, the area on which we fought shrank day by day in the east and west. On March 30, 1945 I received the order from the OKW to transfer my headquarters to the Alpine Fortress, where principally the Führer Headquarters was also to be set up. Obviously the last battles of the war were supposed to take place in this redoubt. The OKW had confirmed to me that the "fortress" was fully ready to mount a defense.

We – Radl and I – found the mountains, the glaciers, the forests, the wild streams all in "their place," but not a trace of military preparation or of fortification. I realized that everything would once again have to be improvised. However my units were scattered, more like destroyed or decimated. It proved difficult to collect several of my soldiers who possessed mountain experience. I was able to have the commander of Commando Unit Center and 250 soldiers assigned to us.

Afterwards I sought out Feldmarschall Schörner north of Olmütz and placed about 100 soldiers of Commando Unit East II at his disposal. This formation's Unit I had been destroyed at Hohensalza. I have described the acts of this commando unit's soldiers elsewhere in this book.

On the morning of April 10, I learned from Schörner's staff that Vienna was already threatened, or more accurately that the remnants of Commando Unit Southeast and Battle Group Danube had been forced to leave the city to defend the so-called Alpine Fortress. However Vienna was my birthplace. My mother, my wife and my daughter must still be there, and perhaps I could help get them out of the battle zone.

I set off in that direction and reached Vienna in the afternoon, accompanied by my adjutant, Untersturmführer Gallent, my driver Anton Gfoeler – who had been present on the Gran Sasso – and a radio operator who had been sent by the OKW. I had been ordered by no less a personage than Generaloberst Jodl to make regular reports on the southern front, which we were abandoning.

Before we drove across the Florisdorfer Bridge we witnessed a spectacle that proved to me that the end really had come. We had just passed a tank obstacle. To the right and left wounded sat in the ditches. On the road a convoy of wagons drawn by teams of six horses. A fat Feldwebel in the company of a young girl sat on the first wagon. One look was enough: this man was a furniture mover. The six wagons were loaded to overflowing with furniture and linen. I tried not to lose my composure and asked the Feldwebel to take along some of the wounded.

"Can't do it," he said. "All full."

Everything happened quickly from that point. We disarmed the Feldwebel and the other drivers. I passed out the weapons to those with minor injuries. The wagons were unloaded and the wounded were lifted onto them. The others took the places of the furniture movers. I said to a Feldwebel who was wounded in the arm, "Drive in a westerly direction to the nearest hospital and take as many wounded with you as you can."

And to the Feldwebel who wanted to rescue the furniture, "You are a proper filthy pig. You and your people get out of here, and if you don't intend to fight, at least try to be less greedy in the future and be more comradely."

We arrived in Vienna as darkness was falling. Cannon were firing. Where was the front? The city seemed dead. Houses burned here and there. We drove on to the Stubenring and past the former war ministry: it was empty. A sentry told us that the command post had been moved to the Hofburg, the palace in the center of the city in which the old Kaiser had lived.

Where were our troops? Who was defending now and who would defend Vienna? I had to turn around at the Schwedenplatz: the rubble of the house in which my brother, who had been called up, lived, blocked the way to the Danube quay. Finally I reached the headquarters of Commando Unit Southeast. The remnants of the unit had withdrawn into the area north of Krems in the afternoon; Commando Unit Danube had likewise evacuated its training quarters in the Diana Baths. I found these soldiers in the following days on my way to the Alpine Fortress and ordered them to Salzburg.

The courtyard of the former Kaiser's palace was jam packed with vehicles. In the cellar an officer reported to me that the Russians had apparently already infiltrated the city and were "being held up and engaged everywhere." By whom? That was a mystery. I wanted to know precisely and decided to continue on my way. I reached the Matzleindorf zone. It was already after midnight. From the left came the sound of battle. Ahead of me a barricade. I got out of the car. Two elderly Vienna policemen appeared, "We are manning the barricade here," they declared to me. "If the Russians show up here, we will surround them and they'll have to give themselves up."

They had always had a sense of humor in Vienna – even if it was only gallows humor!

I drove through the dead streets back to the Hofburg and spoke briefly with Oberstleutnant H. Kurz, the adjutant of the Gauleiter and former Reich Youth Leader Baldur von Schirach. My report left Kurz very skeptical.

"The reports we have," he said, "prove the contrary, that the front has been stabilized. Anyhow you can speak to the Gauleiter yourself."

In his book *Ich glaubte an Hitler* (*I Believed in Hitler*) Schirach claimed that he had installed his headquarters "in the cellars of the Hofburg" from April 6. That is correct, but he had made one room in the cellar into a candle-lit salon for himself. On the floor lay magnificent carpets, paintings of battles and portraits of generals from the Eighteenth Century hung on the walls. The ante-room was used for eating, drinking and kicking up a row. I had to explain to the Gauleiter that I hadn't seen a single German soldier in the city and that the barricades were unmanned. I invited him to undertake an inspection with me. However he declined this invitation and explained to me, bent over his map, how they would save Vienna: two elite divisions were ready to attack. One would attack from the north and the other from the west: the enemy must capitulate.

"Prince Starhemberg used a similar maneuver," he observed, "to lift the siege of Vienna by the Turks in 1683."

Any further discussion was pointless. I took my leave. Schirach looked at me, "Skorzeny, my duty is expressed in three words: prevail or die!"

He undoubtedly meant to say "prevail or retreat," for five hours later the defense commissar of Vienna district left Vienna as fast as he could.

I found my mother's house half in ruins. However a neighbor who crawled from his cellar assured me that my mother had left Vienna with my wife and daughter the day before. I drove to my home in Döbling. The house was untouched. I quickly collected several hunting rifles and took a last look at the home that I was about to leave ready for occupancy by the enemy or looters.

I left the city by the Florisdorfer Bridge and turned around once more: "Auf Wiedersehen, Vienna." Then we took the Waldviertler Road to Upper Austria. In carrying out the mission given me by Generaloberst Jodl, I sent the following radio message: *"All indications are that Vienna will fall today, the 11th of April 1945."*

Notes

1. Himmler maneuvered and intrigued in order to become and remain the head of Army Group Vistula. Guderian stated that Himmler also hoped to receive the Knight's Cross, which many officers of the Waffen-SS had been decorated. He even wanted the Knight's Cross with Oak Leaves, but his hopes were in vain. (Editors' note)

26

NUREMBERG

Grossadmiral Dönitz: "Our Führer is dead..." – Churchill's belated revelations – General Rendulic proposes terms to General Walker – The defense of the South Tyrolean passes was impossible – We become prisoners of war voluntarily – "Have a drink; tonight you will be hanged" – Handcuffs – "Where did you take Hitler?" – Colonel Andrus – Suicide and unusual incidents – The Nuremberg Tribunal – The prison under a state of siege: they fear a surprise attack by Skorzeny and his troops! – "Watched like cobra!" – In Dachau – "Wild Jacob" – Soviet offers – Our trial – Generous testimony by Wing Commander Yeo-Thomas – Acquitted! – I leave the Darmstadt camp

I learned of Hitler's death in Berlin on the afternoon of April 30. The city was surrounded by the Russians and was one great field of rubble. Prominent among the last troops defending what was left of the Reich Chancellery was a battalion of the French Waffen-SS Division Charlemagne.

Hitler dead! After the initial shock we considered this news as unlikely. Adolf Hitler was supposed to go to the Alpine Fortress. There were still troops ready to fight. No! That was impossible! They were lying to us. Perhaps he would yet come.

However the report was soon officially confirmed. The next day when we heard Anton Bruckner's 7th Symphony on German radio we knew what had happened. Before his death he had named Karl Dönitz the German head of state. On May 1 the Grossadmiral addressed the German people:

"Our leader, Adolf Hitler, has fallen... His life was service to Germany. His actions in the struggle against bolshevism were also for the benefit of Europe and the entire cultured world... The Führer chose me as his successor... My first task is to save German people from destruction by the advancing bolshevik enemy. As far as and as long as the achieving of this objective is hindered by the British and Americans, we will also have to defend ourselves against them and fight on... Maintain order and discipline in the cities and in the country, each do his duty in his place..."

I had all my officers and men fall in alongside my command train. There was no need to make a speech. I merely said to them: "The Führer is dead. Long live Germany!" Then my German soldiers joined in the national anthem *Deutschland über alles,* and together with the European volunteers we sang *"Ich hatt' einen Kameraden.*

● ● ●

We all felt that the new Reich President was right and that the struggle must be continued in order to at least keep the way open to the west for as many women, children and soldiers as possible. In spite of a lack of preparation the Alpine Fortress had to and could offer sanctuary to many people. That was my plan since Radl had joined me in Radstadt with 250 men. The economics minister and the president of the Reichsbank had also sent me two of their adjutants and asked me to look after the Reichsbank's treasure. I informed them with the necessary courtesy that I was not a safe watcher but a soldier and that they had the wrong number with me.

Theoretically the Alpine Fortress should have been made into a fortified area 350 kilometers long and 75 wide, which extended from Bregenz in the west to Bad Aussee in the east, through Füssen and Traunstein to Salzburg in the north and in the south to Glurns, Bozen, Cortina d'Ampezzo and Lienz. The last-mentioned line was pulled back to the Brenner Pass following the surrender of the German armed forces in Italy. But after a few days I came to the realization that this fortress never existed and never would exist. Was a dissolution of the allied alliance possible now that Hitler was dead and the national-socialist state had collapsed? I doubted it. However Winston Churchill made the following declaration to the voters in Woodford, and it was an astonishing admission:

"Before the end of the war, when the Germans were surrendering by the hundreds of thousands, I telegraphed Lord Montgomery that he should carefully collect and store the German weapons, so that they could be easily handed out to the German soldiers again if we were forced to cooperate with Germany in the event of a further Russian advance into Europe. My mistrust with regard to Stalin was considerable, for he was doing everything to secure world dominance for Russia and communism."

We thought we must be dreaming! "...in the event of a further Russian advance." But who had made possible this advance into Europe? Nowadays one can smile when he reads that "the German soldier prevented all of Europe from becoming bolshevik." But if we hadn't fought as we did in the east, many of those who have criticized us since 1945 and branded the Waffen-SS as a criminal organization wouldn't have the opportunity to enjoy freedom today; they would also very probably no longer be alive, and if they were they could suffer in silence or break rock in Verkoyansk.

It was clear that the rapid advance by the Soviet armies into the heart of Europe posed an immense danger, not only for the peoples of the old continent but for Great Britain and the United States as well. The belated realizations of the British Prime Minister are proof enough of that. General Guderian assured me that the Wehrmacht could still have inflicted a bloody defeat on the Soviet armies, whose supply lines were already overextended, at the beginning of February 1945 – provided that the western powers gave the Wehrmacht freedom of action in the east. Unfortunately that was not the case.

I also met General Rendulic at this time. He was commanding our Army Group South and at the end held a front reaching from central Austria to the Czechoslovakian border against the Red Army.

Generaloberst Rendulic, who was also an historian, didn't want to just write history, he wanted to make it as well. After the death of Hitler he dreamed that the four armies under his command could not only stop Malinovsky and Tolbukhin in their march to the west, but drive them back far beyond the Danube line. He also sent a negotiator, who gave Major-General Walton H. Walker, the chief of the American 2nd Corps, the following explanation:

1.   Even if those in the United States were of the opinion in 1941 that Germany was a threat to the USA, they must now admit that this threat no longer exists.

2.   Hitler is dead; the German armies are fighting with the last of their strength, and the western allies cannot deny that the real threat comes from bolshevism – in Europe as everywhere.

3.   In the face of such danger the directly or indirectly threatened powers must show their solidarity. Consequently Rendulic asks General Walker to allow the German reserve troops still on hand to pass, so that he can reinforce his four armies and counterattack in the east.

General Walker's reply was sarcastic and negative. Rendulic was four years ahead of the North Atlantic Treaty Organization which was founded in 1949.

● ● ●

Acting on the instructions of the High Command South, which was based by the Königsee, I had concentrated all the surviving and straggling soldiers of my units into a new formation, which was dubbed the Alpine Guard Corps. However it had little in common with an army corps apart from the name.

I received the last order from High Command South on May 1, 1945: I was to organize the defense of the South Tyrolean passes so that the troops of General Vietinghoff, Generalfeldmarschall Kesselring's successor in Italy, could withdraw. At the same time I was to prevent the Anglo-American troops from entering Austria. But it was too late. Our army in Italy had already surrendered without even informing Feldmarschall Kesselring. The officers of the Alpine Guard Corps, which I had immediately sent to the Italian border, were smart enough to return to me as soon as they saw what was happening.

On May 6 Grossadmiral Dönitz issued the order that we were to lay down our weapons on all fronts at midnight on May 8. I withdrew into the mountains with my closest associates to wait and see what would happen. My troops were grouped in small units in the nearby valleys, waiting for my last orders.

Germany had lost the Second World War in spite of the courage of its soldiers. We had really done our utmost to prevent this.

I could have committed suicide; many of our comrades sought death in the final battles or freely took their own lives. I could also have quite easily flown to a neutral country in a Ju 88. But I refused to abandon my country, my family and my comrades in an hour of need. I had nothing to hide, hadn't attempted anything and had done or ordered nothing that would shame a true soldier. I decided to surrender voluntarily and sent two messages to the American division headquarters in Salzburg. In these messages I proposed that the soldiers of the Alpine Guard Corps should go into captivity together. I received no answer. I later learned that the U.S. headquarters had decided that this was a new trick on my part; I could never find out how this, my last "stratagem," was supposed to work.

What I didn't know was that I was being eagerly sought and that the allied press and radio were calling me "the most devilishly intelligent man in Germany." I really had no idea of the legend that already surrounded my name.

● ● ●

On the 20th of May 1945 Radl, Hunke, the officer candidate and interpreter Peter and I, armed and in field uniform, climbed down into the valley. We had asked them to send a jeep for us at a certain bridge near Annaberg. The jeep was in fact there to drive us to Salzburg.

Our driver, a man from Texas, showed a great deal of interest in us. Along the road he stopped in front of an inn. I got out with him. He ordered a bottle of good wine, which I paid for. After we resumed our journey the Texan turned to me and said, "All kidding aside, are you really Skorzeny?"

"Naturally."

"Well then have a drink with your boys, for tonight you'll surely be hanged!"

I therefore drank "to our health." Toward midday we arrived in Salzburg; our driver couldn't or didn't want to find the division headquarters. He dropped us off in front of a hotel that had been taken over by the Americans, saluted cordially and disappeared. In front of the hotel several German liaison officers looked at us in amazement: we were still carrying weapons!

An American major finally took the trouble to listen to us. He sent us back to Saint Johann in Pongau in another jeep. There we were to pick up trucks and other vehicles with which to transport the Alpine Guard Corps from the German office in the prisoner of war camp and from the American units. A German general then sent us to a US battalion stationed at Werfen. I instructed Hunke to stay in St. Johann; if we weren't back in three hours, it would mean that we were prisoners. In this case Hunke was to inform our people and from then on the motto "everyone take care of himself and God everyone" would be the order of the day.

The American battalion had established its headquarters in a comfortable villa on the side of a hill. I had a discussion with a captain. Radl and Peter had to remain at the entrance. Instead of signing the passes I needed to transport my Alpine Guard Corps to Salzburg and prisoner of war camp, the captain led me to the dining room, where four American officers and an interpreter were waiting. Even as I was pointing out on a map where my people were waiting, the three doors and windows were flung open. A dozen submachine-guns were pointing at me and the interpreter asked me to hand over my pistol, which I did. I said to him:

"Be careful, it's loaded, and the last bullet is dangerous."

Then I was frisked and stripped naked. My Mussolini watch was stolen; I had it returned to me but then it disappeared again, this time for good. Finally Radl, Peter and I were put into three jeeps, which drove away between two armored cars. We arrived in Salzburg during the night. They had us get out in the garden of a villa. I had just lit a cigarette when a pair of MPs grabbed us from behind and handcuffed us behind the back. Then I was shoved into a room where a dozen people sat behind two or three desks. There were several reporters and photographers among them. An officer began interrogating me. I stated that I would not speak a word until they removed the handcuffs, which they did. Afterward I walked to the window – the machine-guns still trained on me – and called into the garden, "Radl, Peter, are you still bound?"

"Yes," came the answer from Radl. "It stinks!"

I turned to the major.

"I will not answer as long as my companions are in handcuffs."

I remained standing in front of the window. After some time I heard Radl's voice, "It's alright. Thank you!"

Then I sat down in front of the American major and declared myself ready to answer his questions. His first was, "You had a plan to murder General Eisenhower, didn't you?"

I said that I had not. Further questions followed, questions I was to hear over and over again from American, British and even French intelligence officers in my three years as a prisoner: "If you didn't plan to kill Eisenhower, did you intend to kidnap him? We know for a fact that you intended to kill or kidnap General Bradley! Why didn't the Italian and Hungarian forces on the Gran Sasso and in Budapest fire at you? What were you doing in Berlin at the end of April 1945? Where did you take Hitler? We know from a reliable source that you flew away with Hitler in an aircraft early on the morning of April 30, 1945. Where is he hiding? You know how to fly, don't you? You flew the aircraft; Hitler sat beside you in the cockpit; you can see how well informed we are! ... You needn't deny it: you intended to blow up Montgomery's headquarters, we have proof of it! How do you know that Hitler killed himself in Berlin if you weren't in Berlin at the end of April? Did Hitler give you the order to murder Eisenhower? Who then?" And so on and so on.

After several days I managed to convince Colonel Henry Gordon Sheen, one of the American intelligence chiefs: "If I had taken Adolf Hitler to a safe place," I said to him, "I would have stayed there and not surrendered with my comrades."

"That's a trick," declared the journalists. "Skorzeny is trying to cover up the tracks." The reporters from the *New York Times* and the *Christian Science Monitor* outdid all the others in their skepticism. In his book *Commando Extraordinary*, Charles Foley stated that, "Skorzeny became a character of modern mythology capable of anything."

General Walter Bedell Smith, the high command chief-of-staff, called all the allied press correspondents together in the Hotel Scribe in Paris. Foley wrote:

"The general stated that there had never been a plot against the life and the freedom of General Dwight D. Eisenhower. Military intelligence had been mislead by conflicting orders."

Not satisfied with that, the journalists then asked the general embarrassing questions about the "state of siege" that had existed at Eisenhower's headquarters at the end of 1944 and early 1945, General Eisenhower's double, and the fact that the latter was virtually held prisoner at Versailles by his own troops. General Bedell Smith admitted that it was a case of "mistakes," which had happened on account of faulty intelligence. The journalists remained skeptical, and after lengthy investigations and counter-investigations the allied intelligence services reached the conclusion that something was fishy: my alibis were all too convincing.

I was taken from one prison to another. In the sixth I shared a cell with Generalfeldmarschall Kesselring. On May 29, 1945 I was installed in a wooden hut with Dr. Kaltenbrunner. The shack was copiously equipped with microphones. We talked about our student days; the listening service must have been very disappointed. Dr. Kaltenbrunner had the bad luck to have taken over the post of RSHA chief Reinhard Heydrich, who was murdered in Prague in 1942. He was taken to London and for the first few weeks was interrogated quite thoroughly. Then they locked him up in the Tower of London for seven weeks.

Day and night he had to endure beatings in total darkness, just like those reserved for former Russian prisoners in the Fortress of Peter and Paul: the water slowly rose to a depth of more than a meter in his cell and then flowed out again. This was followed by a cold shower and blows.

Kaltenbrunner was often unable to appear during the trial in Nuremberg on account of three outbreaks of meningitis. I saw him for the last time in July 1946: he was calm and collected, even though he knew that they had sentenced him to death and were going to execute him.

Another fellow prisoner was Dr. Ley, who they had arrested in sky blue pajamas and slippers. As they led him away he reached for a woolen overcoat; as well they placed a tyrolean hat on his head. He did not hold up well to his treatment in prison and soon after he was transferred to Nuremberg prison he committed suicide.

In the Oberursel camp I met Radl, who received permission to share a cell with me. But on September 10, 1945 they once again put handcuffs on me, before taking me to an aircraft which flew us to Nuremberg. Also in the aircraft were Grossadmiral Dönitz, Generalfeldmarschall Keitel, Generaloberst Jodl, Generaloberst Guderian, Dr. Ley – still in pajamas – and even Baldur von Schirach.

On our arrival in Nuremberg Prison the commander of this penal institution, the American Colonel Andrus – he wore a pince-nez and bore a striking resemblance to Heinrich Himmler – almost had a stroke. He found to his horror that Grossadmiral Dönitz and I were still wearing full uniform and badges of rank. Colonel Andrus declared that our uniforms were not permissible and that this was a legitimate provocation. Alerted by his cries, several black military policemen came running. But I had already given the Grossadmiral a military salute. He understood my salute and nodded in approval.

We removed each other's badges of rank without saying a word. Then we saluted and the last head of state of the Third Reich shook my hand.

The prison at Nuremberg was a large building shaped like a five-pointed star. We were guarded by large numbers of black soldiers; our jailer, Colonel Andrus, thought to degrade us in this way. But I always got along well with the blacks, who proved to be much more humane than the whites. One huge young man, a black sergeant, who was extremely friendly, became my friend and more than once slipped me a few cigarettes and chocolate.

We were quite well fed during the first weeks. Older German prisoners, soldiers, who were assigned to kitchen duty, did their best for us – to the annoyance of Colonel Andrus. He was Lithuanian by birth, having become an American citizen only recently, and hated everything German. One day he said to us, "I know that they call you 'krauts' because you like it (sauerkraut) so much. You will therefore get some to eat every day." He saw to it that the food was bland and also of very poor quality.

A young Austrian engineer from the armaments ministry managed to get himself assigned to the kitchen. His name was Raffelsberger, I believe, and he saw to it that I received dumplings. He was the only prisoner to escape from Nuremberg Prison; he did so when he drove into town with several GIs to pick up provisions. He reached South America. At the beginning I was in the wing where the accused were held. My cell was opposite that of the Reichsmarschall. We communicated by way of sign language, for talking was strictly forbidden. Then, just before Christmas 1945, I was transferred to the witnesses wing. Our cells were locked at night and open all day. Andrus issued a draconian decree: whenever he appeared, every prisoner had to stand at attention in the doorway of his cell and had to salute fifteen steps before he passed and twelve after. I found this measure laughable, and each time his illustrious person came into view I ducked into the nearest cell. He noted this and called out to me, "So you refuse to salute me?"

"I will salute you when we are treated like soldiers who are prisoners of war. I refuse to salute you in a subservient way. I am an officer with the same rank as you and not a lackey!"

"I can have you punished for disobeying orders with a month in solitary confinement!"

"You can do whatever you like!"

I believe that the American officers under Andrus hated him more than he did us. I met one of these officers on a flight a few years ago. He recognized me and told me that my behavior toward Colonel Andrus had been pure satisfaction to him and his comrades.

Outwardly the Americans' conduct was "correct." Colonel Andrus therefore let us know that we had the right to complain. In reality not a single complaint was resolved positively. Generaloberst Halder, who was liked by the Americans, had a unique experience. When he remarked to our jailer that he had been treated better in the German concentration camp than in Nuremberg, he received two weeks "in the klink."

Some couldn't take it. Besides Dr. Ley, the good and brave Dr. Conti, the Reich Health Leader who was unjustly accused, hanged himself in the next cell. Generaloberst Blaskowitz jumped to his death from the fourth floor catwalk. And Generalfeldmarschall von Blomberg died in the aid station, where they took him at the last minute. Once, during my weekly walk to the showers, I was allowed to "take along" three bed sheets, one of which I gave to von Blomberg, who was always sick. I gave the second to the Austrian General von Glaise-Horstenau, who had once been the adjutant of Kaiser Franz-Josef. The third I kept for myself. We used them to make clean sleeping bags.

Colonel Andrus was able to introduce even stricter measures as a result of these suicides. There were surprise inspections of the cells day and night. We had to sleep with the lights on, were not allowed to cover our heads and had to face the light bulbs. If we covered our eyes with the blanket while asleep, we were brutally wakened by the guard.

Later, when Reichsmarschall Göring poisoned himself with cyanide, there was a large-scale inspection of all the cells. In Generaloberst Jodl's cell they found thirty centimeters of wire and two sharpened rivets, in Generalfeldmarschall Keitel's a razor blade and in Ribbentrop's a broken bottle.

The worst however, at least for me, was the prison's oppressive atmosphere. The constant spying, the deals they tried to make with the weakest, the use of informants, the denunciations, the false accusations, the servile behavior of certain of the accused and witnesses who hoped to come out of the entire affair with enhanced reputations – they made promises, which they kept, if they proved cooperative – all this had affected my morale badly. I came close to reacting in a way that would have given Colonel Andrus an excuse to punish me hard. There was nothing that he couldn't and wouldn't use against us. We were "tested" by the so-called psychologists. M. Coldensen and "Professor" G.M. Gilbert took me to task several times. We had to take an I.Q. test. The big winners were Doctor Seyss-Inquart, Doctor Schacht and Göring. The Americans were extremely surprised when they found that, by their own criteria, our intelligence quotas proved to be "very above average."

But the main job of these "psychologists" was to report to the prosecutors and create disunity among the prisoners. For example, I was told that so and so had spoken very badly of me – in the hope that I would in turn speak badly of him and reveal something that could be exploited by the prosecution or at least by the press. This trick didn't work on me, but the weak and naive fell for it.

The journalists were hungry for sensational news, and it is not surprising that the international press published such "sensational bulletins" at that time, for the more fantastic a story, the higher the price paid for it. Publishing agreements were concluded by way of middlemen. They asked me for "ready to print" text. I refused. Many prisoners, however, spent the whole day typing, either for the press or for the prosecution – which came to the same thing.

General Warlimont and the "iridescent" Höttl, alias Walter Hagen, worked – no doubt on their defense – from morning until night.

The commentator of Radio Nuremberg also had a news net inside the prison. He called himself Gaston Oulman and allegedly came from a South American republic. In truth his name was Ullmann and before the war he had been on bad terms with the German courts.

The autograph trade was in full swing. Without embarrassing myself, I demanded a package of cigarettes for each autograph. But the more "dangerous" one was, the higher the fee. I knew more than one prisoner who made himself out to be a very dangerous criminal in order to make his stay more comfortable. I don't know whether their false familiarity with the guards was later included in the list of charges or not. At least the friendliness of the catholic prison chaplain Father Sixtus O'Connor, who likewise could have been dangerous in a certain way, was honest. Though the Augustinian order to which he belonged to came from a cloistered community, the father was nothing like a penitent monk – quite the contrary. He had long talks with the prisoners, proved to be conciliatory, friendly and stood up for the prisoners to the extent that Colonel Andrus' decrees allowed. He was Irish, his mother was of German descent, and many of the prison inmates were very flattering to him. Among the keenest were Gauleiter Frank, von dem Bach-Zelewski, General Warlimont, Gauleiter Bohle, Schellenberg and the talented Höttl.

Father Sixtus' sermons were filled with references that everyone could understand, for he did not hold back in his criticism of the Nuremberg Tribunal. On Remembrance Day in November 1945 he preached about the sacrifice of millions of German soldiers who had fallen honorably in battle with the enemy.

Victors who set themselves up as judge and jury and who have the defeated at their mercy for better or worse, have at their disposal the means of exerting tremendous pressure. Thus it wasn't until February 1946 that we were allowed to correspond with our families. However for many of us the joy was short-lived: the bombing raids, the final battles, the occupation by three, then four armies, had claimed many victims.

The "confessions" made at Nuremberg and quite generally the statements made by prisoners under interrogation by the enemy's military-political police must be read by the historian with a great deal of skepticism. Many prisoner gave false testimony in order to be acquitted; I therefore denounce them. One in particular behaved wretchedly: "I have a wife and children," he said to me. "I can't act any other way." As if we all didn't have families to think about!

I was imprisoned in Nuremberg Prison three times: from October 1945 until May 1946, in July and August 1946 and in February and March 1948. The third time I decided to accept a job. In each cell they had replaced the panes of glass with sheets of plastic, which were attached to the window frame with small strips of wood, which frequently came loose. I volunteered to fix the windows.

Apart from the fact that they paid me for this work with a pack of cigarettes each week, I was given the opportunity to go into the cells and talk to my comrades, establish interesting relationships and encourage those whose morale had sunk to zero. At the same time I encouraged myself. When the guards intervened I claimed that I had asked about the prisoner's family or something of the like. I must repeat that a real solidarity existed between us and the black guards, the pariahs. The psychologists made a big mistake when they had us guarded by blacks, who refused to treat us like animals and in doing so gave Colonel Andrus a lesson in humanitarian behavior.

● ● ●

It was the time of the "war crimes trials." In the British occupation zone lengthy investigations were made of 700,000 German officers and soldiers. At the end they found 937 prisoners who were suspected of having committed war crimes. The British military courts sentenced them as follows:

Death penalty:	230
Life imprisonment:	24
Prison (suspended):	423
	—
	677
Acquitted:	260

Six-hundred-and-seventy-seven men had thus fought the war in a way that the enemy saw as incorrect, that meant fewer than one in ten-thousand soldiers.

• • •

In the American zone of occupation, following Brigadier-General Telford Taylor's final report only 570 German military personnel were affected by the famous Law No. 10.[1] Only 177 were brought before the American special court, with the following result:

Death sentence:	24
Life imprisonment:	118
	——
	142
Acquitted:	35

Several thousand persons were arrested in the French occupation zone. The following sentences were issued on the spot:

Death sentences:	104 (carried out)
Life imprisonment:	44
Imprisonment (suspended):	1475
	——
	1623
Acquitted:	404

This meant that 2,442 men were convicted from more than 10 million soldiers, or .024%[2] In the Soviet occupation zone the number of summary executions exceeded 185,000. Of the four million German prisoners of war in the Soviet Union barely thirty percent returned from 1955.

• • •

At the beginning of March we noticed that something unusual was going on in Nuremberg. Colonel Andrus put the Palace of Justice on a state of alert. The guard was tripled. Anti-tank barricades were set up at the main entrances; machine-gun nests protected by sand bags and heavy sheet metal were installed on almost every corner. Small rifle stands with armor protection were set up in the prison corridors, behind which our guards could take cover and fight off an enemy. But what enemy was approaching?

We vainly sought an explanation for these warlike preparations; then Father Sixtus, who had just come from the officers mess, explained it to me. An American general, whose name the father would not betray to me – for he could be very secretive when he had to be – had told him the following: motorized German guerilla units had been sighted near Nuremberg. Their objective was to march into the city, storm the prison and free all the prisoners. These people were all the more dangerous, because they were commanded by Colonel Otto Skorzeny, the one who had kidnapped Mussolini and had nearly kidnapped General Eisenhower.

"But," argued Father Sixtus, "Colonel Skorzeny is here in prison, since September of last year. I spoke to him only yesterday."

"In that case," observed the general, "you can rest assured that you were talking to a phoney Skorzeny, for my information comes from the best of sources. We will clear up this story."

The result for me was intense interrogation, which sometimes degenerated into pure farce. Finally I was able to convince that that I – was myself.

When I was transferred to a camp at Regensburg in Bavaria, I ran into my former radio officer, who explained the whole story. He had discharged himself when the Alpine Guard Corps was dissolved. He reached his family, which lived in Nuremberg. When he learned from the papers that I was imprisoned there, he decided to free me and, if possible, help me flee. A plan was worked out – it was totally impracticable – , but one of the plotters talked and the whole group was arrested. The police informer probably though he recognized me as I walked freely around Germany; therefore the great alarm in the prison, which was maintained for months after the interrogation.

Stars and Stripes, the American armed forces newspaper, took a great interest in me. Under the headline "Guarded like a Cobra," one issue featured an illustrated article on me. I learned that I had successfully escaped four or five times, but that each time I had been picked up. I read this article in bed in the medical station in Dachau, where they had carried out a gall bladder operation on me and where I was in fact "guarded like a cobra," for a guard shared my hospital room with me day and night.

In May 1946 I was transferred to the old Dachau concentration camp. Soon afterward I found myself in a camp in Darmstadt, then back in Nuremberg, then in Dachau again, where I went on a hunger strike to protest against my solitary confinement and against the treatment of the German prisoners in general.

When one speaks of the old Dachau concentration camp one must be clear about one thing: the camp's facilities were relatively comfortable for prisoners in solitary; those sentenced to solitary confinement had a rather large room (about 3.5 x 2.5 x 3 meters), with large, barred windows, wash basin and their own toilet. The Americans built a new bunker inside the camp, with cells for two prisoners each. Each cell was 2.5 meters long, 1.4 meters wide and 2.2 meters high and had a tiny, barred window. We were forced to wash in the toilet. They even showed me the extraordinary kindness of assigning me a habitual criminal for a cell mate. I quickly made it clear to him who was in charge. I don't know what camp they found him in, but I had to teach him how to wash himself.

At least my habitual criminal didn't have the same reputation as Jakob Gröschner, "Wild Jacob," who resided in, as he called it, "good old Dachau" and who played the part of a crazy man. He was as strong as Hercules, smashed everything that he could lay his hands on, set his bed on fire, bent the bars in the window, climbed onto the roof and so on. I don't know why, but I felt sympathetic toward him. Whenever he saw me, even from a distance, he called out, "Always keep a stiff upper lip, Herr Oberst! ... Don't give in an inch ... You are right! ... Forwards!" and the like.

I have already mentioned our trial in Dachau, in which all the defendants were acquitted. One of my supply officers behaved very badly during the trial. Then "Wild Jacob" declared that, "these people are all traitors" and must be "punished severely." No one paid much attention to these remarks until one day Gröschner began beating the poor official with a stick and left him in rather bad shape. I had a great deal of difficulty convincing the American authorities that "Wild Jacob" had acted of his own accord.

Finally the Americans sent him to a clinic. He was released from there as mentally disturbed. In Hannover a Czech intelligence agent approached him with the idea of kidnapping me. Gröschner was able to inform me – even though I had changed prisons – that the Soviets intended to achieve by force in a special operation what they had been unable to do through persuasion.

In fact in November 1945 in Nuremberg I was questioned two or three times by the Soviet prosecutor who, by the way, was extremely correct. We had the following interesting dialogue in the course of the last interrogation:

"It is really astonishing," he said, "that you didn't receive your promotion to Generalmajor. You should have been at least a general!"

"I am an engineer and not a career military man, you know. And intrigues are not my strength."

"I know. Do you like it here? This prison is no friendly surrounding."

"A prison is never a pleasant place to be."

"I see that we understand each other. It would be an easy thing for me to have you called to Berlin by our command posts in two or three days. There you could select a job with us that suits your great abilities."

"Your offer is very well meant. But although Germany has lost this war, it is not yet over for me. I didn't fight alone. I was given orders and I had my comrades carry them out and now I must defend them. I can't leave them in the lurch after our defeat."

"I think you have seen and heard enough to understand. Many personalities who were above you didn't come here at all, perhaps to leave you sitting here now."

"That is the affair of those superiors and not mine!"

He didn't pursue the matter any further, nor did the Americans, who interviewed me next. I must say, however, that after my flight from the Darmstadt camp in 1948 I was warned that a second attempt by the Soviets to bring me to the other side was being prepared. On this occasion an officer of the US Army proved to be a really splendid fellow. I have never forgotten it.

I held the firm hope that I would be released in the summer of 1947. But I had no illusions: at the end of July a certain Colonel Rosenfeld, a prosecutor, informed me of an unbelievable indictment: I was charged with "having mistreated, beaten and killed about one hundred American prisoners of war!"

The struggle between desperation and death began again. Under the influence of excessive propaganda, the victors were convinced that we were all detestable criminals, regular monsters. Everywhere we encountered lies, hatred and a feeling of vindictiveness, as well as stupidity – which was difficult to combat.

We were ten officers of the 150th Panzer Brigade. Five came from the army, three from the navy and two from the Waffen-SS. I had scarcely ever seen six of them.

The German and international press took care of this sensation, which was very well staged. A half-dozen German lawyers immediately declared themselves willing to defend us. One of them, a countryman of mine, the well-known lawyer Dr. Peyer-Angermann from Salzburg, even had himself arrested in order to get to Dachau with a convoy of German prisoners, for the German-Austrian border was closed once again. None of these lawyers had the slightest hope of receiving even the most modest fee: we had nothing at all. I thanked him with my entire heart. Dr. Peyer-Angermann brought with him a complete portfolio on my activities in Austria from 1930-1939, and one could feel that he was prepared to risk his reputation and his career to represent a cause he felt was just.

Apart from that, the tribunal had assigned three officers from the American army as defense attorneys. They were Lieutenant-Colonel Robert Durst from Springfield, Missouri, Lieutenant-Colonel Donald McLure from Oakland, California and Major Lewis I. Horowitz from New York. The latter, I wish to emphasize, was of the jewish faith. The three officers first carried out detailed investigations and interrogations as to my origin, my life in Vienna and my career during the war and proved to be perfect defense attorneys. After all our German lawyers didn't know the "other rules of the game" in an American trial.

The proceedings, which lasted more than a month, began on August 5, 1947. Before that, during the first three, endlessly long days, I was questioned and interrogated by Lieutenant-Colonel Durst, who was armed with files provided by prosecutor Rosenfeld.

"I would like to point out to you," he said, "that I will only take over your defense if I know every detail about your life before and during the war."

I had nothing to hide, and at the end of the third day he offered me his hand for the first time and said, "I am now convinced that you are completely innocent, and I will defend you like my own brother. However I cannot guarantee you a favorable outcome to the trial, if the leadership of the defense is not given to a 'team leader' but to a single defender, namely me. Furthermore it seems to me important that you alone speak for the defense, in your own name and in the names of your comrades."

The so often criticized "leadership principle," which ultimately brought Germany so much misfortune, was used again – but this time with complete success.

Chief presiding judge was Colonel Gardner, called "the hanging gardner," for to that point in time he had only handed down death sentences by hanging. However Colonel Durst was able to have five of the nine members of the military court, who were all colonels, replaced by five other officers – all proven front-line soldiers, Durst told me.

Finally, about halfway through the trial, prosecutor Rosenfeld had to withdraw his charge of murder against us. He was left with only one charge: wearing the uniform of the enemy outside actual combat. Lieutenant-Colonel Durst presented no evidence that the English and Americans had used German uniforms, as I have already shown in this book. But it was already common knowledge that the commander of the Polish uprising had worn a German uniform. They knew that The Americans had penetrated to and fought in Aachen while wearing German uniforms. General Bradley therefore wrote the court a letter in which he assured that he "never had knowledge of these events," but the facts could not be denied.

Apparently General Bradley wasn't aware of what was going on within the army he was commanding. Perhaps too it was the memory of his arrest by the MP, who suspected him of being a disguised German, that caused the gap in his memory that was so uncomfortable for us.

Then came the sensation. RAF Wing Commander Forest Yeo-Thomas, one of the most brilliant personalities British intelligence could boast of, took the witness stand. The decorations he wore on his tunic spoke for themselves; he did not need to be introduced to the court. The French resistance fighters knew him as "the white rabbit."

Colonel Rosenfeld was completely perplexed by the statements made by the RAF colonel, who Eugen Kogon claimed had been killed by the Germans in Buchenwald in his book Der SS-Staat. He declared that the members of his own commando unit had used German uniforms and German vehicles and that under certain conditions his commandos "could take no prisoners."

Lieutenant-Colonel Durst asked him whether he was sometimes forced, "to take and use the papers of German prisoners of war."

"Of course! A prisoner is not supposed to have any papers on him. And if has such nevertheless – all the worse for him."

He added, "As the leader of English commando units I studied thoroughly the actions of Colonel Skorzeny and his units. Therefore I can assure you that the colonel, his officers and soldiers acted like real gentlemen on all occasions."

For a moment I thought Rosenfeld was having a heart attack. Unfortunately I wasn't allowed to shake the hand of this honorable and generous RAF officer. He stood up. I whispered a few words to my comrades: we came to attention in salute to him. Lieutenant-Colonel Durst informed the tribunal that three American officers had placed themselves at the disposal of the defense. After the statement by Yeo-Thomas theirs were seen as superfluous. The judge gave me the word, and using a map I explained as simply as possible the course of Operation Greif. Colonel Rosenfeld asked me a few more questions in his role as prosecutor, but in a more courteous tone. However this did not stop him from requesting the death penalty for us in his closing statements, even though he was unable to prove our guilt; the representatives of the press and radio could only watch in amazement.

Lieutenant-Colonel Durst gave a well-documented and in every respect remarkable defense speech and expressed surprise that the prosecution was still asking for any punishment after its failure to present any convincing proof of our guilt. In conclusion Lieutenant-Colonel McLure turned to the court and said:

"Gentlemen, I would be proud if I had the honor to command such men. We demand a simple acquittal."

During the taking of evidence the presiding judge quite obviously supported the prosecution. An acquittal was to be expected, but it was not announced until September 9, 1947 – in front of a room full to capacity and after much deliberation. A milling crowd of journalists, photographers and radio reporters swarmed around the accused.

As I was about to thank my defenders Colonel Rosenfeld came toward me with outstretched hand. I am not resentful and would gladly have shaken the hand of my accuser, but I didn't believe in the good will of Colonel Rosenfeld. He knew very well that we had neither beaten nor murdered American or other soldiers and that we had no plans to attack Eisenhower's headquarters and liquidate him or any other general. Nevertheless he had tried to associate the 150th Panzer Brigade's action with the allegedly "proven massacre" at Malmedy. He had also produced false statements – concerning the use of cyanide bullets by my units during the Ardennes offensive. The prosecution had even called upon the faithful Radl and Hunke as witnesses for the prosecution! Lieutenant-Colonel Durst filed a protest, but in vain: "They wish to demonstrate that the principal defendant's adjutants disagreed with him."

In truth Radl and Hunke appeared on the witness stand against their will. Radl was uncooperative and gave monosyllabic answers to the prosecution's questions. And as far as our "chinaman" Hunke was concerned, he persistently remained silent. He in fact appeared to be in Peking or Tsientin while Colonel Rosenfeld showered him with questions.

But without the iron efforts of our defense attorneys, without the honorable and generous statements by Yeo-Thomas, we would have been sentenced to death. But the sentences would probably never have been carried out, as in the case of the notorious "Malmedy Trial." None of the forty-seven sentenced to death was executed.

"The defeated German generals were sentenced and done away with. Should another war break out," declared Field Marshall Montgomery in Paris on July 8, 1948, "it would be conducted with even more cruelty, for no one wants to be defeated if it means being hanged!"

We were acquitted, but we were not yet free – we of the Waffen-SS. We fell under the enemy decree known as "automatic arrest." I believe it was on September 11, 1947 when the world press published Colonel Rosenfeld's statement, "Skorzeny is the most dangerous man in Europe!"

The next day, September 12, I learned that Denmark and Czechoslovakia were demanding my extradition. After two weeks they noted that this "was a mistake." Further phoney witnesses were exposed. However I was sent back to Nuremberg, then to the camp at Darmstadt for "denazification."

"They never permitted me a few words with Colonel Yeo-Thomas in order to thank him, so I did so in a letter. Finally I received a note from him: "You did a jolly good job during the war! If you are looking for a place to stay I have a home in Paris... Escape!"

That was my intention too. Three years and two months seemed to me to be enough. I warned the American colonel who was commander of the Darmstadt camp that I had decided to get away. He didn't believe me. But two hours later, on July 27, 1948, I installed myself – with some difficulty – in the trunk of his car. The German driver, who was going shopping for the camp commander, unwittingly drove me through all the checkpoints. I too had chosen freedom.

Notes

1. This law allowed Allied military commanders to set up tribunals to judge those responsible for "war crimes, crimes against peace and crimes against humanity," as defined by the Nuremberg Charter. (Editors' note)

2. Professor J.A. Martinez: *The War Crimes Trials of the Postwar Period*, Paris 1958. (Editors' note)

27

THE MOST DANGEROUS
MAN IN EUROPE

My aim is to earn a living – Denazified "in absentia" – Talks with General Peron, Colonel Nasser, King Hussein of Jordan and Presidents Verwoerd and Vorster – The Daily Sketch is convicted of slander – An absurd invention: "The Spider" – Imaginary kidnappings – My secret army in the Sahara – The attack on Spandau Prison – The train to Glasgow – I am General Dayan! – Sir Basil Liddell Hart: the unnecessary war – The true heroes of the Second World War – The United Nations faces an impossible task – Military conflicts go on – Uprisings in the Eastern Block states – Atomic war = suicide – The German decoding machine in British hands – Special commando units combined with conventional warfare.

Journalists hurried to attribute the most fabulous adventures to the "most dangerous man in Europe," which was sometimes less than welcome for my reputation.

First I was apparently the head of an international plot. In truth I was wondering where I should live; like the vast majority of my countrymen, who had lost everything in the war, I had to start over again from zero.

But before I could earn a living I had to be "denazified." As everyone knows, 3,300,000 Germans were called to appear before the "denazification court" and were affected by this "purge." A good dozen of these civilian courts, which were run by real or alleged "members of the resistance," were in operation in the Darmstadt camp (20,000 prisoners). One of these "judges," before whose tribunal I was supposed to appear, distinguished himself by being especially hard. That was not surprising, for in his time he had denounced many of his fellow citizens to Müller's Gestapo. These measures were forced upon us by the occupying powers. They arranged the Germans into five categories of culprits: to the first group belonged those who had been members of the National Socialist German Workers Party or its related organizations: the Labor Front, professional associations, male or female youth organizations, and so on. Citizens who bore any sort of responsibility within these organizations were placed in two further groups (2 and 3 – less incriminated). Every former officer automatically belonged to the fourth group. Group five formed the "principal culprits," like Minister Dr. Hjalmar Schacht, who was acquitted at Nuremberg.

One could escape the process with a cunning lawyer and three good witnesses to confirm that the accused had "put up sufficient resistance."

I myself was finally "denazified in absentia" in 1952 and was classified as "less incriminated."

After two years in Germany and two in France I found in Spain, a chivalrous land, the opportunity to pursue anew my career as an engineer. As I had none of the "SS treasure" – in contrast to what many writers claimed – this was not easy. With the help of several true friends, one of whom was a friend from my student days who was likewise an engineer and who, luckily for him, had never belonged to the National Socialist Party, I got enough money together to open a small technical office in Madrid.

Luck smiled on me in 1953. I obtained a contract for a large quantity of railroad materials and machine tools. I was able to pay back the money I had borrowed. I know of only one way to live decently: that is to work. That is what I did and continue to do. Naturally they discovered that I represented German firms, among others, and sold their products. It would have been astonishing if I had represented Soviet firms. It is true that I travelled on business to Argentina, where I was received by the late General Peron, and to Cairo, where President Gamal Abd el Nasser told me that he would like to develop Egypt industrially and economically with the help of the west, especially the United States.

There was a German military mission in Cairo in 1951, whose chief was General Wilhelm Fahrmbacher, who had stayed on after the overthrow, and a civilian mission, which included capable rocket scientists, under the leadership of Dr. Voss, a former director of the

Skoda factories. Fahrmbacher and Voss were extremely careful and wanted no former members of the Waffen-SS in their groups at any price. On my second trip to Cairo Nasser gave me a thick volume to read, with about 100 typewritten pages. I had barely skimmed over a few pages when I said to Nasser, who was now head of state, "But these are very secret Egyptian government papers!"

"Read everything please."

It was the text of very favorable Russian proposals for the Aswan Dam and for considerable military aid.

When I had finished reading Nasser said to me: "We Arabs are in no hurry. We can wait. I absolutely do not believe that our arab peoples are susceptible to Marxist-Leninism; it contradicts our religion. I personally am disposed toward the west. But since the west refuses us its help, I see myself forced to accept that of the east. However I will not accept the proposals you have read, not in a month, nor in half a year."

I then asked Nasser whether he authorized me to speak in general terms about this conversation, should the occasion arise. He said that he did.

I knew all to well that I had the American and British secret services on my heels in Cairo. So I was scarcely surprised when, on my return to the Hotel Semiramis, a charming person of Greek nationality but American spirit gave me an invitation to a reception being held that night by the American military attache.

I drove there, and after an hour of general conversation the colonel asked me if we could talk alone. We went into his office.

"Please excuse me for allowing myself the liberty," he said, "but we are soldiers and it is better to speak openly. I know that you were with President Nasser this morning and that your audience lasted for more than two hours. Of course I don't wish to be indiscrete, but may I ask what you talked about?"

"Your curiosity is understandable, and I have authorization to satisfy it. I said little, read and listened."

It turned out that the colonel had reported to the Pentagon some weeks earlier that a decision was needed soon on aid for Egypt. He planned to send a priority telegram that night and asked permission to mention my name. I had no objections.

But there was little change in the policy toward Nasser. Many took him for a communist, and so the Arab world was forced to turn to the Soviet block. Fourteen months after our conversation Nasser signed the well-known aid agreement with the Soviet Union.

In 1969 I met Ibn Talal Hussein, the King of Jordan, a ruler who lived dangerously. How many coup attempts against him have already failed?

In 1965 in South Africa I spoke with Dr. Hendrik, who was murdered by Dimitri Tsafendas, a steward, during a session of parliament in 1966. On that trip I also met the current President, B.J. Vorster, who was then the Minister of Justice. During the war he was interned in Koffeifontein concentration camp with the number 2229342, and was then kept under house arrest, because he was one of the activists fighting for his country's freedom. The independence movement called itself Brandwacht and eighty percent of the Boers between the ages of twenty and fifty stayed in detention camp or prison or were kept under house arrest until the end of hostilities. South Africa achieved its independence after the referendum of October 5, 1960 and left the Commonwealth. The Boers, whose territory had simply been annexed by the British Crown in 1977, had waited for this day for more than eighty years.

I also made business trips to Portugal, the Congo – however I only met the poor President Moise Tshombe later in Madrid, where he lived in exile – Angola, Kenya, Greece, Paraguay and Ireland, where I intended to raise sheep. But no one believed my peaceful intentions.

● ● ●

For thirty years there had existed a sort of "Skorzeny legend." It is impossible to quote even a fraction of this figment of the imagination which has been printed about my alleged activities. I must admit that I devoted a certain amount of attention to this sort of journalism in the Sixties. I even kept several-thousand newspaper and magazine clippings devoted my fictitious adventures. Not that the imaginative scribes had had enough, but their fairy tales had now become boring.

Let us examine my supposed activities since 1950.

First, and even two years before I visited Argentina, I was the Commander-in-Chief of the army of this republic, while General Galland, the former General of Fighters, and Oberst Rudel commanded the air forces there!

After my two-week stay in Cairo, in 1954 the *Daily Sketch* accused me of having for years instructed Egyptian special commandos "in the art of killing British officers and soldiers." There really still were judges and strict laws governing the press in London. I filed suit against the *Daily Sketch*. I was awarded ten-thousand Pounds Sterling in damages as well as costs. I turned 5,000 Pounds over to the Red Cross for the seriously war disabled of Britain and donated 5,000 Pounds to the fund for the German war-disabled.

After Father Sixtus' disclosures at Nuremberg I thought that there must be at least two Skorzenys. The weekly *Wochenend* related the same thing in June 1950. Since 1944 I had a double who was almost as tall as I and whose real or fictitious name was Vohwinkel. A doctor had made the scars on his cheek – impossible to tell us apart. The author of this article wanted to locate a photo of "Vohwinkel" and I together. It seems he was unable to find one. The stupid thing was that they no longer knew which of the two of us was travelling about the world.

But in the time of the cold and hot wars the world press was not unaware that I prepared a few revolutions here and there, and also organized the "Nazi International" (Der Spinne or: "the Spider"), a mysterious mafia with multifaceted, always criminal and subversive activities.

At the end of 1950 *Reynolds News* and the *Münchener Illustrierte* wrote that the heads of the "Spider" were none other than Serrano Suner in Spain, Prince Junio-Valerio Borghese in Italy, the Grand Mufti of Jerusalem in North Africa, Strasser in Canada, Sir Oswald Mosley in Great Britain, Rudel in Argentina, General de Gaulle in France, and so on, together with myself and Martin Bormann, who in reality had died in Berlin in 1945. Only after protracted investigations did the German Ministry of the Interior conclude that the "Spider" had never existed, as proved by a document dated August 30, 1972, which is reproduced here.

Not only had I sunk the "SS treasure" and fished it out again several times from Lake Wahl, Tirpitz or Hinter or even from Lake Neusiedler – they saw it! – which not only mobilized the press but television as well – I also found the secret correspondence between Mussolini and British Prime Minister Winston Churchill, as the Duce "confided in me." Regrettably, I don't know in which matter.

In August 1953 the French government deposed the government of the Sultan of Morocco, Mohammed Ben Jussuf and deported the ruler, who was descended from the Aluit Dynasty which governed in the Eighteenth Century, and his family to Corsica. Soon the French authorities learned that he wasn't safe there. Numerous French and Swiss newspapers confidently claimed that I had been hired by the Arab League to kidnap the sultan and his family. Their reliable sources even informed them that I was paid one million dollars for this operation. So they took the monarch first to Fort Lamy, then to Madagascar. The Laniel government was placed on highest alert.

There was no cause, for I never had any intention of freeing the famous, noble prisoner and his family. I would scarcely have had the time anyway, for Mohammed V returned to Rabat in triumph in 1955 and two years later was proclaimed King of Morocco.

In the same way I must deny that I ever intended to kidnap the Algerian leader Ben Bella and Fidel Castro of Cuba. However, before the head of the revolutionary movement, the so-called "27th of July," seized power in February, certain American reporters told the public that I was his advisor in the guerilla war against Batista.

It soon turned out that I would have to devote almost all my time if I wanted to deny all the "information" published about me by the world press and pursue all the slanderers. That was not possible. Furthermore I was able to determine that the only country whose laws enabled one to defend oneself effectively against lies, slander and systematic defamation was Great Britain. The newspaper editors in that country also knew the laws governing the press better than anywhere else.

During the 1950s the *Sunday Graphic* did not make the same mistakes as the *Daily Sketch*. It had me followed by two officers, or alleged officers, of the intelligence service: Major Stanley Moss and Captain Michael Luke. Their mission was to find me – which was not easy, for "I moved like lightning" – and subsequently interview me about my adventures.

Moss and Luke of course had an aircraft at their disposal. They were lucky to come across my tracks in Sweden, Bavaria, France, Italy, Egypt, in Baghdad and so on. But each time I learned through dumb luck that they were coming, several hours before their arrival at the place in question. This was probably attributed to my being warned in time by the famous "Spider."

I followed my supposed adventures from my desk in Madrid with great interest, and I am sure that Ian Fleming read them too. I lived in the most extraordinary palaces in the world, surrounded by racy blondes or mysterious dark-haired women, who employed their charms in the service of my dangerous activities.

I also heard that I was commander-in-chief of a secret army, whose garrison was located "near Mursuk" in the Libyan desert, "four-thousand kilometers from any civilization" on a rocky plateau "where many peaks exceeded 3,000 meters." On October 13, 1956 the weekly magazine *Samstag* published an account of the adventures of an old Jesuit missionary, Monseigneur Jean Baptiste de la Gravaires. As he knew the Sahara "like his own vest pocket, in the course of his explorations the father was a guest in a mysterious "city" in the desert. This city was the capital of a sort of military empire, whose leader I was.

"Monsieur de la Gravaires" admitted that I had treated him well. I had placed left over units of the Africa Corps under my command, about ten-thousand man, and organized and equipped them. I had at my disposal tanks and aircraft, which "dove out of the steel-blue sky like birds of prey and could land on the smallest surface in this rugged area."

My capital city was protected by "the most modern alarm system," which included infrared beam devices which watched over the area at night; any suspicious approach was detected. *Samstag* noted that organizing an expedition to go there would be very expensive, and there would probably be fighting. The French intelligence service (Le Deuxième Bureau Parisien) therefore had to abandon the idea of an expedition... By the way, "if this phantom city remains unknown to this day, it is because women are forbidden to enter." Pity!

From this mixture of Jules Verne and Pierre Benoit's novel *L'Atlantide*, we come in 1959 to the theft of the treasure of Begum: I was said to have been the instigator. At the same time several newspapers noted that in July 1940 I was supposed to have kidnapped the Duke and Duchess of Windsor, who were in Lisbon at the time. When the papers went looking for more information, they found that in 1940 we in the Das Reich Division were quite simply thinking about how we might occupy the British Isles! But unfortunately this invasion did not take place either.

Apparently I was in constant communication with Martin Bormann. I met him in a forest on the Czechoslovak-Bavarian border, once in the Amazon, or...in Israel, which is even more original. Of course I lived in grand style, owning various castles, a villa on the Riviera, a yacht and fast cars...

But unfortunately they were only castles on the moon! When the telephone rang in my Madrid office, my customers, as always, asked for spiral-welded pipes, sheet metal, cement, a cost estimate for a machine tool and the like.

However in 1962 it was obvious to the *American Weekly* that I intended to storm Spandau Prison and free Rudolf Hess. In the following year, on August 8, 1963, the "hold-up of the century" took place. The Glasgow-London train was stopped at a bridge by a false red light. The mail car was robbed. The thieves got away with more than two-and-a-half-million Pounds Sterling! The affair was prepared down to the smallest detail by a "brilliant mind" and was executed perfectly.

"Who else could this mind be?" asked the French weekly *Noir et Blanc*, if not Otto Skorzeny? It was perfectly clear! I must admit that this magazine did print all the letters of protest sent by me.

From 1957 to 1960 I simultaneously organized an army in India and another in the Congo, supplied and advised both the Algerian FLN and the French OAS, and thanks to my Irish sheep I was also able to take an interest in the activities of the IRA.

Admittedly in the past six to eight years the press has proved to be more objective where I'm concerned. The BBC and French television really exhibited "fair play" and I would like to express my appreciation for their fair judgement of my person.

The most exaggerated information? It was published by the Polish paper *Glos Robotniczy* and the story was immediately picked up by a German paper: Israeli General Moshe Dayan and Otto Skorzeny were, in reality, one and the same person.

This just proves that human stupidity knows no bounds.

EPILOGUE

In concluding his gigantic work on the Second World War, Sir Basil Liddell Hart concluded that the demand for unconditional surrender, the death sentence for the German people, was stupid and dangerous. He stated that "this unnecessary war was thus prolonged unnecessarily," and that the resulting peace "exclusively served the interests of Stalin and gave up central Europe to communist rule." Unfortunately this "unnecessary war" took place. I have tried to point out its true causes and the most important blows which Germany was forced to take. Most of all I would like to give pride of place to the soldiers who saw these battles through with the greatest courage: the simple Russian and German soldier.

In 1941 the former met the onslaught of the German armies with steadfastness and exemplary bravery. Poorly fed and under poor command at the division level, he resisted and often went over to the counterattack in critical situations; his stubbornness and his energy were downright admirable. Together with his opponent, the German soldier, he is the unknown hero of this great war.

Only someone who has fought in Russia, in searing heat or at forty degrees below zero Celsius, in the plains, the forests, the swamps, in the muck, in the snow, in the ice, can make a proper assessment of the Russian and German soldier. The latter fought for five years and eight months; from July 1944 to April 1945 he fought on even though he knew that he had been betrayed.

One should also not forget that for three long years millions of German women, together with their children and older relatives, endured constant bombing raids. Stoically, and with a calmness not seen before, these women endured the terror night after night without complaint. The story of the quiet heroism of the German civilian population and its horrible losses must still be written.

Hitler's Third Reich was born in Versailles on June 28, 1919. What monster was born on September 30, 1946? No one knows yet. In the course of the largest and strangest trial in history, the victors appointed themselves judge in order to punish the defeated.

How could I know in 1939 that I was committing a crime by voluntarily joining the Waffen-SS. A former minister of the British Crown, Lord Hankey, a member of the war cabinet, wrote in his book *Politics, Trials and Errors* (1949), that it was very dangerous for the future of mankind that the "victors *subsequently* invented crimes" and "enacted laws retroactively, "which meant the denial of justice itself." Lord Hankey was also one of the first who declared that a judge could not be the deadly enemy of those he judged.

"The defeated," he wrote, "cannot be convinced that crimes like the deportation of civilian populations, looting, the murdering of prisoners and destruction without military necessity were punished justifiably, when he knows that similar charges were never brought against one or more of the allied victors."

Other personalities also opposed the existence of the Nuremberg Tribunal and its judgements with equal energy: Sir Reginald Paget, the defender of Feldmarschall von Manstein, US Senator Taft, Prof. Gilbert Murray, the Duke of Bedford, to name only the most famous who protested in 1945-1949.

Theoretically the Nuremberg Charter is supposed to prevent crimes against peace, war crimes and crimes against humanity from being committed in the future. The United Nations, like the League of Nations before it, is supposed to outlaw war and apply the charter. Although many German soldiers were the victims of false accusations, we, the other prisoners, thought at first that the United Nations had taken on an honorable mission.

However Hitler and Mussolini, who were designated the chief culprits in the war, were dead. Meanwhile more than fifty large and small wars have been fought since 1946.

France, which had annexed Madagascar in 1896, was forced to quell a serious uprising there in 1946-47. Suppressing it proved difficult, and the island was finally declared independent in 1960. The war in Indochina (1946-1954) cost France 57,687 dead and it was forced to abandon its colony. In 1961 the USA resumed the war; it devoured materiel and men endlessly and brought untold suffering to the population. Holland likewise fought to keep its colonies in Indonesia (from 1946 to 1963), with the same lack of success as France and Belgium, which was forced to quit the Congo.

The hostilities in the Congo were marked by great brutality, just as they later were in North Angola, in Zanzibar, in the Sudan, in Uganda, Biafra, Burundi and so on. The actions by the "Blue Helmets" of the United Nations were bitter, but were criticized, probably justifiably. Racial feuds, anti-semitism and expulsions of elements of populations still plague the African continent, where for a good dozen years coup d'état has followed coup d'état, with no outlook for a "normalization" of the resulting political and social systems.

The Korean War cost the United States 54,246 killed and 104,000 wounded. France lost 30,000 men in the Algerian war and the number of wounded exceeded 55,000. For its part the Algerian Liberation Front estimates "that total losses amounted to one million." The exact number of victims claimed by the Quemoy Islands affair (1958), the wars between Israel and the Arab nations, the guerilla wars in Syria, in Iraq, in Mozambique and so on, and the bloody religious and racial conflicts which had taken place in India since 1947 is unknown.

In most cases these hostilities were carried on in spite of the protests and directions by the United Nations. Never was a war criminal tried according to the Nuremberg Charter, neither for conspiring against peace, nor for war crimes or genocide. Certain officers of the US Army, who were charged with ordering massacres in Viet Nam, were tried by normal military courts – but not in accordance with the Nuremberg Charter.

In Africa and Asia however one sees the methodical elimination of groups of people by others who are better armed and supported by powerful nations. Uprisings in Poland, East Germany, Hungary and Czechoslovakia against the Soviet yoke were bloodily suppressed. How did the western powers react? Not at all. The victors of the Second World War committed the same mistake as at Versailles in 1919, with the difference that they multiplied the causes of conflict all over the world; now any one of them can deteriorate into nuclear war.

• • •

They say that in a future war the "human" factor will be seen as secondary. This is not my view.

No human community accepts its own destruction without defending itself. It was this very feeling that motivated the German people in 1944 and 1945, when the enemy was trying to force them to accept an "unconditional surrender." The world powers that today possess atomic weapons – the USA, Great Britain and even China, France and India – are all aware that a war fought with all the modern means of destruction would be outright suicide.

General Telford Taylor demonstrated in 1955 that a specially trained commando unit could kidnap the President of the United States from a golf course. The operation, in which a vertical takeoff aircraft was used, was carried out so swiftly that it was impossible to determine whether the kidnappers were Russian, Chinese, Czech or German. In my opinion it could also be Americans, although General Taylor did not put forward such a hypothesis.

On the other hand Charles Whiting suspects that one fine day all the members of the Central Committee of the Communist Party of the Soviet Union, together with the supreme chiefs of the Warsaw Pact, will disappear . . .

There is nothing that proves that an atomic war would render the use of special commando units superfluous, as many maintain. The commandos could play a decisive role, while a conventional mass attack would be doomed to failure.

Those general staffs that rely solely on the accuracy and destructive power of their guided weapons would regret it.

Another example of a British commando raid, carried out during the Polish campaign, has only recently come to light. Group Captain Frederick Winterbotham was chief or air reconnaissance in the British secret service until 1945.

A German cipher machine, "Ultra," was captured in the first days of the Polish campaign and immediately taken to England. The cipher machine enabled the English to learn many German operational plans, which made it easier to initiate countermeasures. The above-named English secret service officer concluded the following in his memoirs: allied propaganda, which claims to this day that the Second World War was "a sort of great triumphant, heroic epic" and was won in that way, is false. It would be better if they would think about what would have happened if the "Ultra" device hadn't fallen into British hands.

Perfectly equipped and trained, determined battle groups, which are intelligently led, should always be capable of creating an unexpected situation and producing a decision, perhaps even – as I have said – before a conflict breaks out. During hostilities, commando units of technicians and propagandists could create confusion and perhaps chaos.

Obviously the use of special units can only be planned when their perfectly-coordinated missions are incorporated into the overall process of the war.

● ● ●

As we know, the Laycock-Heyes operation in Beda Littoria in November 1941 failed for several reasons, the main one being that General Rommel wasn't there. But this operation formed only one part of the following whole:

1. Sir Claude Auchinleck, the commander-in-chief of the British forces, who relieved General Wavell, possessed the plan for the offensive which Rommel was to start on November 23.

2. On the night of November 17 the Laycock-Heyes commando unit had the mission of spiriting Rommel away.

3. Auchinleck attacked on November 18, in the belief that Rommel had already been liquidated.

Here is another example of a combination between special action and conventional warfare:

1. Allied troops landed in Italy on July 10, 1943 and on the 23rd occupied Salerno.

2. Sunday, the 24th of July: the Duce is outvoted at a meeting of the Fascist Grand Council. The next day the King of Italy becomes chief of the special command; he sets a trap for his government leader.

The Duce is kidnapped at the exit from the Royal Palace and is spirited away in an ambulance.

3. Hitler gives General Student and me the task of finding and freeing Mussolini. It is a fact that the arrest of the Duce was arranged with the western allies.

What happened in mid-1944?

1. The English and Americans land in Normandy on June 6.

2. During the night of June 19-20 hundreds of Russian special commando units sabotage rail lines, blow up bridges, destroy telephone lines, and so on, in the area of our Army Group Center. The Russian offensive begins on June 22.

3. The western allies enter Cherbourg on June 27, Saint-Lô on July 18; the Russian armies take Pinsk on July 15, Vilna in the north on the 16th, Grodno in the center on July 17.

4. On July 29 Stauffenberg plants his bomb. His co-conspirators inform the chiefs of the German army groups – in the west as well as in the east: "The Führer is dead!"

Can one speak of simple coincidences?

Had the western allies known for certain that the assassination attempt against Hitler was carried out on July 20, 1944, they might have acted – or perhaps they would have done nothing, in spite of the repeated requests by Dulles. In any case the assassination was postponed so often that they didn't believe in it any more. The English and Americans failed to react and left the conspirators in the lurch.

As for me, I wouldn't have been surprised during the night of the 20th of July at the Bendlerstrasse to have received news that two or three battalions of Anglo-Saxon paratroops had landed in or near Berlin. Several units wearing German uniforms would have caused confusion for two or three days at the most. In the critical situation in which our armies in the west found themselves, the English and Americans could have crossed the Rhine at the end of August, beginning of September at the latest.

The enemy's stubbornness to stick to their decision that Germany must surrender unconditionally, prevented them from using outstanding special troops within the framework of a strategic whole – which would have helped achieve victory seven or eight months earlier.

On March 8, 1974 I learned from a German newspaper that I had a rival in Israel. Not General Dayan (this time), but General Ariel Sharon, the commander of Unit 101. Erich Kern, the author of the article, first noted that, "Skorzeny's methods were studied by the Israeli general staff." Consequently, "Sharon and his commando unit crossed the Suez Canal at night. The participants in this operation wore Egyptian uniforms and had about twenty Egyptian tanks. In this way Sharon was able to smash a fairly wide breach on the Egyptian side of the canal."

General Sharon and his Special Unit 101 had more luck than we did with the 150th Panzer Brigade. He crossed the canal – we could not cross the Maas. But this example showed, clearly I believe, that the prospect exists in any war of successfully carrying out a special action and creating a decisive political advantage.

We know that Hitler gave a great deal of thought – as did Lenin, by the way – to Clausewitz's answer to the famous question: "What is war?"

His answer is well known:

"War is only a continuation of politics with other means."

If these means have been fundamentally changed by the atom bomb, only the special action remains as the clearest expression of "continuation of politics." In most cases such an action is more of a matter of politics or economics than actual military science.

Like it or not, a new type of soldier has arisen: an organized adventurer. He must have some of the qualities of a guerilla, a man of science and an inventor, of a scholar and psychologist.

He can emerge from the water or fall from the sky, can walk peaceably along the streets of the enemy's capital or issue him false orders. In reality war is for him an anachronism. In vain the "traditional" generals view him with understandable suspicion. He exists and can no longer disappear from the battlefield; he is the authentic secret weapon of his fatherland.

Also from the publisher

SCORCHED EARTH

THE RUSSIAN-GERMAN WAR 1943-1944

PAUL CARELL

The classic! This new edition of Paul Carell's eastern front study picks up where *Hitler Moves East* left off. Beginning with the battle of Kursk in July 1943, Carell traverses the vast expanse of the Russian War, from the siege of Leningrad and the fierce battles of the northern front, to the fourth battle of Kharkov, and the evacuation of the Crimea, a withdrawal forbidden by Hitler. The book ends in June of 1944 when the Soviet Armies reach the East Prussian frontier. Hundreds of photographs, situation and campaign maps, complete index, and comprehensive bibliography, add to this impressive account. This edition includes a new preface by the author.

Size: 6" x 9"   b/w photographs, maps   600 pages, hard cover
ISBN: 0-88740-598-3 $39.95

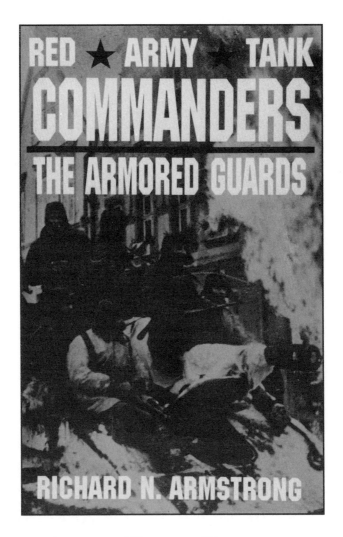

RED ARMY TANK COMMANDERS
THE ARMORED GUARDS
RICHARD ARMSTRONG

This new book profiles six Soviet commanders who rose to lead six tank armies created by the Red Army on the eastern front during the Second World War: Mikhail Efimov Katukov, Semen Il'ich Bogdanov, Pavel Semenovich Rybalko, Dmitri Danilovich Lelyushenko, Pavel Alekseevich Rotmistrov, and Andrei Grigorevich Kravchenko. Each tank commanders' combat career is examined, as is the rise of Red Army forces, and reveals these lesser known leaders and their operations to western military history readers.

Size: 6" x 9" 15 b/w photos, maps 480 pages, hard cover
ISBN: 0-88740-581-9 $24.95

Rommel & the Secret War in North Africa
Secret Intelligence in the North African Campaign
1941-1943
Janusz Piekalkiewicz

A behind-the-scenes look at the intelligence war, and the use of "ULTRA" to defeat the *Afrika Korps*. Also, the German counter-efforts and the initial victories from a new perspective in over 220 photos, maps and documents.
Size: 7 3/4" x 10 1/2"   hard cover   240 pages
ISBN: 0-88740-340-9 $29.95

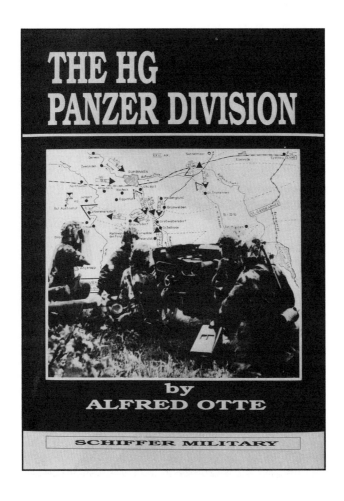

THE HG PANZER DIVISION
ALFRED OTTE

Luftwaffe Panzer division formed from the paratroop corps was one of the elite units in the Wehrmacht and fought in North Africa and Italy. Over 325 photos, documents and maps.
Size: 7 3/4" x 10 1/2"   hard cover   176 pages
ISBN: 0-88740-206-2 $24.95

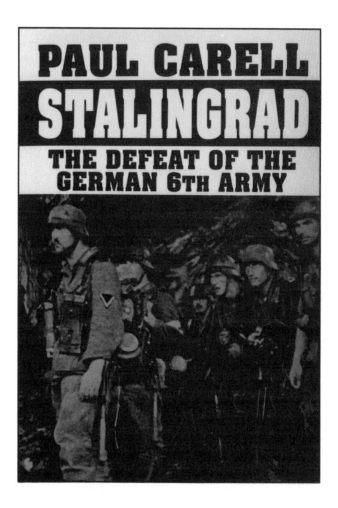

STALINGRAD

THE DEFEAT OF THE GERMAN 6TH ARMY

PAUL CARELL

In this 50th Anniversary book, Paul Carell updates and revises the Stalingrad sections of *Hitler Moves East* and *Scorched Earth,* and reappraises the operations of the 6th Army from the 1942 German summer offensive, through the fighting in the streets of Stalingrad, to the final defeat in January 1943. Paul Carell is also the author of *OPERATION BARBAROSSA IN PHOTOGRAPHS – The War in Russia as Photographed by the Soldiers*, available from Schiffer Military/Aviation History.
Size: 7" x 10"
Hard cover, 352 pages, 190 color and b/w photographs, 27 maps
ISBN: 0-88740-469-3 $29.95